Resounding Voices

School Experiences of People from Diverse Ethnic Backgrounds

Gloria Swindler Boutte

University of North Carolina at Greensboro

Allyn and Bacon

Boston • London • Toronto • Sydney • Tokyo • Singapore

Series Editor: *Traci Mueller*
Marketing Manager: *Amy Cronin*
Editorial Production Service: *Bernadine Richey Publishing Services*
Manufacturing Buyer: *Suzanne Lareau*
Cover Administrator: *Kristina Mose-Libon*
Electronic Composition: *Omegatype Typography, Inc.*

Between the time Website information is gathered and published, some sites may have closed. Also, the transcription of URLs can result in typographical errors. The publisher would appreciate notification where these occur so that they may be corrected in subsequent editions.

Library of Congress Cataloging-in-Publication Data

Resounding voices: school experiences of people from diverse ethnic backgrounds/ [edited by] Gloria Swindler Boutte.
     p. cm.
Includes bibliographical references and index.
ISBN 0-205-31824-X
    1. Minorities—Education—United States—Interviews.   I. Boutte, Gloria.
LC3731.R38 2001
371.82'9'00973–dc21

                                  2001045065

Printed in the United States of America

10 9 8 7 6 5 4 3 2 1   06 05 04 03 02 01

Resounding Voices

To my family (especially my mother),
my children, and anyone whose story has been silenced

Contents

Preface

Resounding Voices was conceived at the 1997 Association for Childhood Education International Study Conference and Exhibition in Portland, Oregon. A small group of educators on the Minority Education Concerns Committee was engaged in a lively discussion of multicultural and racial issues. Adena, a Native American woman, enthusiastically shared a book, *Messengers of the Wind: Native American Women Tell Their Life Stories* (Katz, 1996), that she had recently read. She felt that the stories had awakened residual memories of discrimination that had escaped her conscious thoughts. The stories effortlessly succeeded in helping her understand multicultural issues she had read about in professional articles and books. She was struck by the poignancy of the stories and concluded, "You can do all the multicultural stuff in the world, but unless you touch people's *hearts,* you won't change them." The personal stories in the book were so compelling that she said she was thinking about writing a similar book to tell her own story. Other members of the committee also expressed an interest in such a project.

I was working on a book about my school experiences and was particularly intrigued by the notion that stories make memorable impressions on people. Because the group was multiracial (Native American, African American, and European American), sharing the voices of many racial groups promised to add a much needed and fresh dimension to the literature on the topic. Thus, the rudiments of this book were conceived.

Resounding Voices does not require readers to weave through a web of educational jargon in order to understand the issues. It reflects on the school experiences of people from different ethnic groups. By placing the issues within real contexts, the stories add relevance to theories and research on diversity.

While many books have talked *about* and psychoanalyzed the school experiences of children from different ethnic groups, the actual voices of the people written *about* are seldom heard. This book captures and illuminates the voices of individuals from various ethnic groups who are not usually heard or who have been silenced. Actual stories of individuals shed a deeper level of insight on school experiences than do most of the textbooks currently on the market.

In many education courses, instructors use books such *White Teacher* (Vivian Paley), *Wally's Stories* (Vivian Paley), and *The Water is Wide* (Pat Conroy) to illustrate important concepts about diversity and instruction. Although these books are more than a decade old, they still send powerful, timeless, and invaluable messages to educators. These books appear simple on the surface level; however, the anecdotal and personal nature of the books causes educators to reflect deeply about important educational issues. Personal experiences such as the ones shared by Paley and Conroy add a "real" dimension to the theories and research.

While *Resounding Voices* is written in the tradition of Vivian Paley's and Pat Conroy's work, it adds the perspectives of many different ethnic groups. The uniqueness of this book lies in the diversity of authors from different ethnic groups, family backgrounds, disciplines, and geographic locations. The stories included in *Resounding Voices* are based on interviews with people from the following groups (listed alphabetically): African Americans, Asian Americans, biracial Americans, European Americans, Latino Americans, and Native Americans. The interviewers were from the same ethnic group as the interviewees. The author of each chapter therefore possesses insights about his or her subject matter that may not be readily apparent to others. Each writes with authority and possesses intimate theoretical and practical understanding of the issues discussed.

Another strength of *Resounding Voices* is that the authors are from different geographic regions and from both urban and rural settings in the United States. Additionally, this book includes the stories of whites and biracial individuals—groups often left out of the discussion on multiculturalism and diversity.

Sharing one's stories is like inviting someone into your home. Therefore, we ask readers to treat the stories with the same respect they would extend to a person's home. The stories presented may not be similar to the reader's experiences; however, each person's story (like our homes) is different and valuable in its own right. Once the reader has visited our homes (stories) for a while, his or her understanding of our experiences will be more complete. The stories will prompt readers to explain and reflect on their own lives individually and culturally. These reflections can then be extended to the understanding of both university and school students.

The goal of the stories included in *Resounding Voices* is not to make a prediction about how others in similar situations will behave. Rather, the goal is to understand the nuances of each experience. If we are ever to advance beyond simply looking at similarities so that we can also value differences, we must delve deeply into the lives of individuals while holding their larger cultural context constant. These stories should offer valuable insights about human beings, about patterns as well as about idiosyncrasies and specificities (Ayers, 1989). What the reader learns is not necessarily generalizable because the stories are presented simply as examples of the realities they describe. As Ayers aptly notes, there can be insight and examples without forecast. The conclusions drawn from the stories in *Resounding Voices* are intended to be generalizable existentially, but not statistically. They affirm particular worldviews. Enjoy, appreciate, and understand them as such.

Audience

Resounding Voices is appropriate for a variety of education courses (e.g., introduction to education, multicultural education, methods courses, and curriculum courses). In methods and curriculum courses, the stories can be presented as case studies. Students can examine various methods and curricular decisions in light of their appropriateness to situations presented in this book. These stories—as opposed to generic and abstract examples—lend themselves to specific applications, a dimension that is often missing in methods and curriculum courses. This book will also be useful for sociology, school psychology, anthropology, counseling, or other courses that utilize anecdotal accounts or case studies.

Acknowledgments

Thank you Stephanie and Jonathan for sacrificing "Mommy-time" so I could complete this project. I hope this book inspires you. A special thanks to Dr. Ewuukgem Lomo-David, who helped with the numerous revisions of this book. Appreciation is extended to Eileen Colon, graduate assistant at the University of North Carolina at Greensboro, for her assistance on the revisions of chapters.

My deepest gratitude is expressed to both the authors and the interviewees who welcomed me into their stories and hearts. Thanks for having confidence in me to edit your stories carefully and sensitively. My own life has been enriched by each of you in different but equally profound ways. I also want to thank the following reviewers: Desiree De Florimonte, Morgan State University; Rosario Morales, California State University; and Marilyn J. Taylor, Metropolitan State College of Denver.

References

Ayers, W. (1989). *The good preschool teacher: Six teachers reflect on their lives.* New York: Teachers College Press.

Katz, J. B. (1996). *Messengers of the wind: Native American women tell their life stories.* New York: Ballantine.

Resounding Voices

Overview

Gloria Swindler Boutte

Everyone has a story to tell
—if only someone would listen
if only someone would ask
      —Zimmerman, 1982, p. ix

Conceptual Framework of the Book

This book captures two major and complementary themes. First, it conveys the important role personal stories play in deepening understandings of the educational process. Second, this book is embedded in critical theory and openly acknowledges the role that culture plays in learning and development. It intends to demonstrate that the inclusion of diverse voices is necessary for a comprehensive and complete understanding of schooling. In this postmodern age, educators recognize the importance of personal narratives, the power of stories, and the importance not only of whose perspective, but also of whose voice is being expressed and whose is being heard (Kridel, 1998).

Stories/Personal Narratives

Stories and personal narratives will be used as a method for sharing the voices of individuals from different ethnic groups. Humans tend to make sense of their experiences by discussing them in narrative form (Mishler, 1986). Historically, stories have been used to trace the evolution of individuals in society. Such stories allow individuals to express their perspectives. For example, slave narratives and historical accounts of people such as Frederick Douglas have been used to recount the pain, suffering, joy, and successes of African Americans in this country. The purpose of such stories was not to glorify the person; rather, the tradition has been to make social and political statements or to provide spiritual and emancipatory inspiration to others.

Ayers (personal communication, June 15, 1997) notes that learning the personal stories of individuals helps avoid reducing humans to one-dimensional beings. As soon as one moves beyond superficial interactions and learns a little about another person's life, stereotypes disappear. Understanding a person's circumstances and beliefs gives insight into commonalties shared by all. We quickly learn that the range of normality is vast rather than narrow.

While the authors of each chapter are successful educators, their stories reveal triumphs and challenges that shed insight on their current successes. This book seeks to expose struggles and successes that the authors and interviewees have encountered that may not be readily apparent to a casual observer. The stories highlight how individuals locate and relocate their identities as a result of their participation in the school culture. This book also illuminates what happens when home and school cultures come in contact with one another.

Bruner (1986) defines two kinds of epistemologies (or reasoned ways of knowing): (1) scientific and (2) stories. Both are legitimate in their own right, so the typical dichotomy between the logical (scientific) and intuitive (story) is false. Moreover, the story is a legitimate form of reasoned knowing and is not mere emotive expression (Bruner, 1986). Bruner notes that a key difference between the two ways of knowing is that the scientific works from the "top down" while the story works from the "bottom up." The scientific tradition starts with a hypothesis and searches for instances (and, less often, counterinstances) of the "right" explanation to fit some theoretical framework. However, the work tends to be insensitive to contexts. Contrastingly, the story mode of thought searches for the implicit theory in the story. The two modes of thought represent distinctive ways of ordering experiences and constructing reality. The two modes (though complementary) are irreducible to one another. Efforts to reduce one or the other fail to capture the rich diversity of thought. Because there is an abundance of "scientific accounts" in educational literature, this book will focus on personal narratives and seek to fill in the context that is typically missing from the traditional "positivistic" (scientific) paradigm.

Narrative inquiry is a type of qualitative research design in which stories are used to describe human action (Polkinghorne, 1995). Narrative as a story helps us to understand the fullness of human existence. Narrative reasoning does not reduce itself to rules and generalities across stories but maintains the level of specific episodes.

Although differences exist in the manner qualitative researchers employ the narrative method, this book focuses on "narrative analyses." According to Polkinghorne, narrative analyses produce stories as the outcome of the research process. In this book, the authors have sought pieces of information that contributed to the construction of a story that provided explanatory answers about school experiences. The unspoken questions intended to ascertain the hows and whys by seeking to discover "How did this happen?" or "Why did this come about?" (Polkinghorne,1995). At times, we posed guiding questions, but we sought not to suppress the interviewees' responses by asking specific questions.

A number of scholars herald the use of personal narratives to effect change in schools and society (Apple, 1998; Hatch & Wisniewski, 1995; hooks, 1994). Theory, though academic in nature, should not be disconnected from the everyday experiences of individuals (Pinar, 1988). The power of the autobiographical and biographical method is evidenced by the increased use of journals in university and school classrooms. In the process of exploring meaning and knowledge, the context of historical events and autobiographical experiences cannot be separated (Slattery, 1995). The use of autobiographical and biographical stories allows the voices of the past and present to be heard. By painting a graphic picture of the school experiences of a few people from different walks of life (e.g., poor, economically stable, mainstream, males, females), this book focuses on the *quality* of experiences rather than on quantity.

The intent of this book is *not* to provide a survey of all possible lifestyles or representatives from each ethnic group; the possibilities are almost infinite in some cases. For example, there are currently hundreds Native American nations in the United States, over twenty-five Asian American groups (e.g., Japanese, Chinese, Lao-Hmong, Filipino, East Indian), numerous Latino American groups (e.g., Mexicans, Cubans, Puerto Ricans, Central and South Americans), several European American groups (e.g., English, German, Scottish, Italian, Danish), African Americans from different backgrounds (e.g., African, Caribbean, Latino, biracial), and endless possibilities of biracial or multiracial composition (e.g., Asian-Latino; African-European) (Boutte 1999). Additionally, the book does not aim to focus on ethnic groups with the largest numbers (e.g., Mexicans to represent Latino Americans or Navaho Indians to represent Native Americans). Although experiences recounted by people of similar ethnic groups may be familiar and relevant, the stories should offer valuable insights about human patterns, idiosyncrasies, and specifics of human beings (Ayers, 1989).

Many of the writers and storytellers in this book speak from socially subordinate positions. For example, two of the chapters on European Americans focus on rural settings in two geographically different parts of the United States. Another focuses on White children (economically privileged and working class) who are affected negatively by child abuse in their homes. Each of these stories broadens our understanding of Whites. It is essential that Whites be viewed as part of the multicultural equation and that they are viewed in a multidimensional fashion instead of as primarily mainstream. Such narrow depictions limit our view of ethnicity, reinforce stereotypes, and alienate many Whites who realize that their school and life experiences do not fit the typical definitions. Inclusion of Whites in discussions of culture also helps illustrate that culture plays a role in learning for all ethnic groups.

As McIntosh (1995) observed, whiteness is too often equated with normality. This causes important within-group ethnic differences to be lost. For example, we silence the voices of rural Whites or any other perceived outlier that does not fit the standard of homogenized whiteness. We fail to see whiteness as cultural (Howard, 1993). Whites are therefore omitted as part of the equation for understanding humanity and our ultimate interdependence on one another. The difficulty that many Whites have in recognizing that cultural differences among people of color are valid is probably influenced by their inability and unwillingness (in some cases) to view their own ethnicity in cultural terms (as opposed to "I am just American"). Finally, inclusion of Whites in the book does not in any way ignore structural inequities, which places people of color at a disadvantage and Whites at an advantage in schools and society at large. The structural inequities that exist are evident in the invisibility of people of color and absence of our voices in a substantive manner (versus surface level) in much educational literature. Contrastingly, the stories in this book are told from the perspective of the people represented rather than interpreted by "objective" researchers who present etic perspectives.

This book seeks to provide an in-depth analysis of personal experiences that can be judiciously used to better understand individuals from various cultural groups. The final chapter of this book reflects on how schools are experienced by individuals from diverse backgrounds. As Maxine Greene (1995) advises, once the distinctiveness of the many voices in schools is attended to, the importance of identifying shared beliefs is heightened.

Our hope is that the stories disclosed here will move readers to tap into their own stories and to see the human dimensions of diversity. We realize, though, that the readers' own perspectives affects and modifies comprehension of the stories (Greene, 1995). Therefore, readers must try to see at once through the eyes of the storytellers and through their own eyes. With this in mind, we hope that these stories will assist readers in liberating their minds from the confines of their own culture so they will be able to celebrate the full range of cultural variations among humanity (Boutte & DeFlorimonte, 1998). Fu and Stremmel (1999) refer to this process as "hermeneutic" because encounters with different beliefs, habits, and values make us more aware of our own prejudices and therefore increase our self-knowledge and enable our personal and professional growth. In the hermeneutic process, we become more aware of ourselves as well as of the unfamiliar "other." This does not mean that differences between our thoughts is erased; rather, our range of vision increases and we can view issues from multiple perspectives and vantage points.

Using a range of human stories and looking through multiple perspectives may provoke us (humans) to build bridges among ourselves, to heal and to transform. This book presents the realities of others and asks that readers accept them as valid in their own right (rather than in comparison with others). As Delpit (1993) aptly notes, "We must learn to be vulnerable enough to allow our world to turn upside down in order to allow the realities of others to edge themselves into our consciousness" (p. 139). Rosaldo (1989) reminds us that as "social thinkers" (who are influenced by the thoughts of others) we must take other people's narratives as seriously as our own. We must acknowledge that each individual has the right to, as Freire (1999) puts it, *"say his or her own words, to name the world."* Therefore, the narrative analyses and stories are written from divergent perspectives and are not intended to fit together into a unified master summation that defies the inherent variations and strengths within cultural groups (Rosaldo, 1989). In order to fully understand this, readers must hold two seemingly contradictory concepts constant: (1) culture is too important to be overlooked or disregarded, and (2) information about cultural groups should not be overgeneralized because there is a tremendous amount of variation within cultures. These two key points typically are not presented in a complementary manner in the literature, and educators are often confused about the complexities involved in seeing and *not* seeing the influence of culture (Boutte & De Florimonte, 1998).

Readers are encouraged to allow their interpretations of the stories to be illuminated by their knowledge of cultural influences (e.g., Asian American or Native American culture in *general*). However, readers should not be so blinded by general cultural influences that they overlook unique aspects that account for variations within ethnic cultural groups. The ethnic and/or cultural identification of families varies widely. Many people fall somewhere between the two extremes of traditional versus assimilated. Further, many people vary their degree of acculturation depending on the context. Yet, we do not want readers to reduce the stories to the level of individual (or idiosyncratic) differences and totally negate cultural possibilities. We must see the humanity in all lives, which encompasses not only similarities, but also differences.

Life histories and narratives are person-centered and unapologetically subjective (Hatch & Wisniewski, 1995). Therefore, we admit that all of the authors write based on our cultural lens. To give readers some insight into our biases, each author includes his or her own story. Teaching (via writing in this case) is highly political; therefore, I acknowledge my biases up front. Readers are encouraged to do the same so that they will understand why some points resonate with them while others do not. My story is included in the Appendix. Throughout this book, I will actively oppose race, class, gender, or other forms of oppression and discrimination. The genesis of my passion for taking a stand against oppression is revealed in my story.

Voice and Critical Theory

In this book, *voice* will be defined as the articulation and sharing of one's world, one's experiences, and one's vision (Delpit, 1995; hooks, 1993; Lankshear & McLaren, 1993). The voice of students is important because language is one of the principal ways that people define themselves and establish alliances with others (Gallard, 1993). "In a democracy, people should be educated to tell their stories, to make their own voices heard, and to act together to defend and expand their rights" (Featherstone, 1995, p. 14). In order to become liberated and to participate in the transformation of society toward new possibilities, people must have a voice in the process (Freire, 1999; Greene, 1995).

The fundamental issue of power—in this case, of whose voice gets to be heard in determining what is best for children—is an issue addressed by critical theory. Critical pedagogy addresses the power of language to limit or liberate the human spirit as the individual struggles to redefine him- or herself. Historically and currently, the voices of people like the ones highlighted in this book have been silenced (Delpit, 1995; Greene, 1995; Lankshear & McLaren, 1993). As a result of carefully listening to alternative and nonmainstream points of view, this book provides insight into their lives and trajectories.

Exclusion of a variety of voices from the narrative of mainstream history and culture has tremendous educational and political implications (Lankshear & McLaren, 1993). Silencing of these voices, as has been done traditionally, results in sentencing their lived meanings and their representations of their lives, conditions, and struggles to exile at the margins; at the same time these voices are measured against criteria and demands of the dominant culture. This is oppressive (Lankshear & McLaren, 1993, p. 18). The role of critical pedagogy is to emancipate people who are oppressed, not just from the oppressor, but also from their own perceptions of self in the oppressed state (Friere, 1999).

Critical theory aims to transform structural/historical insights into "new ways of knowing" (epistemologies). Critical inquiry is implicitly "a critique of social, political, cultural, economic, ethnic, and gender structures that constrain and exploit humankind by engagement in confrontation, even conflict" (Guba & Lincoln, 1994, p. 113). Critical theories seek to displace dominant ideologies that oppress people.

Congruent with critical theory, we believe that people are experts on their own lives (Delpit, 1995). While others can only conjecture about the lives of others, going to the source allows for authentic accounts of people's experiences. The appropriate education for children can best be devised in consultation with adults who share their culture (Delpit, 1995). Therefore, the authors of the chapters on various ethnic groups share the culture of their interviewees (except in one chapter); thus, providing additional insights and understandings. This book has enabled people from various ethnic groups to locate themselves in their own histories while simultaneously establishing the conditions necessary for them to function as part of a wider democratic culture (Lankshear & McLaren, 1993). The voices presented in this book are not intended to be peripheral additions to major voices. Rather, they are presented as integral perspectives on the world because they deserve to be given due attention.

Lankshear and McLaren (1993) persuasively argue that many individuals' withdrawal from education and public life has much to do with being silenced and forced to engage in activities and modes of being that are profoundly alien. At the same time, these individuals have generations of history that attest to the fact that successful participation in the educational mainstream often does not deliver on its promise of an enhanced quality of life. Consequently, schooling has come to be strongly devalued by many individuals who have long experienced it as a route to inevitable failure and disadvantage (Lankshear & McLaren, 1993; Ogbu, 1990). Additionally, many marginalized or alienated groups are made to feel distrustful of their own voices and their own ways of making sense (Greene, 1995).

All students come to school with cultural tools, such as language and personal beliefs, that they use to make sense of the world in which they live (Gallard, 1993; Heath, 1992; Irvine, 1990; Ladson-Billings, 1994). Some students come to school with worldviews that are more synchronized with what is valued and considered appropriate in American society. Hence, their cultural tools are more closely represented in textbooks and assessments, and they tend to fare well (Gallard, 1993). On the other hand, students whose cultural orientations are not in synch with schools may not fare well or may have to disassociate themselves from their cultural identities in order to succeed (Fordham, 1988, 1996). Educators frequently do not explore the diverse and multiple realities of their students; that is, they make little attempt to understand the histories and the tensions of these histories that students bring to school (Walsh as cited in Tobin, 1993).

The stories and educational implications in this book inform educators about ways to use students' cultural tools to facilitate learning. As a consequence of the authors' reflections on their school experiences, they are able to offer insights on cultural sensitivity and useful teaching strategies for educators. By including voices of the long silent or unheard, this book will bring renewal to conversations about effectively teaching children from diverse backgrounds. It is hoped that by hearing different perspectives and seeing from unaccustomed angles, readers will realize that the world perceived from one place is not *the* world (Greene, 1995). This book seeks to help break through the silence and invisibility of all too many students.

We encourage educators to open themselves and allow themselves to be affected by and to hear the alternative voices presented in this book. The candor captured by the book would be difficult to obtain if the interviewers did not share the same ethnicity. As noted by hooks (1993), given the realities of daily life in a society governed by white mainstream beliefs, people of color and other disenfranchised groups (e.g., women and the poor) are unlikely to be truthful with mainstream (especially white) interviewers about aspects of their lives. For many groups (e.g., African Americans, Native Americans, Latino Americans, Asian Americans), their survival historically depended on being deceitful in order to avoid being brutally punished or murdered. They therefore learned the art of hiding behind a false appearance—for example, pretending to be stupid or illiterate when in fact they were intelligent and literate. The following quotation from Lunsford Lane, a free black person, illustrates this point.

> I had endeavored to conduct myself as not to become obnoxious to the white inhabitants, knowing as I did their power, and their hostility to the colored people. . . . First, I had made no display of the little property or money I possessed, but in every way I wore as much as possible the aspect of slavery. Second, I had never appeared to be even so intelligent as I really was. This all colored in the south, free and slaves, find it particularly necessary for their own comfort and safety to observe. (from *The Narrative of Lunsford Lane*, published in 1848, cited in hooks, 1993, p. 21)

Even a century and a half later, continued racial and economic oppression causes cynicism that results in people's reluctance to share their viewpoints with mainstream individuals (Ogbu, 1990). Often, people will speak only if they feel that their words will be heard and welcomed (Delpit, 1995; hooks, 1993). The mental and educational well-being of individuals from various ethnic groups is dependent on the capacity to face reality and to allow alternative voices to be synthesized in the dialogue about educational practices (hooks, 1993).

Because this book examines the role of *individuals* within various cultural contexts, it achieves the difficult task of emphasizing cultural differences without overemphasizing them. The stories should help educators seek to become more aware of their students' family lives and of their ease and unease (Greene, 1995).

At the conclusion of this book, readers should return to two major points mentioned earlier: (1) culture is too important to be overlooked or disregarded, and (2) information about cultural groups should not be overgeneralized because there is a tremendous amount of variation within cultural groups (Boutte & DeFlorimonte, 1998). The voices presented should help educators view culturally different students not as mere objects or chess pieces, but in their integrity and particularity (Greene, 1995). The stories should help educators discover how it looks and feels from the vantage point of the person whose world it is.

While this book emphasizes the stories of particular individuals and that cultural groups are not monolithic, losing sight of the larger subcultural contexts would cause problems (Boutte & DeFlorimonte, 1998). The following discussion of "fictive kinship" further illuminates why culture is not negligible.

Fictive Kinship

Many educators think that it is educationally unimportant to know about differences between cultural groups. Indeed, it is easier and less complicated to focus on commonalties among cultural groups than to examine their differences. Yet, differences between cultural groups have important social and educational implications. Even when aspects of one's culture are downplayed, it is difficult to negate the role that culture plays in one's life. For example, people choose places of worship and types of music because of differences in cultural preferences (Fordham, 1988, 1996).

The anthropological concept of fictive kinship refers to a kinshiplike connection between and among persons in a society who are not related by blood or marriage, but who have maintained essential reciprocal social, political, or economic relationships (Fordham, 1988, 1996). Among African Americans, for example, there is a sense of collective brotherhood, sisterhood, or collective social identity. Often, kinship terms such as *brother, sister,* and *blood* are used to refer to one another. Fictive kinship extends beyond skin color and also implies a particular mind-set or worldview. Merely possessing African features or being of African descent does not automatically make one a member in good standing of the group. According to Fordham (1988), people can be denied membership by their cultural group because their behavior, attitudes, and activities are perceived as being at variance with those thought to exhibit appropriate cultural habits and attitudes. The behavior necessary for fictive kinship in one cultural group often opposes and is diametrically different from that of other groups.

The concept of fictive kinship directs us back to the two basic premises presented at the beginning of this chapter: culture is not negligible and cultures are not monolithic. That is, while general social definitions of "blackness" (for example) exist, there are still exceptions and variations among African Americans. Many African Americans choose to disassociate themselves from Blacks and assume what Fordham (1988) refers to as a "raceless" persona. They may be ostracized by the Black community for doing so. Comments such as "She's trying to be White" or "He's not Black enough" may be made about African Americans who assume raceless personae. Yet, these "raceless" individuals add another dimension to the definition of "blackness" because they are still socially defined as African Americans. In order to understand such persons fully, one would still need to know enough about general cultural norms and their specific circumstances. Because race and culture are very influential in this country, even people who assume raceless personae may have deeply rooted residual habits associated with their cultural group that cannot be negated.

While membership in a particular cultural group does not determine behavior, it makes certain types of behavior more probable. Skin color and one's socially defined race are powerful influences on people's experiences in this country. In Schofield's (1997) study of a middle school, educators and students frequently made decisions that were based on skin color even though acknowledging color differences was supposed to be taboo in the school. Although the colorblind perspective may sound appealing because it is consistent with the nation's long-standing emphasis (overemphasis, some would say) on the importance of the individual, it is a subtle, disguised way for prejudice to exist. The colorblind perspective allows actions to be labeled as something unrelated to a person's race and can lead to a misrepresentation of reality and denial of experiential differences based on one's skin color (Schofield, 1997).

Educators are encouraged to be well versed in cultural differences within and between groups. Useful ways of becoming more enlightened about cultural differences include reading educational literature on culture and cultural groups, viewing a wide range of television programs and movies that shed insight into various cultures, reading magazine and newspaper articles about cultures, listening to different types of music, and getting to know members of different cultural groups. Learning about cultural influences from students' homes is particularly insightful and is emphasized in this book.

The stories in the book give a fuller picture of diversity within and between cultures. Within any group, the experience of one person is grounded in specifics of a historical era, social class, geographic region, and family history (migration, mobility, level of assimilation, etc.). What is valuable in the stories are the immediacy and texture of individual lives and the extent to which these individual stories contain generalizable principles.

Definitions

Because *race* is such a difficult and complex term to employ in the United States (Herrnstein & Murray, 1994), it is often used interchangeably with *ethnicity*. In this book, we will use the terms interchangeably also, although we will use the term *ethnicity* in most cases.

Race is not a stable category and has changed over time (Boutte, 1999). The term *race* is used frequently in our society (e.g., on school forms, birth certificates, death certificates, and the like) as if there is total agreement on its definition. However, nothing could be further from the truth. Race has been defined socially, biologically, and geographically, so the definition of race varies depending on the source.

Ethnicity deals with an individual's sense of identification and provides a sense of belonging to a reference group (Slonim, 1993). Table 1.1 provides the breakdown for ethnic groups in the United States. The five ethnic groups listed on Table 1.1 are African American, Native American, Asian American, Latino American, and European American. Mixing of ethnic groups is not uncommon; however, interracial groups are not included on this table because of the infinite number of possibilities. As Table 1.1 indicates, the United States is truly a polyethnic society. As with other ethnicities, there are also many possible White ethnic identities and backgrounds (Fine, 1997).

In this book, nonwhite ethnic groups are referred to as *people of color.* Alternatively, *students of color, children of color,* or some other variations may be used. While this terminology has shortcomings (e.g., it implies that Whites are colorless), it is preferable to the term *minority.* Although the term *minority* is often used to refer to nonwhite groups who make up the numerical minority in the United States, it also connotes *less than* or *inferior.*

TABLE 1.1 *Ethnic Compositions in the United States*

Ethnic Group	*Inclusive Groups*
African Americans	African-Caribbean Native Africans
Native Americans/ Alaskan Natives (approximately 300–500 nations)	Largest tribes include Cherokee, Navajo, Sioux, Chippewa/Aleuts, and Eskimos
Asian Pacific/Americans	Largest groups include Chinese, Japanese, Korean, Vietnamese, Cambodian, Thai, Filipino, Laotian, Lao-Hmong, Burmese, Samoan, Guamanian, Indonesians, Indians (East), Pakistanis, Saudi Arabians, Iranians, Iraqis, and other Arabic-speaking peoples
Latino Americans	Mexicans, Puerto Ricans, Cubans, Central and South Americans
European Americans	English, Welsh, Scottish, German, Dutch, Irish, French, Polish, Russian, Portuguese, Italian, Swiss, Danish, and other European groups

Source: "Family Ecologies of Ethnic Minority Children" by A. O. Harrison, M. N. Wilson, C. J. Pine, S. Q. Chan, and R. Buriel, 1990, *Child Development, 61,* 347–362. Copyright 1990 by the Society for Research in Child Development, Inc. Adapted by permission.

Journeying Through the Narratives

We invite you to travel with us through the stories in this book, to hear the voices of the individuals, to allow them to resonate with you, and to cause you to reflect on your own experiences and preferences. As you read and reflect, ask yourself, "How is he or she (the storyteller) thinking about this? How is it similar or dissimilar to my thinking?"

As you read, imagine a panel of people from different backgrounds telling their own stories. Imagine me as the moderator mediating with my worldview. At times, I will interject cross dialogues and references between chapters. As I edited each chapter, I situated myself in the school settings, homes, times, and places. I invite you to do the same and to view the stories from inside rather than from outside.

Realizing that each of us is inextricably connected to each other, the stories should remind us of our humanity (Boutte, 1999). As Mary Catherine Bateson (as cited in Ayers, 1989, p. xii) has written, " . . . no microcosm is completely separate, no tide pool, no forest, no family, no nation. Indeed, the knowledge drawn from the life of some single organism or community or from the intimate experience of an individual may prove to be relevant to decisions that affect the health of a city or the peace of the world."

Each chapter includes the following information:

    I. Editor's overview of the chapter
   II. Author's story and his/her school experiences
  III. Presentation of stories
- Description of the setting embedded in the story (school, community, etc.)
- Introduction of the interviewee (family profile, grade level, age, etc.)
- Highlights of interviewee's story

  IV. Reflections on each story—Interpretations and analysis by the author of the chapter may be integrated within the story or in separate sections, depending on the author's preference.
   V. Educational implications—Specific implications for schools, teachers, and other educators are presented. Some chapters integrate educational implications within the chapters, while others include them as a separate subsection. Consonant with the critical theory framework, we wanted to empower the interviewees and not silence their voices (or have our thoughts dominate and overshadow theirs) in terms of what their stories mean for others in similar circumstances. Therefore, we consciously tried to capture the essence of the interviewees' stories. In an attempt to reduce the likelihood that information gathered would benefit only the researchers (authors) and not the individuals who willingly and trustingly shared intimate aspects of their lives, many of the stories and implications include direct quotations from the interviewees.

VI. Editor's commentary
VII. Resources for educators—A list of resources specific to each ethnic group will be provided (e.g., agencies that work with particular populations, Internet resources, bibliographies).

At the onset of the project, authors were given the following general guidelines. They selected participants for their respective chapters based on relationships that they had with the interviewees.

1. Interview two to four people—children and/or adults.
2. Obtain informed consent and let interviewees or their parents know that we plan to publish a book that will include their stories.
3. Based on our brainstorming session and subsequent discussions, we agreed that all authors would ask a few standard questions. While each author used her or his professional judgment in terms of other questions and probes, we cautioned authors about asking leading questions which may influence the interviewees' responses. We emphasized that we wanted authentic viewpoints from the interviewees. Hence, questions such as, "Did you have a lot of BAD experiences in school?" were avoided.
4. Each author asked some version of the following questions.
   a. Tell me about your school experiences (sample probing questions: What did/do you like best? Who did/do you play with at school? Why? How do you feel about school? Reading? Math? Favorite subject(s)? Favorite teacher(s)? Least favorite subject(s)? Favorite teacher(s)? Least favorite teacher(s)? Why?).
   b. If adults were interviewed, authors asked how their school experiences compared to their children's. If interviewees had/have unfavorable school experiences, authors probed to find out how they think teachers/educators could have made their experiences more favorable.
   In many instances, the responses to the interviews are captured in direct quotation from the participants and the reader is invited to make her or his own interpretations of the text. However, because the authors and I narrated the stories, our interpretations are inevitably offered as well.
5. Authors sought feedback from interviewees and/or another person(s) who were recommended by the interviewer in order to best capture the accuracy of the interviewees' stories.

Reflective Activity

Realizing the influence of our own life experiences on teaching, write a story (narrative) about your own school experiences and analyze the experiences in reference to yourself as future (or present) educator/professional. What concepts can you identify in your story from educational literature?

References

Apple, M. W. (1998). *The curriculum: Problems, politics, and possibilities* (SUNY Seeing frontiers in education). Albany: State University of New York Press.

Ayers, W. (1989). *The good preschool teacher: Six teachers reflect on their lives.* New York: Teachers College Press.

Boutte, G. S. (1999). *Multicultural education: Raising consciousness.* Atlanta, GA: Wadsworth.

Boutte, G. S., & DeFlorimonte, D. (1998). The complexities of valuing cultural differences without overemphasizing them: Taking it to the next level. *Equity & Excellence in Education, 31* (3), 54–62.

Bruner, J. (1986). *Actual minds, possible worlds.* Cambridge, MA: Harvard University Press.

Delpit, L. (1993). The silenced dialogue: Power and pedagogy in educating other people's children. In L. Weis & M. Fine (Eds.), *Beyond voices: Class, race, and gender in the United States Schools* (pp. 119–139). Albany: State University of New York Press.

Delpit, L. (1995). *Other people's children. Cultural conflicts in the classroom.* New York: The New Press.

Featherstone, J. (1995). Letter to a young teacher. In W. Ayers (Ed.), *To become a teacher: Making a difference in children's lives* (pp. 11–22). New York: Teachers College.

Fine, M. (1997). Witnessing whiteness. In M. Fine, L. Weis, L. C. Powell, & L. M. Wong (Eds.), *Off white* (pp. 57–65). New York: Routledge.

Fordham, S. (1988). Racelessness as a factor in black students' school success: Pragmatic strategy or Pyrrhic victory? *Harvard Educational Review, 58* (1), 54–84.

Fordham, S. (1996). *Blacked out: Dilemmas of race, identity, and success at Capital High.* Chicago: University of Chicago Press.

Freire, P. (1999). *Pedagogy of the oppressed.* New York: Continuum Publishing Group.

Fu, V. R., & Stremmel, A. J. (1999). *Affirming diversity through democratic conversations.* Upper Saddle River, NJ: Merrill.

Gallard, A. J. (1993). Learning science in multicultural environments. In K. Tobin (Ed.), *The practice of constructivism in science education* (pp. 171–180). Hillsdale, NJ: Lawrence Erlbaum.

Greene, M. (1995). *Releasing the imagination.* San Francisco: Jossey-Bass.

Guba, E. G., & Lincoln, Y. S. (1994). Competing paradigms in qualitative research. In N. K. Denzin & H. S. Lincoln (Eds.), *Handbook of qualitative research* (pp. 105–117). Thousand Oaks, CA: Sage.

Harrison, A. O., Wilson, M. N., Pine, C. J., Chan, S. Q., & Buriel, R. (1990). Family ecologies of ethnic minority children. *Child Development, 61* (2), 347–362.

Hatch, J. A., & Wisniewski, R. (1995). *Life history and narrative.* New York: Falmer Press.

Heath, S. B. (1992). *Ways with words.* New York: Cambridge University Press.

Herrnstein, R. J., & Murray, C. (1994). *The bell curve: Intelligence and class structure in American life.* New York: The Free Press.

hooks, b. (1993). *Sisters of the yam: Black women and self-recovery.* Boston: South End Press.

hooks, b. (1994). *Teaching to transgress.* New York: Routledge.

Howard, G. R. (1993). Whites in multicultural education: Rethinking our role. *Phi Delta Kappan, 75* (1), 36–41.

Irvine, J. J. (1990). *Black students and school failure: Policies, practices and prescriptions.* New York: Greenwood Press.

Kridel, C. (1998). Landscapes, biography, and the preservation of the present. In W. C. Ayers & J. L. Miller (Eds.), *A light in dark times: Maxine Greene and the unfinished conversation* (pp. 122–133). New York: Teachers College Press.

Ladson-Billings, G. (1994). *The dreamkeepers: Successful teachers of African American children.* San Francisco: Jossey-Bass.

Lankshear, C., & McLaren, P. L. (Eds.). (1993). *Critical literacy: Policies, praxis, and the postmodern.* Albany: State University of New York Press.

McIntosh, P. (1995). White privilege and male privilege: A personal account of coming to see correspondence through work in women's studies. In P. H. Collins & M. L. Anderson (Eds.), *Race, class, and gender: An anthology* (pp. 70–81). Belmont, CA: Wadsworth.

Mishler, E. G. (1986). *Research interviewing: Context and narrative.* Cambridge, MA: Harvard Press.

Ogbu, J. U. (1990). Overcoming racial barriers to equal access. In J. I. Goodlad & P. Keating (Eds.), *Access to knowledge: An agenda for our nation's schools* (pp. 59–89). New York: College Entrance Examination Board.

Pinar, W. F. (1988). *Contemporary curriculum discourses.* Scottsdale AZ: Gorsuch Scarisbrick.

Pokinghorne, D. E. (1995). Narrative configuration in qualitative analysis. In J. A. Hatch & R. Wisniewski (Eds.), *Life history and narrative* (pp. 5–23). London: The Falmer Press.

Rosaldo, R. (1989). *Cultural truth: The remaking of social analyses.* Boston: Beacon Press.

Schofield, J. W. (1997). Causes and consequences of the colorblind perspective. In J. A. Banks & C. A. M. Banks (Eds.), *Multicultural education/Issues and perspectives* (pp. 251–271). Boston: Allyn and Bacon.

Slattery, P. (1995). *Curriculum development in the postmodern era.* New York: Garland.

Slonim, M. B. (1993). *Children, culture, and ethnicity (evaluating and understanding the impact).* New York: Garland.

Tobin, K. (1993). *The practice of constructivism in science education,* Hillsdale, NJ: Lawrence Erlbaum.

Zimmerman, W. (1982). *How to tape instant oral biographies.* New York: Guarioonex Press.

No More Cotton Picking

African American Voices from a Small Southern Town

Vivian Gunn Morris and Curtis L. Morris

Editor's Overview _____

This nostalgic chapter provides a window into the lives of four African Americans who grew up in a small town in Alabama during the Civil Rights Movement era. The school is the center of this African American community. Teachers reside in the same neighborhood as the students and attend the same churches, so the connections between school and home are seamless. These brief stories demonstrate how the four students experienced the all-Black school similarly in some cases and differently in others. The career trajectories of the two couples are decidedly different, but it is clear that something very enduring, positive, and intangible occurred at Trenholm High School (which served grades one through twelve). This "something" has influenced the lives of the storytellers and their descendants indefinitely. Readers will find timeless messages and implications for educating African American students.

Introduction

Both the coauthors and the two interviewees graduated in the midst of the Civil Rights era (between 1959 and 1962). We attended Trenholm High School, a segregated African American school that served grades one through twelve for more than ninety years before it was closed by a court order in

1969. Trenholm High School, located in the small, southern town Tuscumbia, Alabama, was established as the second high school for African Americans in Alabama. While the school had its beginnings during the 1870s, the high school department was established in 1896 with the financial support of African American citizens and boasted its first four-year graduating class in 1922. By the time the school building was closed in 1969, the physical plant consisted of a brick veneer building with twelve classrooms, a library, science laboratory, separate lunch room, band room, home economics room, auto mechanic shop facilities, and gymnasium. The school building was named in honor of its third principal, George Washington Trenholm, who later became president of Alabama State College (now Alabama State University) in Montgomery. At its height in the mid-1950s, the school had an estimated enrollment of 500 students. The school building was located in the heart of the African American community on a two-acre plot of land that had been donated by African American citizens. The majority of teachers and students resided within a four- or five-block radius of the school building.

If an outsider were to view the school, he or she might notice that classrooms were often overcrowded, that buildings were often too hot or too cold, and that there were too little equipment and supplies and too few books in the library. Despite the lack of financial resources needed to maintain the physical plant adequately and to purchase enough books, supplies, and equipment for the academic program, we generally looked forward to attending classes each day. Students, parents, and community residents attributed this feeling to the caring and committed teachers, programs and activities offered by the school, and the involvement of families and community in the life of the school (Morris & Morris, 2000).

Tuscumbia, Alabama, is best known as the birthplace of Helen Keller, a woman who was deaf and blind who graduated from college and became a writer and an international lecturer who championed the rights of people with disabilities. At one time, Tuscumbia was the center of economic and industrial growth in northwest Alabama and served as a political base for many state and local Democrats (Leftwich, 1935; Report, 1955; Shoals Life, 1998). The town has generally maintained a fairly consistent population of 75 percent White and 25 percent African American. The current population is approximately 8,400, which represents a significant increase over the 5,000 residents during the time we attended Trenholm High School. Presently, Tuscumbia City Schools operates a unitary school system with 1,490 students in four school buildings.

This chapter shares the perspectives of four African Americans who grew up in the same segregated school community. These stories explore the common experiences they had as well as the different experiences of each and how these and subsequent experiences affected their beliefs about schools and teachers. The first two stories introduce the coauthors, who are husband and wife. The two interviewees are also married to one another.

No More Cotton Picking

What is the theme "No More Cotton Picking" all about? I remember learning to chop and pick cotton around the age of nine, primarily in the summer and on Saturdays during the school year. I really hated the dust, the insects, all the weeds, and the cotton balls that caused tears on your fingers, and the heat from the hot sun. We only earned three dollars per day, for nine to ten hours of work, from dawn to dusk. The parts of the day that were bearable included the ride to and from the field, lunch time, and occasionally when clouds covered the sun and we enjoyed a bit of a reprieve from the heat, or when it rained and we could go home.

When my brothers and I were teenagers, our parents purchased a farm where they raised hogs and chicken, had a pear orchard, and grew corn and cotton. I knew then that farming was not the life for me, especially the back-breaking task of picking cotton. Once I enrolled in college, I attended classes during the academic year and summers in order to complete my degree in three years. That also ensured no more cotton chopping or cotton picking during the summer months for me—not ever. I completed my bachelor's degree in May, worked as a receptionist for one of two African American physicians in our college town for the summer, and began my teaching career in September. Since my high school years, I have made it my business to view cotton fields from afar. Those early work experiences were a major motivation for my completing a college degree in order to pursue a career as a professional.

As a young girl, schooling was the center of life in the small segregated town in which I grew up. Following graduation from Trenholm High School in 1959, I ultimately earned a Ph.D. degree from Vanderbilt University in 1973. I grew up with one older brother and one younger brother. Our father was a laborer at the local aluminum production plant and our mother worked at various jobs, including working as a domestic in the homes of White families, a sewing machine operator in a local plant that made bags for baling cotton, a seamstress in a local department store, and a nutrition aide for a local USDA program. But her primary responsibility was being a homemaker. Before my dad got a "public job" (as they called it) at the aluminum plant, both my parents were sharecroppers. For many years, my dad was also the president of the African American aluminum workers union that was later merged with the White local union in the 1960s. Both of my parents were very active in the church and saw that each of us was as well.

Shortly after completing my Ph.D. degree, I was visiting my mother while one of her friends, Mrs. Hankins, was there. Mrs. Hankins remarked, "Now that you are a doctor, you can come back home and take care of us." I quickly informed her that I was an education doctor, not a medical doctor. Like Mrs. Hankins, the only doctors with whom I had been acquainted were the medical doctor and the dentist. As a matter of fact, I really was not totally aware of what a Ph.D. meant when I completed my bachelor's degree. I just knew that professors who were called "Dr." seemed to be in important positions at the college. My understanding of a college education was four years of courses and then I would be ready to teach. Importantly, it meant that I did not have to earn poverty wages as a domestic or field worker.

Neither of my parents had the privilege of completing high school. Dad completed the eleventh grade while Mom completed grade eight. However, they were very persistent in encouraging me and my brothers to do well in elementary and secondary school and attend college in order to pursue professional careers. Mom later completed her GED (with flying colors, as the examiners told her) while my youngest brother was completing his bachelor's degree. Both my brothers completed MBA degrees and are successful businessmen. I have been an educator all my professional life and have taught at every level from preschool, elementary, junior high school, high school, through college levels. As a professor, I have taught at colleges and universities in Alabama, New Jersey, Philadelphia, and Tennessee for more than thirty years. Currently, I am a professor of education at a large, urban university in Tennessee. My husband (coauthor of this chapter) and I are the parents of two adult daughters (one deceased) and a teenage son.

From kindergarten to high school graduation, school was the place to be. It was the place where all the important social, cultural, recreational, and educational activities took place in my community as I grew and matured during the 1940s and 1950s. There were so many things that I liked about school that I don't think there was any one thing that I liked best. I enjoyed the challenge of learning and mastering subject matter, whether it was reading, English, mathematics, science, or home economics. I think I must have read every book we had in our small library collection. At that time, Blacks were not allowed to use the public library downtown. I'd even stay after school to read to my heart's delight. I enjoyed the extracurricular activities as well. I held offices in school clubs, played in the band, sang in the chorus, performed in the spring plays for our parents, attended athletic contests, participated in oratorical contests, competed in field and track events, and played basketball.

The connections between school and home were seamless. My playmates were primarily the girls and boys who were in my class, even though I played with older and younger students as well. We were also neighbors, so most of us had been friends and playmates since we were preschoolers. Many of us were classmates and playmates from kindergarten through grade twelve.

Caring is frequently touted as an important trait for teachers to possess (Kunjufu, 1986; Ladson-Billings, 1994). For me, caring was personified by Mrs. Willie Mae Thompson, my home economics teacher. Mrs. Thompson was like a third mother to me—third only to my biological mother and favorite aunt (Earline). As with my friends, we lived in the same neighborhood (as did most of our teachers and principals). Most families attended one of the four Black churches in the community. Hence, many of the teachers also taught us in Sunday school as well. We were welcome to Mrs. Thompson's anytime and could visit without calling. So it is no surprise that home economics was probably my favorite subject (if I had to choose a favorite). I liked being able to immediately apply what I learned. Because of home economics, my family enjoyed (or suffered) my preparation of foods in new and different ways. School broadened my horizons about different ways of doing things. Thanks to Mrs. Thompson, I made most of my own clothes after taking home economics in seventh grade. But I was also fortunate to have many other outstanding and caring teachers as well.

At the risk of painting an overly idyllic portrait of my school experience, let me point out that children were pretty much the same as they are today. Bullying seems to be a common school experience and is part of my memories as well. In first grade, some of my classmates decided to bully me and threw rocks at me on my way home from school. I reported the incident to Mrs. Magnolia Watkins, my first-grade teacher. Mrs. Watkins intervened and it never happened again.

Weekly school assemblies were an important part of school life in my community. Pictures of famous African Americans adorned the walls of the auditorium. We recited poems that they had written, and our voices echoed as we sang "Lift Every Voice and Sing" (the Negro national anthem), and many other Negro spirituals and hymns. Activities of this nature were repeated daily in our morning devotionals in our homerooms and during recitals, concerts, and plays that were performed in the evenings for our parents and the community.

I loved reading. Each year we purchased the books that we needed from a store located downtown. My parents always purchased the books that we needed and paid the incidental fees (about two dollars) that were used to purchase instructional supplies needed.

My school experiences sharply contrast with those of my children. I attended a small, segregated, African American school in the South, while they attended much larger, desegregated schools in both the South and the Northeast. For example, our daughters earned their high school diplomas from a school that had a student population of 2,400—a small town in our estimation. For the most part, the schools they attended were not neighborhood schools, and they often rode the bus to school, while I lived three blocks from my school building (first through twelfth grade). Our children have often been the only African Americans in their classes or in the vast minority in terms of ethnicity. They knew few of their teachers outside the school building, while the majority of my classroom teachers were our neighbors, and they also sponsored social, civic, and religious activities for school-age children in the community.

My children's schools provided textbooks and instructional supplies. There were adequate books in the libraries, appropriate audio-visual equipment, and spacious physical plants. The school I attended always appeared to be understaffed, with little equipment, scarce resources, and a poor physical plant. The toilets never seemed to work. They overflowed and water often stood on the floor. The stalls were doorless except for one for the teachers, so there was no privacy. Although poor facilities such as these have been associated with low-quality schools, this was not the case at Trenholm. Our competent and caring teachers, good academic programs, a wide range of extracurricular activities, and a community that worked with the principals and teachers made our school a good school for children in our community. The quality of the graduates from this small segregated school provides clear evidence of the quality of the education that was provided. The graduates from my class have fared extremely well. Three-fourths of the nineteen students pursued a postsecondary education—they either attended or completed technical college or a four-year college or higher. Many of our children have attended or completed college as well. So it seems that my motivation not to end up picking cotton has spanned another generation.

Could I Really Be President—a Leader— Curtis's Story

What is college? What does it mean to go to college? As I was nearing my high school graduation, I was not sure what it really meant. No one from my immediate family had attended college, but I knew there was something for me beyond high school other than working at one of the local plants. I knew I needed education beyond high school in order to pursue a career as a "professional." I had heard of the famous place called Tuskegee that Booker Taliaferro Washington had founded and where Dr. George Washington Carver had been a scientist. That sounded like the best place for me to go since I always strived for the best.

Like Vivian's (my wife) father, my father also worked at the Reynolds Metals Aluminum Plant after returning from active duty in World War II. The similarities in our lives are not surprising given the context that we both grew up in. Although my mother's primary responsibility was being a homemaker, which included caring for me and my younger brother and sister, she occasionally worked as a maid at a hotel and was also a domestic in the homes of White families.

Both Vivian and I attended the same, small, African American high school and graduated in 1959, two years after we were married. After graduation, I attended Tuskegee Institute (now Tuskegee University) and Alabama A & M College (now Alabama A & M University), two historically black colleges. I was not able to finish college at the time because I had to work either full time or part time to take care of my young family. Later, I completed my bachelor's degree in business administration from Florence State College, a historically White, state-supported college that was six miles from Tuscumbia, Alabama, the town in which I grew up. Interestingly, when

I earned my high school diploma in 1959, it was a violation of state law for African Americans to attend Florence State College (now the University of North Alabama).

In 1972, I earned a master's degree in urban studies from Alabama A & M University. I have also pursued professional development opportunities in accounting, corporate planning, business management and related courses at other universities and institutions. During the earlier stages of my career, I held management and executive positions in training/job placement, planning, and fund raising/allocations with companies in Alabama, New Jersey, and Pennsylvania. Currently, I am employed with Memphis City Schools, the largest urban district in Tennessee, where I am responsible for facilitating the renewal of the district's strategic plan and coordinating the accreditation/school improvement activities for 164 schools that serve over 118,000 students.

It is not surprising that I ended up working for a school district, since school always played a prominent role in my home and community. Our high school (grades one through twelve) was the center of activity for the African American community.

My playmates were my classmates, some boys who were younger, and some who were older. But we all attended the same school. It seemed sort of natural because this group was engaged in similar activities at school. The same group of boys and girls played in the band, sang in the chorus, or participated in sports with me.

I benefited from academics and extracurricular activities, but in different ways. Academics were stimulating, and sports helped me develop leadership and organizational skills and the type of discipline needed to get things done from day to day. Of course, excelling in school was expected of me. My grandparents, uncles, and parents constantly conveyed the importance of school to me. Doing well in school was not negotiable.

Reading is one of my great passions. I guess this is one of the reasons I really enjoyed being in plays during my elementary and high school years. You had to learn the scripts and I would also read further to learn more about the environments in which the plays were set. I would rehearse the scripts with my family. As I look back, I probably didn't read as much as I would like to have because of the lack of resources. There were few books in my home. The books we brought home from school, newspapers, our Bible and Sunday school materials were pretty much the extent of reading resources in our home. I enjoyed reading magazines such as *Life* and *Look* that were found in our small school library. Magazines featuring African Americans were becoming popular, like *Jet* and *Ebony,* and I looked forward to reading them as well. Our school library wasn't very appealing in terms of a place to go to find out about the world. I saw it as a resource to help me complete a class assignment. All of the books appeared to be very, very old to me, no real appeal. Maybe that's why I like bookstores and libraries so much now. They are right in the middle of the community and they have attractive and appealing resources. Now, I can't find enough time to spend in bookstores or libraries. When I go to the very nice ones, I often overstay my time because of my interest in the printed word.

When I was in elementary and high school, mathematics was just another subject that I had to pass. I didn't see the emphasis placed on it that related to real life until I got to college. Mathematics became a really important subject when I got to college because the professors helped me to see it as an important tool—how it could be used and how to use it.

I began to discover the importance of mathematics in every aspect of my life. However, as I look back, a major practical use of mathematics for me while still in high school was reading music to play the trombone in the marching and concert bands and singing tenor in the high school choir. No one explained the relationship of mathematics and music at that time.

I can't remember having a least favorite teacher. I would really have to stretch to think of one because I was so turned on with school itself that I guess I never thought in those terms. One of my favorite teachers was Mrs. Garlor Hyler, my seventh-grade English teacher. She was a no-nonsense teacher who really taught me all the basics in English that took me through my college years. Mrs. Hyler had a great command of the content and could expand on the subject far beyond what was in the textbook. That was very impressive to me. It really caught my attention.

Coach Charles Mahorney was another favorite teacher of mine. In addition to coaching me in football and field and track, he taught all the health and physical education courses at my school. While I was a junior or senior in high school, Coach Mahorney taught a segment of the health and physical education course that dealt with family living. I especially liked the book we used in that class. It was one of the few new books we used and it included lots of graphs and other illustrations that enhanced the narrative. We discussed the concepts of dating, courtship, and marriage, and many other practical ideas that related to real life. We had opportunities to explore these concepts through discussions from our own point of view as well as others. This course really held my attention. Perhaps this education helped me deal with the challenges of being a married teenager.

There was not a lot of variation in socioeconomic status in our small-town school, where families were either poor or poorer. I never really thought about the issue of race and culture as it related to school. Looking back, I do recall celebrating Negro History Week in February of each year. We always included Negro spirituals and music by African Americans in our repertoire of songs we sang at assemblies and recitals and the songs we played in the concert and marching bands. A vivid memory of mine is literally passing by the White school (elementary school was near my home) on my way to Trenholm High, my school. The board of education was right up the hill from where I lived and my White neighbors walked in one direction to school and I walked in another. And I had quite a ways to walk. Even though the White school was right across the street or within a block of the Black children's homes, we had to walk quite a distance (e.g., eight blocks to two miles) in rain, sunshine, sleet, or snow to get to the Black school. A few families who could afford to have cars drove their children to school or sent them in cabs. Many of the teachers at Trenholm lived within a four-block radius of the school. A few of the children did too—like Vivian. Vivian lived three blocks from the school, so her walk was a lot less than mine.

What can schools and teachers do to help students have a more successful experience? It appears to me that schools must first create compelling environments that stimulate learning, that make it convenient for students to learn, and place in that environment teachers who are equipped to manage classrooms in order to help students learn. In addition to teachers having earned degrees in a particular subject, they must also have some practical experience in using that subject matter in life and be able to communicate that to their students. Teachers need to be able to relate their subject matter to how the world really works and how students can use that subject matter content in a world that demands performance. For example, how does the content relate to a future vocation or in the role of being a good citizen who contributes to the lives of individuals and the community?

Before I attended first grade, my paternal grandfather asked me what I wanted to be when I grew up. I said, "I want to be president!" Well, I haven't become president of the United States yet, but I had opportunities to serve in many leadership roles throughout elementary and high school at our small, segregated, African American school in northwest Alabama. I served as president of my homeroom classes for several years, president of the student council, and captain and cocaptain of my high school football teams. I was also a leader in the high school band and choir, Boy Scouts, and in the Trade and Industrial Education Club. I had many opportunities throughout my elementary and high school days to appear before audiences of students, teachers, and other community residents. I was also a teen leader in the local church where my family attended. My school and community experiences helped to provide the confidence needed to take on leadership positions in my professional, religious, and community life after completing college. So with caring schools, communities, and homes, children from all walks of life can be leaders, and even president.

We Were Shortchanged!—Wilson's Story

Wilson graduated from Trenholm High School a year later than we (Vivian and Curtis) did, in 1960, and immediately began working in a local grocery store in his neighborhood. He is married to Madeline, his high school sweetheart, and they have three adult children, two boys and one girl. A few years after graduation from high school, Wilson began working at the local Reynolds Metals Aluminum Plant where his dad and many other friends and neighbors had worked from their early years until retirement. Reynolds Metals reduced its local operation in northwest Alabama when Wilson was in his forties, so he took early retirement at that time along with many other employees who had worked at the plant for many years.

Like both of us, he really enjoyed school. He liked the surroundings, being with people, and learning how to associate with people as well as academics. He fondly recalls his clan—he and three of his closest friends. Wilson noted that they just did "young men" things, whatever young men were doing at the time. Extracurricular activities were very important aspects of school life for Wilson also. He played football and basketball, acted in school plays, sang in the chorus, and played in the concert and marching bands.

Reflecting on his experiences in school, Wilson says, "I feel great that I had an opportunity to attend there [Trenholm High School]. And right now, I am more appreciative about it than I was at that time." While in school, Wilson excelled in mathematics but disliked English, even though his twelfth-grade English teacher was one of his favorite teachers. He noted, "I guess one of the reasons [that English was his least favorite subject] was that I never could speak it too good. But I don't know. I loved the teacher, Miss Marie Long. English, I didn't hate it, but I didn't seem to be able to master it as well as other things I was involved in." He also stated that Miss Long did all that she could to help students learn. Some of Wilson's impressions of his school experiences echo ours. He speaks favorably of teachers. He fondly recalled the principal who was also his twelfth-grade government and economics teacher: "He would have you climbing in your social studies book and on test day, he'd give you a test on just what was going on in the world." But Wilson's memories are also laced with bitterness.

Wilson stated that he was glad when the segregated African American school that he attended was closed in 1969 because he believed they were shortchanged on education. He indicated:

> I figured as an all-Black school, we were being shortchanged on education. If you were exceptional, you had a shot, but at Trenholm, some teachers didn't know as much as some students. I was glad to see it go, I just wished I could have attended Deshler, integrated. I really wish that. Opportunity was so much greater; everything was greater. I was glad to see Trenholm High School go. Being an all-White school [Deshler], the opportunity was there for them [his children].

Comparing his school experiences with his children who attended integrated schools, Wilson feels that his children are a lot better off. He feels that the money that was available for resources at the desegregated high school was what contributed to the differences in opportunities for students as compared to the segregated, African American school that he attended. Sadly, inequities between schools for low-income, rural, and urban children continue to exist across the United States (Kozol, 1991). Often, children of color bear the brunt of schools having lower per-pupil expenditure, inadequate facilities, and the like (Boutte, 1999; Kozol, 1991).

While Wilson sees many advantages of the desegregated school, he emphasizes that discipline is missing from schools today. When he was in school, not learning was not an option: "I had no choice. I had to like those books." Like both of us (Curtis and Vivian), Wilson had too many favorite teachers to mention. We wonder how many African American children today can say this with confidence and without hesitation. Perhaps, despite the lack of adequate facilities and resources, something more enduring and positive took place at Trenholm High. Wilson's wife, Madeline, thinks so.

And It All Really Came Out Good— Madeline's Account

Madeline graduated from Trenholm High School in 1962. She was the third child of a family of six that included four girls and two boys. She has worked for the board of education for the past twenty-eight years; she is manager of one of the elementary school cafeterias. She and Wilson have three children.

Madeline's sentiments about the school are favorable: "I was a pretty good student in school. I did my best. And it all came out really good. I didn't go to college, but I applied myself so that I can make it all right." School brings back memories of close friendships for Madeline. Madeline indicated that she had three best girl friends from school with whom she did lots of things like spending-the-night parties and attending school socials (dances) and ball games.

Defying stereotypes that females tend to do less well in mathematics, Madeline indicated that mathematics was one of her favorite subjects and that English was her least favorite subject (like her husband). Madeline shared, "I did well, but I just didn't like English that much. I did my best." Yet, her favorite teacher was Mrs. Barbara Stewart, librarian and teacher of junior high English. Madeline added that Mrs. Stewart was just one person that you could really talk to if you had a problem: "You know, even after teaching, you could go to her with problems and sit down and talk."

Madeline still holds a great deal of respect for many of her teachers:

Mrs. Deloris McCree was one fantastic teacher. And you know, you read the chapter before you go [to class]. You didn't take books to class. When you got there, she'd ask you questions. I remember I answered a question one day. She asked it and I answered it, and I was wrong but I told her that's what was in the book. And she told me no and I told her yes. She asked me where was my book and I told her in the library and she told me to go and get my book. And I showed her and I was right. That was in the book, but she said the company made a misprint. She was just smart. She didn't give me a bad grade for it. You know she was just smart. That was the way it was.

Madeline reflects on how teachers and schools could help student have more successful experiences:

You know, it's hard to say what teachers can do. First, we need our children to show that interest level, what they want out of life. If a teacher sees that a child wants something, that can happen. But there are a lot of kids who go in there [classrooms] and they don't want anything. And it's hard. We have a lot of good teachers who will reach out to a child if they see that he really wants something. But I don't know, maybe that's not it.

Unlike her husband, Madeline indicated that she wasn't happy when the African American school she attended was closed, but she believed that the desegregated school offered more opportunities for African American children. For example, she indicated that when her younger sister attended Deshler [the desegregated school], they had more classes and more opportunity to get higher-level classes than Trenholm did. Each of her children also graduated from Deshler High School, the previously all-White school in the town.

Discussion and Analyses

There are some common themes that are reflected in the stories of the interviewees and the coauthors that may be due in part to their growing up in the same community and attending the same school from grades one through twelve. On the other hand, some of the recommendations for improving schools are quite different, which may reflect the divergent experiences of the coauthors and interviewees following their high school years. The importance of caring, competent, and committed teachers was reflected in the stories and was selected by this school community as the number-one factor that made their small-town, segregated, African American school a good school (Morris & Morris, 2000). In each of these stories, some of the favorite teachers exhibited caring by being confidants of the students, providing personal guidance, and treating the students as family members. This concept of caring as an important teacher characteristic is appearing more frequently in recent teacher education literature and has emerged especially as a critical theme in case studies of segregated African American schools or of African American teachers (Ceceleski, 1994; Dempsey & Noblit, 1996; Edwards, 1996; Foster, 1997; Irvine & Irvine, 1983; Ladson-Billings, 1994; Rodgers; 1975; Sowell, 1976; Walker, 1996). Dempsey and Noblit (1993) noted that in the context of African American education, "Caring about a child meant that teachers taught valued information and nurtured and sustained the child" (p. 48). They noted the essentials of caring as continuities of purpose, place, people, and curriculum, which is reflective of the work by Noddings (1992) on developing caring relationships in school environments. Most of our teachers at Trenholm High School were also residents of the school community; they sponsored community organizations that supported the school; they were Sunday school teachers of the children they taught during the week; and their children attended the school as well. Ladson-Billings's (1994) work also highlights the importance of strong school–community connections for successful teachers of African American students.

Wilson expressed some doubts about the competence of some of his teachers at the segregated, African American school, while the coauthors and Madeline felt confident that their teachers were smart and provided a very good education for the students. Each of the former students communicated their participation in a wide variety of social, recreational, and leadership activities that were provided through the school and supervised by their classroom teachers. They appeared to have many opportunities throughout their school years to develop their talents in a wide variety of areas with support from the school faculty and staff and from parents and from the community.

Many southern, African American public schools, like Trenholm High School, were originally established by African American families who purchased land and buildings that were later donated to the local boards of education in order for the schools to become a part of the public school system. Most of these schools could not have survived without the continuing support of the African American communities in which they were located.

Lightfoot (1978) noted the importance of collaborating with families and the community in order to be successful in teaching African American children. In the recounting of the story of Caswell County Training School in rural North Carolina, Walker (1996) emphasized the important relationship that exists between the school and the community. Ceceleski (1994) tells how one African American community refused to allow its school to be closed and of the struggle that took place to succeed in that mission. And Sowell (1974) reported that parental involvement was a key variable in creating academic excellence in schools.

The coauthors, Wilson, and Madeline spoke of the scarce instructional resources and the poor physical plant at their segregated school building. However, their children attended desegregated schools where they had spacious physical plants, ample instructional resources, and a much wider range of upper-level courses. What appears to be noticeably missing from the descriptions of their children's schools are references to the relationships with teachers, the social environment in the school, and the support and involvement of families and community in the life of the school. In a recent study of this school community (Morris & Morris, 2000), Trenholm High School graduates note that at the segregated African American school

1. they trusted and respected their teachers
2. teachers knew their students well both as the students participated in activities during school hours and outside the school
3. teachers demonstrated in a variety of ways that they cared about students.

It seemed clear that students viewed the Trenholm school community as a family where everybody cared about each other and looked out for each other. Students also felt that teachers were their friends. Graduates noted that teachers helped students to develop a strong sense of self and provided activities for students in-class and outside of the classroom to help develop talents of individual students. Teachers valued the active involvement of parents and other community residents in the life of the school, so there was a continuity of shared values. Students believed that teachers enjoyed their work with the students and were competent in their subject matter areas. (p. 237)

Trenholm High School, the African American high school that the coauthors, Wilson, and Madeline attended, was closed in 1969, and African American students were assigned to attend the desegregated high school (the former all-White high school in the town) outside their immediate community. Morris and Morris (2000) noted that:

They [African American students] enrolled at a desegregated school outside their community that had a superior physical plant and equipment, appropriate school supplies, and textbooks. However, many African American students felt that the major problem that they faced at Deshler High School was racial discrimination. They believed that the environment was a hostile one for them. The students reported that they were underrepresented in school activities, were excluded from the decision-making process, experienced a loss of ethnic identity, received little or no counseling, felt a lack of support from White teachers, and experienced feelings of not belonging. In addition, Trenholm students and families lost their school colors, their symbols, and their mascot. All of these symbols were important socially and emotionally to the students and to the African American community. It was around these symbols that the school community rallied. There was no longer the maroon and gold and the Trenholm Wildcats, but red and White and the Deshler Tigers. (p. 239)

Trenholm High School students bore the brunt of school desegregation efforts, as did African American students in other communities (Foster, 1997; Irvine & Irvine, 1983; Walker, 1998).

Both Wilson and Madeline communicated a need for stricter discipline in schools because of some of the changes in society since they attended school. Madeline believed that drug use by students today, as compared to when she attended school, was one of the major changes. She also felt that students had a major responsibility in improving their school experiences.

This feeling was reflected in her statements when she said, "First we need our children to show that interest level, what they want out of life. If a teacher sees that a child wants something, that can happen. But there are a lot of kids who go in there [classrooms] and they don't want anything. We have a lot of good teachers who will reach out to a child if they see that he [the child] really wants something."

Educational Implications

We believe that we need principals who come from a cadre of highly qualified teachers, who are strategic planners and servant leaders. Teachers deserve no less. Within this context, schools need teachers who: (1) care about the children they teach, (2) are competent in their subject areas, (3) have developed a variety of teaching strategies that are appropriate for meeting the needs of the children in their classrooms, and (4) are effective in working with families in order to involve them in the education of their children. Teachers must also be good classroom managers in order to focus the majority of their class time with children engaged on educational tasks. Good teachers will have high expectations for their students and will teach to those expectations. In order for teachers to be able to do this work well, schools must provide the financial and technological resources to support their efforts. This support entails providing appropriate continuing professional development activities for both novice and veteran educators.

Developing Caring Relationships

Noddings (1992) reports that caring in education requires strong relations of trust; these require both time and continuity to build. This kind of caring was evident in the stories told by the interviewees and the coauthors. In this school community, caring was communicated and reciprocated as teachers provided instruction in classrooms, served as advisors for extracurricular activities, and worked with parents in social and civic organizations to support the work of the school. Students enrolled at Trenholm High School for most of the years it was in operation remained in one school building for twelve years with a small student body of no more than 500 students. Especially in junior high and high school classes, students were often taught by the same teachers for a number of years; for example, the mathematics teacher taught junior high mathematics, algebra, and geometry. The majority of the students and their teachers lived within a four- or five-block radius of the school building, so they were friends and neighbors as well. Teachers and their students at Trenholm had many opportunities over an extended period of time to build the trust required for building caring relationships (Morris & Morris, 2000).

If developing caring relationships between teachers and students is still important to enhancing the motivation to learn today, what can schools and teachers do to nurture the development of such relationships? Teachers today often live in different communities from the children they teach. So the proximity of residence that was a plus for the Trenholm school community is not present in most school communities today. Trenholm was a very small school compared to many contemporary elementary and high schools, where some buildings enroll enough students to constitute the population of a small town. Are some school enrollments so large that size alone is a major deterrent to developing caring relationships?

Klonsky and Klonsky (1999) indicate that recent shootings in schools have revived interest in small, supportive school communities where caring adults play leading roles. In Chicago, for example, small schools have been formed within a large school setting where a team of teachers may work with a small cohort of students for three to four years. As a result of these efforts, schools are showing significant gains in attendance rates, student achievement on standardized tests, violence reduction, and increased graduation rates. Schnitzer and Capro (1999) report that school officials in Norfolk, Virginia, used a similar concept at the Granby High School to establish four academies in the high school, which has a total enrollment of 1,600. Each academy houses an estimated 450 students in grades nine through twelve, who remain in a specific academy with the same team of teachers for four years. Schnitzer and Capro write that "Teachers get to know students and their families. Students feel more comfortable because they do not have to adjust to an entirely new group of teachers each academic year" (p. 47). Staff members have reported increased achievement and a significant decrease in discipline problems. Granby staff members believe that the decrease in discipline problems is due to the fact that students "are more comfortable; have a greater sense of security; and know that *caring* [authors' emphasis] adults are present to supervise, counsel, and interact with them" (p. 48).

Looping is a school organization concept used in some elementary schools that extends the time a teacher spends with a group of children to at least two years. Little and Dacus (1999) found that looping at one school resulted in increased confidence in students and improved parent–teacher relationships, both of which can contribute to enhancing educational outcomes for children. In this particular school, parents have requested a third year with the same teachers.

Caring is one of the six standards that undergird what Rogers and Renard (1999) describe as relationship-driven teaching, which can enhance students' motivation to learn. School must be: (1) safe, (2) valuable, (3) successful, (4) involving, (5) caring, and (6) enabling. They note,

> Students are motivated when they believe that teachers treat them like people and care about them personally and educationally. When teachers apply in the classroom their knowledge of human needs, amazing things happen. These teachers treat students with respect; offer meaningful, significant choices; create valuable, fun, or interesting learning opportunities; and foster relationships

that help students see teachers as teachers and not as dictators, judges, juries, or enemies. Teacher and students collaborate for high-quality learning, and inappropriate behavior becomes a nonissue. (p. 34)

Teacher Competencies

While developing caring relationships with children and their families is central to our promoting positive academic achievement in the children we teach, this teacher attribute must be combined with competence in subject matter and pedagogy in order to meet the needs of children in today's society. The National Commission on Teaching and America's Future (1996) states that "A caring, competent, and qualified teacher for every child is the most important ingredient in education reform and, we believe, the most frequently overlooked" (p. 3). Morris and Morris (2000) report that graduates of Trenholm High School believed that in addition to their teachers caring about them, they also (1) maintained orderly classrooms (Dempsey & Noblit, 1996; Edmonds, 1982; Henderson, Greenberg, Schneider, Uribe, & Verdugo, 1996; Sowell, 1976; Walker, 1996); (2) were fair (Henderson et al., 1996); (3) were competent in their subject areas (Foster, 1997; Henderson et al., 1996; Sowell, 1976; Walker, 1996); (4) made practical applications of subject matter (Dempsey & Noblit, 1996; Hauser & Thompson, 1996); (5) had high expectations of students (Dempsey & Noblit, 1996; Hauser & Thompson, 1996; Henderson et al., 1996; Walker, 1996); and (6) made learning fun. In addition to these competencies, teachers at Trenholm High School worked effectively to involve families and the community in the life of the school. These are the kinds of teachers we need today in schools for all our children.

Supporting Teachers

Teachers need support from principals, parents, central office staff, local boards of education, universities, local and national legislators, and policy-makers in order to be the caring, competent, and qualified teachers that we need in every classroom in this country. A brief discussion of some of these supports follows.

Mentoring and Induction Programs. Novice teachers should be involved in effective mentoring and induction programs during the first three years of teaching to avoid the "sink or swim" phenomenon. Each new teacher should be assigned a seasoned teacher as mentor; this mentor should have received the appropriate training to assist and support the teacher. Both the novice teacher and the mentor benefit from this relationship. Many states, school districts, and universities have rather recently developed formal, structured, mentoring programs designed to meet the needs of beginning teachers (Ebert, 1997; George, 1989; Huling-Austin, 1990; Krupp, 1987; Mitchell, Scott, & Hendrik, 1996; Taylor, 1987; Zanting, Verloop, & Vermunt, 1997).

Continuing Professional Development for K through Twelve Faculty and Staff.   Irvine (1991) indicates that the most significant teacher variable associated with school success is the quality of the staff development and inservice program and that the more specific and focused the training, the greater the effect. Morris and Morris (2000) note that "professional development activities should be designed to build the capacities of the teachers, principals, and other staff at the building and classroom levels" (p. 259). Professional development activities should be driven by the school improvement plan developed by the faculty with input from all stakeholders in the school community.

Continuing Professional Development for University Faculty.   A large portion of the courses included in most teacher preparation programs across the country are taught by arts and sciences faculty due to the focus on subject matter mastery. It is therefore imperative for both teacher educators and arts and sciences faculty to be involved in continuing professional development in order to effectively meet the needs of preservice and veteran teachers who enroll in their programs. These professionals must not only be able to "talk the talk," but also be able to "walk the walk." That is, they must be able to model in their university courses the best practices that they advocate for prospective and practicing teachers.

Preservice Teacher Education.   All of the basic teacher competencies noted above must be a part of preservice programs. In addition, preservice teachers must have ample field experiences in a variety of settings that expose them to the real world of teaching in schools; courses and simulation experiences on university campuses are not enough. It is also important that practicing teachers and administrators become part of the teaching teams for prospective teachers.

The Consortium on Renewing Education (1998) summarizes very succinctly what we believe is needed to significantly improve the educational achievement of children in our schools in the twenty-first century:

> The quality of the nation's public schools chiefly depends on the competence of the teachers and principals who staff them; the commitment of students, parents, and communities who animate them; the adequacy and judicious use of dollars that support them; and the prudent application of emerging technologies that enlarge them. Together these human, social, financial, and technological resources comprise a school's capacity to promote learning. (p. 25)

Editor's Commentary

Vivian's and Curtis's stories resonate with me, probably because there are many similarities between their lives and my own. Like many African Americans who lived in rural areas, small town, and urban cities in the United States during the Civil Rights era, we were the first generation to attend college—not because our parents were any less intelligent or motivated than their White peers, but because of systematic efforts to exclude them and structural barriers (institutional racism and classism) that typically precluded even envisioning a college education as a viable option.

Since the authors chose to focus primarily on school experiences, we get only a glimpse of Vivian's mom. Although Vivian's mother had not been able to complete high school, she eagerly worked for and received her GED later in life. Her efforts personify determination and a deep valuing of education. Likewise, I applaud my mother and uncles (and numerous others) who completed high school during an era and in a place where this accomplishment was formidable. These stories need to be told and heard.

While these stories demonstrate that many African Americans historically and currently value education, this value may not be readily apparent in other cases. Anthropological and educational literature has shown that some African Americans (in the working class for the most part) may associate academic success with assimilation into the White culture and with loss of (Black) culture. African Americans may therefore deliberately disassociate themselves from educational pursuits and school success (Fordham, 1995; Ogbu, 1990). On the other end of the continuum, Fordham (1995) eloquently demonstrates that to succeed in school, many African Americans assume a "raceless" persona and disassociate themselves from Black culture (e.g., language, music). Fordham laments that losing one's culture is often a Pyrrhic victory; the cost (loss of one's psychological balance) is too great. I agree. The broader insight from the four stories in this chapter is that there is a tremendous amount of variation within ethnic groups in general, and African Americans in this particular instance.

A key theme of this chapter is that there are many historical and current examples of African Americans valuing education and not viewing it as the domain of Whites. The dichotomy between being smart (raceless) or Black is therefore false and unnecessary. Even in the face of difficulty, the family is the first place where many African American children learn about the importance of education (Arnold, 1995; Halle, Kurtz-Coastes, & Mahoney, 1997). To suggest that this essential aspect of African American culture (valuing education) is formed primarily in reaction to Whites limits our awareness that Blacks have historically viewed education in a manner that extends beyond the influence of Whites. That is, education is an inherent African and African American value. The stories in this chapter are certainly concrete reminders of this. Even though Wilson and Madeline did not attend college, it is obvious that they value education and passed this value on to their children.

It is not surprising that Vivian, Curtis, Bessie (Chapter 3), and I are employed in the education profession. For many small town and rural African Americans raised in the middle of the civil rights era, teaching was one of the few professions open to us. Additionally, teachers were highly regarded in the Black community. Although teachers, preachers, and other service professionals were considered to be middle class by mainstream society, they were regarded as upper class in many rural African American communities in the South in the 1950s and 1960s (Persell, 1997). When teachers are referred to in Vivian's and Curtis's stories, their names are revered. They are called by their whole names: Mrs. Willie Mae Thompson, Mrs. Garlor Hyler,

Coach Charles Mahorney, etc. Teachers' names are local legends in their small community. Interestingly, my teenage daughter has difficulty recalling some of her previous teachers' last names! I wonder if the differences in the two generations represent a reflection of the impressions (or lack thereof) that teachers make on their students. In the case of Trenholm graduates, the powerful and sustaining impressions are likely reinforced by the strong community links shared by teachers and students.

Like my own story, attending kindergarten was not part of the educational equation for rural African American students. On the other end of the education continuum, those who did matriculate in college had to attend historically Black colleges and universities—there was little choice. In this story, Tuskegee and Alabama A & M were highly regarded by Vivian and Curtis (and probably the community as a whole). In my home state, South Carolina State College and Benedict College were highly regarded in the Black community. Without these invaluable institutions, much human capital in the Black community would have likely been lost.

Finally, a common theme expressed in the four stories was the important role that reading played in broadening children's horizons. However, I hasten to add that children should be critical readers, as Madeline learned when her teacher concluded that her textbook was in error (Apple, 1992; Freire, 1999). Although Madeline deferred to her teacher, she likely learned that textbooks and other sources of knowledge can be questioned rather than simply accepted as legitimate knowledge. Just like the school experiences of the four people in this chapter, books are open to multiple interpretations.

And so the legacy of Trenholm High is complex and different for all involved, ranging from themes exclaiming "No More Cotton Picking," "Could I Really Be President— A Leader?" "We Were Short-Changed," to "And It All Really Came Out Good." But one thing is clear, it was a powerful experience regardless of the interpretation.

Reflective Activity

Think of what life might have been like if you grew up as an African American in the 1940s and 1950s in a small town in Alabama. What would be different for you? Similar? What can you learn from the four stories that will inform your experiences working with rural, African American students from similar circumstances?

Resources for Educators

Books and Articles

Amez, N. (1978). Implementation of desegregation as a discriminatory process. *Journal of Negro Education, 47,* 28–45.

Anderson, J. (1988). *The education of Blacks in the south, 1800–1935.* Chapel Hill: University of North Carolina Press.

Ashmore, H. (1954). *The Negro and the schools.* Chapel Hill: University of North Carolina Press.

Ayers, B. D., Jr. (1973, November 19). Southern Black mayors give Wallace standing ovation at a conference. *The New York Times,* p. 25.

Bauer, C. M. (1977). *John F. Kennedy and the second reconstruction.* New York: Columbia University Press.

Blacks at bama. (1979, Winter). *The University of Alabama Alumni News, 60* (1), 6–23.

Boddie, J. L. (1997). Making the grade in high school: Success for African American males. *The High School Magazine, 5* (2), 50–55.

Bond, H. M. (1969). *Negro education in Alabama: A study in cotton and steel.* New York: Octagon Books.

Bullock, H. (1967). *A history of Negro education in the south.* Cambridge, MA: Harvard University Press.

Caladas, S. J., & Bankston, C., III. (1998). The inequality of separation: Racial composition of schools and academic achievement. *Educational Administration Quarterly, 34* (4), 533–557.

Ceceleski, D. (1994). *Along freedom road: Hyde County, North Carolina, and the fate of black schools in the south.* Chapel Hill: University of North Carolina Press.

Chavkin, N. F. (Ed.). (1993). *Families and schools in a pluralistic society.* Albany: State University of New York Press.

Coffin, G. C. (1972). The Black administrator and how he's being pushed to extinction. *The American School Board Journal, 5,* 159.

Cooper, R. Detracking reform in an urban California high school: Improving the schooling experiences of African American students. *Journal of Negro Education, 65* (2), 190–208.

Crain, R. (1968). *The politics of school desegregation.* Chicago: Aldine.

Delpit, L. (1995). *Other people's children: Cultural conflicts in the classroom.* New York: New Press.

Dempsey, V., & Noblit, G. (1993). The demise of caring in an African American community: One consequence of school desegregation. *The Urban Review, 25* (1), 47–61.

Dempsey, V., & Noblit, G. (1996). Cultural ignorance and school desegregation: A community narrative. In M. J. Shujaa (Ed.), *Beyond desegregation: The politics of quality in African American schooling* (pp. 115–137). Thousand Oaks, CA: Corwin Press.

Du Bois, W. E. B. (1935). Does the Negro need separate schools? *Journal of Negro Education, 4,* 328–335.

Du Bois, W. E. B. (1903/1995). *The souls of black folk.* New York: Penguin.

Edwards, P. A. (1996). Before and after school desegregation: African American parents' involvement in schools. In M. J. Shujaa (Ed.), *Beyond desegregation: The politics of quality in African American schooling* (pp. 138–161). Thousand Oaks, CA: Corwin Press.

Fleming, W. L. (1905). *Civil war and reconstruction in Alabama.* New York: Columbia University Press.

Foster, M. (1990). The politics of race: Through the eyes of African-American teachers. *Journal of Education, 172* (3), 123–141.

Foster, M. (1997). *Black teachers on teaching.* New York: The New Press.

Franklin, V. P., & Anderson, J. A. (Eds.). (1978). *New perspectives on black educational history.* Boston: G. K. Hall.

Fry, P. G., & McKinney, L. J. (1997). A qualitative study of teachers' early field experience in an urban, culturally diverse school. *Urban Education, 32* (2), 184–201.

Futrell, M. H. (1999). Recruiting minority teachers. *Educational Leadership, 56* (8), 30–33.

Garibaldi, A. M. (1997). Four decades of progress and decline: An assessment of African American educational attainment. *Journal of Negro Education, 66* (2), 105–120.

Goodwin, A. L. (1997). *Assessment for equity and inclusion: Embracing all our children.* New York: Routledge.

Grantham, T. C., & Ford, D. Y. (1998). Principal instructional leadership can reverse the under-representation of Black students in gifted education. *NASSP Bulletin, 82* (595), 101–109.

Haberman, M. (1995). *Star teachers of children in poverty.* West Lafayette, IN: Kappa Delta Pi.

Halford, J. A. (1999). A different mirror: A conversation with Ronald Takaki. *Educational Leadership, 57* (7), 8–13.

Henderson, R., Greenberg, N. M., Schneider, J. M., Uribe, O., & Verdugo, R. (1996). High-quality schooling for African American students. In M. J. Shujaa (Ed.), *Beyond desegregation: The politics of quality in African American schooling* (pp. 162–184). Thousand Oaks, CA: Corwin Press.

Hess, F. M., & Leal, D. L. (1999). Computer-assisted learning in urban classrooms: The impact of politics, race, and class. *Urban Education, 34* (3), 370–388.

Irvine, J. J. (1991). *Black students and school failure: Policies, practices, and prescriptions.* New York: Praeger.

Irvine, R. W., & Irvine, J. J. (1983). The impact of the desegregation process on the education of Black students. *Journal of Negro Education, 52* (4), 410–422.

Jones, T. J. (1969). *Negro education: A study of the private and higher schools for colored people in the United States.* New York: Amo Press and the New York Times.

Jones-Wilson, F. C., Asbury, C. A., Okazawa-Rey, M., Anderson, D. K., Jacobs, S. M., & Fultz, M. (Eds.). (1996). *Encyclopedia of African-American education.* Westport, CT: Greenwood Press.

Ladson-Billings, G. (1994). *The dreamkeepers: Successful teachers of African American children.* San Francisco, CA: Jossey-Bass.

Lightfoot, S. L. (1978). *Worlds apart: Relationships between families and schools.* New York: Basic Books.

Menkart, D. J. (1999). Deepening the meaning of heritage months. *Educational Leadership, 57* (7), 19–21.

Morris, J. (1999). A pillar of strength: An African American school's communal bonds with families and community since Brown. *Urban Education, 33* (5), 584–605.

Morris, V. G., and Morris, C. L. (1981). The beginning of Black public education in Tuscumbia. *Journal of Muscle Shoals History* (9), 66–73.

Morris, V. G., and Morris, C. L. (1995). Early schooling for Blacks in Tuscumbia, 1877–1896: Before the arrival of George Washington Trenholm. *Journal of Muscle Shoals History,* (14), 82–90.

Morris, V. G., & Morris, C. L. (2000). *Creating caring and nurturing educational environments for African American children.* Westport, CT: Bergin & Garvey.

Muller, C., Katz, S. R., & Darie, L. J. (1999). Investing in teaching and learning: Dynamics of the teacher–student relationship from each actor's perspective. *Urban Education, 34* (3), 292–337.

Murrell, P. C., Jr. (1999). Chartering the village: The making of an African-centered charter school. *Urban Education, 33* (5), 565–583.

Parks, S. (1999). Reducing the effects of racism in schools. *Educational Leadership, 57* (7), 14–18.

Quality Education for Minorities Project. (1990). *Education that works: An action plan for the education of minorities.* Cambridge, MA: Author.

Rand, D., Parker, T. T., & Foster, S. (1998). *Black books galore! Guide to great African American children's books.* New York: John Wiley & Sons.

Reitzug, U. C., & Patterson, J. (1998). I'm not going to lose you: Empowerment through caring in an urban principal's practice with students. *Urban Education, 33* (2), 150–181.

Rodgers, F. A. (1975). *The Black high school and its community.* Lexington, MA: Lexington Books, D. C. Heath.

Sheeler, J. R. (1945). George Washington Trenholm. *The Negro History Bulletin,* 17–20.

Shujaa, M. J. (Ed.). *Beyond desegregation: The politics of quality in African American schooling.* Thousand Oaks, CA: Corwin Press.

Sowell, T. (1974). Black excellence: The case of Dunbar High School. *Public Interest, 35,* 1–21.

Sowell, T. (1976). Patterns of Black excellence. *Public Interest, 43,* 26–58.

Trenholm, G. W. (Undated). Concentration on public high schools in the south rather than multiplying private secondary schools. Presentation made at the National Association of Teachers in Colored Schools. Source: Washington, DC: Howard University, Moorland-Spingarn Desegregation Research Center.

Trenholm, G. W. (1912, April 4). Status of Negro education in Alabama. Annual address of G. W. Trenholm, President of the Alabama State Teachers' Association, delivered at Selma, AL. Source: Washington, DC: Howard University, Moorland-Spingarn Research Center.

Walker, V. S. (1996). *Their highest potential: African American school community in the segregated south.* Chapel Hill: The University of North Carolina Press.

Walker, V. S. (1998). Focus on diversity. *Briefs, Newsletter of the American Association of Colleges for Teacher Education 19* (12), 4–5, 8.

Yarbrough, T. E. (1981). *Judge Frank Johnson and human rights in Alabama.* University: The University of Alabama Press.

Useful Web Sites

African American Directory: http://www.handilinks.com/catl/a/36048.htm.

African American Education: http://africanmetropolis.com/news/afiedu.atm.

African American Education: http://www.cannylink.com/educationaaeducation.atm.

African American Education: http:/jupiter.land.osaka-u.ac.jpl~krkvls/afed.html.

African American Education: http://www.nd.edu/~rbarger/www7/african.html. Paper compares the beliefs and accomplishments of W. E. B. Du Bois and Booker T. Washington.

African American Education—Collection Titles: http://www.system.missouri.edu/whmc/afedu.htm. Special collection of papers related to African American education.

AFC's African American Education Curriculum: http://www.afc-online.com/Education/curriculum/curr8.html.

African American History: http://www2.ocls.lib.fl.us/Usefulsites/African.html. General resources, Martin Luther King, Jr., art and literature, and science and inventions links.

African American History: http://www2.ocls.lib.

African American Literature: http://www.libmemphis.edu/instr/afrolit.htm. Includes books, audiovisuals, periodical articles, reference works, and Web links.

African American Resources: http://www.ops.org/mne/multi.af-am.html. Lists of books and reference works for the professional and videos for the professional and students. Books for students are organized in the categories of primary, intermediate, and secondary levels.

African American Resources: http://page.prodigy.net/urbansounds/bh-links.htm.

African American Women: On the Net. http://www.gencom/ani/aframwmks.htm. Numerous related links from A to Z.

ADAH References: African-American Research: http://www.archives.state.al.us/afrp/afro.html. Alabama Department of Archives & History Web sites with resources "From Reconstruction to the Civil Rights Era: Records about the African American Experiences in Alabama."

American Studies, Black History and Literature: Writing Black: http://www.keele.ac.uk/depts/as/Literatur/amlit.Black.html. Links to texts and resources on the Web, historial texts, and other libraries and indexes.

Fred D. Gray of Tuskegee is among first recipients of ABA spirit of excellence awards. (1996, January). Chicago: American Bar Association. Web site: http://www.abanet.org/media/jan96/tuskegee.html.

Frederick D. Patterson Research Institute: http://www.patterson-uncl.org/.

Famous African Americans in the Humanities: http://www.ithaca.edu/library/htmls/humafro.html.

A Guide to African American Documentary Resources: http://www.unc.edu/lib/mssinv/afam.html.

The Intersection of Race, Gender, and Class: http://saber.towson.edu/itrow/rgc.htm. Bibliography lists in several related categories.

MosaicWeb—African-American Education: http://www.mosaicweb.com/afric_edu.htm.

National Urban League: http://www.nul.org.org/.

Publications about Black Americans (UNC-CH): http://www.unc.edu/pubs/bib/Black/subject/file.7.html.

Schomburg Center for Research in Black Culture: http://gopher.nypl.org/research/sc/sc.html.

Urban Institute Resource Library: http://www2.edu.org/urban/list.asp. List of recent books and articles, includes abstract of each.

Urban Minority Families: http://ericweb.tc.columbia.edu/families/index.html.

We Shall Overcome: Historic Places of the Civil Rights Movement: http://www.cnps.gov/nr/travel/civilrights/.

What2Read—African American Literature: http://www.what2read.com/cgibin/softCart.exe/home.html?

Literature

Campbell, B. M. (1995). *Your blues ain't like mine.* New York: Balantine. A moving fictional account of the 1955 lynching of Emmett Till. The book presents the parallel tales of the black and white families set in the midst of the Civil Rights Movement.

Johnson, D. (1998). *All around the town: The photographs of Richard Samuel Roberts.* New York: Henry Holt & Company. Photos of women, children, and men in one African American community in South Carolina during the early twentieth century. Offers a window into one African American community (reading level: ages four to eight).

Johnson, D. (1999). *Sunday week.* New York: Henry Holt & Company. This celebratory picture book travels through daily activities in an African American community. Readers get a peek into church, home, and education activities in this community (reading level: ages four to eight).

References

Apple, M. W. (1992). The text and cultural politics. *Educational Researcher, 21* (7), 11–19.

Arnold, M. S. (1995). Exploding the myths: African American families at promise. In B. B. Swadener & S. Lubeck (Eds.). *Children and families "at promise." Deconstructing the discourse of risk* (pp. 143–162). Albany: State University of New York Press.

Boutte, G. (1999). *Multicultural education: Raising consciousness.* Atlanta: Wadsworth.

Ceceleski, D. (1994). *Along freedom road: Hyde County, North Carolina, and the fate of black schools in the south.* Chapel Hill: University of North Carolina Press.

Consortium on Renewing Education. (1998, December 16). 20/20 vision: A strategy for doubling academic achievement in America by the year 2020. *Education Week, XVIII* (16), 24–25.

Dempsey, V., & Noblit, G. (1993). The demise of caring in an African American community: One consequence of school desegregation. *The Urban Review, 25* (1), 47–61.

Dempsey, V., & Noblit, G. (1996). Cultural ignorance and school desegregation: A community narrative. In M. J. Shujaa (Ed.), *Beyond desegregation: The politics of quality in African American schooling* (pp. 115–137). Thousand Oaks, CA: Corwin Press.

Ebert, C. (1997). A new institution: The emerging educational community in an effective professional development school. *Action in Teacher Education, 19* (2), 52–62.

Edmonds, R. (1982). Programs of school improvement: An overview. *Educational Leadership, 40* (3), 4–11.

Edwards, P. A. (1996). Before and after school desegregation: African American parents' involvement in schools. In M. J. Shujaa (Ed.), *Beyond desegregation: The politics of quality in African American schooling* (pp. 138–161). Thousand Oaks, CA: Corwin Press.

Fordham, S. (1995). *Blacked out: Dilemmas of race, identity, and success at Capital High.* Chicago: The University of Chicago Press.

Foster, M. (1997). *Black teachers on teaching.* New York: The New Press.

Freire, P. (1999). *Pedagogy of the oppressed.* New York: Continuum Publishing Group.

George, M. (1989). Maximizing the expertise of mentor teachers: An evolving process. *Mentoring International, 3* (2), 21–24.

Halle, T. G., Kurtz-Costes, B., & Mahoney, J. L. (1997). Family influences on school achievement in low-income, African American children. *Journal of Educational Psychology, 89,* 527–537.

Hauser, M., & Thompson, C. (1996). Creating a classroom culture of promise: Lessons from a first grade. In B. B. Swadener & S. Lubeck (Eds.), *Children and families "at promise": Deconstructing the discourse of risk* (pp. 210–223). Albany: State University of New York Press.

Henderson, R., Greenberg, N. M., Schneider, J. M., Uribe, O., & Verdugo, R., (1996). High-quality schooling for African American students. In M. J. Shujaa (Ed.), *Beyond desegregation: The politics of quality in African American schooling* (pp. 162–184). Thousand Oaks, CA: Corwin Press.

Huling-Austin, L. (1990). Teacher induction programs and internships. In W. R. Houston (Ed.), *Handbook of research on teacher education* (pp. 535–548). New York: Macmillan.

Irvine, J. J. (1991). *Black students and school failure: Policies, practices, and prescriptions.* New York: Praeger.

Irvine, R. W., & Irvine, J. J. (1983). The impact of the desegregation process on the education of black students. *Journal of Negro Education, 52* (4), 410–422.

Klonsky, S., & Klonsky, M. (1999). Countering anonymity through small schools. *Educational Leadership, 57* (1), 38–41.

Kozol, J. (1991). *Savage inequalities.* New York: Crown.

Kunjufu, J. (1986). *Countering the conspiracy to destroy black boys: Vol. II.* Chicago: African American Images.

Krupp, J. A. (1987). Mentor and protege perceptions of mentoring relationships in an elementary and secondary school. *International Journal of Mentoring, I* (1), 35–40.

Ladson-Billings, G. (1994). *The dreamkeepers: Successful teachers of African American children.* San Francisco: Jossey-Bass.

Leftwich, N. (1935). *Two hundred years at Muscle Shoals.* Birmingham, AL: Multigraphic Advertising.

Lightfoot, S. L. (1978). *Worlds apart: Relationships between families and schools.* New York: Basic Books.

Little, T. S., & Dacus, N. B. (1999). Looping: Moving up with the class. *Educational Leadership, 57* (1), 42–45.

Mitchell, D. E., Scott, L. D., & Hendrik, I. G. (1996). *California mentor teacher evaluation: Technical report.* Riverside: University of California, California Educational Research Cooperative.

Morris, V. G., & Morris, C. L. (2000). *Creating caring and nurturing educational environments for African American children.* Westport, CT: Bergin & Garvey.

National Commission on Teaching & America's Future. (1996). *What matters most: Teaching for America's future.* Woodbridge, VA: Author.

Noddings, N. (1992). The challenge to care in schools: An alternative approach to education. New York: Teachers College Press.

Ogbu, J. U. (1990). Overcoming racial barriers to equal access. In J. I. Goodlad & P. Keatings (Eds.), *Access to knowledge: An agenda for our nation's schools* (pp. 59–89). New York: College Entrance Examination Board.

Persell, C. H. (1997). Social class and educational equality. In J. A. Banks & C. A. M. Banks (Eds.), *Multicultural education: Issues and perspectives* (3rd ed.) (pp. 87–107). Boston: Allyn & Bacon.

Report of visiting committee on evaluative criteria of Trenholm High School. (1955). Tuscumbia, AL: Author.

Rodgers, F. A. (1975). *The black high school and its command.* Lexington, MA: Lexington Books, D. C. Heath and Company.

Rogers, S., & Renard, L. (1999). Relationship-driven teaching. *Educational Leadership, 57* (1), 34–37.

Schnitzer, D. K., & Capro, M. J. (1999). Academy rewards. *Educational Leadership, 57* (1), 46–48.

Shoals life: Tuscumbia. (1998). Times Daily Website: http:www.timesdaily.com/tuscumb.html.

Sowell, T. (1976). Patterns of black excellence. *Public Interest, 43,* 26–58.

Taylor, S. E. (1987). The California mentor teacher program: A preliminary evaluation of one district's program. *International Journal of Mentoring, I* (1), 27–34.

Walker, V. S. (1998). Focus on diversity. Newsletter of the American Association of Colleges for Teacher Education 19 (12), 4–5, 8.

Walker, V. S. (1996). *Their highest potential: African American school community in the segregated south.* Chapel Hill: The University of North Carolina Press.

Zanting, A., Verloop, N., & Vermunt, J. (1997). Accessing the practical knowledge of mentor teachers by student teachers. Paper presented at the annual meeting of the American Educational Research Association, Chicago.

3

Listening to the Voices of African American Males

Bessie L. Gage

Editor's Overview

This chapter introduces us to two African American college seniors who are enrolled at one of the historically Black colleges and universities in the Southeast. During their primary and middle school years, they were labeled as "bad" or "troublemakers" by schools. They were placed in classes below their academic and motivational levels, but they persisted and succeeded. Ray and Harold defy common stereotypes about Black males as they unapologetically share their interpretations of schooling. Conventional profiles of people most likely to be successful in school and life are markedly different from the author's, Harold's, and Ray's stories. When we closely examine the three stories in this chapter, we gain insights about what schools can do to help African American students from low-income and working-class families succeed.

Author's Story

I grew up in a small textile town in the Piedmont region of South Carolina during the 1950s and 1960s. I was the oldest of eight children in a single parent home. I have four brothers and three sisters. During the first eleven years of my life, we lived on old, abandoned farms.

I do not remember many of my childhood experiences before the age of six. It was around this time that I lost my great-great-aunt-Bessie ("Annee"), first to mental illness and eventually to death in the summer of 1956. I have a few spots of memory of her loving care and concern in the

43

years before age six. Annee had also raised my mother. My mother had great love and devotion for Annee and gave me her name. After Annee's death, we moved in with my great-grandmother. I began school in the fall of 1956. Since we lived in the rural part of the county, I had to walk about a mile and a half to catch the school bus to the small, segregated primary school in town.

New Primary School had eight classrooms, seven teachers, and a teacher/principal. The school had four first-grade classrooms, two advanced first-grade classrooms and two second-grade classrooms. The organization of the school was based on the assumption that half of the children would not pass to second grade. This meant that half of the children in the school would be placed in advanced first grade (instead of second grade), even if they made good grades.

I was unfortunate to be assigned to the classroom of the teacher/principal. My impression of her is not favorable. She was a mean, older woman who was harsh with all of the children. It also seemed like the teachers feared her. She used her fist to beat children. I had almost gotten through the school year before she beat me in my back with her fist for an offense I did not commit. We were sent to the coatroom to get our coats by rows and the student that went to the coatroom after me told the teacher/principal that I marked on the wall with a crayon. The marks were on the wall when I went in the coatroom to get my coat. She saw the marks on the wall and beat me in my back with her fists. I did not even own crayons. After that experience, she never asked me any questions and I never said a word in class the rest of the year.

I was one of the students placed in one of the advanced first-grade classrooms. There was a new baby in the family, and I stayed out of school for five or six weeks because I needed some shoes. When I came back to school, the teacher had given my seat to a new student. As I stood by my former seat, the children in the class said, "Teacher, she came back." Miss Davis was a young, pretty teacher who was very kind. She worked to help me catch up with the work I had missed while I was out of school. I was still very quiet and I do not remember playing with many of the children. Two new children had been assigned to our class during my long absence. These were children of teachers in our school system. They were placed in the advanced first grade because they had already completed all of the first-grade work.

My second-grade teacher, Mrs. Mary Ethel Sims Moorer, was my favorite elementary school teacher. She liked me. She allowed me to be her helper. I took the milk money to the cafeteria and was paid with free milk. I worked very hard to please her. It was in her class that I began to love school. Mrs. Moorer was a very special person in the Black community, although I did not know that when I was in her second-grade classroom. To me, she was just a kind, beautiful teacher. She was the daughter of the founder and first principal of our high school. She was married to the second principal and legendary football coach of our high school who is now in the South Carolina Hall of Fame. I ran into her on the day of my graduation from South Carolina State College. She had come to pick up her daughter, who was in the sophomore class. She was delighted about my success. Many years later, I found out that Mrs. Moorer had attended high school with my mother. My mother had been a student assistant to Mrs. Moorer's mother in high school.

Many of my elementary school experiences are vague. The ones that I remember are not very favorable. In fourth grade, my teacher, Mrs. Hunter, whacked me on my leg because she said that I was running up the steps from the playground. I told her that I was not running and so did the girls who were running. All of the girls in the classroom were spanked.

Mrs. Hunter had two daughters who were very bright and skipped grades. One was moved ahead to my advanced first-grade class. Her daughters were admired by all of the children and teachers.

My family moved to a brand new public housing project in town during the summer of 1961. This was an exciting time for our family because we had not lived in a house with electricity and indoor toilet. We moved to Horseshoe Circle; a horseshoe-shaped street of duplexes with a playground and recreation center in the center of the neighborhood. This was mostly a neighborhood of working-class families. A few professionals lived on Horseshoe Circle. For a number of years, my ninth-grade homeroom teacher lived in the other end of our duplex. For a short period of time, the Black high school football coach lived across the street from us. Most families felt pride and privilege to live on Horseshoe in the early years. At that time, this was some of the best housing for Blacks in our segregated town. Most of the families on our street eventually bought their own homes, including my mother.

After we moved, I lived ten minutes from my new school, Cohen Street Elementary (grades five through seven). Sixth grade was tough for me because I was in the classroom of my friend's mother. We sat together and her mother was hard on both of us. I remember having worked very hard that year.

I was ill most of the seventh grade. From September of 1963 until February of 1964, I was in three health care facilities. I spent two weeks in the local hospital, three weeks in the regional hospital, and three months in the South Carolina Home for Crippled Children. I had rheumatic fever and was not expected to have a normal life. I did not have any school while I was in the hospital. We did have a teacher for half a day at the Home for Crippled Children. We were visited often by people from the community and across the state who brought gifts for us. I had many new experiences, including piano lessons, and even appeared on the television news during one of the several Christmas programs held at the home.

My High School Years

Sims High School was the pride and joy of the Black community. It was a large county high school serving all of the Black students in the county in grades eight through twelve.

High school was a wonderful experience. I excelled in the average ability section that I was assigned to in ninth grade. I had the highest GPA in my homeroom class and received a lot of attention and encouragement from my teachers. Of course, this made me study harder to do well. I did so well in ninth grade that I was assigned to the top section of tenth grade. I was unsure about this assignment because this homeroom class included the best and the brightest students, including our class valedictorian. In addition, these were scary teachers. This was college prep. The teachers were also the best and the brightest. They had master's degrees from northern universities. They set very high expectations for their students.

I was a late bloomer. High school became very exciting for me. I loved all of my classes except mathematics. Mathematics continued to be a struggle for me throughout my doctoral studies. The school library was a joy. This was the first school that I attended that had a library. I also made my first visit to the local public library. A news magazine carried a story on the topic I wanted to write on for a history research paper; however, the magazine was not in our school library. My history teacher sent me to the public library. The public library had been segregated until recently, and I was afraid to go to the library. I wanted to change my topic, but my teacher insisted that I go to the public library and check out the magazine. I went to the library, and a lady met me at the door and asked if she could help me. I told her that my history teacher told me to come and get a magazine for my research paper. She told me to wait at the door and she would get the magazine. She came back with the magazine and filled out some papers and told me when to return the magazine. I thought the librarian was nice, but I realized later that she probably did not want me sitting in the library reading the magazine.

This history class sparked my love of history that continues to this day. I was fortunate enough to have my history teacher for the tenth grade as well. Overall, I enjoyed most of my high school classes and subjects. I particularly enjoyed biology and for many years kept one of my biology projects. I drew fairly well so I was able to provide great details and information in my drawing and I earned an A on the assignment. However, my teachers and classes in English, home economics, and Spanish also had a profound influence on my future.

My tenth-, eleventh-, and twelfth-grade English and literature teacher was one of the most respected teachers in our school. During our senior year, when most of the students cut class as a senior privilege, they never cut her classes. Most of my friends thought I was crazy for taking an English literature class as a senior elective, but she had advised us to take this course as a preparation for college.

I was also drawn to home economics and excelled in the classes. I took my first clothing class in the ninth grade and by the end of my second clothing course in tenth grade was making garments for the people in my community. Since I did not always have money to buy cloth, I would make a garment for a customer free if they purchased the fabric and allowed me to use it as a class project. By my junior year in high school, I was making garments for some of my teacher's customers. When my teacher was too busy to take in sewing, she would refer the customer to me and another student in our class. I was not able to work outside my home much due to my illness, so sewing became my means of earning money for my high school needs. I was also able to help my mother by making all of the clothes for the five females in our family. Sewing continued to be a source of income for me throughout high school, college, and my first few years as a beginning teacher. I was not permitted to take clothing in my senior year because my teacher thought I did not need any more clothing instruction. I was encouraged to take child development and food and nutrition. I had decided to attend two of my home economics teachers' alma mater, South Carolina State College, and major in home economics.

The summer before my senior year, my home economics teacher got me a summer job with Head Start as part of the federal summer work program for low-income students. The job was to give me experience in working with children in preparation for the child development class I would take in the fall of my senior year. When I reported to the center for work as a teacher's assistant, I was told to start cleaning upstairs. I told the director that I was supposed to work as a teacher's assistant. He said that cleaning was the only job he had for me. I asked to call my teacher. He then assigned me to be a teacher's assistant in a classroom on the second floor. There was a teacher and two other high school students (children of friends of the director) sharing a Head Start teacher's assistant position. This was a wonderful summer experience. I got to know some of the other high school students working in the program. It helped me to decide that working with young children would become my profession.

By 1968, although all of the students at my school were Black, we had several white teachers. I had my first two White teachers in my Spanish class during my junior year. When my Black teacher went on maternity leave, Miss Darcy, a White missionary from Portugal, took over the class. She taught more Portuguese than Spanish. A White, male student teacher joined the class for the last six weeks before our teacher returned. I fell in love with Spanish language and culture. The class worked hard to put on an assembly program in Spanish. The student teacher told us that if we worked hard on the program and earned 100 on our six-week test, we would get a 100 on our report card! Teachers at my high school would not give students a 100 even if we had a 100 average for the grading period. I was one of the two students to earn the 100. During my senior year, I was elected Miss Spanish Club.

By the end of my senior year, I had decided to be a teacher of young children. During my junior year, I had joined the Future Teachers of America. I had worked as a substitute teacher in elementary schools. At the beginning of my senior year, I was elected president of the Future Teachers of America Club, to the surprise of some of the teachers. I was told that the president would have to do her own work this year. Another one of my teachers and my best friend assisted me with all of my club paper work and activities. After graduation, many of my classmates went to work in the local cotton mills. About 15 percent of our class went to college immediately after graduation. Our class of 1969 was the last class before desegregation.

Two college acceptance letters arrived on the same day. My sisters and brothers encouraged me to go to the college with the lowest acceptance fee. However, that college did not have the lowest tuition. In the fall of 1969, three of my classmates and I matriculated at South Carolina State College, the only state-supported college for Blacks in South Carolina. I enrolled in the School of Agriculture and Home Economics to pursue a major in child development and preschool education.

I earned a bachelor of science degree in home economics with a specialization in child development and preschool education from South Carolina State College in 1973. I taught first grade and prekindergarten in rural South Carolina before earning my master's degree in early childhood education from Atlanta University (now Clark-Atlanta University) in 1977. I joined the faculty of a historically Black university in North Carolina in the fall of 1977. I taught early childhood courses and supervised students for nine years before taking an educational leave to earn my doctoral degree. I spent three years as a full-time doctoral student at Southern Illinois University at Carbondale to earn a Ph.D. in curriculum and instruction with a specialization in early childhood. I returned to my university as department head in the fall of 1989.

My school experiences, and first two degrees, were in Black settings. However, my public school experiences, doctoral studies, and experiences in professional organizations have been in majority-White settings. My experiences in Black settings provided many opportunities for growth and development. I have found that I received the necessary preparation for ease, comfort, and success in majority settings. I have also found that historically Black colleges and universities prepare African American students very well for success in our diverse society.

Education and Development of African American Males

I became interested in the growth and development of young African American boys while teaching primary and preschool children. It seemed that the African American boys were always in trouble. They were often labeled as "bad." I often wondered why some of the boys in my classes were "bad" when they were in other settings outside of my classroom. I often got reports that a few of the boys had caused others problems. People would say, "I peeked into your classroom and saw that all of the children were well behaved." I was asked, "Why do you not have problems with the boys?" There were several very active, African American boys in my prekindergarten class. I was a new teacher in the school that year and some of my colleagues said I had been given all of the "bad" children. I viewed my class as a wonderful group of four-year-olds. I had half boys and half girls and the class was 75 percent African American and 25 percent White. Most of the boys were very active and several seemed to cause problems outside of the classroom. My teacher assistants had great difficulties managing two of the African American boys.

I never sent a child to the office for behavior problems. Administrators wanted to know why I did not send the "bad" children to the office. I would say I do not have "bad" children in my class. I did talk with parents each day about "good" and "bad" behavior as well as academic progress when they picked up their children. Many of the parents indicated that their child behaved better at school than at home.

I think that my success in working with young African American boys resulted from my background in child development and caring for my seven younger siblings, including four brothers. I had a great deal of experience with African American males through my brothers and their friends growing up in public housing. I observed that the "bad" boys were often very bright. Therefore, I set high expectations for all of the children in my classes, and most of the students worked hard to do their best.

Early in my teaching career, I began teaching at a small historically Black university in North Carolina. At that time, all of my students were African Americans. We had a few male students in early childhood education. Many of the male students dropped out of the university or changed their major. As their teacher and advisor, I often gave encouragement and suggestions. I know that most of the African American male students had the potential to be successful. Many of the African American males did not exhibit good work habits, study skills, and time management skills, but occasionally they would do good work.

Three years ago, in an effort to recruit more African American males and students from other ethnic groups, I wrote and received two grants that helped us to increase the number of African American males in our program from one to ten. I began to question whether we needed to work with our male students differently from the female students in our program. I found that the males need a little more encouragement and nurturing than the females. As a matter of fact, female students also provided nurturing and encouragement for the male students. Nine of the ten African American male students successfully completed the program.

My interest in Black males is also personal. As I work with my nephews, I am interested in finding ways to help them to become prepared for college. I decided to talk with African American male students who were struggling to succeed in college to determine the nature of their school experiences and the impact those experiences had on their success in college.

The two African American males interviewed for this chapter are attending a small historically Black university in the South. The students are from the Midwest and the Northeast. Pseudoymns are used to protect the interviewees' identities. The first interview is with Harold.

Harold

Harold grew up in Stamford, Connecticut, and was raised primarily by his mother, although he stayed with his father from time to time.

Harold recalls elementary school as "a pretty good elementary experience," except for a short stint in third grade at a Catholic school. His mother wanted to "try something new," so she sent him to Catholic school. Harold reflects,

> That didn't work out too well. I mean, I don't know what it was—maybe it was the environment, but I didn't do too well at the Catholic School, so I was placed back in public school. . . . It was . . . It was . . . It was just entirely different. We had to wear uniforms. The whole environment was different. We had to pray. It was more religious and I mean we focused on the academics, the math, the reading, all of that, everyone was all in one big class. So . . . ability really wasn't a thing, but I don't know. I don't know if it was just me or the teacher, but it just didn't go well in the third grade in Catholic school.

Harold continues,

> They actually wanted to keep me back in the third grade. It wasn't that I didn't understand the material, but I guess I was what you would call that Bad Kid in the Catholic school.

It is not amazing that Harold internalized messages about him and perceived himself as "bad." But when we examine the circumstances, it becomes apparent that Harold's misbehavior may have been influenced by a number of things. He shared that he did not know anyone in the Catholic school: "(T)here weren't many kids in my neighborhood that went to Catholic school." Parents and educators sometimes underestimate the impact of winging it alone in school with little or no peer support. This theme is echoed later in Chapter 4 as we hear about a Korean child's experiences.

Harold explains,

The school itself. I would say it was alright, but me being from where I was from and going to that type of school . . . I was living in what you would call the projects. You know what I'm saying . . . and in the projects, if you ride the little bus, you know . . . we were that [dumb]. They [friends] knew that I was not dumb, but I was on the little bus, going to a Catholic school. . . .

Children with disabilities rode the buses, so Harold felt that he was stigmatized by this. "I kinda felt like an outcast. . . . You know what I mean? It kinda made me feel like an outcast, because . . . everybody having gone to that school since kindergarten. So everybody basically moved together. There was only one teacher for one grade, so I kinda felt I was the outcast 'cause I was new and everybody pretty much knew each other. The kids, they didn't know me, you know."

To make matters worse, Harold also disliked the uniforms, so he was delighted to return to public school.

[I]t was a new school as well . . . it was a newer school that I went to, but I knew people there from the previous school. We had moved to another section of town. Some of the kids I had grew up with and some other schools, but they changed the district, so I pretty much knew everyone in that school. But as far as the schooling, [it] was good. The teachers were good and I learned.

Math was something that I was good at, I mean I like . . . dealing with numbers and I pretty much like helping everyone else with math. And that was my thing. I was with the brightest groups in math, like the second highest in reading.

In elementary school, Harold "hung out with everybody. Everybody I hung out with, the people they called nobodies, nerds. 'Cause, you know, I was in the highest math class, so I knew that."

Although Harold was confident that he was a good student, his middle school placement threw him for a loop.

Middle school . . . at first, I didn't like it because when I first got there, they had groups. They had the first, second, third, and fourth group. And when I arrived there, they had me in the fourth group, and I didn't understand it at first. . . . The rumor was that whatever you made on your standardized testing, that was how they placed you in the seventh and eighth grade. And I had a problem with that because the work I was given in the seventh grade at the beginning of the year, it was pretty easy. You know . . . and I tried to excel and actually I did excel and my mother called the school and they moved me up. They moved me up to the third group. And the third group I figured, you know, I wasn't going to move up any more. I figured they . . . They said this was where I belonged. So I kinda acted like, you know, I belonged there. I was doing well, I had all A's and B's and I tried myself to talk to my teacher to move me up again. But it just never happened. For the seventh grade I just stayed in that group. I think I was working under my ability, but they didn't hear that so. . . . I mean the work . . . the work they taught us . . . it was effective, but me at my level I thought that I could have done better, even at that age. The same thing for the eighth grade.

Once placements in school are made, they often become permanent (Boutte, 1999). Educators seemingly give little reflection to the theoretically dynamic nature of placements and often perceive them as difficult to change even when warranted, as in Harold's case:

Eighth grade I remained in the same group, but they had changed it. It was no longer 1, 2, 3, 4, they had changed it to letters W, X, Y, and Z. And, you know, the kids in the school were acting like X is the highest, Y is the second, like it was in order. I was in the Z. I talked to my teacher about it but they basically said that the Z and the W, that one is not higher than the other. They fed me all that and . . . I wasn't in the X and the Y . . . so . . . I just knew that once again I was at this level and I was going to do this thing and I did well. I got awards and everything.

It is easy to see why some African American students become disenfranchised from school. Ogbu (1994) explains that "in a racially stratified society with a job ceiling, the type of schooling provided for racial minorities is often one that prepares them for their respective place in the job market" (p. 73). In Ogbu's research, African American students were often "herded" into classrooms that neither expected much from them nor acknowledged within-group differences in the amount of effort students put forth. But Harold continued to try to succeed in school even though he was powerless to change his situation.

High school for Harold followed the same trend as middle school because his guidance counselor picked out classes for him. But Harold and his mother protested. Harold recalls,

And I had a talk with the principal at [name of high school] where I attended. Me and my mother and he told me . . . that if I felt these classes were not in my level, then "I'm gonna give you the opportunity to make your own schedule, and at the end of the semester we are gonna see how you're doing. And we will see about making the right decision." And that's what happened. I was able to pick my classes. I was in all the (advanced) groups and I think I had one honors class. I think that was for math. He said since I did well in math I could pick an honors course in math. So I picked a honors course in math and I did well my freshman year of high school.

Harold was also in the choir, on the yearbook staff, and tutored elementary students in the school across the street from his high school. He tutored younger children for three years.

Harold's decision to go to college was influenced by his church:

My church told me about the college tour that happens every year and that's when I knew I was going to college. I knew I had to work hard just being around campuses and stuff like that. That encouraged me to work hard and I pretty much knew that I was coming to college in the eighth grade.

So this child who perceived himself as "bad" is doing well in college, and it turns out that he is not bad after all. In the next story, we will meet another "troublemaker," Ray.

Ray

Ray was raised in a small town—Niles, Michigan. It had one high school, one middle school, and three elementary schools. Ray didn't like being in a small town and wanted to get out and see the world. The town is predominantly Black, but generally racially segregated by neighborhoods. Ray grew up in a Black neighborhood and was raised by his grandmother and father. Family and church were important parts of his childhood. Although his grandmother and father did not get past high school, they always stressed to Ray the importance of getting an education. Ray will be the first one in his family (he has two older brothers) to finish college.

As Ray reflects on his school experiences, he says,

The farthest I can think back to . . . All my elementary years, I was told I was a troublemaker. I was in trouble a lot. Now that I reflect on it, I do not think that my teachers understood me because not only was I a troublemaker, but I was put in the low tracks in reading. . . . I do not think that they knew how to handle me. Like, for instance, I recall getting in trouble. I said something or did something to one of the White kids in the class, and the teacher ended up putting me in the corner. I couldn't go out to recess for almost a whole month. Every recess time, I had to go sit in the corner by the office. And um, I can recall other times where I felt that I could do the other stuff that the higher reading groups were doing. But instead I had to stay in the lower reading group because I do not think that she [the teacher] really wanted to deal with the other aspects of my behavior and attitude. It was kind of like she put us off in a group where we didn't have . . . we were the ones that didn't get a lot of attention. . . .

Ray recalls that there were several boys who were labeled "bad"—one of them was a White boy named Danny. However, sixth and seventh grades were turning points for Ray:

I started to work with teachers, I guess they knew how to handle me better. Maybe I had more experience. So, they started to experiment and put me in higher reading groups. They kept on telling me, "You could do this." I mean, whenever I did not do something up to my ability, they would always let me know. They would not let me get away with shortchanging them—myself, actually.

The power of teacher expectations coupled with student determination is apparent. Two of Ray's seventh grade teachers were particularly influential:

Mr. McKinley and Ms. Noble . . . just, they always encouraged me. They wouldn't let me just do an assignment, just to hurry up and finish it. I think it paid off 'cause once I got to high school, . . . I had accelerated all through my high school years.

High school was a period of awakening for Ray:

That's when everything started to change. . . . My relationship with White people started to change. I learned so much about the history between White people and Black people and then I was able to learn, be able to pick up on racial slurs and stuff like that. Before then I had not recognized it. When it hit me, the whole social population I hung out with changed. There was a point that I did not deal with White people too much.

Ray's awakening regarding the role of race in America collided with (or was initiated or propelled by) Eurocentric school materials and instruction:

On my part, I did well in school. They placed me in accelerated English classes, but I just did not like the way they dealt with . . . young Black boys, and they would try to kick us out of school. One of the ways we expressed ourselves was through fashion. All my buddies were always in trouble. I was in an accelerated English class and I was the only Black person in the class. There was one instance that made me angry and that was with Mr. Kelly. There was an instance in class where we had to read *Huckleberry Finn* and they say "nigger" a lot in that book. First of all, I did not agree with reading that. I didn't think that was appropriate. And I did not feel comfortable. And every time the class would read "nigger," I felt that the whole class was looking at me. You could see them looking out the corner of their eyes, so I went and told him about it. . . . Yeah. I told him about it and he came to me and told me something along the lines that this is literature and that I was being selfish to say that it was wrong. This is something that needs to be read and that I should not focus on that. It really made me upset, and that was one of the situations that I really remember.

Teachers often saw Ray's "potential," and, hence, would

pull me to the side and tell me stuff like I was not like the rest of my friends and that I should not hang out with them and that I really had the potential to go places and I could do this and that. I heard this throughout most of my high school years. I guess I really should not have taken offense at that, but I did.

Ray's African American friends were placed in shop classes—"a class just to fill the time slot. Stuff that they [teachers] knew they [students] would get nowhere with." One of Ray's friends is in jail right now. The rest of them are at home, working, and two of them went to college, but Ray thinks that they dropped out.

While it is certainly difficult to ascertain which factors play a heavier role in success or nonsuccess of students, the general invisibility of people of color in the curriculum sends the message that education is the domain of Whites. Ray recalls that ". . . everything was culturally, racially, leaning towards White children. Helping them out. Helping them learn about stuff that they thought was important. There was a lot of stuff that I learned that I felt was not important. The only [Black] person that I learned about was Martin Luther King." Having just completed a research paper on multicultural education, Ray recommends that teachers

just try to implement and try to research African Americans, Hispanics, and Mexicans. Just need to study more of their behaviors and their characteristics and the way they learn, instead of teaching them in the way that they [teachers] learned as children. Instead of talking about things that White children are interested in—to look into other topics. I mean, that would help a whole lot. A lot of times I would get in trouble and I would think that I wasn't that bad, but they didn't understand. They were not used to that. I had a lot of energy. I always wanted to be doing something. They wanted always for me to be sitting in my seat. All the time and sit up there, I mean. For African Americans, get some learning experiences where they could be more mobile instead of sitting in their seat.

Ray's story concluded when he was asked whether there was anything else he wanted to share about his school experiences. He responded, "Nothing beside the fact that my experiences made me feel like education—even though they say that education is made for everybody—it was basically made to assimilate every other race and culture into the White way of belief, the White way of culture."

So, like Gloria Boutte, Ray fled to the refuge of a historically Black college. He wants to be "a real good teacher" and then move on to become either an assistant principal, principal, or counselor. "Something like that [counselor or principal]. Because I think counseling and just extra social and mental [psychological] support is what a student needs."

Editor's Commentary

> *"I am not included within the pale of this glorious anniversary! Your high independence only reveals the immeasurable distance between us. The blessings in which you this day rejoice, are not enjoyed in common. The rich inheritance of justice, liberty, prosperity and independence, bequeathed by your fathers, is shared by you, not by me. . . ."*
> —Frederick Douglass, My Bondage and My Freedom, *(Douglass, 1855, p. 441)*

The title of this chapter, "Listening to the Voices of African American Males," is appropriate. Too often, the voices of people like Harold and Ray are silenced and we hear the all-too-familiar refrain "Black males don't do well in the classroom." Seldom do we hear the real reasons why African American males are not faring well in classrooms or how they are purposely excluded (Boutte & McCoy, 1995). Even less frequently do we hear success stories about Black males in school.

Stories like Harold's and Ray's haunt me even more than the ones about Black males losing interest in school by fourth grade (Kunjufu, 1985; Ogbu, 1994). Students like Harold and Ray want to do well, but the system works against them by holding low expectations and saddling them with negative labels like "bad."

Neither of the young men in this story internalized the negative messages about them. Despite the discouragement from school and educators, they persisted and insisted on being allowed to work up to their potential. Harold's mother's support and leadership were vital as well. She was savvy enough to try Catholic school and, later, when he returned to public school, she had him removed from a placement that was much below his level. Many parents of color may be unaware of the politics of school placements and may seldom question the school's authority.

The young men's actions in this chapter continuously shout, "I am smart and intelligent, regardless of what you say!" At a very deep level, they refused to accept an outside (etic) assessment of them, regardless of how pervasive it was. Many African Americans define themselves from the standpoint of their families and communities rather than rely on the perceptions of schools and society (Hale-Benson, 1986).

Although I celebrate Harold's success, it is difficult to remove all doubt that his potential was not dampened in some way. And this gnawing question about what could have been (that is impossible to answer) sends a chill down my spine. When I think of the tremendous loss of "human capital" among African Americans (in general) due to structural inequities in schools and society (Ogbu, 1994), I cringe. The most insidious part is that the system is on autopilot and the vast majority of educators do not fully know or understand how they unintentionally contribute to inequities every day. Hence, the importance of liberatory/emancipatory pedagogy (Delpit, 1995; Freire, 1999) is magnified by Harold's and Ray's stories.

Ray's and Harold's stories hit close to home since I have a five-year-old, African American son. I have already tackled numerous issues with my 17-year-old daughter and can only anticipate that the issues already faced will be compounded for my son. I'd like to think that I'm wrong about this or being overly pessimistic, but my personal and professional experiences with school, supported by a preponderance of educational literature, do not support this position. So I ponder what Harold's and Ray's stories mean for my own five-year-old, African American son. Although information on the African American male "problem" is pervasive (for example, when preparing to react/comment to this chapter, I went to my bookshelves and was readily able to pull eleven books about Black males and issues that they face), and most school officials are familiar with it, most of it is rhetoric that is seldom applied at the classroom and school level. Therefore, it is difficult to remain optimistic because most educators think of themselves as "nice people" but do not realize that even nice people can harm children unless they make conscious efforts not to. I doubt if any of Ray's or Harold's teachers understood how their (teachers) action could have been potentially damaging and devastating to their students. Often, when children do not do well in school or when schools are not "ready" for the children, the blame still falls on the child and her or his family. Ironically, when children do well, educators and schools readily claim responsibility for their success (Boutte, 1999).

Black males are bombarded with negative stereotypes in the media, in society, and at school (Ogbu, 1994). Therefore, schools can be quite hostile places for them. As we will see in the next two chapters, Asian Americans are stereotyped at the other end of the continuum, which carries burdens of its own. It is important for educators to become adept at becoming intimate with educational (and popular) literature on various ethnic groups and at using it as a general guide, not overemphasizing it when making instructional, curricular, and disciplinary decisions (Boutte & DeFlorimonte, 1998). The reader can refer to Chapter 1 for a more thorough discussion of these two complementary concepts.

At one point in high school, Ray became angry at the White power structure and immersed himself in Black culture. According to Cross's (1991) stages in the Black Racial Identity Development Model (Table 3.1), Ray's constant encounters with racism (albeit well disguised under the veil of tracking) may have led him into the "Immersion/Emersion Stage," in which he immersed himself in Black culture and

TABLE 3.1 *Black Racial Identity Development*

Preencounter Stage
- Seeks to assimilate into White culture.
- Absorbs many beliefs and values of dominant White culture.
- Distances him/herself from other Blacks.
- Believes race is not a relevant factor in own success.
- Social significance of one's racial group membership has not yet been realized.

Encounter Stage
- Event(s) (positive or negative) force acknowledgment of effects of racism.
- Faced with the reality of not being White. Focuses on own identity or race.

Immersion/Emersion Stage
- Desires to surround oneself with symbols of one's racial identity and avoid symbols of Whiteness.
- Explores own history and culture.
- White-focused anger dissipates.

Internalization Stage
- Secure in own sense of racial identity—less defensive.
- Willing to establish meaningful relationships with Whites who are sensitive to his or her self-definition.
- Ready to build coalitions with other oppressed groups.

Internalization/Commitment Stage
- Finds ways to translate personal sense of Blackness into a plan of action or general sense of commitment to concerns of own racial group, which is sustained over time.

Note: Research has demonstrated that other people of color (e.g., Asian, Latino, and Native Americans) also go through the same stages of racial identity.

Source: Cross, W. E. (1991). *Shades of Black: Diversity in African-American identity.* Philadelphia: Temple University Press. An edited excerpt. © 1991 by Temple University. All rights reserved.

developed a deep sense of racial pride (an important stage on the road to being able to forge alliances later with other disenfranchised groups in the collective fight against many types of oppression—for example, race, class, and gender oppression).

It is not surprising that racial cleavages occur in a race-conscious society (Ladson-Billings & Tate, 1995; Tatum, 1997). As Beverly Tatum (1997) observes, by the time many students get to high school, they have segregated themselves by ethnic groups (e.g., Latino Americans, Asian Americans, European Americans). Having the emotional support of someone (e.g., friend, parent, educator) who understands your plight cannot be underestimated, as we shall hear again in Chapter 4, when a Korean American high school student shares the same sentiments.

The choices that the school offered Ray and his friends were extremely short-sighted. They could either do well in school or be involved with their African American friends. Ray's story echoes Fordham's (1988) findings that Black students in her study who assumed raceless personae (disassociation of oneself from one's culture) were rewarded by the organizational structure of the school (e.g., they got good grades and officials begged them to take AP courses). For their part of the bargain, the Black students who assumed raceless personae continued to believe firmly in the "American dream." These students hoped that assuming raceless personae would mitigate the harsh treatment and severe limitations in the opportunity structures that were likely to confront them as African Americans. While some may think that disassociating themselves from their cultural group in order to "succeed" in school is a viable prag-matic strategy, Fordham (1988) asserts that this choice ends up being a "Pyrrhic vic-tory" because it is too costly in terms of psychological well-being and the losses are too great (loss of a culture). So for many students of color, the American dream becomes a nightmare.

What does it mean that many schools view success for black males as an anom-aly or rare spectacle? Although "White culture" is glorified in school curricula and many White students are advantaged by systemic practices (e.g., testing, placements, high expectations) (Boutte, 1999; Ogbu, 1994), White students do not have a monop-oly on school success and doing well in school should not be equated with "acting White." Indeed, Blacks have a history of success even when confronted with adverse situations such as those faced by Harold and Ray. Yet, as Ray lamented, schools offer little information about these successes in their curricula. Hence, Carter G. Woodson's comments made in the 1930s are still pertinent to the current discourse on race:

> *The same educational process which inspires and stimulates the oppressor, with the thought that he is everything and has accomplished everything worthwhile, depresses and crushes at the same time the spark of genius in the Negro by making him feel that his race does not amount to much and never will measure up to the standards of other people. (1933/1977, p. xiii)*

Are schools set up only for children who come to school already familiar with mainstream culture? It would seem so. Children from low income and nonmain-stream homes are often stigmatized in school. The stigma attached to one's home is unknown to young children. Like my own story, Bessie expressed pride in her fam-ily's move to a "brand new public housing project." In fact, this area was "some of the best housing for Blacks" in Bessie's segregated town. Educators in public schools are responsible for teaching children from all walks of life, not just those from the most advantaged homes. Educators have to be prepared to recognize and build on strengths that children from low-income homes possess.

I would be remiss if I did not mention how much things HAVE changed in schools. During Bessie's era, children with disabilities were segregated and often not allowed to attend public schools. It is shameful that "crippled children" were isolated in special "homes." Today, children with disabilities are included to the fullest extent in public schools.

All but two of Bessie's teachers shared her ethnicity. Yet, her impressions of some of them are not favorable. Although some argue that White teachers have extreme difficulty teaching African American children (Sleeter, 1993), others point out that if teachers are willing to offer culturally relevant pedagogy, they can be effective regardless of their race (Ladson-Billings, 1994) (Ladson-Billings' study profiled three White and five Black teachers who were successful at teaching African American students.) Approximately 88 percent of the teaching profession is White, and all indications suggest that these trends will continue. Therefore, it is especially important for White teachers to become adept at culturally relevant teaching. Indeed, Bessie's White, male student teacher made a significant impact on her life. He dared to give her the grade of 100 that she worked hard to get. African American teachers must also realize the importance of culturally relevant teaching and cannot assume that shared ethnicity alone is sufficient (particularly since most teacher education programs are Eurocentric in nature). Also, African American teachers may share their ethnicity with Black students, but not necessarily their socioeconomic status or gender.

One year, Bessie had two new teachers during the school year. While this is inevitable in some cases, one caveat should be mentioned. Too often children of color, children from low socioeconomic homes, and children labeled as "low ability" are given teachers who are least prepared (e.g., new teachers). Contrastingly, White students, children from middle- or high-income families, or "high-ability" (e.g., honors) classes are given the "best teachers" (Oakes & Lipton, 1994). This self-perpetuating system typically relegates students like Harold and Ray to inferior positions in school and later in life. In Harold's and Ray's cases, they were able to beat the odds. They offer their resounding messages that Black males are capable. We are challenged to listen beyond the pervasive negative stereotypes of black males. Schools should heed the call of black males such as Harold and Ray and teach them accordingly.

Reflective Activity

Interview Black males from middle socioeconomic statuses. Find out how their experiences are like and unlike Harold's and Ray's stories.

Resources

Children's Literature

Curtis, C. P. (1999). *Bud, not buddy.* New York: Delacorte.
Franklin, K. L. (1992). *The old, old man and the very little boy.* New York: Atheneum.
Greenfield, E. (1988). *Nathaniel talking.* New York: Black Butterfly Children's Books.
Greenfield, E. (1991). *Night on neighborhood street.* New York: Dial.
Greenfield, E. (1993). *William and the good old days.* New York: Harper Collins.
Lauture, D. (1992). *Father and son.* New York: Putnam & Grosset.
Lester, J. (1998). *Black cowboy wild horses.* New York: Dial.
Mead, A. (1997). *Junebug.* New York: Bantam Doubleday Dell.
Mead, A. (1999). *Junebug and the reverend.* New York: Bantam Doubleday Dell.

Mendez, P. (1991). *The Black snowman.* New York: Scholastic.
Pinkney, B. (1994). *Max found two sticks.* New York: Simon & Schuster.
Polacco, P. (1992). *Mrs. Katz and Tush.* New York: Bantam.
Smalls-Hector, I. (1992). *Jonathan and his mommy.* Boston: Little, Brown.

Adult Books

Bowser, B. P. (1994). *Black male adolescents: Parenting and education in community context.* New York: University Press of America.
Boyd, H., Allen, R. L., & Feelings, T. (1996). *Brotherman: The odyssey of black men in America—anthology.* New York: Ballantine.
Bush L. (1999). *Can black mothers raise our sons?* Chicago: African American Images.
Davis, A. C., & Jackson, J. W. (1998). *Yo, little brother: Basic rules of survival for young African American males.* Chicago: African American Images.
Davis, J. (1999). *African American males in school and society: Practices and policies for effective education.* New York: Teachers College Press.
Davis, L. E. (2000). *Working with African American males: A guide to practice.* Thousand Oaks: Sage.
Gates, H. L., Jr. (1997). *Thirteen ways of looking at a Black man.* New York: Random House.
George, J. C. (1993). *The Black male crisis.* Cincinnati: Zulema.
Harris, W. G., & Boudreaux, G. D. (1999). *The African American male perspective of barriers to success.* New York: Edwin Mellon Press.
Hill, P. (1992). *Coming of age: African American male rites of passage.* Chicago: African American Images.
Hopkins, R. (1997). *Educating black males: Critical lessons in schooling, community, and power.* Albany: State University of New York Press.
Hrabowski, F. A., Maton, K. I., & Grief, G. L. (1998). *Beating the odds: Raising academically successful African American males.* New York: Oxford University Press.
Hutchinson, E. O. (1996). *The assassination of the black male image.* New York: Simon & Schuster.
Kunjufu, J. (1985–1995). *Countering the conspiracy to destroy black boys* (Vols. I–IV). Chicago: African American Images.
Majors, R., & Billson, J. M. (1992). *Cool pose: The dilemmas of black manhood in America.* New York: Touchstone.
Mincy, R. B. (1994). *Nurturing young black males: Challenges to programs and society policy.* New York: Urban Institute Press.
Reese, M., & Smith, T. (1997). *Successful African American males: Teacher makes a difference.* New York: Educational Resources Press.
Tukufu, D. S. (1997). *A guide toward the successful development of African-American males.* Richmond Height, OH: Tukufu Group.
Williams, G. (1997). *Boys to men: Maps for the journey.* New York: Doubleday.
Wynn, M. (1992). *Empowering African-American males to succeed: A ten-step approach for parents and teachers.* Marietta, GA: Rising Sun.

References

Boutte, G. (1999). *Multicultural education: Raising consciousness.* Atlanta: Wadsworth.
Boutte, G. S., & DeFlorimonte, D. (1998). The complexities of valuing cultural differences without overemphasizing them: Taking it to the next level. *Equity and Excellence in Education, 31* (3), 54–62.
Boutte, G. S., & McCoy, B. (1995). Excluding the Black male in school and society. *Kappa Delta Pi Record, 31* (4), 172–176.

Cross, W. E. (1991). *Shades of Black: Diversity in African-American identity.* Philadelphia: Temple University Press.

Delpit, L. (1995). *Other people's children: Cultural conflict in the classroom.* New York: New Press.

Douglass, F. (1855). *My bondage and my freedom.* NY & Auburn: Miller, Orton & Mulligan.

Fordham, S. (1988). Racelessness as a factor in Black students' school success: Pragmatic strategy or Pyrrhic victory? *Harvard Educational Review, 58* (1), 54–84.

Freire, P. (1999). *Pedagogy of the oppressed.* New York: Continuum.

Hale-Benson, J. (1986). *Black children: Their roots, culture, and learning styles.* Baltimore, MD: Johns Hopkins University Press.

Kunjufu, K. (1985). *Countering the conspiracy to destroy Black boys.* Chicago: African American Images.

Ladson-Billings, G. (1994). *Dreamkeepers: Successful teachers of African American children.* San Francisco: Jossey-Bass.

Oakes, J., & Lipton, M. (1994). Tracking and ability grouping: A structural barrier to access and achievement. In J. I. Goodlad & P. Keating (Eds.), *Access to knowledge: An agenda for our nations's schools* (pp. 187–204). New York: College Entrance Examination Board.

Ogbu, J. (1994). Overcoming racial barriers to equal access. In J. I. Goodlad, (Ed.), *Access to knowledge: The continuing agenda for our nation's schools* (pp. 59–89). New York: College Entrance Examination Board.

Sleeter, C. E. (1993). How white teachers construct race. In C. McCarthy & W. Crichlow (Eds.), *Race, identity, and representation in education* (pp. 157–170). New York: Routledge.

Tatum, B. D. (1997). *Why are all the Black kids sitting together in the cafeteria? And other conversations about race.* New York: Basic Books.

Woodson, C. (1933/1977). *The mis-education of the Negro.* New York: AMS Press.

4

Six Buckets of Tears

Korean Americans' School Experiences

Lea Lee

Editor's Overview

This chapter chronicles a second-grade, Korean American child's experiences as a new immigrant to the United States. Although the school is in a rural location where few people of Asian descent reside, the teacher makes efforts to make Min-Woo feel welcomed. Because Min-Woo does not speak English, the first few months are emotionally turbulent for him and his family. He feels homesick, as can be expected, but ends up adapting to the new environment. As for many first-generation immigrant children, American culture becomes more compelling than Min-Woo's native culture. As the author notes, success for children should encompass more than just academic performance. Choosing one culture over the over is too great a psychological sacrifice. As noted in Chapter 1, biculturality should be the goal.

"Six Buckets of Tears": My School Experiences in the United States

"Wow! How could you become a professor in America as a native Korean who came over here as an adult?" This type of question is frequently asked by admiring young Korean students at the university where I teach. My response is always very simple: "Six buckets of tears are needed to do that."

The tears represent the hardships I have experienced after coming to a totally new country from Korea. They also symbolize my endurance and perseverance during six years of schooling. I vividly remember lots of difficult moments in the United States when I was adjusting to a culture diametrically different from the one in which I was raised.

Early in my life, I had developed the dream of going abroad to see a different world and to learn more advanced academics. When I was very young, I had read several biographies of great Korean people. Most of them had experience studying in foreign countries, such as Japan, Germany, France, Greece, India, England, and America. They did this at a young age and returned to Korea to dedicate their skills and knowledge toward the development of their home country. As I grew up in Seoul, I always wanted to be a college professor. Upon entering college, I realized that the best way for me to achieve my life goal was to go abroad to acquire higher degrees in the education field. After I graduated from college with a valedictorian honor, I asked for my parents' permission to go to America. That was the first obstacle I had to overcome, even before I got on the airplane to the United States. Korean children must consult with parents and get approval from parents to be away from home. Since letting a girl go away from home before finding a husband is uncommon in the Korean culture, I had to convince my parents to let me come to the United States. As modernized Korean parents, they believed that educating girls (up to the college level) was important. They knew that a higher education would guarantee their daughter's meeting an educated man, which is tied with a comfortable life in Korea. However, they could not understand why I wanted to further my studies at a place far away from home. They finally reluctantly gave their consent to me, after they realized that my life's dream was to become a scholar.

During the entire flight across the Pacific Ocean, I prayed for a safe arrival at the right destination. Yahoo! I was so excited! One hot summer day in 1988, I eventually arrived at O'Hare Airport in Chicago after my long journey. Before coming to the United States, I had spent many hours learning English and becoming familiar with American culture. However, I could never have been prepared to function well in a new country where so many customs were the opposite from those in my native country. Even though I had gone through four years of intensive training and preparation during my college education in Korea, there were so many things I had to learn after arriving in the United States. Many seasonings and ingredients used in Western food were also different from what I was used to. One day, I bought a package of cheese to practice eating cheese as Americans eat it. I ended up throwing it away, due to its terrible smell. Over the years of being in the United States, I gradually developed a taste for Western food and enjoyed the new seasonings and ingredients.

On the first day in an American university, I could not find my classroom. Would you believe that a grown-up with a B.S. degree could not locate a classroom, even though I knew the room number? School buildings in the United States are sometimes designed like a maze, where a classroom is hidden behind another classroom. I was not familiar with this type of American school architecture. For at least a week, I really needed a mentor or guide who could assist me, until I picked up basic information about American culture.

I could not stop bowing each time I ran across my teachers in school buildings on campus. Since I had been trained for twenty-two years to bow to my teachers, it was natural for me to bow to my teachers here in the United States. I was shocked by American students' attitudes toward teachers. When I saw students waving their hands at the teacher, it was very hard for me to understand. A student would never wave to a teacher in Korea! The classroom atmosphere was also extremely strange to me. In the United States, interaction between the professor and students occurred frequently during the lecture. Students could express their opinions and ideas, even if they were not consistent with the professor's beliefs. In Korea, students usually sat still and listened, without questioning the professor in class. When a student had clear knowledge of a topic that was questionable during the lecture, the student would go to the professor's office to present his/her opinion passively. Also, when a professor points to a specific student and calls his/her name during the class, the student must stand up and respond to the professor's question.

Making friends in the United States was almost impossible. Most of the students I met in school had jobs and busy personal lives. Simply put, they had neither the interest nor the time to spend with a foreign girl who could not speak English very well. Sometimes, while I was eating lunch, alone in the school cafeteria, I hoped someone would approach me, wanting to be my friend. Only one "minority" student demonstrated an interest in me occasionally. As a Korean, I had learned to appreciate foreign people living in Korea and to show excessive kindness to any visitors to the country. I craved for some warm and sincere friends. When I initiated the formation of a study group in preparation for the final exam in my class, one African American female, Linda, showed an interest. Linda was willing to meet me at the library on a Saturday afternoon. Consequently, I developed a long-lasting friendship with Linda, who also helped me complete schoolwork on several occasions.

Many education courses required some type of fieldwork. The fieldwork included activities such as visiting a public school, child development center, hospital, or museum. It was not an easy task for me since I didn't have a car and didn't know how to get there. When I needed help, my good friend Linda was there for me. I could never forget the true friend who could see my needs and who sacrificed much time and effort for me. Linda comforted me when I was frustrated and scared with stress and overwhelming burdens. Whenever I was sad, lonely, and homesick, Linda gave me a big hug and talked to me. Linda included me in her family gatherings at times and treated me as one of her family members. Linda understood how much I was missing my parents and siblings back in Korea.

The first major U.S. holiday I learned about was Thanksgiving. One afternoon in class, my adviser and professor invited me to spend the holiday with him. He announced to the class that he would have me as his guest for the Thanksgiving holiday. I was so embarrassed that my face turned red. I knew immediately that my professor was treating me differently from the other students. I was very excited and happy about the invitation. I also appreciated the professor's thoughtful and kind invitation. However, I didn't want the whole class to know about the professor's special treatment of me. As a foreign student, I appreciated the invitation by my teacher, yet I didn't want to be recognized as different from my classmates. I was also very nervous, because I didn't catch the date and time to meet him when he announced it to the class. It would have put me at ease if he had written the invitation on a card and handed it to me privately.

I learned how an American breakfast menu (foods such as cereal and milk) was different from the Korean menu on my first Thanksgiving morning. Staying overnight at a typical middle-class home, I had the opportunity to learn about an American family relationship and living style. The best way to learn American customs was through actually observing/visiting an American home and interacting with the family members.

While I was learning and adjusting to the new culture, I also studied hard to achieve my goal in the United States. Because my decision to study was made by me without any outsider's pressure or will, I really did my best to be academically successful. I dedicated an average of ten hours a day for self-study at the library or dorm room. The weekend was not used for relaxation or for enjoying my young life. Weekends were used to catch up on readings and schoolwork. Even though I didn't share my studying style or studying duration with anyone, my professor noticed it and repeated, "No sweat, no sweat, no sweat," and, "No sweat." Of course, I didn't know the meaning of the phrase at that time. I still could not figure out why the professor made that comment. I later learned that he had noticed my hard work and wanted me to relax and take it easy.

All of the school experiences were difficult for me. From taking lecture notes in class and taking exams to writing term papers, I struggled with the language barrier. I really wanted to understand the entire lecture. I understood only 30 to 40 percent of the information received during lectures during my first semester. I needed a guide who could show me how to study and how to be an outstanding student. Often, instructors don't consider that international students have special needs and require some adaptations during lectures and exams. It would have been a great help if the instructor had assigned a buddy who would have allowed me to copy lecture notes. No matter what type of problems I faced, however, I never gave up. I searched for solutions to problems so that I could achieve my goal. For example, when I could not understand a subject, I read textbooks repeatedly. I even memorized the text so that I would be able to pass the course with a good grade.

After tolerating many painful years, I finally became a professor and scholar in America. My ceaseless efforts were necessary, but not sufficient to achieve my goal. Without my friends and instructors, who were encouraging and willing to give support, I know that I would not be who I am today. Many of my true friends had high expectations for me, which helped my confidence level. My friends embraced the Korean culture and even tried to learn and implement some of the beliefs, daily living styles, and customs of Korea into their own lives. They respected the Korean culture and encouraged me to be proud of my culture. Those friends' names and faces will live deep in my heart for a long, long time.

I can only imagine what it would be like to be a small Korean child living in America. Some of my feelings and frustrations are reiterated through the voice of Min-Woo, a Korean boy growing up in a rural town in Kentucky.

Min-Woo's Voice

Cuckoo!! Cuckoo!! Cuckoo!! Cuckoo!! The alarm clock is waking Min-Woo's family. It is time for Min-Woo, who is seven years old, to get up. He has to get up early to catch the yellow school bus. It is the most difficult thing he needs to do in America. He has to beg for the mercy of his mom for a few more minutes of sleeping everyday. He says to his mom with dozing eyes, "Uhm ma, jo gum mahn duh jah go ship pah yoh" ("Mom, I would like to sleep a blink moment of time"). Sleepily, he visualizes himself boarding the school bus that is as cute as a toy bus. But it is hard to go to school so early in the morning. He enjoys riding the school bus, which is new to him. He has never seen such a thing in South Korea, where he is originally from. He used to walk to school in Korea, and he had to be there by 9 o'clock.

Min-Woo lives in a small rural town in Kentucky. He loves to hear birds singing, smell green grass, watch blooming flowers, and feel fresh air in the morning. Min-Woo loves to go to the city park in front of his duplex and ride his bike. He also loves to play under big, tall trees around his house with his younger brother, who is four years old. Min-Woo thinks trees in America are giant compared to trees in South Korea. He tried several times to hug some big trees. It was not easy to put his arms around some trees. Sometimes, he and his brother held hands to be able to reach around the trees.

Min-Woo moved from Korea eight months ago with his parents. He finished the first semester of second grade (from March to July) in a public elementary school in Seoul, Korea, before he moved to America. When he entered an American school in September 1996, he was assigned to the second grade again. At the time I wrote this story, he was in the second half of second grade in Kentucky.

For Min-Woo, math is a very easy task. He is practically the best student in math in his class. What he is learning in school is addition and subtraction, which is too easy for him. He already mastered not only addition and subtraction, but also multiplication and division in Korea. However, he does not consider himself the best in math. Whenever he gets his math papers back from the teacher, he misses a few questions. That is why he thinks he is doing average work. His mom and dad scolded him for his frivolous work several times. When he declared, "Mee kook san sook ga nuh moo shee wuh you" ("The math questions were too easy here in America"), they advised him to take time and be more careful before answering the questions.

Recess is Min-Woo's favorite activity in school. He likes to participate in chasing games and play basketball with his American friends. His heart beats with delight when the friends understand what he is saying on the playground. He still does not want to do writing. Writing in English is a very difficult task for him.

Min-Woo's favorite American friend is Mary, who always wants to hug him. Min-Woo is very delighted about living in America. He used to say that he missed his friends and teachers in Korea. When he came home from school, he used to be very irritable and cried easily. He screamed with a crying voice to his mom, "Uhm ma naa Seoul ae dae rhee go ga sei yoh!" ("Mom, please take me back to Seoul!") Min-Woo's parents were shocked when they heard that.

He used to say he wanted to go back to Korea where grandma lives. He used to say that he missed his friends and teachers in Korea. Now Min-Woo says that he loves his American friends and teachers more than the ones in Korea. This new information was a contradiction to what his parents had known about their son's feelings. They were anxious to find out the reason and the time when he changed his attitude about America.

Min-Woo explained to his parents that his American friends and teachers are more caring. They want to hug him very often. His Korean friends and teachers never hugged him. His American friends also want to know more about Korea. They came to him and asked about Korean schools, language, and food. "How do you say a car in Korean?" "Do you have Christmas?" Min-Woo said to them, "A car in Korea is called 'chaa.'" "Yes, we have Christmas." He also enjoys finding the location of Korea on the globe with his American friends.

The first day of school in America was especially memorable. As soon as he walked into the class, all the children in the class said, "an nyeong haseyo," which means "hello" in Korea. He felt a special and warm welcome. It was quite an emotional moment to know that they wanted him to be here. One day when he was running late for school, his classmates again showed that they were happy to see him. They waved their hands and tumbled down to the floor with him. They all said "hi" when he arrived at school late. Based on a few experiences he has had, he believes everyone loves him.

Min-Woo's special talent is drawing. He draws various characters in cartoons, robots, and animals. He watches cartoons on TV and draws what he saw "off the top of his head." He cuts out the characters and animals and role plays with them. He has a list of friends anxiously awaiting his drawings. He likes to pass out the drawings to friends as gifts. His parents are very proud of his talents and encourage him to be an artist, if he is happy with what he is doing. (See Figure 4.1 for a sample of Min-Woo's drawings.)

Min-Woo's favorite teacher is Mr. Brown, who teaches art. He appreciates Mr. Brown's protection and acceptance. Min-Woo remembers clearly that Mr. Brown said to class, "Do not hit him because he is my friend." He thinks it is cool that the teacher calls him "my friend" in front of other children. He has boasted about the incident to his parents many times, "Uhm Ma, sun sang nim yee na rul chin guu ra go bul ruh yoh" ("Mom, my teacher thinks that I am his friend").

He loves his American classroom, where he finds many colorful toys and games. His freely moving around and talking with friends during class is quite a strange atmosphere for him. It is different from his second-grade class in Korea, where he had to sit quietly at his desk all day, except for a few minutes of transition time. He feels that he is playing most of the time in school. It has been a joyful school experience for Min-Woo because he can play in school.

However, it was not all that much fun when he could not understand a word of what he heard in school during the first few months. He was very stressed and frustrated. He hated America and cried sometimes whenever he missed his grandma. Even though he wrote a letter to his grandma, teachers, and friends in Korea, he was not emotionally satisfied. He just wanted to go back to Korea to see them.

A major crisis in Min-Woo's family was when Min-Woo's parents found out that he did not do anything in school without the Korean bilingual tutor who assisted him for an hour each day. He did not want to write or read unless the tutor was around him in the classroom. He did not like to speak English in the classroom either. He simply sat quietly at his desk and played with his hands and papers instead of being actively engaged with the assigned work. He worked on reading and writing with the tutor during the class and after-school tutoring session. Otherwise, he did not want to write. He did not want to read. He did not want to speak.

Min-Woo's teacher and the school principal invited his parents to the school to discuss the problem he was having with English. That was the parents' first official visit to talk about their son's schoolwork. He had only

FIGURE 4.1   *Min-Woo's Sample Drawings*

attended school about two months at the time. The teacher and principal said that Min-Woo needed special attention to improve his English ability.

Min-Woo's parents were upset to hear the comments and decided to give intensive English instruction to their son. Since then, his mother has spent one hour a day including weekends teaching him English. Fortunately, they had English textbooks for beginning learners from Korea. They used the books as instructional materials. As a former lawyer, his mother had the educational background and ability to teach beginning English. To express herself better in English, the mother has attended English classes conducted by retired senior citizens at a local church while Min-Woo is in school.

Min-Woo also spends two hours a day for math and piano lessons at home after school. His parents purchased "Daily Math," which was published by an educational company for second graders in Korea. Doing the "Daily Math" is not a new thing to him because he did it in Korea since he was four. Sometimes, Min-Woo speaks his opinion about the extracurricular lessons to his parents when he is tired of studying: "Whae na man, mae ill gong boo hae yaa haa na yoh?" ("Why am I the only person who has to study everyday?") His mother thinks he is speaking pretentiously and acting rude since he has been attending an American school.

Min-Woo's father also pays attention to his son's progress in learning English, even though he is busy with his own schooling. As a full-time student studying for an MBA at a university, his father cannot spend much time teaching, but he disciplines his children based on his careful observation and information given by the mother.

Due to the dual effort both at home and at school, Min-Woo is able to communicate in English. It has been only eight months since he moved to the small town in western Kentucky. He can now truly enjoy going to school and understand what is going on in class. Min-Woo prefers to speak English when he has visitors even though they are Korean. He is amazed by the fact that he can listen to, speak, and write in English. He wants to use English all the time now so that he can test himself. He trusts his own ability in terms of expressing himself in English and has very high self-esteem. He raises his hand in class very often, whenever he does not understand the meanings of words. As his English problem diminishes, he demonstrates a stronger leadership in the class while playing and learning. As he becomes more proficient in English, he is less homesick. He is a very outgoing child. He is happy here and he loves his American friends.

Min-Woo and his mother were in a good mood during the school's "Spring Swing." Spring Swing was a fun festival for children and parents to play in school. Min-Woo's mother was a ticket receptionist in his class during the Spring Swing. He was very comfortable seeing his mom in the classroom.

The teacher is amazed at how fast he learns English. The parents are thrilled about his improvement in English competence and reassured that they made the right decision about moving to America. Teaching English to their two sons was one of the main goals they wanted to achieve in America.

The family is planning to move to a bigger city as soon as Min-Woo's school is over. The town is very peaceful and safe. They do not need to worry about crime and drugs in the school and in the community, but there is not much to see around this town. The father wants to show bigger cities and different things in America to his two sons. The mother wants to acquire an advanced education. The children want to have friends who have a common background with them. Min-Woo does not want to be the only foreign child in his class.

Reflections on Min-Woo's Voice

Min-Woo recognizes the environmental differences between Korea and America. The streets in Korea were busy with many people and cars, and he had a hard time riding his bike around his house. He also realized that going to school in America is to actively play with toys rather than sitting quietly. He likes to receive physical expressions from friends and teachers, such as smiling, holding hands, and hugging, that are refrained from in Korean family and society. He will be able to do that reciprocally in the near future, but he is still too shy to initiate showing his affection. He is a very happy and self-confident child, like many Korean students, such as the one in Park's (1995) study. Park surveyed 207 Korean students in America to identify their special needs or concerns. The students' grade levels ranged from second grade to freshmen in college, although the majority (85 percent) of the sample was at the junior and senior high school level. According to Park, the majority of the Korean students appeared to be well adjusted to life in the United States and happy about their schools, families' lives, and friends. They also appear healthy in terms of their self-perceptions and proud to be Koreans living in America. Some of the specific item ratings and percentages from Park's study are shown on Table 4.1.

Min-Woo is also a very busy child. After he comes home from school, he spends many hours learning math, English, Korean, and piano. He rarely expresses discontent about his parents forcing him to study when he does

TABLE 4.1   *Korean Students' Responses about School Experiences (Park, 1995)*

Comments	Percentages
I am happy living in the United States.	97%
I feel good about myself.	97%
I have many friends.	94%
Teachers like me.	88%
My parents love me.	97%

not want to. He usually does what his parents say, because he has been taught to respect and obey his parents.

Min-Woo's parents regard education not only as a means of success, but also as a measure of one's self-worth. As cited in the *Handbook for Teaching Korean-American Students* (California State Department of Education, 1992), Korean children feel obligated to receive high grades and are imbued with the notion that their academic success is linked to the family's reputation. Thus, Min-Woo's parents instilled in him very early the idea that the parents' acceptance is contingent upon high performance in school. His parents also taught Min-Woo that he must obey his parents' wishes.

He does not have much free time, but he spends most of his free time, after he completes the expected study, drawing and playing with his cartoon characters. He is happy to hear from his teacher comments such as "He is an artist" and "He is the teacher's friend." He wants to be close to the teacher and to be recognized by the teacher (see the letters written by Min-Woo to his teacher and principal in Figures 4.2 and 4.3). He is proud to share information about Korea with classmates.

During the last eight months, Min-Woo has changed a lot. At first, he was very frustrated and didn't like America, mainly because he didn't understand English. As in Min-Woo's case, Koh and Koh (1988) describe Korean children as invariably experiencing environmental and psychological stresses when they move from one culture to another. According to them, stresses faced by Korean children are often greater due to their lack of English proficiency and the cultural differences between Korea and the United States.

However, collaboration among teachers, parents, and a Korean tutor hired by the school and Min-Woo's own motivation to learn English helped him to learn English successfully. Min-Woo is now well adjusted to the new language, food, culture, and school. Currently, he prefers to play with American friends and teachers. After experiencing difficulty for six months, he now enjoys English, cartoons, parks, trees, birds, and, most of all, American friends. However, he still thinks that he cannot do a great job in his writing in English.

There is sometimes a major conflict between Min-Woo and his parents. When he does not talk softly and politely to his parents to express his opinions and when he does not obey their requests, he gets a scolding or a punishment. Although he cannot freely say what he wants to say to his parents yet, he is learning in school how to speak up and express his ideas straightforwardly. Min-Woo is struggling to adjust to two diametrically different value systems. Min-Woo's parents try to convey a message to him to develop new values in America and simultaneously understand and develop cultural traits represented by their Korean family and community.

According to Paulston (1978), Park (1995), and Yao (1988), newly immigrated Korean parents and children are seriously challenged by acquiring

FIGURE 4.2 *Min-Woo's Sample Story and Drawings*

new cultural behaviors and attitudes while trying to retain attributes from their native culture. It has been found that Korean parents may hold ambivalent and often inconsistent expectations concerning the cultural choices their children make in finding their place in American life (Kim, Sawdey & Meihoefer, 1980). Min-Woo has been told by his parents to keep learning

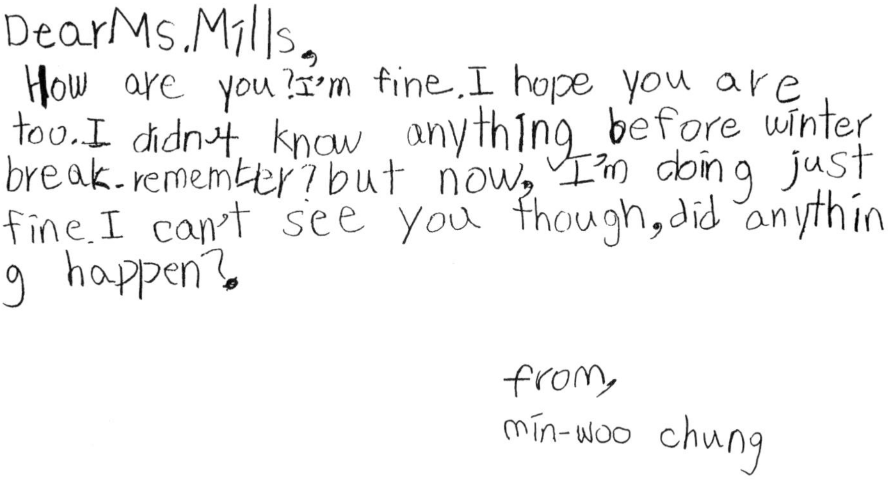

Dear Ms. Mills,
How are you? I'm fine. I hope you are too. I didn't know anything before winter break. remember? but now, I'm doing just fine. I can't see you though, did anythin g happen?

from,
min-woo chung

FIGURE 4.3   *Min-Woo's Letter to the Principal*

American values without substituting them for Korean values. Parents and educators alike should recognize that cultural adaptation is developmental. Korean children need emotional support as they make the transition from the traditions of their native culture to the values of their new environment. Parents need to learn about the differences in the two cultures and support the process (California State Department of Education, 1992). By adopting a bicultural approach in which children add new values while keeping their original culture, they can build a strong psychological foundation for high self-esteem and a clear identity.

Min-Woo's parents had a difficult time accepting that their child had a problem in school. His parents took the teacher's remarks about their child too seriously. In Yao's opinion (1988), teachers should be careful criticizing Korean newcomers and selecting languages they use when talking about their children. He recommended that teachers talk first about strengths, then about problems or weaknesses, explain the remediation plan, and finally ask for help and support from the parents.

The parents wanted to hear what he would be able to do in two months rather than what he could not do or what he would not be able to do. The first six months must be considered as an accommodation period. The child's lack of understanding in class must be accepted as part of the developmental process, rather than criticized.

Min-Woo's parents instilled in their children very early the idea that they have high expectations for them and that parental acceptance is contingent on high performance in school. Kim (1988) found that Korean parents' expectations for their children's achievement often reach an unrealistically high level. These expectations are supportive for those students whose interests and abilities make such expectations or goals realistic. Korean parents are willing to go into debt to pay for expenses related to extracurricular lessons and education. Min-Woo's parents are also willing to hire instructors who specialize in music and art. His mother specially organizes her time for tutorial sessions at home for Min-Woo. The persistence and economic sacrifice of Korean parents demonstrate their commitment to their children's education.

Min-Woo's parents are actually his primary teachers. Min-Woo's parents are well educated and his family has a high social class background. Min-Woo must study with his mother every evening, which is a typical style of Korean families. He does not like his mother sometimes because she tells his father whenever he does not obey her. Min-Woo is afraid of his father. He tries hard to listen carefully to what his mother asks him to do, to prevent his mother from reporting his behavior to his father.

Min-Woo's family came to the United States for two reasons. First, his parents wanted their children to obtain a high-quality education. The parents are typical Korean parents who regard education as the single most important contributor to their children's future success, and they will take extraordinary measures to ensure that their children have every opportunity to obtain the best education (Yu, 1988). Second, the parents decided to come to America to complete their own education at a university. The father is one of the Korean graduate students composing the fourth largest group of foreign students attending universities in the United States, demonstrating the keen interest in education and the dedicated pursuit of academic excellence prevalent in Korea. Both the mother and father gave up their careers as a lawyer and an administrator in a newspaper company, respectively, in Korea to provide better educational opportunities for their children.

Large Korean communities are found throughout the United States, particularly in New York, Chicago, Atlanta, Seattle, San Francisco, Los Angeles, and Honolulu. The state with the largest number of Koreans is California. Min-Woo's family will soon move to California to pursue their original plan and goals. Min-Woo's school experience in Los Angeles will be somewhat different from the one in the small town in Kentucky. First, there will be more Asian students in the school, with whom he can exchange feelings. Min-Woo can talk about his pleasant and frustrating experiences with other Korean children who have similar experiences and learn the skills needed to cope with new values and cultures. Min-Woo will not be alone or isolated from friends.

There will be more teachers who have more background knowledge and are familiar with Asian cultures. They may be more understanding of the diversity that Min-Woo and his family are bringing to the community.

This acceptance will make his assimilation easier into the new school and the area. At least, he will not be called "a Chinese boy," as he was called while attending a school in Kentucky, where he was the only Asian boy. Those children failed to distinguish Koreans from Chinese. At least, people will be less likely to follow him or stare at him when he goes into a restaurant or store.

In California, classrooms will contain more Korean decorations, materials, children's books published in Korea, and learning activities about Korea, so that Min-Woo can engage in a school curriculum that is relevant to him. The teachers and classmates in Los Angeles will be more likely to share their knowledge of Korean culture with Min-Woo, which will help him to be more proud of his Korean heritage.

Children in Los Angeles will probably recognize a popular and common Korean lunch menu item, Kim Bob, rolled rice and vegetables with dried seaweed. They may even want to have some of Min-Woo's lunch, prepared by his mom. In Kentucky, he was ridiculed for eating Kim Bob when his classmates in the small town school saw it at first. The food was too strange for some of his former classmates. Min-Woo felt a distance from them when they could not enjoy the food and discuss the taste. Traditional recipes of Korean dishes are usually passed down, orally, generation by generation. Thus, the same Korean food has many variations. Korean children cheerfully discuss and compare how their mothers prepare the dish. By sharing their food during lunchtime, they develop a strong friendship and emotional bonding. Min-Woo missed this type of special joy in the small Kentucky town. Furthermore, he hesitated to open his lunch box completely after he encountered the first negative responses from his classmates.

In California, Min-Woo will actively participate in school events such as a Korean day, arranged by the school system, during which Korean students and parents present Korean history, culture, food, costumes, music, stories, poems, and art. Although Min-Woo has found his niche in the rural Kentucky school, there are many times that his Korean-ness places him on the periphery of the curriculum, instruction, and interactions. His family recognizes the importance of his heritage and look forward to moving to California, where they anticipate more synchronization between the school and his home.

Suggestions for Teachers

The following list of suggestions can be used as general guidelines for teachers or school personnel who interact with Korean or Korean American students and their parents. Although some of the recommended ideas are directly applicable to Min-Woo's case, most of them can be applied to various situations while working with Korean families. Suggestions are divided into four categories: (1) working with Korean Children in the classroom, (2) working with Korean families, (3) developing an awareness of Korean culture, and (4) helping Korean parents and students learn about school.

Working with Korean Children in the Classroom

Provide substantial guidance and direction until they are comfortable in child-centered classrooms.   Korean students who have recently come to the United States are used to structured and formal activities. They will benefit from gradual introduction to spontaneous, informal activities. They should be encouraged to seek help from peers, make some decisions on their own, and express themselves creatively over time (California State Department of Education, 1992). Thus, the teacher may provide assistance in choosing activities and planning for the day until they become accustomed to a child-centered classroom. Teachers should understand that Korean children experience difficulty in making choices. In Korea, most Korean children are trained to obey and follow directions given to them.

Provide ESL teachers or native-speaking teacher aides.   Korean students who immigrate to the United States will have to make significant adjustments to new social and academic norms. To facilitate the shift to a different life in a new country, these students and their parents may need help from sensitive teachers and counselors who are familiar with the family's native language (California State Department of Education, 1992). Thus, the school with Korean students needs to consider hiring at least a native speaking part-time teacher. Administrators should seek Korean–English bilingual staff. Qualified Korean teachers and/or instructional assistants can usually be found in the community or at a nearby university. Some Korean students attending a university are willing to spend their time helping Korean children and parents.

Learn a few words in Korean.   Teachers should learn simple Korean words such as "hello" (*ann nyung ha sei yuo*), "love" (*sa rang hae yuo*), "bye" (*ann nyung hee ga sei yuo*), and "thank you" (*kam sa ham mi da*). This demonstrates a positive attitude toward the child's language and culture. Teachers may consider teaching simple Korean songs to young children. It is not that difficult for students and teachers to learn rhythmic Korean children's songs and basic words. It also benefits American-born children to learn songs in a language other than English.

Reflect Korean culture in the classroom.   Teachers need to reflect Korean culture in the classroom by posting signs written in Korean. Most Korean parents are willing to devote their time to such efforts. Have children's literature or materials from Korea in class. The classroom environment and materials should represent Korean culture and must be nonbiased, respectful of diversity, and culturally sensitive. When the cultural uniqueness of Koreans is reflected in school programs, Korean students can more easily overcome their feelings of inadequacy and the lack of self-confidence brought about by language difficulties and bewildering cultural phenomena found in the United States (California State Department of Education, 1992).

Conduct a unit on Korea.   Instructional materials for learning activities may be borrowed from parents or from local Korean churches and community centers. Parents are often willing to serve as a resource for such units. Korean parents can plan for a Korean culture day. They can prepare food, drinks, toys, music, and ornaments from Korea, donating the income to the school. This is a great fund-raiser and an opportunity to share Korean culture. The unit should be part of ongoing efforts to diversify the curriculum (rather than a one-time isolated unit).

Give specific assignments to the Korean student.   Korean students feel an obligation to accomplish what has been assigned to them by the teacher. Teachers should make specific assignments for English improvement, especially when children are struggling with it. Generally, when Korean parents do supervise their children's schoolwork, it is easy for them to make the children work because it is required by an authority, the teacher. Yet it is advisable not to assign too much and recognize that learning to speak English is a developmental process. The process should be enjoyable rather than laborious.

Reject the stereotype that Koreans are smart in math.   Math is introduced much earlier in Korea than in the United States. Therefore, it may seem that Korean children are talented in math. But, in reality, not all of them are. They may have a private tutor at home teaching math. Teachers need to be careful about marking "wrong" on math worksheets for Korean children with a language problem. Instead, they need to pay attention to the children's reasoning before marking it wrong. If it is a word problem, they may have misunderstood the English used.

Be sensitive to stress resulting from cultural conflict between the two cultures.   Korean children are often confused and stressed by cultural differences. Things that are not accepted for children in Korea are encouraged in America. For example, Korean children are often taught to look down or avoid direct eye contact when a teacher says something directly to them. In America, the expectation is to maintain eye contact. Understanding such differences is a key factor in helping children negotiate both cultures.

Repeat directions several times for Korean students.   Koreans with limited English may need individualized attention from the teacher. Teachers may need to speak slowly or repeat directions. Teachers should inform children of what to do when they do not understand words.

Working with Korean Families

Find out Korean students' and parents' immediate needs or problems.   Do not automatically assume that Korean children and parents have language problems. A great deal of diversity exists in the rate and amount of English they acquire. Therefore, teachers need to find out each individual's needs and provide appropriate services. Obviously, second-generation Korean children will not likely have problems with English. However, they may have other cultural issues that teachers should be sensitive to.

Arrange a home visit and enjoy tea or food.   Teachers can learn a lot about the family through a home visit. It is not imposing or intrusive to initiate a home visit. Koreans often prepare food or tea for their guests. During the visit, teachers are expected to begin the eating, since they are held in high esteem. It is customary for Korean parents to wait for the teacher to initiate eating.

Let parents know that it is important to use Korean language at home. Most Korean parents want their children to continue speaking their native language, but they are unsure whether it will interfere with learning English and attaining high levels of academic success. Teachers should encourage children to be bicultural. Teachers need to tell them that it is a good way to maintain their unique tradition and that speaking Korean at home will not interfere with their learning in school.

Plan educational programs for Korean parents.   Schools put tremendous effort into teaching children English at school. However, many immigrant parents do not gain English proficiency. They remain non-English speaking while their children speak perfect English. To bridge the gap between generations and to help limited English proficiency parents participate in their children's education, classes that teach English, school traditions, American culture, and customs could be developed. There is a great need for educational programs to provide Korean parents with opportunities for learning more about the American educational system, philosophy, and curriculum. For example, Korean families can meet at a school for two hours each week to work on learning English and other American cultural practices.

The Internet may be used to search for local activities, community service organizations, and historical and cultural resources for Korean American children and families. Unlimited information is available on the

Internet. Resources, which may be helpful for teaching Korean children, can be located.

Be clear and firm about meeting times, but understand cultural differences in perceptions about time. Koreans perceive time as a process that lets different things happen at the same time. Westerners schedule events one at a time. Thus, Korean parents may come late for an appointment without apologizing. It may be helpful to communicate the importance of appointment times and to let parents know that other families are scheduled before and after their designated time.

Korean parents may also feel uncomfortable about their limited English proficiency and may not attend conferences. Also, many Korean parents work long hours, which interferes with their availability for conferences.

Make it clear that a child's academic or psychosocial problems are not a source of shame. Some Korean parents of children who need special services in school may reject these programs, such as ESL or bilingual instruction, because they fear their children being stigmatized as "slow learners." Educators should point out that bilingual education offers students the opportunity to maintain their Korean language without jeopardizing their learning of English and academic subjects.

Developing an Awareness of Korean Culture

Understand the personal, social, cultural, and psychological background of each Korean child and family. Sharing and communicating with families is crucial to creating a culturally sensitive environment for children and their families. By asking about their families, Korea, and Korean culture, teachers and families can construct a foundation of trust and acceptance.

Respect the tradition of respect toward elders. Teachers need to be aware of the Korean tradition of respect toward elders and teachers. Korean parents highly respect school administrators and teachers. They believe that their role is to listen and follow educators' professional judgment. They may be reluctant to participate in school functions and confer with teachers, because they defer to the authority of educators. Such behavior should not be misconstrued as a sign of the parents' lack of interest and responsibility in school affairs. To solve this conflicting situation, teachers need to understand/accept their own immense authority in front of Korean parents and children. Teachers also need to explain to Korean parents that parent involvement is welcome in school. Active parent involvement in class in preparing materials, assisting teachers, and supervising children may be a new expectation for Korean parents. Thus, specific encouragement and directions for parent involvement must be given to them.

Korean parent volunteers can have a role as mentors for newly arrived children and their families. Each child can be assigned a mentor who spends at least an hour each day interpreting for and helping the student.

A tradition in Korea is that parents can come to class on the first day of school simply to stay with the child. Therefore, parents of new Korean students should be allowed to stay in class until the child is used to the new school.

Express an interest in Korean culture.   Korean students tend to respect their traditional roots when the teacher shows interest in and a positive attitude toward Korean culture. It is important to encourage respect for their heritage while also helping them become bicultural. Students who are taught to respect their traditional roots emerge as healthier individuals.

Become familiar with Korean cultural practices.   Koreans are accustomed to bowing to greet others. Teachers and children may learn how to bow to each other.

Many Koreans worship their heads. They believe the head must be toward the bright side where the sun rises. Some parents may find it offensive if their children's heads are toward the west during school nap.

Use written communication.   Koreans learn written English in middle school, high school, and at the university level. They may not understand what you are saying, but they can easily comprehend the English that is written. Therefore, written communication may be used to convey information to parents.

Understand that smiles often express embarrassment and confusion, not pleasure.   Korean parents may smile or slightly laugh when teachers seriously discuss the child's language problem. Teachers need to laugh right along with them since it is the same as accepting their apology.

Helping Korean Parents and Students Learn about School

Allow a transitional period for children to adapt to the new school.   Instead of being anxious or worrying about slow improvement in English competence, teachers should send directions of what to do at home to Korean parents for the first few months. Most immigrant children need approximately six months as an accommodations period. Because of language difficulties, Korean children may sometimes behave as if they did not hear what the teacher said. They may not follow a teacher's direction. In that case, teachers should be careful about labeling them as having behavioral disorders or hearing impairment.

Provide a tour of the school to both Korean children and parents. Provide a tour of the school. Parents and children need to be familiar with the locations of school facilities such as gym, cafeteria, office, teachers' lounge, and playground.

Conclusion

While the practices suggested may benefit all children, they are particularly important for children and families who have recently immigrated to the United States. Despite the misconception that Koreans tend to assimilate easily, as Min-Woo and my story illustrate, the process is socially, emotionally, cognitively, and physically challenging. Therefore, teachers and schools should make special accommodations in order to ensure children's psychological as well as academic well-being.

Editor's Commentary

Koreans are one of the major Asian immigrant groups whose populations have mushroomed since the enactment of the 1965 Immigration Act (Asian Indians and Vietnamese are the other two major groups) (Min, 1998). The majority of Korean Americans came to the United States as a consequence of this law. In the 1980s, more than 30,000 Koreans immigrated to the United States every year, making them the third largest immigrant group of the decade, following Mexicans and Filipinos. The 1990 census counted approximately 800,000 Koreans in the United States (28 percent of this population was born in the United States). Despite their short immigration history and small group size, they have attracted a great deal of attention—probably more than most other Asian groups—from the media and researchers, primarily because of their concentration in small businesses and Korean's merchants' frequent conflicts with African American customers (Min, 1998).

Although Korean Americans are often reputed to "assimilate" easily into American culture, Min-Woo's adjustment was difficult for his family and him. Imagine how his family felt when Min-Woo's teacher and principal invited them to school to discuss the problem he was having with English. The tremendous amount of anxiety and embarrassment experienced by his parents because "authorities" conveyed disappointment in their child (whom they are very proud of) cannot be underestimated. Even though it seemed as if Min-Woo adjusted to school after a few months, the emotional and social impact of this experience should not be underestimated and we cannot assume that all is well. Like many students of color, the difficulty of balancing two cultures is constant.

Reflecting on his school experiences, Clifford, an 18-year-old Korean American who was born in this country but spent seven years in Korea, stated, "I feel comfortable around people who are like me—minorities in general, people who other people identify as being not American or white—because we both have a culture, a separate heritage that we can identify with" (Oei & Lyon, 1996, p. 59). Clifford's comments illustrate the dilemma of being raised in a race-conscious society in which structural and social inequities exist (Ladson-Billings & Tate, 1995; Ogbu, 1994; Tatum, 1997). They direct us back to the two complementary concepts presented in Chapter 1 that explain that while culture should not be overemphasized, it is also too important to be negated. While Min-Woo and his parents wanted him to fit in at school, his parents also wanted to move to California, where they could have a better cultural support base in the Korean community. It is not surprising that Min-Woo's family chose California as a preferred place to live. According to the 1990 census, approximately 32 percent, or 260,000, of all Korean Americans reside in California (Min, 1997). Los Angeles provides an extra advantage to Korean Americans because "Korea town," a physically segregated location, is there. Although there is a large majority of Hispanic Americans in Korea town, the area serves as a commercial and residential center for Korean Americans. Approximately 3,500 Korean-owned businesses, complete with Korean language signs, are located there. The vast majority of Korean businesses serve native Korean cuisine and sell groceries, books and magazines, and sundries. Businesses also provide services for other distinctively Korean cultural tastes (Min, 1997).

Living in a place where their lives are not constantly "on stage" or viewed as exotic is a benefit that Min-Woo and his family can enjoy if they move to California. Being the only one (or two) persons of one's ethnic group can be an uncomfortable and isolated position for students. The level of assimilation into mainstream culture among people of color varies widely. Some children may want and try to fit into the classroom, others may resist, and still others may fall somewhere in between. Therefore, educators' assessment of the level of support and most effective strategies should consider numerous factors (e.g., level of acculturation, socioeconomic status, aspirations, and values). Ongoing communication with families is important.

Because Min-Woo appears happy on the surface and fits in well in school, his emotional needs may be overlooked by teachers as long as he thrives academically. Min-Woo is lucky that his mother has the expertise and time to tutor him in English. A challenge that bilingual children face is becoming proficient in English, which is necessary for school and societal success in general. Yet maintaining their "home" language is equally important (Delpit, 1995). This formidable task of maintaining the Korean language may be easier in Min-Woo's case because Koreans as a group tend to be homogeneous in terms of culture and historical experiences (more homogeneous than any other Asian group, with the exception of the Japanese) (Min, 1997). Having a single language gives Koreans an advantage over other multilingual Asian immigrant groups, such as Indians and Filipinos, for maintaining their ethnic ties and group solidarity. Younger-generation Koreans may therefore be more likely to preserve their language and subculture. A group of children being able to speak, read, and write in one language makes it easier for schools to facilitate bilingual education. Second-generation Korean children also regularly attend Korean churches with their parents (Min, 1997). These trends may change for third-generation Korean American children, and the likelihood of losing Korean culture may increase.

Min-Woo's family looked forward to moving to California because teachers there would likely be more familiar with Korean culture. Min-Woo's physical appearance would more likely be distinguished from that of Chinese and other Asian ethnic groups. Non-Asians commonly stereotype people of the Asian disapora as "all looking alike." Such negative stereotypes invisibilize many Asian ethnic groups. Asian Americans are frequently overlooked or viewed as "exotic" or "foreign" (even if they are born in the United States) (Oei & Lyon, 1996; Takaki, 1994). Clifford, the student interviewed by Oei and Lyon (1996), laments, "One of my Korean friends feels like people exclude him. But of course they do *exclude him: He can't communicate as well, he dresses different, he's outcast. And so you end up with a lot of little Asian cliques that speak their same language, and their English hasn't advanced, and people identify them as FOB—Fresh Off the Boat" (p. 54).*

Children like Min-Woo and like many other children of color often try to straddle two cultures. They receive messages in school and at home that they need to succeed in American society, but achieving success in both cultures simultaneously may require conflicting beliefs and practices. Clifford (Oei & Lyon, 1996) expresses the pressures and expectations of Koreans trying to succeed in America: "My parents said to me, 'Living in the white man's world, to compete with them, you have to be able to hang with them in society—you have to be able to speak like they do, know their culture. You don't want to be an outcast. Yet you want to be above their standards of intelligence, because if it comes down to the worst, a white person is going to hire a white' " (p. 56).

However, Clifford discovered that living in the "white man's world" comes with other caveats. How is it possible to fit into this world when people continue to group Asian Americans into one conglomerate? Clifford complains, "I think expectations of me are different because I'm Asian. My friends used to say to me, 'Oh, Cliff, you must have it worse,' because stereotypically Asian parents are harder on their kids. A lot of teachers said I wasn't the typical Asian student. I was sort of rambunctious in class. I was never the quiet one" (p. 53).

Clifford's comments demonstrate that although he did not want to be lumped into the generic Asian category, his teachers and peers often typecast him as a "model minority." Like many children, Clifford and Min-Woo seek to fit in with their peers. Hence, they are attracted to American culture and tend to drift away from Korean culture. Clifford says,

> *Some Asian people consider me sort of whitewashed because I've been here so long they don't identify me as an Asian. Sometimes I don't identify with Koreans as well as I'd like—sometimes I'm intimidated by Koreans because I lack so much of what real Koreans have—the tradition, the history they know. I've forgotten a lot of history and Korean folklore, things I was taught as a little kid. (pp. 52–53)*

Clifford's comments seem ambivalent at times. On one hand, he talks about his preference for friends who are similar to him, but he also discusses his alienation from Koreans (perhaps he is only comfortable with "whitewashed" Koreans?). The tension between the two cultures is probably due to implicit "melting pot" notions permeating U.S. society (e.g., school instruction and curriculum and the media) coupled with influences from the Korean community to maintain Korean culture. The difficulty of balancing two cultures is compounded by unspoken (often) insistence that one choose one culture over the other, which for most children is impossible. Biculturality is often not seriously presented as an option.

Just as Min-Woo struggled to fit into his new American school, we also see Lea's (the author's) extraordinary efforts to succeed after her entry into the United States. Her frustration and anxiety level were extremely high. Lea's story illustrates her determination and also illuminates how lonely the walk to success can be for an international student coming to the country. Lea's alliance with Linda, an African American, defies the idea that Koreans and African Americans do not get along. As mentioned in the Preface (citing Bill Ayers), as soon as one moves beyond superficial interactions and learns a little more about another person's life, stereotypes disappear.

If the conflicts between Korean and American culture were overwhelming for Lea as an adult, it is difficult to conjecture the impact on a child like Min-Woo. Lea found many aspects of American culture to be diametrically opposed to Korean customs. She had to get accustomed to the informal interactions with professors (she couldn't stop bowing and could not imagine waving at a professor). Additionally, the protocol for responding in class was different and, while she spoke and read English already, studying in English was a laborious task. The architecture of the buildings was different, and she missed her family. I can only imagine how disempowering this must have felt. And yet, Lea triumphed. But as her telling of Min-Woo's story indicates, she has not forgotten the trauma (six buckets of tears) of the transition and is proud of her Korean heritage.

Lea's pride and understanding of the strengths of Korean culture are as important as her acculturation. For example, the respect awarded to elders and teachers is admirable. The manner in which students in Korea approach their professors is no better or worse than the way it is done in the United States. It is simply different and both are defined by the context. The trajectory to normalcy varies widely. Recently, I had the pleasure of hearing a Korean scholar present a paper titled "Beyond Authoritative Parenting." The title was provocative and I was enthralled with her discussion. The presenter noted that she was weary of all of the negative connotations much educational literature places on what it terms authoritarian parenting. Many Korean parents, like Min-Woo's, and many African American parents (Delpit, 1995) would be labeled "authoritarian" because of their "strict control" over their children. According to Baumrind's (1972) classic work on parenting styles, children of authoritarian parents tend to be withdrawn rather than independent. However, Baumrind discovered that African American girls raised by authoritarian parents were self-assertive and independent (Lamb & Baumrind, 1978). Findings such as these suggest the importance of interpreting familial practices and outcomes on the basis of the particular context rather than from a mainstream context. In other words, the trajectories to independence are likely to differ for Korean American and European American individuals. So while Min-Woo's parents may seem controlling according to traditional Western psychological wisdom, the predicted effect of withdrawn personality needs to be interrogated. The manner in which children and families interpret and experience situations varies widely. Lea grew up in Korea and was raised with "traditional" Korean values. Yet, her level of independence does not appear to have been hampered. When we take a moment to examine closely how many psychological theories are defied by people of color, we may learn to listen more closely to their stories to understand what their lived experiences mean to them. We should ask, "What can we learn from people of color's inside (emic) view?"

The Korean scholar who problematized authoritative parenting raised several important issues. What does it mean that independence is stressed over interdependence? She expressed her shock at discovering elderly people in the United States living alone or in convalescent homes while their grown-up children lived halfway across the country. In Korea, adult offspring typically take care of their aged parents with honor. Many African and Asian countries share this tradition, as do African Americans and other ethnic groups in the United States. Does the value of one person's independence, needs, desires, and so on take precedence over the welfare of the family and community? There is no one correct response to this query, and voices like Min-Woo's and Lea's invite us to consider alternative possibilities. It is likely that our response will fall somewhere in between the dichotomies of independence and interdependence.

If we reexamine the desired goal of independence through a different lens, we can recognize that it is valued differently depending on the context. We will find that independence may be developed and demonstrated differently and that there is no one formula. Varying degrees of independence (and interdependence for that matter) are required, and there is no one correct way to grow up or to parent. "What we are talking about is creating a new tradition, telling 'new stories' that are fundamentally different by virtue of the role that the lives of the historically oppressed have assumed in their construction. This is a matter of redefining American culture, not once and for all, but in the negotiated meanings that are always emerging. . . ." (Perry & Fraser as cited in Erickson, 1997, p. 57).

Finally, one caveat about focusing on cultural groups in classrooms should be mentioned. Although food, music, and other "visible" aspects of culture are important and have the potential for helping children and educators become less ethnocentric, they should not be the entirety of multicultural efforts (Boutte, 1999; Erickson, 1997). Continuously demonstrating both similarities and differences among humanity as well as "invisible" (unspoken, implicit) aspects of culture facilitates the development of broader perspectives. And with broader horizons, perhaps a society as diverse as ours would not continue to demand "six buckets of tears" from newcomers.

Reflective Activity _____

Imagine moving to another country to increase the economic and/or educational quality of your family's life. How would you feel if you had to assimilate into a culture (of your new country) that is diametrically different from your own (in terms of, e.g., language, food, music, social etiquette)? Is assimilation too high a price to pay to fit in? Why or why not?

Resources _____

Children's Literature and Korean Language Material

Audiobooks

Taylor, Theodore. Tuck triumphant. Prince Fred. (1921). (Theme: Dogs, Adoption)

Fiction

MacMillan, D. (1982). My best friend, Mee-Yung. Seoul, Korea: Seoul Computer Press. (Theme: family life, friendship).

Messner, J. (1989). Kim: Meeting a Korean-American family. Englewood Cliffs, NJ: J. Messner.

Folklore and Folktales

Ha, T. H. C. (1958). Folk tales of old Korea. Seoul, Korea: Yonsei University Press.

Han, S. C. (1991). Korean folk and fairy-tales. Elizabeth, NJ: Hollym. (Theme: human nature).

Kim, Y.-K. (1990). Brave Hong Kil-dong. Elizabeth, NJ, and Seoul, Korea: Hollym. (Theme: social justice).

Kim, Y.-K. (1990). The tiger and the persimmon. Seoul, Korea: Hollym Publishing Inc. (Theme: foolish tiger).

Poitras, G. Y. (1985). The woodcutter and the fairy. Seoul, Korea: Si-sa-Yong-o-sa.

Vorhees, D. (1990). Mr. Moon and Miss Sun. Seoul, Korea: Hollym Publishing Inc.

Vorhees, D. (1990). The greedy princess. Elizabeth, NJ, and Seoul, Korea: Hollym.

Vorhees, D. (1990). The lazy man. Elizabeth, NJ, and Seoul: Hollym. (Theme: diligence).

Vorhees, D. (1990). The ogres' magic clubs. Elizabeth, NJ, and Seoul, Korea: Hollym.

Vorhees, D. (1990). The seven brothers and the big dipper. Elizabeth, NJ, and Seoul: Hollym.

Vorhees, D. (1990). The snail lady. Elizabeth, NJ, and Seoul: Hollym.

Vorhees, D. (1990). The son of the cinnamon tree. Elizabeth, NJ, and Seoul: Hollym.

Yu, C.-S. (1986). Korean folk tales. Toronto: Kensington Educational.

Korean Language

Chang, S.-I. (1982). Modern Conversational Korean. Seoul, Korea: Seoul Computer Press. (Theme: language material).

Poetry

Yoon, S.-J. (1990). Big brother's big brother's. Seoul, Korea: Woong Jin Publishing Company. (Theme: family and friends).

Useful Resources about Korea

Art

Adams, E. B. (1986). *Art treasures of Seoul with walking tours.* Seoul: Samhawa Printing.

McCune, Evelyn. (1962). *Arts of Korea.* Seoul: Dong Hwa History Publishing.

Business

Janelli, Roger L. (1993). *Making capitalism: The social and cultural construction of a South Korean conglomerate.* Stanford, CA: Stanford University Press.

Cookery

Ha, Suk chfong. (1985). *Traditional Korean cooking.* Seoul, Korea: Soodo.

No, Chin-hwa. Cn. (1985). *Practical Korean cooking.* Elizabeth, NJ: Hollym International Corp.

Games & Recreation

Chooe, Sang-su. (1985). *Han.guk minsok nori.* Korea: sfongmun.

Chooe, sng-chofol. (1987). *Chfulgfoun orak kkeim.* Korea: Taea choulpoansa.

Koh, Frances M. (1997). *Korean games.* Seoul: East West PR, ISBN 0-9606090-8-3.

Pak, choang-yfong. (1989). *Lejo rekofurieisyfon.Silnae.* Korea: Llsin Sfojfok Kongsa.

Literature
Chung, Chong-wha. (1985). *Love in mid-winter night.* Boston: KPI; Distributed by Routledge and Kegan Paul.
Chung, Chong-wha. (1989). *Korean classical literature: An anthology.* New York: Kegan Paul International, distributed by Routledge, Chapman, and Hall.
Chung, Chong-wha. (1995). *Modern Korean literature: An anthology.* New York: Columbia University Press.
Kim, Jaihiun J. (Ed.) (1987). *Korean poetry today.* Seoul: Hanshin.

Music
Pratt, Keith L. (1987). *Korean music: Its history and its performance.* London: Faber Music, in association with Jun Eum Sa Pub. Corp., Seoul, Republic of Korea.

Religion and Philosophy
Chun, Shin-Yong. (1982). *Korean thought.* Seoul: Si-sa-yong-o-sa Publishers.
Guisso, R. W., & Yu, Chai-Shin. (1988). *Shamanism: the spirit world of Korea.* Berkeley, CA: Asian Humanities Press.
Wfon, fui-bfom. (1992). *A history of Korean Buddhist culture and some essays.* Seoul: Jip Moon Dong.

Society and Culture
Ha, Tae Hung. (1968). *Guide to Korean culture.* Seoul: Yonsei University Press.
Joe, Wanne J. (1972). *Traditional Korea: A cultural history.* Seoul: Chung.ang University Press.
Korean Overseas Information Service Committee. (1993). *Facts about Korea.* Seoul: Republic of Korean Overseas Information Service.
Publication Committee. (1986). *Korean arts and culture.* Seoul: Seoul International Publishing House.
Publication Committee. (1997). *Korea: 5000 years of mystery.* Chicago: Korean National Tourism Organization. (205 N. Michigan Ave, Suite 2212, Chicago, IL, 60601)
Shalant, Phylis. (1995). *Look what we've brought you from Korea: Crafts, games, recipes, stories, and other cultural activities from Korean-Americans.* Parsippany, NJ: Julian Messner.
Unknown slide photographer. (1992). *Korea: Its culture and tradition.* Seoul: Art space publishing.

Software
Publication Committee. (1995). *Korea folk art festival.* Seoul: Ministry of Culture and Sports.
Publication Committee. (1997). *Exploring Korea culture.* Chicago: Korean National Tourism Organization. (205 N. Michigan Ave., Suite 2212, Chicago, IL, 60601)

Video
Plumber, T. (1987). *Family and home.* New York: The Society.

Useful World Wide Web Pages

Korean American Museum of Art and Cultural Center (KOMA): http://koma.org/.
Korean American Family Service Center: http://koma.org/freedom.html.
Korea's Weekly Top International News: http://koma.org/weeklynews3.html.
Korean American Guide: http://sopo.com/kordoc/guide.htm.
Kids Place: http://www.cyberkorean.com/kids.htm.
Sae Jong Camp, for families with adopted Korean children: http://members.aol.com/saejong/saejongcamp.html.
Korean Cultural Night explores the American Dream: http://www.dailybruin.ucla.edu/db/issues/96/5/17/ae.korean.html.

References

Baumrind, D. (1972). An exploratory study of socialization effects on black children: Some black-white comparisons. *Child Development, 43*(1), 261–267.

Boutte, G. (1999). *Multicultural education: Raising consciousness.* Atlanta: Wadsworth.

California State Department of Education. (1992). *Handbook for teaching Korean-American students.* (ERIC Document Reproduction Service No. ED 342 248).

Delpit, L. (1995). *Other people's children: Cultural conflict in the classroom.* New York: The New Press.

Erickson, F. (1997). Culture in society and in educational practices. In J. A. Banks & C. A. M. Banks (Eds.), *Multicultural education: Issues and perspectives* (pp. 32–60). Boston: Allyn & Bacon.

Kim, B., Sawdey, B., & Meihoefer, B. (1980). *The Korean-American child at school and at home: An analysis of interaction and intervention through groups.* Washington, DC: U.S. Department of Health, Education, and Welfare.

Kim, C. (1988). *Korean-American students' attitudes toward American society.* Doctoral dissertation, The University of the Pacific, Stockton, California.

Koh, T. & Koh, S. (1988). *Cognitive and affective adaptation of Korean American school children in Chicago: Service and research priorities* (ERIC Document Reproduction Service No. ED 299183).

Ladson-Billings, G., & Tate, W. F. (1995). Toward a critical race theory of education. *Teachers College Record, 97* (1), 47–68.

Lamb, M. E., & Baumrind, D. (1978). Socialization and personality development in preschool years. In M. E. Lamb (Ed.), *Social and personality development* (pp. 50–69). New York: Holt, Reinhart, & Winston.

Min, P. G. (1998). The Korean-American family. In C. H. Mindel, R. W. Habernstein, & R. Wright Jr. (Eds.), *Ethnic families in America: Patterns and variations* (pp. 223–253). Upper Saddle River, NJ: Prentice Hall.

Oei, T., & Lyon, G. (1996). In our own words: Asian American students give voice to the challenges of living in two cultures. *Teaching Tolerance, 5* (2), 48–59.

Ogbu, J. (1994). Overcoming racial barriers to equal access. In J. I. Goodlad (Ed.). *Access to knowledge: The continuing agenda for our nation's schools* (pp. 59–89). New York: College Entrance Examination Board.

Park, E. (1995). Voices of Korean-American students. *Adolescence, 30* (120), 945–953.

Paulston, C. (1978). Biculturalism: Some reflections and speculations. *TESOL Quarterly, 12,* 369–380.

Takaki, R. (1994). The myth of the "model minority." In R. C. Monk (Ed.), *Taking sides: Clashing views on controversial issues in race and ethnicity* (pp. 55–61). Guilford, CT: Dushkin/McGraw-Hill.

Tatum, B. D. (1997). *Why are all the black kids sitting together in the cafeteria? And other conversations about race.* New York: Basic Books.

Yao, E. (1988). Working effectively with Asian immigrant parents. *Phi Delta Kappan, 70,* 223–225.

Yu, E. (1988). Korean-American communities and their institutions: An overview. *Korean Culture, 9,* 33–45.

5

When East Meets West

Asian American Students' Success through the Lens of One Chinese Family

Wenju Shen, Ph.D.

Editor's Overview _____

In this chapter, we meet a Chinese American family—mother, father, two daughters, and a son. We glimpse how they are influenced by both Chinese and American culture. The concept of biculturality is personified as we examine how both generations find their places in the United States. The portrait Wenju Shen paints provides an inside perspective on what it is like to balance two diametrically different cultures. The author also shares aspects of her entry into the United States, her family's subsequent immigration here, and their determination to make it in "the land of opportunity."

My School Experience in The Land of Opportunity

It was New Year's Day, 1985. I was looking out of the window from the guestroom on a college campus in West Pennsylvania. The entire campus was blanked with snow, not a trace of life as far as I could see. It seemed I was trapped in the dormitory on New Year's Day, but my heart was full—full of joy, full of excitement, full of ambition. Almost two decades after I had received my B.A. degree, I became a student again and would now pursue the degree of Master of Education. I had come to this university four months earlier as a visiting professor. My job description focused on teaching noncredit courses and giving seminars and speeches about Chinese culture and language. I had enjoyed the experience, but I felt more challenged culturally than academically. I had always been a good student, but due to the infamous Cultural Revolution in China, I had been deprived of the opportunities to further my education. Instead, like millions of other Chinese people in that era, I went through despicable tortures and spent thirteen years of my life in house prison, military camp, and "in exile" in places where tap water and electricity were luxuries.

Lost time cannot be replaced, but a lost dream can be found. I felt I was standing on top of the hill again, looking into the future. But at the same time, my heart was filled with worries too. It had been so long since I sat in a classroom taking notes from the professor. Did I still have what it takes to be a successful student? I learned from my previous four months' experiences that there were so many things in the American culture that I had not yet comprehended. English is my second language. There were times at social gatherings that I found myself totally at a loss at people's jokes. To what degree would things like this affect my absorbing textbooks and professors' lectures? And, of course, there was my family. When I left China, I left my husband and two preteen children at home with a promise that I would return as soon as my one-year contract was fulfilled. Now the separation would have to be longer. Could I do it? Could they? I did not get much sleep these nights. A decision was made, not without difficulty, but with determination.

School was everything I had expected. During the first semester in my graduate program, I took fifteen semester hours (five courses), including research, curriculum, and psychology. I was not an education major in my undergraduate program and because of the Communist Party's closed-door policy in those decades, we were not exposed to anything from the outside world. The textbooks and the class discussions I now encountered were therefore foreign to me in every sense. The professors were generous enough to let me tape the lectures, and I spent hours and hours listening to the recordings and looking up words in my Chinese–English dictionary. My visiting professor's contract had not been fulfilled yet; therefore, I needed to continue with those responsibilities. I also worked twenty hours per week as a graduate assistant to help pay the tuition. During those six months, my sleeping hours were counted not by day, but by week. At the end of the first semester, I received four As and one B. Looking at that piece of paper lying beside the dog-eared dictionary and textbooks, my heart was filled with joy again. I had made it.

I was awarded the degree of Master of Education at the end of 1985. I had planned to go home after I graduated, but my advisor and major professor convinced me that I should stay in the States pursuing a doctorate degree. Knowing my primary concern, she went through all the red tape and sponsored my family (all three of them) so they could come to the States to join me. Meanwhile, I applied for doctoral programs that would provide scholarships and/or financial aid. By the beginning of January 1986—one year after I started my graduate study—I was notified that I was granted a graduate assistantship from another university in Pennsylvania starting immediately. I was an official doctoral candidate! By then, I was more familiar with the American higher educational system and felt more at home with the program. My family came to the States after I passed the candidacy exam. Having been apart for two years, we were finally all together at the other end of the world.

Things seemed to get better and better. I was selected from the doctoral students in the College of Education for the position of "teaching associate"—assuming half the teaching load of a full-time instructor. This arrangement not only allowed me to have firsthand experience teaching American students but also provided financial security for the family.

Both our children were in junior high school. My husband decided that he would pursue his graduate studies. (He was later also selected for the teaching associate position.) For quite a few years, ours was a family of four students. In our apartment, the most decent furniture was the four desks and the four lamps—our investment for the American dream. To make ends meet and save some money for the children's extracurricular activities, my husband and I drove sixty miles one way to work in a Chinese restaurant on weekends. For years, our time was divided by studying, teaching, and working in the restaurant until I completed all my course work. My GPA was 4.0. Although my status was ABD (all but dissertation), I accepted a tenure-track position at a state university in Kentucky.

Currently, both my husband and I are college professors. Our daughter, who has a degree in business, works as the head of a department at a major company; our son is in graduate school pursuing the same dream we pursued years ago.

Looking back, I saw myself leaving the library Saturday evenings, smiling apologetically at the librarians for their patience. I saw a capital letter *A* in bold red ink on my paper and remembered how relieved I felt. I saw my husband and me crawling on the highway for eight hours during a storm one night returning home after a long day waiting on tables. I saw myself sitting with my children looking up all the biology terminology in the dictionary and telling them, "We will make it." Then I saw each of us in cap and gown accepting flowers from each other. "We made it!" This has been the utmost congratulation in our family.

The story of my school experience will not be complete without commending my professors for their generous support. Every step on the way towards my goal, I had a star shining over me. My advisor and professor in my master's program reunited my family, making it possible for me to stay and further my education in the States. My advisor (who later became my husband's advisor, too) and major professor in my doctoral program called us his "extended family." He meant it in every possible way. It was he who greeted my family at the airport and brought them "home." It was he and his wife who gave my children their first Christmas gifts. My father was critically ill during my comprehensive exam time. I was torn between a daughter's love and a student's commitment. It was he, my professor, who went to see my father in Shanghai (he was attending a conference in China) and brought back a tape of my father's injunction that I should not leave school. There were so many others: professors who believed in me, students who trusted me, and classmates who challenged me.

I cannot help but remember one incident in my student life. In one statistics course, there were only two students who received As for the final grade. I was one of the two. One American student commented that I received an A because I am an Asian student, meaning the professor lowered standards for me. I insisted that the professor compare every single assignment that I had completed with hers. I was naturally pleased with the results, but I was really touched by the support I received from the entire class, including the professor, regarding this matter. I was persecuted in my own country; yet I found trust, respect, and, most of all, friendship in this country. I often ponder over the meaning of "land of opportunity." To me, the utmost opportunity is not a house with a white picket fence. It is the freedom to pursue one's goal. It is the freedom to reach self-actualization. It is the freedom to be a better person.

This is a great country. This is the land of opportunity.

Introductory Comments about Asian American Students

For a long time in this country, Asian American students have been viewed as high achievers. Their images have been supported by impressive statistics, from the percentage of students who are awarded Presidential Scholarships to winners at local spelling bee contests. But recent studies (Schneider & Lee, 1990; Shen & Mo, 1991) have indicated that Asian American students are not all "whiz kids." A great number of studies have questioned the myth of the universal success of Asian American students. Some probed into cultural roots for explanation (Pang, 1990; Sue & Okazaki, 1990); others set foot in the territory of school counseling and communication with parents (Morrow, 1989; Shen & Mo, 1991). In these studies, discussion seems to be focused on the validity of Asian American students' success in school. When a positive correlation between Asian American students' success in school and their cultural background is challenged, concerns about those who are experiencing difficulties in school become apparent.

The Family

I know a Chinese family, the Lins. This family started twenty years ago as a young couple. The husband was a former college professor and a promising candidate for a law degree in an American university; the wife was a registered nurse. Like many other new immigrants, they were ambitious and industrious. They saw themselves as two fighters creating a future of quality life in the land of opportunity. However, life made other plans for them. First, the husband experienced language barriers in his studies and, consequently, lost financial aid. Then, the wife became pregnant. Their firstborn child and three more children in the following years completely changed their perspectives of success. They drew a new blueprint for their future in which the happiness and success of the children assumed primal priority. They stored away their own career ambitions and opened a restaurant so that the family would have financial security and to provide a stable home for the children.

I have known this family for years and have always been amazed by their lifestyle. Even though they have been in this country for two decades and all four children were born in the States, in many ways this family is very "Chinese"—the closeness between the family members; the sacrifice parents are willing to make and have made for children; the absolute obedience the children have to their parents; and the fact that, after three girls, the parents were determined to have a son. And then there are some things in this family that are very "American" too—taking pride in the children's independence and individuality, a willingness to invest in the children's extracurricular activities, the valuing of practical experience and social skills as opposed to mere book knowledge.

The children's accomplishments are extremely impressive. Amy, the 17-year-old eldest daughter, is graduating from high school this summer. I have a copy of her resume. Here are some highlights: a G.P.A. of 4.0; a class rank of 1 in a class of 397; a 1590 on the SAT; and a 4 on the AP calculus exam, a 4 on the AP U.S. History Exam, and a 5 on the AP English Literature Exam. Among the honors and awards she has won are high awards in spelling, piano, and art competitions; being named to Who's Who Among American High School Students; being named a Furman Scholar, a National Merit Semifinalist, a Beta Scholar Nominee, and a Presidential Scholar Nominee; being elected a Girls State County Commissioner; and being named to the Governor's Honors Program and the Duke University TIP Program. She is also involved in the school literary magazine, debate club, science problem solving bowl team, the math club, and ballet. All the above are not quite half of her record.

Victoria, the 15-year-old tenth-grader, and Diana, the 14-year-old ninth-grader, also have outstanding records. They were both in the Duke University Talent Identification Program last summer. Ming, the nine-year-old son, was recently the sixth-place winner in the District Writing

Competition (the seventh-place winner was a tenth-grader) and won first place in the District Spelling Bee Contest.

What are the keys to the family's success? Is there any relationship between their success and the deep structure of their value system? My hypothesis is that a harmonious application of Chinese traditional values in mainstream U.S. society plays an important role.

I spent many hours observing the family's environment and behaviors, interviewed the parents and the children, and interacted with them in daily routines. I tried to identify activities and behaviors that can be traced back to Chinese traditional values and those that are more "Americanized." I also looked for a "happy medium"—an integration of the East and the West. Over the past months, I accumulated stacks of notes, tapes, and supporting documents. My findings are strikingly interesting and the syntheses of my observation notes with interpretations will offer an insider's view on the issues to be described and discussed.

The family operates a Chinese restaurant, which is located in the less prosperous area of their town. Most of the customers are lower-income families and employees of local stores. There are usually more "take-out" than "eat-in" customers. When looking at the sparsely occupied parking lot, one will probably wonder whether the restaurant is open. But once inside, the liveliness and energy can be felt immediately. I visited with the family in the restaurant one afternoon—between lunch and dinnertime. The children had just arrived home from school except Amy, who was still at school preparing for a coming art exhibit. I found Victoria in the "study room" making wontons while flipping some index cards. She told me she was reviewing some notes from that day's history class. Diana was busy putting a school project together. Ming was at the cash register taking care of a customer. Mr. Lin was in the kitchen; Mrs. Lin was everywhere and with everybody. I followed her around, starting my interview.

After much talk with the family and observations of their daily operations, I have a better understanding of the value system practiced in this family. I have seen abundant evidence of a beautiful marriage between the East and the West. To provide a clearer picture of the two cultures, my discussion will be organized into the categories of Chinese values and American values.

Traits Rooted in Chinese Culture

Obligation to Family

The Confucian ethical code, which is the essence of Chinese culture, holds that the first loyalty is to the family. The family represents a religious, political, and social unit. Academic achievements and upward mobility are viewed not as personal matters, but as part of children's obligation to the family (Shen & Mo, 1991). Chinese parents view their children as their investment, something related to their own honor, pride, and happiness. It's not unusual among Chinese people to hear a compliment concerning a friend's young child's academic accomplishment immediately followed by a statement such as, "You don't need to worry about anything for old age."

In the Lin family, two messages were made loud and clear to the children from the very beginning: (1) they should do better than their parents because they are provided with a stable, worry-free environment; (2) they should do better than their relatives and friends at home because they are in the land of opportunity. The children grew up with such high expectations that they don't see any other way. Amy wrote in one of her essays, "I, Amy Lin, [will] make something of myself, become famous, be one of the few who did not become another faceless entity, another speck in the crowd of specks." In the same essay, she offered, "But then I thought of my father. He tried so hard, succeeded, yet, strangely, he failed. And I think he would do it again, the same way, the same hard path. And I vow not to become another faceless speck—I vow to make my name famous, to break the cycle of drudgelike monotony." Obviously, to Amy, striving for success, or "not to become a faceless speck," is not just the goal of her life, but also her determination to change the family image.

Amy not only set an example to her younger siblings; in a way, she helps reinforce the parents' messages to the other children. All the other children look up to their older sister, follow her footsteps (e.g., winning contests, excelling in standardized tests). "We want Dad and Mom feeling proud of us" is the children's motto. Indeed, their parents are proud of them.

Parents' Sacrifice and Possible Guilt Induction

Mr. and Mrs. Lin do not remember when they have ever dined out or seen a movie as a couple since the birth of their first child. Everything they do is for the children. As small restaurant owners, they work long hours and often feel overwhelmed by take-out orders and all kinds of chores. It is not unusual for them to forget whether they have eaten lunch or not, but they never fail to pick up each child at school and take them to different after-school activities. They have a rule in the house that each child must leave the day's work at the kitchen counter before going to bed. No matter how late the couple finishes the restaurant work, they go over each child's work and make notes of necessary follow-ups, such as to talk to the teacher about certain subjects. Their restaurant opens six days a week (most family-run Chinese restaurants open seven days a week). Because they want to spend Sundays sitting down with the children and listening to what they want to say, they do not open their restaurant on Sundays. They are not Christians, but they take the children to church every Sunday because they believe it is good for the children. Every summer, they close the restaurant for a few weeks to take the children "to see the world." The child with the most impressive accomplishments will choose the place to go. This year is Amy's turn—she is graduating and has been offered full scholarship by different prestigious universities. The entire family will go to China.

Mr. and Mrs. Lin are the most loving couple I have ever known. It was touching to watch the way they looked at each other when they talked. I asked Mrs. Lin if there were times that they felt exhausted and would want to take time for themselves. Her answer was very simple: "We have decided that children's interests come first."

Recently, I was intrigued by a report I read from *HXWZ* (the most influential Chinese electronic journal) about how young parents sacrifice for their children in today's China (Kuo, 1997). The parents are all professionals—office supervisors, teachers, and even military officers. After their children had been accepted to a prestigious musical institute in Beijing, the parents all resigned from their jobs and went to Beijing to accompany their children. They were afraid their children were too young to tell right from wrong and would be too homesick to concentrate on study. They lived in temporary housing facilities near the boarding school, made home-cooked meals for the children, and literally studied with their children. According to the report, these parents have placed too much pressure on the children, the school, and even the city. The report appeals that it is time to put an end to this sacrifice/investment-pressure/payback cycle.

I recall one of my students in China many years ago. This student was the first one in the whole village to become a college student. His parents sold their last share of crops to buy his train ticket. Everybody in the village pitched in, a few eggs, some buns, a dollar or two, along with many, many expressions of admiration and wishes. This student came to the provincial university carrying a load of expectations and pride that his parents and fellow villagers had for him. University life was not easy for this country boy. For a year or two, he struggled against cultural shock, poverty, alienation, and academic challenge. Finally, he gave up and committed suicide. His last words were "Can't face parents and fellow villagers."

Amy and her siblings are among the lucky ones. Nevertheless, they feel the pressure, too. Mrs. Lin told me during one of our chats that Amy had decided to study law. She said her father gave up his dream of becoming an attorney for the children. She wanted him to see his dream realized in his daughter. She said she would open a law firm so that her father could eventually work as a lawyer. Heart-touching dream. I sincerely hope this is from nothing but love, and maybe a young woman's ambition.

No Pains, No Gains

Chinese parents tend to value efforts over innate ability. The Chinese people have a household fable. A young boy played truant one day, wandering in the village. He saw an old woman by the river grinding a thick iron rod. When asked what she was doing, the old woman said she was making an embroidery needle. "If you have the perseverance, you will eventually make an embroidery needle out of an iron rod." The boy learned the lesson and returned to the classroom. This boy later became the nation's best-known poet. "No pain, no gain." "Practice makes perfect." These sayings typically reflect Chinese values. When a student fails in school, the only acceptable reason is that the child did not study hard enough. This probably can be traced back to a Confucian saying that the father is to blame if he only gives life to his son but does not teach him properly. A parallel belief among Chinese parents is "ends justify means." Whatever parents do is considered for the good of their children. In China, there are very few cases in which a child is taken away from the parents. On the contrary, there are many examples, fiction or reality, in which the child becomes "good-for-nothing" because the parents spoiled him. Usually, the ending is that both parents and child have remorse for the consequences when it is too late.

As I am writing this, an incident stands out in my mind. Mr. Lin insisted that all four children take piano lessons. He set up the piano in the restaurant so that he could make sure the children had enough practice. The middle girl is not particularly interested in piano, but she does not really have any choice. Often, when practicing, her mind would wander off a little bit, but each time her father or mother, regardless of where they were (in the kitchen or with a customer), would appear beside her to pull her back on track. A few times later, Mrs. Lin made a point that whenever this girl sat down at the piano, she would drop everything and sit by her side, with a stick in hand. I do not know whether she has actually used the stick, but the result was her daughter later played in the church and won a second-place prize in one of the contests.

Authority and Obedience

In my observation, in the Lin family, there is seldom any haggling between the parents and the children. The children have absolute respect for and obedience to the parents and the parents never seem to have doubts that they might have been just a little unreasonable. Once I visited with them during prom time. At first, Mr. Lin found it very hard to say yes to Amy's going out all dressed up with a boy. After much consideration, he finally said yes, but with a stipulation of no dancing afterwards. I shared my children's prom stories with Mr. Lin, assuring him that the prom can be a very positive experience in children's lives. I wondered whether that had anything to do with Mr. Lin's eventually changing his mind about the rule. But during the whole process, I never heard any complaints from Amy other than "My dad is old fashioned." I have no doubt that if Mr. Lin had not changed his mind, Amy would have stayed home that night without complaints.

I could not help but feel amazed by the children's filial obedience to the parents. After all, these are American-born children. But later I found the answer in my other observations. Mr. and Mrs. Lin do not just expect respect and obedience from their children. They practice what they preach. One time, I met Mrs. Lin's father in their home. It was a touching sight to see the middle-aged parents of four children so attentive and respectful to their father. Rome was not built in one day.

I recall a story my mother used to tell me. A poor man's mother was very sick. Her last wish was to have a bowl of fish soup. It was freezing winter. The son did not have the money to buy a fish. So he went to the frozen river and lay on the top until the ice was melted by his body heat. A fish jumped out of the water, and the son's filial piety was remembered and praised forever. It really makes me ponder how deeply rooted cultural values are in people's minds and hearts. They cross the barriers of time, space, language, and environment.

Traits Found in American Culture

Parental Involvement

I was often asked by American teachers why the parents of their Asian students seem to lack interest in getting involved in their children's school activities. "Not necessarily," I always responded. "It is the culture." I still remember my son's elementary years in China. It was a lab school affiliated with the university in which my husband and I were teaching. The school had absolute authority over parents. The relationship between teacher and parents was unidirectional and could be well described as "give-and-take orders." Any signs of questioning the teacher or school would be considered as lack of respect and poor manners.

Many Asian parents have experienced difficulties in meeting teachers' expectations for their involvement in school activities. But I never witnessed any hesitation in Mr. and Mrs. Lin's involvement in their children's school activities. I commended them one time, saying that they must have a computer chip in their mind to store every child's schedule. During different talks with Mrs. Lin, I found she knew what each child was doing at a particular time. "It's ten-thirty Thursday morning. Amy is having history class. She is probably doing her presentation now about Abraham Lincoln. Victoria is having the big algebra test. Diana is probably very nervous about giving her book report. Ming's teacher is taking the class on a trip to the farm." I often wonder how she manages to remember all of this in addition to all the restaurant details.

Parental involvement in this family is far beyond knowing the children's schedules and schoolwork. This family has a rule that when a child has a special event, at least one parent will be there. Mrs. Lin demonstrated her level of commitment to the children's education when I witnessed her planning one weekend's travel itinerary. Mrs. Lin's brother had planned a party for their father's eightieth birthday in Los Angeles on that weekend, but Ming, the nine-year-old boy, had a spelling bee contest in the district that Saturday. Mrs. Lin had not seen her father for a couple of years and her other siblings for many years, but she had to attend Ming's contest as her husband needed to stay at the restaurant for business. She decided to go nonstop from restaurant to contest to airport even though it meant she could stay in Los Angles for only a few hours and would be really exhausted when she came back to her routines. I saw Ming's eyes light up when he knew that his mother was going to his spelling bee contest. I knew she had made the right decision.

Mr. and Mrs. Lin are not very fluent with the English language, but that does not hinder them from discussions with teachers about the children's curriculum or extracurricular activities. They have frequent meetings with teachers, counselors, and administrators—required or spontaneous. These meetings cover a wide range of topics: elective classes, summer programs, swimming, the children's feelings about certain things, and many more. One time, I tried to ask about the possible language barriers when communicating with the teachers, and Mrs. Lin gave me a witty smile: "I do my homework." I knew that meant she would spend time looking up words in the dictionary and writing down what she wanted to ask and rehearsed at home before the meetings.

The literature on parental involvement in child and adolescent education in American schools conveys the clear assumption that parents' involvement benefits children's learning (Chavkin, 1993; Eccles & Harold, 1993; U.S. Department of Education, 1994). In studies that are focused on "unsuccessful" students among new immigrants' children, the theme "lack of parental involvement" is very loud (Zhang & Carrasquillo, 1996). I learned that for Asian families, "parental involvement" means letting go of the "old" way and trying to adapt the home culture to the mainstream society. It will not be easy, but it is imperative.

Investment in Children's Extracurricular Activities

As discussed above, the "no pain, no gain" belief is rooted in many Chinese people's minds. Studying requires serious, even painstaking effort. Knowledge and academic accomplishments are usually measured in terms of information-based test scores. As a result, the Chinese educational system has produced students with impressive test scores, but not matching practical knowledge and skills. A relative of mine, a college student in China, broke the world's record for total GRE exam score last year. However, when he tried to use English in our conversation, he discovered he has a long way to go before he can use the language functionally.

I recall the Asian students' protest a few years ago against Berkeley's new admission standard, which has as a component leadership skills and extracurricular activities, in addition to academic record. I am not commenting on the protest or the standard here, but I hear a loud message that Asian students will meet a challenge along the path to success if they focus solely on academics to the detriment of extracurricular activities.

In this vein, consciously or not, Mr. and Mrs. Lin have paved the way to their children's success from the very beginning. This couple is very generous in investing in their children's extracurricular activities—they give both money and time. Take the piano lesson as an example. They have the town's best and most expensive piano teacher coming to the restaurant on a regular basis for all the four children. They go to every one of the recitals is which any one of the children plays.

They close the restaurant on Sundays because they want to spend time with the children. I remember the first time I met the family on a Sunday morning. Mrs. Lin and the three younger children were in the public library. The two girls were reading by themselves; Mrs. Lin was reading a chapter in a book to the boy, then six years old. She told me that children learn not just in classrooms. For the same reason, they put aside a certain amount of money every month just for summer traveling. They could have spent the money in many other ways, but they have their priorities. They believe "to see the world" is as important an education process as school.

Individuality and Independence

One thing I noticed about Mr. and Mrs. Lin is that they are often torn between keeping the children under their wings and letting them go out into the real world. Although it has not been easy, this couple always encourages the children to be on their own. In summer, the children usually participate in different programs. Some of the programs require that the children leave home for a sustained period of time. I was touched to learn how the parents lost sleep during those nights and how they struggled not to pick up the phone every day. The children are now used to those activities. Their ability to take care of themselves is admirable.

Although the children are obedient to their parents, they never hesitate to speak up about things that are important to them. The parents encourage the children to voice their opinion. As a matter of fact, the Sunday meetings are structured for this purpose. Many of their "doings" are too subtle for an outsider to capture and comprehend, but I definitely see "American" values in this family's practice.

Not the Final Word

The purpose of this chapter is to explore the factors that have a positive impact on Asian American students' success in school. To provide a definitive answer to such a question is too ambitious for one chapter. Therefore, this chapter should not be considered "the final word" on Asian American families. It does, however, provide an insider's glimpse, which provides insight to others seeking to better understand Asian American students.

The data I collected from my observations and interviews with the family seem to support my hypothesis that a harmonious application of traditional values in the mainstream society may be the key to Asian American children's success. With the increasing number of new immigrants from the East in the past decades, a concern about these students' adaptation to the American school system has arisen. While the adaptation involves many variables, I appeal to teachers and parents to look for "the happy medium." Human traits, in many ways, are universal. If we could look beyond arbitrary barriers and into the common values of human beings, we would see a vast territory called universality. To live and succeed in a multicultural society, as Confucius says, "we need to find the mean."

Editor's Commentary

As this book progresses into each chapter, I move further and further from the familiar realm of my own culture. My struggle with responding to this chapter is how to do so without contributing to the stereotype of the "model minority." The basic connotation that Asian Americans are prototypes for other people of color further divides all ethnic groups. Additionally, the model minority concept is typically presented from the viewpoint of people outside the Asian culture.

I recall enthusiastically sharing two chapters in Richard Monk's (1994) book presenting opposing viewpoints on the question "Are Asian Americans A 'Model Minority'?" with a Chinese friend, Chun. I shared the readings with my Multicultural Education classes and wanted to know whether Chun thought they captured the essence of issues faced by Asian Americans in general. After a few weeks of seeing Chun and noticing that she had not commented on the chapters, I finally asked her what she thought of the readings. Chun had guessed that I thought she would enjoy the chapters, so she had decided to say nothing in order to avoid hurting my feelings. But having been pressed for a response, she reluctantly responded, "I didn't like them."

For additional support, she said she had shared them with her husband and he also didn't like the chapters because they further separated Asian Americans from other groups and so underlined the tremendous discrimination and problems that Asians face in the United States. Chen, her husband, who had been in the living room, joined Chun and me in the dining room to continue the conversation.

Although Ronald Takaki (1994) had argued in one of the chapters that Asian Americans are not a model minority and highlighted major problems that they faced as a group, simply posing the question of whether any group can be a model for others is troublesome. Chun and Chen conveyed that Asian Americans in this country do not have any unifying support group organizations because of the tremendous cultural variations and language differences among Asian Americans. In fact, Chen

*said that it seemed to him that African Americans are more organized and have a bet-
ter collective sense. This was a surprising analysis to me because a frequently touted
viewpoint in the Black community is that we are divided and that there is no collective struggle. But Chen explained that injustices suffered by Blacks are frequently
brought to the limelight by groups such as the NAACP or the Urban League. Asian
Americans, he continued, don't have such groups to support them when something
unjust happens—which led Chen to another point. Both Chen and Chun added that
Asian Americans are always negatively portrayed in the media (many Blacks hold
parallel viewpoints).*

*After recovering from hearing their unexpected analyses of Black culture, I bet-
ter understood how similar (yet different) our experiences were. The audacity of the
"White power structure" to decide that of all of these (insignificant) "minority"
groups, one would be awarded the title Model Minority enraged us. This "award" undermines the strengths of other people of color. Furthermore, as mentioned in Chapters 3 and 4 (and echoed by Chun and Chen), the award for being the "model
minority" is a Pyrrhic victory. Appraising people of color using a Eurocentric yardstick is problematic. Is the intent to dole out an award to one group so that others will
seek the same "praise"? Comparing diverse ethnic groups using one standard is counterproductive at best. Each ethnic group has to define its successes in the U.S. context
in its own way. This definition cannot be imposed by others.*

*So, my reflections on this chapter are especially difficult because I am outside
the Chinese cultural perspective and experience. My intent, then, will be to capture the
family's strengths as well as challenges. I will refer to the stories presented in this
chapter as well as educational literature that seems to echo the messages in this chapter in my attempt to present a rounded view of Chinese Americans.*

*Although the Chinese are the largest of various Asian American groups, they
comprise less than 0.5 percent of the total U.S. population (Mindel, Habernstein, &
Wright, 1998). The Chinese were the first Asian immigrants to arrive in the United
States (DeGenova, 1997), and have been present in the United States in significant
numbers for almost a 150 years. They were attracted by the discovery of gold and other
precious minerals in California and by jobs that became available as the American
West "developed." At the same time, they were forced to emigrate because of a poor
economy and unstable political conditions in China. The Chinese were also the first
group of Asian immigrants to face blatant hostility in the United States, which cul-
minated in institutional and legal discrimination (e.g., The Chinese Exclusion Act of
1882) (DeGenova, 1997).*

*Today, Chinese Americans are a diverse group of people who originated from
various parts of China. However, the Chinese population in the United States can be
divided roughly into two main groups: Cantonese- or Toisanese-speaking Chinese and
Mandarin-speaking Chinese. The former group is made up primarily of immigrants
who came to the United States for economic reasons before World War II (DeGenova,
1997). The majority of Cantonese-speaking immigrants were former peasants whose
socioeconomic status in China was low. They tended to settle in urban Chinatowns
and worked as unskilled laborers. Contrastingly, most Mandarin-speaking Chinese*

are recent immigrants. They tend to be from the middle class and are more likely to be professionally oriented than entrepreneurial. Because Chinese Americans typically emigrated to the United States on a more-or-less voluntary basis, Ogbu (1994) refers to them as "immigrant minorities." Distinguished from groups who were initially brought to the United States against their will (e.g., African Americans) or who were conquered (e.g., Native Americans and Hispanic Americans in the southwestern United States), immigrant minorities believed that coming to this country would lead to increased economic well-being, better overall opportunities, or greater political freedom. Ogbu explains that these expectations continue to influence the way Chinese Americans perceive and respond to their treatment by White Americans and the societal institutions controlled by the latter.

Ogbu (1994) stresses that, like other disenfranchised groups, immigrant minorities are confronted with economic, political, and social barriers. They may suffer personal, intellectual, and cultural derogation, and they are often denied true assimilation into the mainstream of American life. Ogbu's research showed that, when confronted with these collective problems, Chinese Americans (and other immigrant minorities) tend to interpret them as more-or-less temporary problems that they will overcome or can overcome eventually with hard work and education. Ogbu explains that one thing that helps immigrants maintain this optimistic view is that they compare their present situation with that of their former selves or their peers back home. Typically, immigrant minorities conclude that they have better opportunities in the United States. On the whole, Ogbu argues that immigrant minorities tend to accept the folk theory of the White middle class that anyone can get ahead in the United States through hard work and education.

Another factor that helps immigrant minorities adjust is that they bring with them a sense of who they are (cultural identity), which they had before emigrating to the United States. That is, their cultural and language differences did not develop in opposition to White American culture and language. Groups such as Chinese Americans may therefore believe that while there are barriers to overcome because they are in a foreign land, they do not give up their own culture, language, or identity in the process. Finally, immigrant minorities tend to trust or acquiesce to White people more than do "involuntary minorities" such as African Americans.

Ogbu's anthropological work presents one way of understanding the family in this chapter. Indeed, Wenju's theme, "the land of opportunity," conveys her belief in the American ethos and her expectations. Whether it rings true to the Chinese American community in general is an assessment only they can make. Perhaps the congruence of the Confucian emphasis on education and families with the American ethos influences the impressive academic records of this family. Yet, as Wenju notes, the pressures to succeed can sometimes be too great, as in the case of her student in China who committed suicide. So there are always many perspectives on what success means.

Because of the heterogeneity of the Chinese American community, Chinese American families cannot be described simply. However, filial piety is possibly the strongest value in Chinese American families (DeGenova, 1997). Amy's respect for her father's decision-making process in his deliberations about allowing her to go to the prom conveys how the Chinese notion of filial piety goes beyond the American value of respecting one's parents. A much stronger sense of obligation and parental respect is expected by Chinese parents.

As mentioned in Chapter 4, a sense of interdependence is deeply embedded in the Asian American family's relationship. All three children seek not to bring shame to their family and, therefore, they seek to excel in school. The focus is not on the individual, but on the family. This theme is reflected even in the intergenerational stories like the one Wenju's mother told her about the mother on her death bed who asked for a bowl of fish soup as her last wish. The extent that the son went to in order to please his mother reflects the filial piety at play in Chinese families. But the relationship goes both ways, as evidenced by the sacrifices that the parents in this chapter make for their children. The father gave up his career, they are actively involved in the educational process both at home and in school, they do not take time to dine out without the children, they work extremely long hours, they seek out extracurricular activities and experiences that they think will enhance their children's success—the list goes on and on. In turn, the children will take care of them when they are old, as was also mentioned in Chapter 4. In this vein, obligation and obedience to one's parents takes on a more circular (as opposed to unidirectional) trajectory. That is, each person helps someone and is helped in turn, and the cycle continues. Once again (as in Korean culture), we see that the road to a "healthy" development is broad rather than narrow. It has many different faces and dimensions.

As Wenju noted, there is a tremendous amount of pressure on the children to do well. But I'm not sure if this is interpreted by the children in this *family as pressure or as just part of what life is about. Likewise, from my perspective, the parents seem to have extremely stressful lives, but perhaps they do not perceive it that way.*

The Lin family balances both American and Chinese culture, and it is obvious that both are important to them. So while the children excel beyond most American parents' imagination, Wenju concludes that still "in many ways this family is very 'Chinese.'" Wenju's message demonstrates that culture is dynamic and that healthy adaptations of cultures is not a dichotomous process—families do not have to choose one culture over another—and that the process varies depending on the family.

Reflective Activity

What are some of your stereotypes (positive and negative) of Chinese Americans? Are these fair assumptions? Where did they come from?

Write down the names of as many successful and/or famous Chinese Americans (living or dead) you can think of. Does your list show much diversity in terms of professional field (e.g., politics, economics, education, medicine, law, social work, journalism)? If you made such a list for other ethnic groups (e.g., European Americans, African Americans, biracial Americans, Latino Americans, Native Americans) how would it look? Are the contemporary versus historical images of each group balanced? Comment on the general invisibility of Chinese Americans in the media (television, movies, books) in light of the label "model minority."

Resources

Trade Books (Fiction and Nonfiction)[1]

Ashley, B. (1992). *Cleversticks*. New York: Crown.
Bishop, C. H., & Wiese, K. (1989). *The five Chinese brothers*. New York: Coward-McCann.
Cao, G. (1996). *The attic: A Memoir of a Chinese landlord's son*. Berkeley University of California Press.
Carter, A. R. (1994). *Chinese past Chinese future*. New York, NY: Franklin Watts.
Coerr, E. (1988). *Chang's paper pony*. New York: Harper and Row.
Fritz, J. (1988). *China's long march: 6000 miles of danger*. New York: Putnam.
Jiang, J. L. (1997). *Red scarf girl: A memoir of the cultural revolution*. New York: Harpercollins Juvenile Books.
Kort, M. G. (1994). *China under communism*. Brookfield, CT: Millbrook Press.
Liyi, H., & Chic, C. (1993). *Mr. China's son: A villager's life*. Boulder CO: Westview.
Pitman, H. C. (1986). *A grain of rice*. New York: Hastings House.
Russell, C. Y. (1994). *First apple*. New York: Boyds Mill Press.
Yang, R. (1997). *Spider eaters: A memoir*. Berkeley: University of California Press.
Yep, L. (1975). *Dragonwings*. New York: Harper and Row.
Yep, L. (1977). *Child of the owl*. New York: Harper and Row.
Yep, L. (1993). *Dragon's gate*. New York: Harpercollins.

Websites

China Expo's Chinese Culture: http:www.chinaexpo.com.culture.
China Vista: http:www.chinavista.com.
China World Link: http:www.chinaworldlink.com.
Chinese Culture Center of San Francisco: http:www.c-c-c.org/home.html.
Chinese Historical and Cultural Project: http:www.chcp.org.
Chinese History, Culture, and Entertainment: http:www.Newton.mec.edu/Angier/DimSum/chinadimsumaconnection.html.
Hanlong Meta Index for Sites of Chinese Culture: http://www.hanlong.com.
Six Paths to China: http://www.knpacbell.com/wired/China/index.html.

Organizations

American Association for Chinese Studies, 300 Brick Hall, Ohio State University, Columbus, OH 43210, Tel: (614) 292-6681
Asian American Business Association, http://www.usclub.com/aaba/aboutus.html.
Center for Chinese Research Materials, P.O. Box 3090, Oakton, VA 22124, Tel: (703) 281-7731
Center for Teaching About China, 1214 W. Schwartz, Carbondale, IL 62901, Tel: (618) 549-1535
Chinese Culture Association, P.O. Box 1272, Palo Alto, CA 94302-1272, Tel: (415) 948-2251, http://stlouis.sinanet.com/org.
Chinese America Forum, http://stlouis.sinanet.com/org/CAF.
Chinese Information and Culture Center, 1230 Avenue of the Americas, New York, NY 10020-1513, Tel: (212) 373-1800
Institute of Chinese Culture, 86 Riverside Dr., New York, NY 10024

[1]All resources compiled by Jianhua Feng

References

Brand, D. (1987). The new whiz kids: Why Asian Americans are doing so well, and what it costs them. *Time,* pp. 42–51.

Chavkin, N. F. (Ed.). (1993). *Families and schools in a pluralistic society.* Albany: State University of New York Press.

DeGenova, M. K. (1997). *Families in cultural context: Strengths and challenges in diversity.* Mountain View, CA: Mayfield.

Eccles, J. S., & Harold, R. D. (1993). Parent–school involvement during the early adolescent years. *Teachers College Record, 94,* 568–587.

Kuo, G. (1997). Save today's young parents—A report from Beijing. *HXWZ,* pp. 22–28.

Mindel, C. H., Habernstein, R. W. , & Wright, R. (1998). *Ethnic families in America: Patterns and variations.* Upper Saddle River, NJ: Prentice Hall.

Monk, R. C. (1994). *Taking sides: Clashing views on controversial issues in race and ethnicity.* Guilford, CT: Dushkin.

Morrow, R. (1989). Southeast Asian parent involvement: Can it be a reality? *Elementary School Guidance of Counseling, 22,* 289–297.

Ogbu, J. (1994). Overcoming racial barriers to equal access. In J. I. Goodlad (Ed.), *Access to knowledge: The continuing agenda for our nation's schools* (pp. 59–89). New York: College Entrance Examination Board.

Pang, V. O. (1990). Asian-American children: A diverse population. *The Education Forum, 55* (1), 49–66.

Schneider, B., & Lee, Y. (1991). A model for academic success: The school and home environment of East Asian students. *Anthropology & Educational Quarterly, 21,* 358–377.

Shen, W., & Mo, W. (1991). *Reaching out to their cultures: Building communication with Asian-American families.* ERIC Document Reproduction Service, ED 351 435.

Sue, S., & Okazaki, S. (1990). Asian-American education achievement. *American Psychology, 45 (8)* 913–920.

Takaki, R. (1994). The myth of the "model minority." In R. C. Monk (Ed.), *Taking sides: Clashing views on controversial issues in race and ethnicity* (pp. 55–61). Guilford, CT: Dushkin.

U.S. Department of Education (1994). *Strong families, strong schools: Building community partnerships for learning.* Washington, DC: Author.

Zhang, S. Y., & Carrasquillo, A. L. (1996). *Four Chinese junior high school "unsuccessful" students: Language, culture, and family factors.* ERIC Document Reproduction Service, ED 383780.

6

Shades of Differences

Biracial Influences

Janet H. Mason

Editor's Overview _____

In this chapter, we meet two women (the author and her sister) and one man who are biracial. The women's mother was Black, and their father was White. The man's father is Lumbee Indian, and his mother is White. The stories in this chapter are told primarily in their own words. We gain insights about what it is to grow up with two different heritages—one (White) that is privileged in the United States and another (Indian or African American) that has historically been marginalized.

Neither White nor Black

During the late 1930s and early 1940s, South Carolina was not a terrific state to live in for people of African American heritage. People whose skin was of a darker hue were victims of racial discrimination in varying degrees, from grown Black men being called "boy" to mob lynchings of Black men and boys with no consequences for the perpetrators. With few exceptions, race was the divider between the "haves" and the "have-nots." Langston Hughes's reference to his "White old man" dying in a mansion while his "Black old mother" died in a shack is symbolic of this racial divide and comes very close to describing the circumstances of my own beginnings, which profoundly influenced my life.

I was born in the late 1930s in South Carolina to a beautiful Black woman who was one of twelve children and educated only through the elementary grades. My father was a tall, Irish stone mason, twenty years her senior. He was well known and respected in the White community. They had six children together but were denied the freedom to legalize their relationship because marriage between "colored " and White was illegal. Thus, my siblings and I grew up in that never-never land of racial identity defined by our light skin and different hair texture. Always knowing that merely one drop of African blood decided our racial identity, our struggle for individual identity was further complicated by the unpleasant stigma "bastard children." As a mature adult, I later decided that if one drop of African blood had such influence, it must be powerful stuff! The law forbade my parents from marrying even though couples of the same race who lived together for seven or more years became married by common law. In fact, the law forbidding miscegenation was officially removed from the South Carolina books of law only in 1998! The children of such a union had no escape from being negatively labeled. Perhaps because of the legal distinction, my parents never shared the same house on a permanent basis. My father visited once or twice a week but never actually stayed in the country house he provided for my mother and her children for more than one or two consecutive days.

I was the fifth child of my mother and father and the ninth child of my mother. My mother had four children before my father became a part of her life. Sadly, my mother was a murder victim when I was only three years old. She left eight of her ten children under the age of adulthood, including a six-month-old baby. It doesn't take much imagination to picture the dismal circumstances created by this distressing situation. Primarily my maternal grandmother, who had been prematurely widowed about six months earlier, assumed our care. My father sparingly provided for our financial support but contributed even less of his personal time to our day-to-day care. He, like all the players in this scenario, was a product of the political, social, and economic environment in which we all lived. This would have been a challenging predicament for any family—Black or White and regardless of their geographic location. Add biracial children to the mix in the racially turbulent southeast United States, and the challenge becomes a bit more complex.

"Mama"

From the time of my mother's death until I was six years old, I was lovingly cared for by my chocolate-brown maternal grandmother. She was the county's midwife, and in spite of her lack of any formal education, she was respected in the community because of her excellent skills at delivering babies to both Black and White mothers. My grandmother was no stranger to delivering pale babies to Black mothers and, on rare occasions, she delivered honey-colored babies to White mothers. The latter were the deliveries that caused her the most grief. Given the racial situation in South Carolina at that time, a White woman involved intimately with a Black man placed mother, father, and baby in grave jeopardy. She developed clever strategies designed to rescue terrified clients from these delicate situations.

As I grew up and reached school age, my grandmother tried to prepare her biracial grandchildren for the realities of a less than perfect world. This was an era during which very dark people were most discriminated against. Even my grandmother and other older relatives reinforced common notions that light skin was better. They taught me and my half-White siblings to appreciate our lighter skin and Caucasian-like hair texture. My grandmother, whom we called Mama, told us we were beautiful. She instilled confidence by continually reminding us that our biracial status was not a handicap, but an asset.

By the time I was halfway through the first grade, I had begun to believe her. The year was 1943, the country was deeply involved in World War II, and my oldest brother had been drafted along with my uncles and cousins—off to fight for a country in which they were harassed if they attempted to register to vote. The school I attended, New Zion Elementary School, was for "colored" children only. Needless to say, the schools for colored children were little more than rundown shacks. Our textbooks were the dog-eared discards from the White schools. Biracial children, like all children with any trace of African heritage, were racially defined as colored. Unlike South Africa, where the political system, apartheid, classified people by skin color, there was no official distinction between African American children and biracial children. We were all "colored." Consequently, I was relegated to the limited public resources available for colored children. For example, my older school-age siblings quickly learned the town's only library was available to White students six days a week but allowed colored students access only one day a week. Of course, they were never allowed to be in the library on the same day as the White children. Teachers in the colored school were all Black and few had been educated beyond the eleventh grade.

Color distinctions were often made within the African American community. In the first grade, I benefited from my light skin and long straight hair. In preparation for the May Day Festival, a May Day King, Queen, Prince, and Princess were selected each year. The all-Black faculty selected my very fair-skinned older sister as the queen and yours truly as the princess. One of my fair-skinned second-grade cousins was selected to be the prince, and another fair-skinned eighth-grade boy was identified as the king to reign with my sister.

Discussions I overheard between my grandmother and other older relatives confirmed that having lighter skin and other Caucasian features were valued in the Black community, and those values resulted in our selection to represent royalty in the May Day Festival. I remember a common chant by my grandmother and others:

If you're black, get back.
If you're brown, hang around.
If you're yellow, my fellow.
If you're white, alright!

Unfortunately, my light physical characteristics did not always endear me to my darker relatives and classmates. It was apparent that colored people in the United States had been brainwashed into believing the standard for beauty was measured by the appearance of White people. My grandmother (1885–1949), whose parents had been slaves, often told us stories about the White "masters" who fathered children with selected Black females on their plantations. My grandmother's stories are confirmed in the literature on slavery. For those of us who share a biracial history, the current theory that President Thomas Jefferson fathered children with his slave Sally Hemmings is not very difficult to believe. As shown in the excerpt by Harriet Jacobs, coercive relationships and rape involving White men and Black women were a way of life during slavery and the postslavery era.

It haunts me that most biracial (Black/White) children born during slavery were the result of rape:

> Sir Charles Lyell said that "one of the most serious evils of slavery is its tendency to blight domestic happiness; and the anxiety of parents for their sons, and constant fear of licentious intercourse with slaves is painfully great." This "evil" not only blighted the happiness of the white family but was one of the powerful forces operating to weaken the slave family altogether. The extensive miscegenation that went on was largely the result of people living and working together at common tasks and the subjection of slave women to the whims and desires of white men. There was some race mixture that resulted from the association of black men and white women, but this was only a small percent of the total. Despite all the laws against the intermingling of races, the practice continued, and its persistence is another example of the refusal of the members of the dominant group to abide by the laws that they themselves created. (Franklin & Moss, 1947/1994, p. 139)

Because of this shameful history, the children of Black/White unions have been at once ostracized and advantaged. Mama believed it was advantageous to have light skin and Caucasian features because she had witnessed their privileges as children of the "master." On the farm where she was raised, in the postslavery era, light-skinned people had more desirable chores—often inside the "Big" house out of the hot sun. They were often allowed to acquire limited schooling, or to learn the skills of craftsmen. Thus, the seeds of racism within the African American community based on shades of skin color was imbedded centuries ago and continues to impact African American children and families today.

Harriet Jacobs Remembers Her Life as a Young Slave Girl

But I now entered on my fifteenth year—a sad epoch in the life of a slave girl. My master began to whisper foul words in my ear. Young as I was, I could not remain ignorant of their import. I tried to treat them with indifference or contempt. The master's age, my extreme youth, and the fear that his conduct would be reported to my grandmother, made him bear this treatment for many months. . . . He tried his utmost to corrupt the pure principles my grandmother had instilled. . . . But he was my master. I was compelled to live under the same roof with him—where I saw a man forty years my senior daily violating the most sacred commandments of nature. He told me I was his property; that I must be subject to his will in all things. My soul revolted against the mean tyranny. But where could I turn for protection? No matter whether the slave girl be as black as ebony or as fair as her mistress. In either case, there is no shadow of law to protect her from insult, from violence, or even from death; all these are inflicted by fiends who bear the shape of men. The mistress, who ought to protect the helpless victim, has no other feelings towards her but those of jealousy and rage.

From Harriet A. Jacobs, *Incidents in the life of a slave girl written by herself.* [As cited in Franklin, J. H., & Moss, A. A., Jr. (1947/1994). *From slavery to freedom* (7th ed.). New York: Alfred A. Knopf, p. 138.

My brother, Herbert, whose appearance often gets him mistaken for White, shares this story from his teen years in a rural South Carolina town in the late 1940s. Herbert was about sixteen or seventeen years old, over six feet tall, and working as a laborer with other young African American men whose skin was dark. On their way home from work one day, they stopped at a White-owned store to get a snack. The other fellows all preceded him at the counter and each ordered a bag of pork skins and a bottle of soda to wash it down. When he attempted to order the same thing, the clerk, a young White female, thinking he was White, whispered, "These pork skins are not fresh. They are fine for those colored boys, but you ought to take the potato chips, because they are fresh." Herbert didn't know what to do. He believed the clerk was flirting with him—a behavior that could get him a death sentence. At the same time, he was feeling an uncomfortable separation from his coworkers. In his dilemma, he told the clerk he only wanted a soda and would not take the pork skins or the potato chips. He did not reveal his racial identity to the clerk, nor did he share her confidence with his coworkers. It was for him a perplexing, awkward situation. It was the beginning of many such scenarios that continued to permeate his life.

Brothers and Sisters Never Known

My father was born to Irish immigrant parents sometime in the mid-1870s. Before meeting and establishing a relationship with my mother in the late 1920s, he had married a woman who shared his ethnicity, and together they had five children, one son and four daughters. We were told that his first family lived in Chase City, Virginia. I vaguely remember my "other" (White) brother visiting with my father when I was a very young girl. The two "brothers" one White and one Black shared a brief visit at my father's house, but the Southern racial divide was too powerful for any further interaction between his six half-Black children and their five all-White siblings. Separated by about 250 miles, we might as well have lived on two different planets.

In describing Shirlee Taylor Haizlip's (1994) book, *The Sweeter the Juice,* a family memoir about Black/White relationships, Alvin Poussaint, M.D., a clinical professor of psychiatry at Harvard University, wrote the following:

> This is a compelling and enlightening memoir giving voice to an often ignored legacy of slavery. Millions of African Americans have White branches of their family tree which are hidden from them. The peculiar American definition of race, and the continuing racist perception of Black blood as a taint, continues to cause psychological damage to so-called White and Black Americans. I highly recommend this book to anyone seeking to understand the complexities of the American racial dilemma.

In this saga, Haizlip goes in search of her mother's biracial siblings who have "passed" into the White world. Her quest was motivated by a sadness she detected in her aging mother, the youngest child of a large biracial family and the only one who remained colored. I was in envy of her mother's reunion, at age seventy-five, with her eighty-year-old, White sister, whose husband, children, and grandchildren were completely unaware of her "tainted" heritage.

Throughout my childhood and adult life, the question "How many brothers and sisters do you have?" it always caused me a moment of hesitation. I have never verbally included my father's five children by his White wife, but mentally and emotionally I have wondered about who and where they are. Will their children's and grandchildren's paths ever cross those of my children and grandchildren? The mystery and the tragedy of our obsession with race continue to strangle the personal freedom of too many Americans.

Making Sense of It

Many years after my Black mother and my White father were dead and gone from my life, I emotionally arrived at a secure place about who and what I am. Being raised in a Black world, I had denied my White father almost entirely. Since marriage was denied my parents, I carried my mother's family name. In early and middle childhood, when asked my father's name, I supplied my maternal grandfather's name. I was too embarrassed to give my real father's name because it was a familiar local white surname and it was culturally different from mine. During my young years, there was little open dialogue about the dilemma of half-White children and even less was written on the topic. We had no forum to speak in. We had no champion for our cause. More important, we had no choice. Given the standard American definition of race, we were colored, or Negro, or Black, or African American, depending on the era. As a teen and young adult, whenever I filled out applications that requested racial identity, I was tempted to write "other."

Here, it is important to note that many of the African American teachers of my early years in those segregated schools helped me to build a foundation that allowed me to climb to the next level of understanding. I attended many different schools between the second and tenth grades. By age three, my mother was gone, and by age eight, my father had joined her. My grandmother passed away when I was twelve. I lived in South Carolina; Washington, D.C.; Newark, New Jersey; Philadelphia, Pennsylvannia; and Bordentown, New Jersey. In each of these locations, I lived with a different relative and attended all-Black schools, except in Newark. Most of my teachers were Black and communicated their concern for a biracial, parentless youngster.

In contrast, when I was moved to the home of my oldest sister in Newark and attempted to register for my eighth-grade classes in a predominantly White school, the vice principal asked me to identify my nationality. I told her I was colored (the prevailing term of that era). She took from my hand the eighth-grade class schedule that I had just been given by a counselor and told me that I could not possibly do their level of eighth-grade work after spending my first seven years in "colored" schools. I can only suppose that if I had claimed my White heritage, she would have assumed I was intellectually equipped to succeed at the eighth-grade level. Thanks to my former Black teachers and my grandmother, I refused to allow this judgmental person to define my level of intelligence. I insisted that she take another look at my excellent report card from the seventh grade and, as much as a thirteen-year-old could, I demanded that she test me for my ability to perform eighth-grade work. She did. I passed!

Fortunately, I was assigned to the homeroom of a most caring Jewish teacher who had lost both her parents in the Holocaust. She went far beyond her required responsibilities to nurture my learning. She loaned me her personal books, encouraged me to write papers on African American heroes, and openly addressed my biracial appearance in a positive manner. To my surprise, she familiarized me with the names and accomplishments of a few biracial historical figures, including Prince Hall, who organized the first chapter of the Prince Hall Masons, a prestigious international organization of African American men. This dear lady was the epitome of a concerned teacher who individualized her students effectively.

I had come to Newark from an all-Black junior high school in Washington, D.C., where I had been the victim of a few mean-spirited students. For example, the science teacher changed my seat several times because, in her small classroom, my eighteen-inch-long braids often fell on the desk of the student behind me. My fellow Black classmates—mostly girls—thought it was amusing to poke the tips of my braids in their ink wells, ruining the precious few blouses and sweaters I owned. That same year, I was provoked to engage in my one and only school fight, with a student who continually harassed me, calling me "yellow, half-White, and sh—-colored."

As occurred later in the eighth grade, a sensitive, caring teacher, Miss Evans, provided me comfort and guidance. Based on her appearance, I believe she was also biracial. She was my English teacher. During that time, I spoke with a southern Black dialect, often causing the children in Washington, D.C., to laugh when I read aloud or shared in the class discussion. I began to turn inward and was becoming shy and insecure as a result of my speech patterns and the pranks that targeted students who looked like me. Miss Evans often stayed after school and tutored me one-on-one to "correct" my pronunciation.

She was the first teacher in my life who cultivated a love for reading, which has continued to be a big part of my world even today. She had a simple strategy. She told me to read, read, read. My assignment was to use the dictionary every time I encountered a word I did not understand and to use that new word in conversation as soon and as often as possible. I told her about the pranks aimed at me, which were often accompanied by the accusation "You think you are cute!" or "Janet Harrison is stuck up." When I shared my pain with Miss Evans, she replied, "Well Janet, would you rather be stuck up or stuck down?" She encouraged me to look to the future and not to be too concerned with such adolescent pranks. I think she helped me to grow up quickly. I learned to use humor to diffuse potentially adversarial situations.

By the time I finished high school, graduating number-two in my class behind my best friend (who years later became a vice president of Merrill Lynch and rated among the highest-paid African American women in the United States), my vocabulary scores were ranked with second-year college students and my southern dialect was nonexistent. This, in spite of the fact that I had no parents; had changed schools and cities eight consecutive years; lived in eight households, not always with my siblings; and most frequently did not look like my Black or White fellow classmates. Without a doubt, a few very good teachers were pivotal influences in my life during those challenging adolescent years.

In his autobiography, *Life on the Color Line*, Gregory Howard Williams (1995) relates a story that is sometimes heartwarming but too often heart-breaking. For the first ten years of his life, he was raised as a White child. When his parents divorced, he discovered that his father was half Black and had been passing for White. His White mother agreed to him and his younger brother moving with their father to a distant city to live with their Black relatives. Williams recounts his amazing journey, which I found to contain great similarities to my own life along the color line, including startling contrasts between the Black and White worlds. I could empathize with Williams when he discussed what it felt like to be in the presence of Whites and to hear them speak negatively about Blacks without knowing that I was Black (I am often mistaken for Asian or Latino American). Like Williams, I have encountered racism from both Blacks and Whites. And also like Williams, I received a great deal of encouragement from Blacks and Whites, especially teachers.

Reaching a Comfort Zone

At age eighteen, one year after finishing high school, I married my wonderful husband, the brother of my ninth-grade algebra teacher. We started our family early, postponing college indefinitely. Thirteen years after graduating from high school, in my early thirties, while maintaining a home for my husband and two children (who were in elementary and middle school), I became a college freshman. I enrolled in a teacher education program at a small, conservative school in New Jersey. For the first time, with the exception of the eighth grade, I was immersed in a school culture with both Black and White students. Prior to attending college, the eighth grade year in Newark, New Jersey, was the only school experience I had had that was not for Black children only. In the middle of my junior year, I transferred to California State University at Long Beach. I graduated in 1973, magna cum laude with a bachelor's degree in physical education. I embarked on my professional teaching career in Southern California, which is home to a large community of Hispanic people. I was frequently mistaken for a Hispanic person because of my skin color and hair texture. I continued my education in graduate school, gaining a master's degree in my field and a second master's in school administration. I grew intellectually, emotionally, and psychologically. My academic world expanded my horizons. I learned to accept my unique place in the world and recognized that I was not responsible for other people's attitudes.

During my years as a teacher and middle school administrator, I have consistently felt a keen sensitivity for the plight of biracial children. The nineteen years I was employed as a classroom teacher and school site administrator were all served in Long Beach, California. Southern California is the home of many nationalities and ethnicities. Biracial children who have White, Black, Hispanic, or Asian heritage are rapidly becoming commonplace. Students bring to the schools of California all the shades and cultural features known to human beings. My skin color, between Black and White, often gave these mix-hued youngsters a faculty member they could relate to.

While I was serving as a high school activities director in 1986, a tall Samoan girl who was a member of the student council that I sponsored came into my office and said, "Mrs. Mason, I am graduating this year, and I have a present I want you to have." She handed me a colorful box and asked me to open it. I opened the box and stared at a beautiful tropical mother-of-pearl necklace with matching earrings. This was not the typical style of jewelry to be found in American "Island" shops. She explained that her mother had ordered this especially for me from Samoa. In some amazement, I asked what had I done to deserve such special consideration. She explained that in her twelve years of schooling in the California school system, I was the very first Samoan teacher she had ever had! I almost blurted out her error. But after I gathered my wits about me, I decided not to burst her bubble and let her graduate with this treasured bit of happiness. I gave her, instead, my heartfelt thanks. It was a nice feeling.

Time Brings about a Change

In 1993, at age fifty-seven, I retired from the California public school system, and, with my husband of thirty-eight years, returned to my roots to live out our retirement in South Carolina. As a school administrator, I had become troubled by the lack of classroom management skills demonstrated by new teachers emerging from our nation's colleges and universities. Their knowledge was not keeping pace with the changing demographics of our nation's classrooms. Myriad changes in the social, economic, and political environment were negatively impacting classroom behavior. Many young teachers were unable to meet this challenge. After my retirement, I offered my services to the College of Education at the University of South Carolina to teach my version of classroom strategies to preservice teachers. My offer was accepted—with a counter offer that I enroll in a doctoral program and receive a generous teaching scholarship. I accepted the offer and became a graduate teaching assistant in the fall of 1993. Thus, I only remained retired from June to August!

As I went about my duties and responsibilities as a scholar and teacher on that old, prestigious university campus, I would often reflect upon my humble, uncertain beginnings in this state to which I had returned. I was ever mindful of the changes that time has wrought. During my childhood, people of color, biracial or otherwise, would have been welcome at the University of South Carolina only to cook or clean. Biracial students who chose to "pass" into the White race would have been accepted if their African heritage was never revealed. Such stories were whispered in the Black communities. Although race is still a problem, my mix-hued children and grandchildren are free to attend the schools of their choice; the only barrier is tuition. Couples of mixed race, who would have risked death in my childhood years, stroll across campus with relative impunity.

I earned my doctorate in December 1996 and assumed a full-time position at the university. At my hooding ceremony, I looked out at my honey-brown, three-year-old granddaughter and thought, "This day is a down payment on her future." With this achievement, I am writing a check that she can cash in the years to come. Silently, I said to Miss Evans, my seventh-grade teacher, "I have chosen to be stuck-up rather than stuck-down."

I am at peace with who I am. The peaks and valleys of my life have made me more cautious in attaching identity labels on others. I know that the issue of race in our country will continue to be controversial for many years to come. I have long since forgiven those who caused me pain in my youth. I know forces largely outside of their control shaped their lives. I will always treasure those who helped to pave my way. Especially, I thank God for the caring teachers who responded to the needs of a troubled child at critical times. I am aware that many of those challenges served to make me stronger and helped to shape my character. I feel that I have not just survived the complexities of my background. I have triumphed over them.

The Mulatto to His Critics

Ashamed of my race?
And of what race am I?
I am many in one.
Through my veins there flows the blood
Of Red Man, Black Man, Briton, Celt and Scot.
In warring clash and tumultuous riot I welcome all,
But love the blood of the kindly race
That swarthes my skin, crinkles my hair
And puts sweet music into my soul.

Joseph Seamon Cotter (1918)

Although Ruth, my sister, and I grew up in the same family, our lives were different in ways I am only now coming to realize since engaging her in conversations/interviews for this chapter. Ruth is much older than I am, and her skin is much lighter than mine (she could easily pass for white). The differences in our interpretations of our experiences are probably due to these two factors. In talking with Ruth, I discovered that she had more of a relationship with our father than I had. Since I was very young when he used to pick her up from school, I do not have any recollection of this and was totally surprised by this revelation. However, both of us encountered painful situations because of our biracial heritage. But I will let Ruth, who is now sixty-six, tell her own story.

Ruth's Story

While attending a racially segregated elementary school in South Carolina from the first to the third grade, I was one of approximately a half dozen biracial children. Occasionally, my father, who was White, would come by the school to pick me up. My father was many years older than my mother and therefore was many years older than most of the fathers of the children in my school. I remember being embarrassed when my father would come to pick me up. Invariably, a student would call out to me so that everyone could hear, "Hey, Ruth, that ol' White man is here to get you."

During my sixth-grade year, my grandmother allowed me to go and live in Washington, D.C., for a year with my uncle (my deceased mother's brother) and his wife, Aunt Agnus. At the end of my school year, they put me on the train to send me back to South Carolina to spend the summer with my grandmother. At that time, trains between Washington, D.C., and all points south were segregated. There were many passenger cars for White passengers and few passenger cars for colored passengers. Naturally, Uncle Pete and Aunt Agnus put me in the colored passenger car. After the train left the station, an African American porter came to me, took my hand, and said, "Little miss, you're in the wrong spot, come with me." He walked me through two or three passenger cars that were filled with people of color, until we reached a passenger car that was all White. Then he said, "Now this is where you have to ride." He was very kind in his efforts to help me. I was scared to death! I had never been surrounded by all White people for such a long time. I sat quietly throughout the trip and talked to no one except the porter.

After leaving South Carolina when our grandmother died, I attended a junior high school in Philadelphia that was segregated by de facto segregation. Although segregation was not legal in the neighborhood where I lived with an older sister, economics separated the colored and White children. Predominantly White neighborhoods had bigger houses and schools that served predominantly White children. Neighborhoods with less expensive houses served predominantly colored children. At Shoemaker Junior High School, where I attended during the seventh grade, I will always remember with a warm heart my seventh-grade math teacher. Because my skin color is especially fair, the math teacher, who was White, was apparently sensitive to my unique situation. I felt that he continually tried to protect me from other kids that he perceived as too rough. He helped me with my homework. He would often ask me to stay after school to help me, and I knew he was doing this so that most of the kids would have left the school grounds by the time I left to walk home. On one occasion, he overheard a classmate call me a "White nigger" and offered consolation to help me try and understand my predicament.

Although the math teacher was very helpful, my all-time favorite teacher was my seventh-grade English teacher. Up through the seventh grade, I was afflicted with a speech impediment. I had a stuttering problem. She arranged for me to get help from a speech therapist and helped me to gain a great deal of self-confidence. She would recommend good movies that I ought to see. Sometimes, when I told her I had no money for the movie, she would give me money from her personal funds to help me. She too was biracial, and I felt a strong kinship with her and I think she felt a kinship to me.

By the time I reached junior high school, my favorite subject was history, especially learning about Native Americans, whom we called Indians. I loved to read about Indians and see movies that had Indians in the storyline. I believe I liked learning about Indians because their appearance looked like somebody who was neither White nor Black. I had gradually become very conscious of being in that never-never land of neither Black nor White. I also developed an appreciation for the fact that Indians refused to be slave victims for White people and chose death over slavery.

As a teenager, living with yet another older sister in New Jersey, I was doing domestic work for a lady who was White and who encouraged me to further my education. She had a little girl about five years old. In view of the fact that I had always loved sewing, I offered to make her little girl a skirt for a special occasion. The lady was so impressed, she suggested I take a course in detail sewing at the local high school in her neighborhood. She suggested that additional skill in this craft would help me to get a job that would improve my quality of life. She advised me to use her address when I registered for the class. Apparently, she knew no one would recognize my Afro-American heritage, although she never said that.

About halfway through the course, which I was thoroughly enjoying and I was learning a lot, the instructor for the class seemed also impressed with my skill and ability and gave me a lot of attention. I was aware that I was the only non-White person in the class, but for the sake of my future, I chose not to talk about it. Then one day, there was a rude awakening. One evening, while we were all in class, the instructor was showing me how to make French seams. She was literally sitting beside me showing me how to handle the material to make the French seam when there was a knock on the door. The instructor went to the door and stayed a minute or two and came back and announced to the class that a nigger was trying to register in the class. To my shocked ears, her precise words were, "Imagine having to be that close to a nigger every day." The pain I felt was excruciating, but I was too afraid to speak out. I stayed until the class was over that evening, but I never went back.

School experiences for my children and grandchildren were very different from my own for several reasons. My ex-husband, who was the father of my children, is African American. Therefore, my children, although obviously of mixed heritage, were closely related to their African American heritage. Additionally times had changed. My children were students during the 1960s and 1970s, when civil rights legislation had begun to make life a little less difficult for racially mixed children. Their public school experiences took place in Cleveland, Ohio, a large industrial city that boasted many ethnic groups. Unlike me, they always attended schools that were racially mixed and were never subjected to many of the experiences to which I was victim.

Currently, my grandchildren are attending schools in Cleveland; Philadelphia, Pennsylvania; and San Diego and Walnut, California. Even though they are three generations removed from their White great-grandfather, their appearance still denotes their biracial heritage. In conversations with my grandchildren, they rarely report incidents, either negative or positive, relating to their racial mixture.

Terry's Story

Terry Cumbee is a thirty-two-year-old biracial male of Native American and European American parents. His father is a member of the Lumbee Tribe of Robeson County, North Carolina, and his mother is White. As we shall see in Terry's story, he identifies heavily with his Native American heritage and comments little about his European American lineage. His strong identification with Indian culture is seemingly influenced by three major factors: (1) Terry has Native American features (e.g., black hair, dark eyes, and skin color that looks more "Indian" than "white"); (2) school and society responded to Terry in part based on his physical features; and (3) he shares his gender with his father.

In his story, he talks very little about his mother's influence. Native American culture was more compelling, and his mother did not seem to understand what it meant (psychologically and socially) to try to assimilate into mainstream culture in a society that viewed Terry as different. Terry tells his own story.

In Terry's Own Words

I grew up in a small town on the South Carolina–Georgia border with my mother, father, and two brothers. We were in a semi-rural area, that is to say that there was a sizable city within fifteen miles of our house. But we grew up in a middle- to lower-class neighborhood.

We had many conflicts in our household due to the differences in the cultures. Many times, my father would be teaching my brothers and me his traditions and my mother would stop him. He [my father] believed that my brother and I should learn the secrets that the Earth had to share via the forest that was behind our house. He taught us that it was better to have the ability to survive in the forest than to read books about Sammy the seal or

George the monkey. This really infuriated my mother because she wanted us to read, while my father wanted us to learn life skills to help us survive in the world. He put more value in what a person could do with his hands than in books "because books," he said, "were written by the people who stole his culture" (as a Native American).

Other times, when he would tell us stories of his escapades in the North Carolina woodlands, my mother would intervene also, since she considered the stories "fairy tales." His religion was a mixture of Baptist and native traditions. He would tell us of the one Spirit that shared itself with all living things to bring life into the world, which she considered sacrilegious since she was raised in a Catholic home. But, as boys, we were always eager to learn from our father, even at the expense of chastisement from our mother.

One of his escapades that they both agreed upon as being true happened when my mother was pregnant with my older brother. My father had left her and returned to North Carolina so that he could aid the tribe's [armed] demonstration against the Ku Klux Klan in the late 1950s. This was another conflict between my mother and father. He taught us to fight for our brothers and sisters, whether they were actually relatives or not, and my mother regarded this as nonsense. She was of the opinion that we should "look out for our own welfare" and avoid physical confrontation at any risk. Another major clash between my mother and father was the ownership of weapons. My father believed that weapons should be kept in order to hunt and also for self-defense; therefore, I was always carrying a hand-made bone handle knife [that he made for me] with me wherever I went.

First of all, I would like to say that there are literally millions of different peoples who have suffered far greater maltreatment due to their race than me, and my past can in no way be compared to others such as the Black American experience. However, my experiences have had major effects upon my life. They are my personal experiences, and I am a product of them today. As I said, I did not grow up in the Lumberton, North Carolina, area around my father's tribe. (I should explain, the Lumbee Tribe does not have a reservation. This is because the Tribe never signed a treaty with the U.S. government. However, the state of North Carolina recognizes the tribal land and, in 1887, established an All American Indian training school for the Lumbees. Today, this institution is known as the University of North Carolina at Pembroke.)

Consequently, I grew up in an area where the population knew nothing about Native Americans except for the images that they saw on television and, at that time, what was written about the "Indians" in the textbooks. This was before the texts were revised to tell the truth, and, therefore, the "Indian" was viewed as the "bad guy." Additionally, my features matched my father's moreso than my mother's. I had a dark complexion, dark eyes, and dark hair, and above all, I was different than the other children in my elementary school. When I first entered my elementary school, the venerable, ragged edges of the former name of the school, which had recently been removed, were still visible to the onlooker—Belvedere All White Elementary School. I remember staring at the faded outlines as a child thinking to myself, "I'm not White, but I'm not Black, either." I often wondered, at that age, what color was I? I was darker than the White kids, but lighter than the Black kids.

I had thought that our family was the normal family, until I entered school. One of the differences I came to find to be different from the community was language. My father spoke a sort of uneducated, broken English. He didn't pronounce words "correctly," and I entered elementary school with this virtually outlandish vocabulary that I had learned at home that no one in my elementary school could comprehend. That was when I first remember experiencing a cultural clash. All of my teachers thought that I was "slow" or that I had a learning problem because I could not pronounce their words in the "right" way and also because I used words that were not recognized as "words" to them. They had quickly labeled me as a problematic child.

One of the first conflicts that I remember in elementary school was in the second grade with Ms. Period. I still remember her face, name, and voice. Every time we were at recess, Ms. Period was the playground supervisor. We played many different games that involved "good guys" and "bad guys," as all children do at this age. I was always elected as the "bad guy" because I was different. So I decided that I must really be a "bad guy." One day while Ms. Period was teaching, I put a dried chicken bone that I had broken in half and arranged in each one of my nostrils, put feathers in my hair so that I could match their concept of an Indian, and peered through the classroom window from within the bushes outside so that all the students could see the "Indian-bad guy." The whole class erupted with laughter that did not end until Ms. Period came outside and snatched me from the bushes to present me the very first (of many) paddling lessons that I received in elementary school. I learned that the paddlings were not so bad. I guess that I had built up an immunity of sorts to physical pain from the many camping trips with my father.

My father's beliefs caused other conflicts for me in school. For instance, he believed that if a child was born with a "veil," or thin layer of skin over their face, this child would have the ability to see spirits. I was born with the veil. I remember in the fourth grade (I guess at that time I was at an age when I could better comprehend what was going on around me), I was in Ms. Green's class and the subject of ghosts was brought up because it was near Halloween. That class, that day, and that moment when I decided to express my beliefs changed my educational career. I decided to tell Ms. Green, in my fourth grade naiveté, that spirits did exist and that I had actually seen them personally. The class erupted with a riotous laughter that seemed to last for ages. All eyes were upon me, fingers pointing, open mouths showing me only their missing teeth. Then, when Ms. Green regained control of the room, she stated that this was nonsense that I had made it up as a joke. (I was a liar and a joker?) This changed my fourth-grade-bulletproof self-esteem into helter-skelter.

Who was I to believe? What was real? Did I imagine the spirits? I wondered who I should trust, this school, which to me was a single entity that consisted of the community around me who laughed at me and designated me the "bad guy," or my family, who lived in their own little world at 410 Audubon Street, where spirits were real and where manhood was achieved through learning to fight, survive, and work with hands, not books. I was so confused that I stopped participating in class discussions and kept to myself. Sometimes when I walked home from school, the other kids would pick at me, but this is where I had the advantage. My father had taught me to fight because he knew. He knew that the day would come and that I would not back down from the "others." He had been taught that we were different and needed to know how to defend ourselves. Many times mom had to pay for all the other kids' lunches at school when some foolish kid would try me or make fun of me in the lunchroom and I would tear the entire lunch room apart with the kid who had made the mistake of calling me some name. My father had taught me that if my family were disgraced, there was only one solution, only one remedy; to fight, and I did, and I always won because I carried the rage within me from Ms. Green's class, and Ms. Period's paddling stick, and the wide-open mouths with teeth missing that laughed at me. I won when I fought and I fought against everything that represented this community that would not accept me.

I virtually stopped participating in school and kept to myself mainly, with the exception of two of my friends, who decided to become my blood brothers in junior high school. We cut our wrists, lashed leather strips around our arms for a few minutes so that our blood would mix and, therefore, we would become family. At this time, my junior high school principal found the wounds on my wrists and promptly decided that I had tried to commit suicide. Then I had to visit a psychologist, who was very understanding of what had happened but tried to explain the dangers involved. However, then, as before, I was automatically designated a child with problems. In my view, I didn't have problems; the society in which I was living had problems with my culture.

Nevertheless, I was headed for failure and I had planned to drop out of school. However, providence had a different plan for me. I enjoyed writing stories during my childhood, only I did not understand the rules of English grammar. I had written a story about a boy who had decided to run away from his home and live in the forest. Well, my older brother, who did not have the least interest in writing, elected to turn in my story to his teacher instead of attempting to write a paper on his own. Well, this teacher praised him so much for this composition that he felt guilty and told her the truth. This is when one of the best experiences happened to me in school. This English teacher actually came to my house to talk with me about my potential as a writer. I could not believe that a teacher would come to speak to me, the "bad guy." It was the best feeling that I had experienced in my young life at that point. She had confidence in me: IN ME! I will never forget that conversation. She essentially told me that I was intelligent. Me! This had a profound effect on my life.

After I had finally recovered some of my self-confidence thanks to the thoughtful teacher who visited my home, I decided that I would endeavor to decipher the foreign (to me) techniques involved in writing in English. So, English became my favorite subject, and I found that the English teachers that I had were more open to exploring my culture through writing than the other teachers. However, when I arrived at the University of South Carolina, I decided to try a course in Education. That is where I met the teacher who has had the most profound effect upon my life. I wanted to find out if I could possibly be interested in becoming an educator, so I took an introductory course in education. That is where I met my mentor, Dr. Janet Mason. She was the first teacher who accepted me as a human being and judged me upon my work instead of my race. She has been, and continues to be, a powerful inspiration in my life today. It is to her that I can attribute my discovery of my life quest to become an educator. It was through her constant devotion and dedication to helping me uncover my strengths and talents that I found my true vocation, my calling—to become an educator. I am going to dedicate my career as a teacher to guarantee that the damaging experiences that I suffered in my childhood will never occur in my classroom when I become an educator.

Editor's Commentary

If the lives of children of color are complex in our race-conscious society, the lives of biracial children are seemingly even more convoluted. As Audre Lorde (as cited in Hill Collins, 1993) emphasized, "the true focus of revolutionary change is never merely the oppressive situations which we seek to escape, but that piece of the oppressor which is planted deep within each of us" (p. 25). Hill Collins (1993) aptly notes that locating that piece of oppression inside us is difficult to do. If we agree with this statement, and I do, then the stories in this chapter beg the question regarding the extreme difficulty of locating the oppressor when one's heritage is represented by one ethnic group that has historically been the oppressor (European American) and another ethnic group that has historically been oppressed by Whites (e.g., African Americans and Native Americans).

The stories in this chapter all reflect the conflicts involved in trying to balance two cultures in a society that continuously makes demands on biracial individuals to choose one or the other (Poston, 1990; Root, 1990). Despite the abolition of legal barriers to interracial marriages, marriages and relationships across racial lines continue to be subjected to considerable mixed reactions (Wehrly, Kenney, and Kenney, 1999). Couples involved in interracial relationships and their children are generally faced with questions, stares, discrimination, inappropriate comments, and, often, rejection. The degree of difficulty experienced by interracial couples and their children varies based on the couple's socioeconomic level, on their educational background, and on the community in which they live (Wehrly et al, 1999). Most of the literature on couples in interracial marriages deals with African American and European American unions, although this coupling represents the smallest proportion of interracial marriages. Nevertheless, Black–White unions are by far the most controversial and therefore subject to the most negative and racist attitudes (Wehrly et al., 1999).

All three of the individuals in this chapter struggled with their identities. As shown in Table 6.1, choosing to identify with one or both of one's ethnic groups can be a viable and healthy option depending on the children, family members, and context (Poston, 1990). Part of the difficulty Terry had was that his mother and father differed dramatically on major issues. It is important that spouses respect each other's culture and learn something about it (Wehrly et al., 1999).

In all three stories, we find evidence of the effects of oppression outlined by Freire (1999). Freire explains that regardless of the nature or type of oppression (e.g., racism, sexism, classism), there are four fundamental dimensions. The first dimension is the necessity for conquest or control. The histories of African and Native Americans make

---

TABLE 6.1   *Stages of Biracial Identity (Poston, 1990)*

1. *Personal Identity.* The individual is still a child, and the sense of self is largely independent of his or her ethnic heritage.
2. *Choice of Group Categorization.* Biracial youth feel pressures to choose one racial orientation, but limited cognitive development makes it unlikely that a biracial identity will be chosen.
3. *Enmeshment/Denial.* A mixture of confusion, self-hatred, and guilt from pressures to choose one identity and to deny the other heritage is experienced. Negative feelings must be resolved to move to an appreciation of both racial backgrounds.
4. *Appreciation.* Individuals may still be identifying with the group chosen in the second stage, but they are working to learn more about and to value the racial roots of both parents.
5. *Integration.* "Individuals at this stage experience wholeness and integration" (Poston, 1990, p. 154).

---

it obvious that this dimension exists and is maintained in many ways beyond the scope of this discussion. Suffice it to say that both were conquered, exploited, and killed in large numbers by Europeans.

The second dimension, which has been mentioned several times in this book, is that the oppressor must keep the oppressed divided in order to remain in power. The within-race color issues discussed by Janet and Ruth are evidence of the "divide and rule" dimension. Although Janet and Ruth were lighter than their peers, many of their human rights were still denied because of the "one drop of African blood" that they possessed. Freire astutely observed that as long as the oppressed are isolated and the rifts among them are deepened, unity cannot occur. Hence, the people in power will maintain their position. As I have noted in previous chapters, divisions between and within groups of people of color are counterproductive to their goals to be liberated and to have all of the human rights endowed to all people. So, although Janet and Ruth were sometimes elevated by society because of their closeness to Whiteness, they were still socially regarded as African Americans in some settings and identified themselves with African Americans. Both of them wisely rejected division between them and other Blacks but did not deny their White heritage as well. Ruth could have easily passed for White, but she chose not to.

The third dimension of oppression is manipulation. Freire observed that marginalized groups are manipulated by myths about their cultural groups and about the dominant elites. Manipulative acts are used to make the masses conform to the objectives of the dominant elites. One of the methods of manipulation is to inoculate individuals with the bourgeois appetite for personal success (as opposed to collective success). This dimension works to ensure that only a few people will be part of the dominant elites. In Janet's and Ruth's cases, people helped them become successful because of their lighter skin, which also, by default, ensured the likelihood of nonsuccess among people in their community having darker skins. The existing power structure of the United States and the South manipulated their school and community to define beauty in terms of closeness to "White" features, thus condemning darker skin.

The fourth dimension discussed by Freire is cultural invasion. In this phenomenon, the oppressors penetrate the cultural context of another group. The oppressors disrespect the potentialities of the oppressed and impose their own view of the world and inhibit the creativity of the invaded by curbing their expression. "For cultural invasion to succeed, it is essential that those oppressed become convinced of their intrinsic inferiority" (Freire, 1999, p. 134). Consider the following quotation from Janet's story:

> *I spoke with a southern Black dialect, often causing the children in Washington, D. C., to laugh when I read aloud or shared in the class discussion. . . . Miss Evans often stayed after school and tutored me one-on-one to "correct" my pronunciation.*

Janet received feedback from the children that there was something wrong with her speech—that it was inferior. Cultural conquest leads to the cultural inauthenticity of those who are oppressed so that they begin to respond to the values, stan-

dards, and goals of the invaders. The more they mimic the invaders, the more stable the position of the invaders becomes. In Janet's case, it is not surprising that the students who denigrated her speech were also Black because they also had been taught to value the "language of power" as better than others' language systems or dialects.

One of the myths put forth as part of the cultural invasion process is that a person's language (an essential part of one's being) is inferior. African American language has historically been regarded as inferior by our society, in which the rules for the standard are based on White mainstream speech (Boutte, McCoy, & Davis, 1995; Delpit, 1995; Heath, 1992; Lindfors, 1987; Perry & Delpit, 1998; Smitherman, 1977). African American language is a structurally rich, rule-governed language system, even though it is not the language of power (Delpit, 1995; Perry & Delpit, 1998). Yet, the strengths of the African American language system are disregarded, and it is still regarded as substandard by many educators. Speakers of this language system are therefore viewed from a deficit perspective when they enter school rather than as children who are proficient in one language system which needs to be maintained.

While speakers of African American language need to learn Standard English (the "language of power") as Delpit (1995) coins it, their language system should not be eradicated or denigrated (Heath, 1992). Yet, Janet, Ruth, and Terry were given the distinct impression that there was something wrong with their language. The language of the oppressor was thereby glorified and aspects of their culture (language) were invaded and interpreted through the eyes of the oppressor. This also successfully condemns people in their families and communities, as was the case with Terry:

> *My father spoke a sort of uneducated, broken English. He didn't pronounce words "correctly," and I entered elementary school with this* virtually outlandish *[emphasis added] vocabulary that I had learned at home that no one in my elementary school could comprehend.*

Imagine the shock and insult at being told that the person closest to you is inferior. Terry, like most children, had accomplished the magnificent feat of mastering the language of his home. Upon entering school, children like Terry are punished for this major accomplishment, while children lucky enough to be born in homes where standard English is spoken are rewarded and advantaged.

The cultural invasion of Terry's culture is more blatant than the general invisibility of African Americans in the curriculum experienced by Janet and Ruth. In Terry's case, cultural invasion took the form of inaccurate and mythical portrayals of Indians in his textbooks and on television. Basically, everything that his father taught him was contradicted. His mother unknowingly contributed to this invasion with little effort because she was more familiar with the culture of power. Freire (1999) notes that well-intentioned professionals (and others) use cultural invasion not as a deliberate ideology, but as an expression of their own upbringing. According to Freire, denying the rightness of a person to create and value their own way of being human is an oppressive act.

Terry's spiritual beliefs were not understood or validated as legitimate. Other aspects of his worldview were dismissed and ridiculed. Cultural invasion is an act of violence, although it is seldom recognized as such. Its effects are detrimental. In Terry's case, he was on the verge of dropping out of school. Given the cultural assaults that people of color, and Native Americans in particular, face, it is not surprising that Native Americans have the highest dropout rates of any students of color (Barba, 1995; Kasten, 1992). Terry conveys that with the help of an excellent and caring teacher, he was able to "recover" some of his self-confidence. Recover is a pivotal word in Terry's statement, convincing me that he, like most children, came to school confident. Too few children of color exit school that way.

Terry's father taught him to fight for the rights (humanity) of his "brothers and sisters." Using the idea of the unity of humanity broadly and the right to be treated humanely, his father saw past the societally defined use of differences among the races as a basis for discrimination.

Perhaps the sense of brotherhood and sisterhood is what drew Ruth to the study of Indians. She recognized the parallels between the plight of Indians and African Americans in the United States. She —like Janet and Terry—rejected categorical constraints that society put forth, as did their parents, who dared to develop cross-racial unions. While cross-racial unions are not without major challenges, they have the potential to destroy simplistic beliefs about the superiority and inferiority of various ethnic groups. As Patricia Hill Collins (1993) notes, it is dangerous to take a stance that seeks to compare and rank which group is the most oppressed. While we may differ in shades, as the title of this chapter conveys, we also share the common need to be treated humanely regardless of our color or lineage.

Reflective Activity

Referring to Table 1.1 in Chapter 1, make a list of ten ethnic sub-groups, two from each of the five major ethnic groups. Cut the list into strips, leaving one ethnic group per strip. Fold the strips so that the names of the ethnic groups are concealed. Randomly choose two of the strips. Imagine that one of your parents is from one group and the other from the other group.

1. Based on what you know about the two chosen groups, speculate about possible aspects of their cultures that might affect your perspectives/orientation (e.g., preferences, habits, beliefs, and physical features).
2. What within-group cultural attributes might affect your perspectives (e.g., social class, neighborhood, family, geographic region).
3. How would you identify yourself? (How would you respond if asked the insensitive question "What are you?" or what would you write on applications requesting your race?)

Repeat the activity with different combinations. Think about challenges you might face as well as the strengths of being biracial.[1]

[1]Activity adapted from Alethia Rollins' (graduate student at the University of North Carolina at Greensboro) presentation in HDF 602, Spring 2000. Adapted and used with permission.

Resources

Books

Frederickson, George M. (1971). *The Black image in the White mind.* Middletown, CT: Wesleyan University Press.

Gaskins, P. F. (1999). *What are you? Voices of mixed-race young people.* New York: Henry Holt.

Gatewood, W. B. (1990). *Aristocrats of color: The Black elite, 1880–1920.* Bloomington: Indiana University Press.

Gibbs, J. T., & Larke, N. H. (1989). *Children of color.* San Francisco: Jossey-Bass.

Higginbotham, A. L. (1978). *In the matter of color: Race and the American legal process, the color period.* New York: Oxford University Press.

Hodes, M. (1999). *White women, Black men: Illicit sex in the nineteenth century South.* New Haven, CT: Yale Press.

McBride, J. (1997). *The color of water: A Black man's tribute to his white mother.* Berkeley, CA: Berkeley Press.

McLaurin, M. A. (1991). *Celia, a slave.* Athens: University of Georgia Press.

Nash, G. B. (1999). *Forbidden love: The secret history of mixed race America.* New York: Henry Holt.

Nash, R. (1995). *Everything you need to know about being a biracial/biethnic child.* New York: Henry Holt.

O'Hearn, C. C. (1998). *Half and half: Writers on growing up biracial and bicultural.* New York: Pantheon Books.

Piper, A. (1993). Passing for White, passing for Black. *Transition, 58,* 4–32.

Russell, K., Wilson, M., & Hall, R. (1992). *The color complex.* New York: Harcourt Brace Jovanovich.

Spickard, P. (1989). *Mixed blood: Intermarriage and ethnic identity in twentieth-century America.* Madison: University of Wisconsin Press.

Williams, G. H. (1995). *Life on the color line.* New York: Penguin.

Williamson, J. (1984). *New people: Miscegenation and mulattoes in the United States.* New York: Free Press.

Children's Books/Adult Novels

Flagg, F. (1999). *Welcome to the world baby girl!* New York: Ivy.

West, D. (1996). *The wedding.* New York: Doubleday.

Williams, V. B. (1990). *More, more, more said the baby: Three love stories.* New York: Harper Collins.

References

Barba, R. H. (1995). *Science in the multicultural classroom: A guide to teaching and learning.* Boston: Allyn & Bacon.

Boutte, G. S., McCoy, B., & Davis, B. D. (1995). Helping African American students maintain *and* adapt their communication styles: A challenge for educators. *The Negro Education Review, XLVI* (1–2), 10–21.

Delpit, L. (1995). *Other people's children: Cultural conflict in the classroom.* New York: New Press.

Franklin, J. H., & Moss, A. A., Jr. (1947/1994). *From slavery to freedom: A history of African Americans* (7th ed.). New York: Alfred A. Knopf.

Freire, P. (1999). *Pedagogy of the oppressed.* New York: Continuum.

Haizlip, S. T., *The sweeter the juice.* (1994). New York: Simon & Schuster.

Heath, S. B. (1992). *Ways with words.* New York: Cambridge University Press.

Hill Collins, P. (1993). Toward a new vision: Race, class, and gender as categories of analysis and connection. *Race, Sex, & Class, 1*(1), 25–45.

Kasten, W. C. (1992). Bridging the horizon: American Indian beliefs and whole language learning. *Anthropology and Education Quarterly, 23* (2), 108–119.

Lindfords, J. W. (1987). *Children's language and learning.* Boston: Allyn & Bacon.

Perry, T., & Delpit, L. D. (1998). *The real ebonics debate.* New York: Beacon.

Poston, W. S. C. (1990). The biracial identity development model: A needed addition. *Journal of Counseling and Development, 69* (2), 152–155.

Root, M. P. (1990). *Racially mixed people in America.* Newbury Park, CA.: Sage.

Smitherman, G. (1977). *Talkin' and testifyin'.* Boston: Houghton-Mifflin.

Wehrly, B., Kenney, K. R., & Kenney, M. E. (1999). *Counseling multiracial families (Multicultural aspects of counseling series, Vol 12).* Thousand Oaks, CA: Corwin.

Williams, G. H. (1995). *Life on the color line.* NY: Plume Books.

7

Out in the Boondocks

Rural School Experiences and Education That Is Multicultural for White Students

Carol E. Marxen

Editor's Overview _____

This chapter provides an intergenerational view of the rural lives of the author and four other European Americans in small, midwestern towns. As each of their stories unfolds, we discover that their lives are not as worry free as some might think. Issues of class, religion, and ethnicity are addressed. The author discusses how rural Whites can straddle rural culture and more global perspectives.

"Those People" Who Live on a Dairy Farm

"Where do you live?" inquired a tenth-grade classmate who asked me to go to a party with him. "On a dairy farm, four miles west of Brighton, in Maple Park," I replied. "Oh, you live out in the boondocks. Why don't you drive into Park Center and meet me at the party?" he asked. "I will have to check with my parents to see if I can use the car. Call me tonight," I told him. "Is it long distance?" he asked. "No," I said, wishing that I lived in the suburb where he lived rather than on a farm out in the boondocks. Despite the disappointment of driving to the party by myself rather than being escorted, I was excited. A boy had actually asked me out on a date! As a high school sophomore, this was my first official date, and the party was with the "in crowd."

My next step was convincing my parents that, first, it was safe for me to go to the party and, second, that I should be allowed to use the family car. I decided to wait until my dad was in the barn milking before I asked him because he was always in a better mood when he was milking cows. When I got home from school, I did all of my barn chores and helped my mom with supper. I did not want to give my dad or mom an excuse to say no to my request. Besides being teased by my older brothers about a boy asking me out, I was interrogated with predictable questions: "Where is the party?" "Will there be adult supervision?" "Who are you going with?" "What do his parents do?" "Where does he live?" "Is he Catholic?" These anticipated questions were answered and my parents followed up my answers with their customary comments: "I don't like you going to parties in that area." "We don't know these people." "They have different values than we do." "You have to check with your brothers to see if they need the car." "Maybe your brothers could take you to the party and pick you up." And my favorite: "If the boy really wanted to take you out, he would drive out here to get you so we can meet him." This was only one of numerous interrogations I had with my parents about friends, parties, and dates with "those people from Park Center."

It wasn't until much later in life that I realized the concerns my parents had about my "suburban friends" were based on cultural stereotypes. The cultural differences surfaced because in the 1950s, the state mandated rural schools to consolidate with larger schools. This forced our small rural school to consolidate with Brighton School District. Brighton School District included the small town of Brighton and also the growing suburb of Park Center. My father, a school board member of our rural school district, opposed school consolidation. Maybe his reluctance to accept the suburban culture and its people was an expression of the loss he felt as our country school was taken away and the suburbs were closing in on our farm of three generations.

My Story

I grew up on a dairy farm in the midwestern, rural community of Maple Park, located four miles from the small town of Brighton and thirty miles from Hartland, a major metropolitan area. In the 1950s and 1960s, Brighton's population was approximately 1,000 and Maple Park was a small community scattered with dairy farms. Although we were within a half-hour drive to downtown Hartland, our community was considered rural.

I am the youngest of six children. I have three brothers and two sisters. Until I entered school, my brothers and sisters were my only playmates.

When my sister, who is two years older than I am, started school, my mother, a piano teacher, gave me piano lessons so I would have something to do while my sister was in school.

Country School

When I was five years old, I began first grade at District 100, a one-room country school one mile from our farm. The enrollment varied from thirteen to eighteen students in grades one through eight (Figure 7.1). The boundary of our small district was approximately a two-mile radius around the school. We were all White, Protestant, European Americans. Our diversity consisted of which Protestant church we belonged to and whether our parents owned a farm or just lived in the country.

Miss Condon, our teacher, rented a room from a family that lived across the road from the school. The families in the school would take turns inviting her to dinner. It was a big event when she came to our house. I remember her as a wonderful and caring teacher. The school had one large classroom. Our desks were bolted to the floor and the teacher conducted grade-level lessons at a large table in the front of the room. Our library was a long narrow room with books on shelves from the floor to the ceiling. The bookmobile stopped at our school once a month.

FIGURE 7.1 *My One-Room Country School.*

There was a small kitchen with a stove, sink, and refrigerator, and mothers took turns coming to school to prepare our hot lunches. Hot lunches were made up of surplus commodities such as canned stewed tomatoes or spinach served in coffee cups to complement our cold lunches brought from home. Although most of us did not appreciate the "hot" part of our lunch, we had to eat it.

Until I was in the third grade, the school's only bathroom was an outhouse. When the new bathroom facilities were installed, our library got smaller. It also meant that I could no longer hide my cup of hot tomatoes or spinach under my coat, ask to go to the outhouse, and dispose of it. Consequently, I missed the outhouse!

Our curriculum included the 3 Rs, art, music, recess, and the annual Christmas program. The reading curriculum was "Dick and Jane." Phonics was not part of our reading program; we learned to read by sight. Art and music lessons were taught to all eight grades at the same time and the older students helped the younger ones. Listening to the teacher instruct another group of students at the front of the room was one of the ways we learned. I remember listening to the seventh- and eighth-graders' geography and map lessons. Discussions about different cultures, however, were absent.

We went outside for recess every day. The playground consisted of swings, teeter-totters, and a merry-go-round. "Anti-Anti-Over" and "Pom-Pom Pull-Away" were our favorite games. There was a creek across the road from the school, and in the winter we would go sledding down its banks. When we were outside, the older students played with and looked after the younger students.

Regardless of this being a public school, religion was part of our school life. We spent the month of December practicing for the Christmas Program, which was a community celebration. A huge stage was built at the front of the schoolroom, the desks were unbolted from the floor and replaced with chairs for the audience. We all had parts to learn and songs to perform. The Christmas Pageant was the highlight of the night and the girl who was chosen to portray Mary felt honored (Figure 7.2). After the program, Santa Claus appeared with bags of peanuts and candy for all the children. And best of all, we got to stay up late (Figure 7.3).

Cultural Change

District 100 consolidated with Brighton School District when I was nine, and my secure, sheltered, protected life came to an abrupt halt. When I climbed aboard the school bus in September 1952, I was a very shy, scared fifth-grader. I suddenly had sixty classmates rather than one, and I did not know anyone in my class.

Geographically and socially, I was isolated from my classmates who lived in Brighton and Park Center. Even if I was invited to a classmate's

FIGURE 7.2 *Annual Christmas Program at My One-Room School.*

FIGURE 7.3 *Santa Claus Brings Candy for All the Children.*

house, my mother did not drive and my father and older brothers did not have time to "cart me around." In addition to the distance barrier, my parents were skeptical of my new classmates' families, especially the ones from Park Center. Could they be trusted? They did not live on farms or in a small town, and their fathers and mothers worked in factories. They did not have the same values that we did. Many of them were Catholics. I was not encouraged to make friends with anyone outside of Maple Park or Brighton.

In junior high, interaction with my classmates outside of the classroom continued to be minimal. I did, however, find one way to meet new friends and attend extracurricular school functions: I joined the band. Luckily, my mother was a musician and she encouraged me to participate in band. I was allowed to go to home and away ball games to play in the pep band, attend band contests, and join the summer marching band. Participating in the marching band provided me opportunities to make my very first trips outside of the state to Chicago, Illinois, and Winnipeg, Canada.

Culture and Ethnicity

One of my first introductions to a different ethnic group was a play presented by District 100's Mother's Club. Every year the Mother's Club put on a play to raise money for a spring field trip. In this particular play, one of the mothers played the part of a southern "mammy" (Figure 7.4). I do not remember the plot, but I do remember my friend's mother making her face and hands Black for the play.

Another experience by which I learned about a different culture occurred during Bible school at my country church. A friend of my older sister was a missionary in New Guinea and showed slides of the "natives." She talked about their culture and language, and I remember her saying that missionaries were helping the people in this backward country become civilized.

When I was six, television introduced me to people who were from different cultural and ethnic groups. We watched *The Jack Benny Hour, I Love Lucy,* or *Charlie Chan* movies. In my early years, people from different cultural and ethnic groups either lived far away, were on television, or were stereotypically portrayed.

Throughout my elementary, junior, and senior high school days in the 1950s and 1960s, I interacted with people having different religious and societal cultures, but I had no opportunity to build relationships with people from other ethnic groups. Moreover, the curriculum in our school addressed cultures and ethnicity from a historical perspective, but it did not include current issues. We were busy memorizing historical dates and the sayings of famous White Americans.

It wasn't until I went to college that I had the opportunity to interact personally with people from diverse ethnic and cultural groups. I found out

FIGURE 7.4   *Annual Mother's Club Play Featuring the Role of a Southern Mammy.*

that they were real people—not just people in plays, in other countries, and on television. Black women were not all "mammies" and Black men were not all tap dancers, nor were Black individuals to be feared. People with Asian heritage were American citizens, and they did not talk like Charlie Chan.

Although I shed some stereotypes in college, my teacher education program did not address multicultural education in the curriculum. After graduation from college with a degree in elementary education, I taught in an all-White suburban school for eight years and then moved to a very remote, White, rural community, where I taught for twelve years. It was when I was living in this rural community that I realized children who grow up in remote, rural, White, monocultural settings need multicultural education infused in their curriculum more than do the children who live in multicultural settings. For it is the absence of positive images, the lack of diverse perspectives, and the omission of discussion about different cultures and ethnic groups that create prejudices and stereotypes.

Only when individuals explore their diverse roots and branches can they fully understand the whole, and only when individuals respect differences can we become one society. When individuals understand diversity, they can appreciate our common humanity (Ramsey, 1987). Following Ramsey's suggestion to explore one's roots and branches, I took a trip back through my school experiences. By taking that trip, I am more aware of who

I am and the changes I need to make within myself to live in a world full of diversity. I am also aware that my ways of knowing influence the students in my classes. By looking back, I can feel comfortable accepting my students' differences and, thereby, move forward.

Consequently, my interest in rural schools and multicultural education is personal and multifaceted. First, I was raised in a small, rural, farming community and had attended a one-room country school for four years when I was thrust into a different school culture. Second, as an adult, I moved from teaching in a large, White, suburban area to teaching in a small, geographically isolated, White, rural community, where I observed latent and covert racist attitudes. And, currently, I am a White, female teacher educator at a university located in a small, rural community preparing mostly White, young females from the surrounding rural areas or suburbs to teach in an increasingly diverse world.

This chapter is a small part of my struggle to understand how people in small, rural communities view diversity and multicultural education and to take this information to better prepare White, female teacher education students to teach effectively in a diverse world. To begin to better understand the complexities of a rural culture, I interviewed four individuals from a small, midwestern, rural community about their lives and school experiences. The participants are a mother and daughter and a father and son whose lives span fifty-five years in the same rural community.

To help the reader understand the context of ruralness, the next section begins with background information on rural communities and schools. Next, portraits of the participants' life and school experiences are shared. The benefits and barriers of growing up in a rural community that emerged from the participants' stories are discussed, as are changes that occurred across the two generations. Finally, taking seriously the suggestions from the participants and current literature on effective rural education, a rural multicultural education model is proposed.

Rural Communities and Schools

Ask people on the street what images they have when they hear the word *rural*. Depending on which part of the country a person is from, the picture might be of a small fishing village in New England, a dairy farm in Minnesota, a cattle ranch in Montana, a cabin in northern Michigan, an Indian village in South Dakota, or a shack in the Appalachian Mountains. Rural communities may be ethnically homogeneous, like a Hispanic community in Texas, a Black community in Louisiana, a White community in the Midwest, or a Navajo community in Arizona. In contrast, other rural communities are diverse, and recent demographic data show that more new immigrants, particularly Mexicans, are settling in rural areas.

Rural Stereotypes

For some people, *rural* may conjure up terms such as *peaceful, safe, secure, scenic, togetherness,* and *contentment.* In contrast, it is more likely that people associate *rural* with *uncultured, crude, unsophisticated, backwoods, old fashioned, underdeveloped,* and *provincial.* Terms used to describe rural residents include *hicks, country bumpkins, naive, ignorant,* or *hillbillies.* Haas (1991) concluded, "Just as other minorities are stereotyped by the larger society, knowledge about rural folk is remarkably stereotypical in nature. Labels generally carry a negative connotation and represent an urban 'putdown' of rural people in rural life" (p. 422).

Murray (in Weisman, 1990) maintained that the association of *rural* with *unsophisticated* or *dumb* sends a negative self-image to rural schoolchildren. Elementary social studies texts and the media add to the unflattering illustrations about rural communities, schools, and people. Speaking to this issue, Herzog and Pittman (1995) reminded us that "even though our times are characterized by a heightened awareness of and sensitivity to cultural differences, it is still considered socially and politically correct to poke fun at 'rednecks,' 'hillbillies,' and 'hicks' " (p. 114). When students in rural schools consistently hear and see negative stereotypes, they may question their competence and consequently lack the confidence needed to succeed outside or inside their rural community. Their lack of self-esteem may become a barrier to success. Haas (1992) summarized our love/hate relationship with rural America: "As a nation, we have idealized rural America on one hand, and ignored it on the other" (p. 7).

Definition of Rural

From a more objective point of view, the U.S. Census Bureau described "rural" as places "with fewer than 2,500 inhabitants or fewer than 1,000 inhabitants per square mile" (Herzog & Pittman, 1995, p. 114). Until 1990, any community that was not urban or metropolitan was classified as rural (Haas, 1992; Herzog & Pittman, 1995). Others (e.g., researchers, educators, sociologists) used a combination of criteria such as size, scarcity or density of population, distance and isolation from an urban center, economic and social conditions, sociocultural values, and self-designation (Haas, 1991) to define rural areas. Phelps and Prock (1991) maintained that "ruralness derives its definition from its isolation, both geographically and demographically, its labor intensive income base (farming), and pervasive poverty" (p. 274).

Since the rural decline in the 1980s, people living in rural communities face the challenges not only of stereotypes and geographic isolation, but also of high poverty rates, low growth rate of jobs, decline in population, and a population that is aging (Flora & Christenson, 1991). On the brighter side, the strong economy in the 1990s has improved employment and income figures in rural America. Despite the favorable conditions, Huang (1999) revealed that rural America still has plenty of problems to solve:

> In 1995, the rural poverty rate was 15.6 percent, compared to the urban rate of 13.4 percent. This rural–urban gap has remained constant since 1991. Moreover, a large portion of rural residents (26.3 percent) lived just above the poverty line, compared with the urban rate of 18.2 percent. Such a large proportion of the population having a marginal income status makes rural families particularly vulnerable to changes in national and regional economics and setbacks in their personal lives. (p. 2)

Despite increased employment in rural areas in the 1990s, rural employees still earn about four-fifths of what urban employees earn, in spite of the fact that more than 60 percent of rural employees have two incomes. An interesting side-note is that teachers in rural areas did not gain in real income in the 1990s (Huang, 1999).

During the 1990s, there was an increase in the rural population, especially of people under age sixty-five. One of the reasons for the increase is that telecommunications technology makes it possible for professionals to work outside metropolitan centers. In addition, immigrants are moving to rural areas (Huang, 1999). Although most immigrants settle in metropolitan areas, two percent live in rural areas. Of these, 57 percent are Mexican (Effland, & Butler, 1997). On average, the immigrants who settle in rural areas are younger and have less education than those who settle in metropolitan areas; they are also younger than the "native" residents in rural communities (Huang, 1999). The economic and demographic changes that occurred in the 1990s provide opportunities and challenges for the communities and schools in rural America.

Western County and Ricefield

The interviews for this chapter live in Ricefield. Located in a remote area in a midwestern state, Ricefield is the county seat of Western County. The majority of residents living in this rural area have been here for generations. Their ancestors were immigrants from Germany and the Scandinavian countries. Because there is an Indian reservation in close proximity, Western County has always had a small Native American population. In 1990, there were 126 Native Americans living in the county.

Similar to most rural areas today, Western County and Ricefield have a declining population. In 1950, Western County had a population of 8,053, but the numbers have been spiraling downward. In 1980 the population was 5,542, and by 1998 it was 4,350. Ricefield's population fell from 2,100 in 1960 to 1,643 in 1998. The population of the area meets the U.S. Census Bureau's criteria (fewer than 2,500 inhabitants or fewer than 1,000 inhabitants per square mile) of rural. There are three other towns in the county; in 1998, they had populations of 720, 116, and 70 respectively. The closest large city, Melford (which in 1997 had a population of 33,812), is 90 miles away. The state's major metropolitan area, Hartland, is 200 miles from Ricefield. Four small towns with populations of approximately 3,000 to 7,000 are within a 60-mile radius of Ricefield. Simply put, Ricefield is located in a geographically isolated rural area.

As the county seat, Ricefield has the advantage of housing the county court house, highway department, and county social services department. It also hosts the county fair. The town has a community hospital, a public library, and a liquor store. It has a golf course, a baseball field, and two small parks. Main Street has a grocery, appliance, department, and drug store; two banks; a law office; numerous insurance agencies and gas stations; a local newspaper office; three cafes; and two taverns. There is a funeral home with an adjacent furniture store that is managed by the funeral director. The town has six churches, which serve Catholics, Presbyterians, Missouri Synod Lutherans, American Lutherans, Convenants, and Jehovah Witnesses. Ricefield has an elementary school building and a high school building. The major economic bases of the county are large grain and cattle farms. Since the 1980s, there has been an active economic development group. Although the group has solicited small industries to come to Ricefield, they have met with limited success. Two small industries have located in Ricefield and have created minimum-wage jobs for a small number of people. One company left after five years, and one remains active.

Schools

As in most rural areas, Western County once had many one-room schools that educated children in grades one through eight. During the school consolidations of the 1950s and 1960s, they were annexed to Ricefield School District, and by 1966, all the one-room schools in the county were closed.

Ricefield School District opened its first school in 1885, its first nine-month school in 1892, and a new school building in 1899. By 1911, in addition to classes for children in grades one through twelve, the school building housed an agricultural department for area farmers and a normal training department to train teachers. In 1932, a nine-week spring primary class was opened for preschoolers. Students from the teachers' training department taught the class until the department closed in 1948.

Increased enrollment in the Ricefield School District was a direct result of annexing the country schools. Consequently, a new elementary school was constructed in 1953. The high school remained in the original 1899 building and its 1916 and 1955 additions. On April 1, 1972, a devastating fire destroyed much of the high school. A new high school was constructed and opened in the fall of 1974.

The graduation classes from Ricefield School District range from 44 in 1950, 51 in 1960, 73 in 1970, 82 in 1972, 76 in 1980, 44 in 1985, and 42 in 1990. The school's declining enrollment from the 1970s to the 1990s is characteristic of rural America.

Portraits of Rural America in the Midwest

The following portraits tell the school experiences of four individuals who grew up and attended school in Ricefield and/or in one of the Western County country schools. Their experiences are a sampling of rural living from two generations of Ricefield school graduates that span fifty-five years. The portraits are of a mother (1961 graduate) and her daughter (1983 graduate) and a father (1960 graduate) and his son (1986 graduate).

Elizabeth

Elizabeth, who is fifty-six years old, was born and raised on a farm five miles from Ricefield in Western County. Although her parents were primarily grain farmers, they had some pigs, chickens, and dairy cows on their farm. Elizabeth has two older sisters and a brother who died at thirteen from a muscular disease. There is an age span of eleven and sixteen years between her and her sisters.

Over the years, Elizabeth has not traveled too far from Ricefield. Her first trip to Hartland was in high school for a 4-H demonstration at the state fair. She has been out of the state for weddings and church events but has only been on one vacation involving travel by air.

Elizabeth attended District 42, a one-room county school, for grades one through seven. The school building had one large room with a library on one side. A wood-burning stove heated the room. There was no kitchen or indoor plumbing. The outhouse doubled as a prop for playing "Anti-Anti-Over" during recess.

The school enrollment varied from seven to twelve students. There was only one other student in Elizabeth's grade. During the seven years Elizabeth attended District 42, she had four teachers. The teachers were responsible for planning everything for all eight grades, starting the wood-burning stove in the morning, and keeping the school clean. Elizabeth liked all of her teachers except one, whom she described as "an older lady, with her hair in a bun type thing. I don't remember her as being very enthusiastic. She was a somber, rigid person."

Elizabeth does not remember anything outstanding, special, or challenging during her seven years at her one-room country school: "You had your time with the teacher where you went to the front of the class, you sat at a table with that teacher, and you went through your lessons." She remembered spending a lot of time on penmanship, "making the letters just so." Reading at the library table was one of her favorite activities.

During recess, the students played games such as "Captain May I," "Pom-Pom Pull-Away," or "Anti-Anti-Over." In the spring, county schools in the same area would get together for a "play day." Says Elizabeth, "The most major thing I can remember happening was when one kid in the wintertime stuck his tongue on a cold pipe! This was our excitement."

Elizabeth's ethnicity is German and her religion is Missouri Synod Lutheran. Elizabeth's classmates were also her playmates outside of school: "When families got together on Saturday for an evening of playing cards, the kids went along. They would be the same kids you went to school with." Many of the same families attended the rural German Lutheran Missouri Synod church on Sunday morning: "Church was actually a once-a-week outing!" Elizabeth described life in her rural community as being part of a big "extended family."

Although Elizabeth's family was poor, she did not view herself as poor until she was in high school. She explained that everyone she interacted with in the farming community had about the same and there were no outside influences such as television. Therefore, it wasn't until she went to Ricefield to school that she realized her family did not have as much as other families.

Throughout her life, Elizabeth's schoolmates and friends have been White (European Americans). Religious diversity, "basically Catholics against Protestants," is the only diversity she recalled: "I can't remember the first time I saw a Black person. It was probably on television, and we did not have a television until I was in eighth grade. But I know that as far as actually meeting a Black person, it was after high school." She recounted learning about Blacks when they studied the Civil War in social studies, but learned nothing about the legalized discrimination against Blacks still current in the 1950s. Elizabeth recalled, "The only current things we discussed were in a paper like a *Weekly Reader.*"

With an Indian reservation only thirty miles away, Elizabeth assumed that "most Native Americans lived on reservations and were pretty self-sufficient. They weren't part of our culture because we didn't see them or hear of them." Again, Native Americans were discussed in school only in the context of the past.

After consolidation in 1956, Elizabeth went into town to begin eighth grade in the Ricefield School District. She was apprehensive about "going from a one-room school to one where there are many different floors and rooms. You feel like you're getting lost. Besides all the new people—more than fifty in my grade rather than one. The experience was very different and very scary."

Elizabeth's extracurricular activities were minimal because "my folks didn't want to be driving back and forth to town for those things." Library club was an after-school activity that she joined, but she missed many meetings because she didn't have a ride. Most of Elizabeth's activities when she was in high school revolved around her family and church.

Although Elizabeth admits she is not athletic and was never the first person chosen to be on a team, she cannot remember ever being harassed about it. Nor was she ever teased because she wore thick glasses. Elizabeth explained, "Everything was so simplified then. You weren't out. You were with your extended family most of the time and we didn't have a lot of time to socialize during school."

Elizabeth's favorite subjects in her new school were English, history, home economics, and bookkeeping. She laughed when she recalled that she did not like typing, because most of her jobs since high school have required extensive typing.

Elizabeth graduated from Ricefield High School in 1961 with forty-nine classmates. After graduation, rather than leaving Ricefield to seek employment or attend a postsecondary institution, she worked as a bookkeeper at a hardware store in Ricefield for two years. Elizabeth explained why she did not go to college:

> I didn't go to college because my parents said they couldn't help pay for college or a car. I don't know why I didn't check into loans and riding to school with someone. At the time, I think I thought I could start at the bottom at a place of work and after a few years of experience, I could work my way up into a better position. Probably thought experience counted as much as a college education.

Elizabeth married her high school sweetheart in the fall of 1962. Because they lived in the country, twelve and one-half miles from Ricefield, and they had only one car, Elizabeth quit work. A daughter, Allison, was born in 1965 and a son, Joseph, in 1969. Elizabeth worked at the Western County Court House in the treasurer's office from 1966 to 1968. They moved into town in 1969. Since 1974, Elizabeth has worked part time for doctors at the local clinic filing insurance papers. In 1994, she started another part-time job for the county social service department as an account clerk. Currently, she spends the mornings at the clinic and afternoons at the social service department.

Elizabeth believes that, for the time and place she went to school, she received a good education. She still uses her typing and bookkeeping skills and believes she has a good command of English. She attributes her English skills to her love of reading.

In her current jobs at the clinic and social services, she interacts with Native Americans and Hispanics and feels comfortable with her ability to relate to them in the office. But she does not feel qualified to do more. She stated, "If I had to go into their home and work with them, I don't know their culture well enough that I would understand their thoughts and way of thinking. I do think we need to understand these cultures better because there are going to be more Blacks, Native Americans, and Hispanics moving into rural areas. We have a few Hispanic people that stay year round now." In this respect, she does not believe she learned enough about other cultures in school. On the other hand, she defended her educational experience by stating, "That is the way they taught in those days."

After reflecting on her life, Elizabeth regretted, "I wish I would have gotten out of Ricefield at some time to experience other areas and to get an education." She doesn't blame her lack of adventure on the rural community in which she grew up, but more on her personality: "I'm afraid to get out and do different things. In other words, I'm in a rut. Basically, I am and have always been a very shy person."

To help students in today's rural schools become prepared for postsecondary education or employment, Elizabeth believes that parents need to be involved in their child's school experiences. She is an advocate for the arts and sciences:

> Parents need to encourage kids and teachers to be involved in things other than sports. Sports is good for teamwork, but I think they also need to encourage kids in arts and sciences, and some of the cultural things that we miss out on in the rural community. . . . Arts and sciences get cut because of money problems easier than sports.

Because of her work at the clinic and social services office, Elizabeth maintained that we need to educate students about the Native American, Black, and Hispanic cultures because there are an increasing number of people with diverse cultures moving into the area: "Whites are going to be the minority—maybe even in Ricefield, and we need to understand their culture."

Allison

Allison, Elizabeth's daughter, is thirty-four years old. She was raised on a farm until she was four, when her family moved to town. Her father, like Elizabeth, grew up on a farm near Ricefield, attended a rural country school, and graduated from Ricefield Public Schools the same year as Elizabeth. After high school, he farmed with his dad for a couple of years. Poor crops forced him to quit farming, and he went to work at a farmer's cooperative in Ricefield for five years. He was employed at a men's clothing store in Ricefield and eventually purchased the business. In 1984, with a declining population and poor rural economy, he sold the store and worked as an insurance agent. Allison has one younger brother.

Allison, like the rest of her family, has not ventured too far from home. The first time she went to Hartland was in high school to compete in a state choir contest, and, at thirty-one, she took her first airplane flight. When she was young, going to Melford was considered a "big trip." If they went shopping, it was more common for them to go to one of the smaller towns within a sixty-mile radius of Ricefield.

Allison described her community and school culture: "Pretty much everybody in the community is either Nordic or German. The big difference was between the Lutherans and the Catholics. Everybody was a Christian, so they were all on the same wavelength. In school, everybody celebrated Christmas, everybody sent Valentine's Day cards, everybody celebrated Halloween and did all of the traditional holidays that they aren't allowed to celebrate now."

Allison attended elementary and high school in the Ricefield School District. Ricefield started a nine-month kindergarten program in 1967, just three years before Allison started school. Due to lack of space, kindergarten classes were held in a large room above the bowling alley. It was located just across the playground from the elementary school. Allison recalled that the children who lived in town went to school in the morning and the children who lived in the country went to school in the afternoon, and except for her relatives, she "didn't meet any of the farm kids until first grade."

Allison recalled two of her fondest elementary school memories. One was her elementary music class, where they sang songs from different countries. Another was in sixth grade, when each student studied a country and made a presentation to the class on "cultural day." Allison described how the students were assigned a country to study: "Because a lot of people were vying for Germany, the teacher assigned us to different countries, because nobody would have wanted to take some of the Third World countries. What little boy or girl who is German and Swedish would want India?" Allison does not remember which country she was assigned.

In high school, Allison's favorite subjects were English and photography. She loved to read science fiction and Greek and Roman mythology. Physics was another favorite class, but she attributes that to the teacher:

> I think 90 percent had to do with the teacher. He was a wonderful teacher. He was probably my favorite teacher. On the other hand, I hated algebra and the teacher was a female. She talked over everybody's head and assumed that everybody knew everything. And here's a woman in a traditionally man's professional field. My physics teacher did a heck of a lot better job at helping people understand how math is relevant. And, you know, it's kind of funny because algebra is so relevant in everything I do today. I work with Excel spreadsheets and all the formulas and everything that you use in there is all based on algebra so I wish I had been able to understand it better in high school.

In high school, Allison said the "in crowd" did not like her. The popular students played sports, and she excelled in vocal music. Allison competed in regional and state contests and received star ratings at the state level for her solos. The year she graduated, the girl's basketball team went to the state tournament. Allison did not like sports: "I hated physical education with a passion. It was the only class I ever got a C in. When I complained, they raised it to a B–." She further explained, "My value system is different from theirs too. The in crowd drank, smoked, and partied all night. I liked to read, study, and sing." Allison recalled one group of girls in her grade who would "talk about you behind your back. If you walked by them, they'd get out of the way. If there was a seat somewhere, they would quick put their books on it so you couldn't sit there. It was over time and consistent. Over time, it really undermines your self-confidence." She concluded that if you were female and did not participate in sports, it was impossible to be accepted or popular.

During the summers of her high school years, Allison worked at a Dairy Way. While she attended community college, she was a waitress in a restaurant in Ricefield during the weekends and summers.

Allison graduated from Ricefield High School in 1983 with fifty-two classmates. She was a member of the National Honor Society and was ranked fourth in her class. After graduating from high school, she attended a two-year community college located thirty-five miles from Ricefield. Allison chose the community college because her few close friends were going there. She explained, "I really considered myself to be quite naïve when I was in high school and it was close to home and my friends were going there. It was comfortable."

Allison completed three associate's of science degrees in three years: legal secretary, word processing specialist, and business management. Since graduation from the community college in 1986, Allison has worked for a prospering technology firm that has its corporate office in Melford. The company has expanded and now does business nationally and internationally. Allison is married, has an infant daughter, and lives in a small, rural community twenty-three miles from the city in which she works and seventy-five miles from her hometown, Ricefield.

Despite Allison's academic success in high school and community college, she has no desire to go back to school for an advanced degree. She explained,

> I really have no desire to go back to school because my experiences in school weren't happy. Maybe it's because in school I always felt like I didn't measure up because I didn't have friends. But academically I was good, and I was proud of that. There were a lot of frustrating times, there were a lot of times that I was made fun of. School means unhappy. I am happy where I'm at. I'm accepted and I enjoy what I am doing. I have a lot of friends, I get along with people, and I am very well respected at work. It's like here I was in high school and I was this ugly duckling; well, now here I am at work, and I'm a swan. And it's

amazing because these people didn't know me when I was in high school and have no preconceived notions of what a nerd I was in high school.

Allison believes that her education did not prepare her to interact with people of different cultures. Allison remembered studying about Native Americans when they studied their state history in fifth and sixth grade. In high school, they spent a little time studying the Civil War and slavery, "but we didn't spend the time on it like I think we should have." Allison recalled that in a class called Current Events, they would read the paper during class and then talk about it: "That was probably the most we ever talked about different cultures and what was currently happening. There really wasn't a lot of experience with people of other cultures."

The one Black student enrolled in school was Allison's third cousin and four years younger. She was adopted and moved to Ricefield when she was eight. "She really had a tough time and was teased a lot," Allison remembered. "She was retained in junior high. That was hard on her. They would call her names in grade school and shun her in high school. But my brother, who was in the same grade after she was retained, was kind to her."

Allison herself felt discriminated against at times because she has very fair skin coloring: "Because of the color of my skin I was picked on a lot, because I have such a fair complexion. They actually called me an albino. And that's why nobody's safe in school. Everybody finds something to pick on about somebody."

Being discriminated against because she grew up in a rural community and graduated from a small high school, however, was never a problem for Allison. She admitted that the reason is probably because she has never been in a situation where the majority of people were not from small towns or rural communities. Most of the students in the nearby community college she attended and most of the employees where she now works are from small towns in the Midwest. And she prefers it that way. Melford is the largest town in which she wants to work, and she plans always to have her home in a rural area.

When Allison attended community college, she remembered that there were Black and Asian students, but she did not have classes with them. She maintained, "They really stuck to themselves. They would gather in their circles and didn't associate outside of their culture." Allison wishes she had taken advantage of the opportunities to learn about other cultures when she was in college:

And now I am working with an international company and find it really enjoyable and refreshing because I do work with someone who came from China or Africa. To help us learn about other countries, once a month we have a luncheon where they bring in speakers about another country. They show a slide show. The only thing that prepared me was my company. They have done a lot to help educate our employees, because most of our employees are from the Midwest and we need to understand the culture of people we interact with. Our company really values diversity.

On the other hand, Allison talked about the influx of migrant workers from Mexico who have made Melford their home. Allison stated, "That's one area where there is a strong prejudice, it is against the migrant workers." There are no Mexican Americans working at her company. The only person of color that she works with is part Philippino, and Allison said, "until somebody else mentioned it, it had never even crossed my mind to wonder what her background was." Most of her work with people of other cultures is through the Internet or telephone.

Through her experiences at work, Allison has come to believe that personal contact makes the biggest difference in understanding people from different cultures. She realizes that this is a difficult task for small rural schools but "maybe the Internet holds the greatest opportunity for them to actually talk to other people from other cultures." Allison also thinks that schools should talk about the current problems of Blacks, Native Americans, and Hispanics, as well as their history. In social studies, she believes, the curriculum should stress the different cultures across the United States as well as global cultures.

Along with the study of other cultures, Allison advocated that students should have the opportunity to take a foreign language. She regrets that when she attended Ricefield High School, foreign language was not offered: "I would have taken German, because I am three fourths German."

Allison argued that ethics and values should be taught in schools: "If there was something that I, as an employer, would look for is someone who has a strong work ethic and is willing to go the extra mile for the team." But she concluded by saying that most students in high school are looking only at the present and at being popular, not what they need to succeed in life.

Allison believes that her high school education adequately prepared her for community college and the workplace. She explained that she always knew she wanted to be in office management and took classes in shorthand, typing, and bookkeeping. Ricefield even had a couple of computers: "Although they are not the computers like I use at work today, the experience helped me not to be afraid of them."

Allison and her husband want a rural experience for their year-old daughter, Tanya. That is one reason they live twenty-three miles from Melford: "There may not be a variety of curricula, but she sure has the opportunities to participate in them, whether it be sports, choir, or band. We did not want our kids to go to school in Melford and have them graduate with a class of 600 people. Not even know her classmates."

George

George is fifty-seven years old. He was born and raised in Ricefield. Because his mother was sixteen and unmarried when he was born, his grandparents adopted and raised him. Although many of the elder residents of Ricefield knew who George's father was, he did not find out until six years ago. He is proud to learn that his father was a graduate of a university and a pilot. George never got to know his father because he was killed in a plane crash.

When he was growing up, George's friends were neighborhood kids. He did not play with farm kids because they rarely came to town. George and his neighborhood friends were poor. He concluded, "There were two classes of kids and I was in the lower class. Our dads were not businessmen. I don't know if they did or not, but we thought they had money. Those were the ones who eventually went off to college."

From the time he was very young, George had a job of one kind or another. One of his first jobs was mowing lawns: "I pulled the lawn mower around with my bike. And then I got an old car and I still mowed lawns because it was a good job and one of the only ones in town." After he got older, George worked for a machine parts store in town.

George's heritage is German, Danish, and Irish. As a boy, he attended the German Lutheran Missouri Synod Church in Ricefield and is a member of the same church today. When he was young, his grandparents were good friends with their minister and they spent many New Year's and sometimes Christmas at the minister's house. George contended that since they spent so much time at the minister's house, "they weren't the wrong-side-of-the-track type of people."

George laughed when he described the "religious discrimination between the Catholics and Lutherans. I dated Catholic girls, but was told by our pastor that we should never get serious with them." His grandparents never said anything directly to him about Catholics, except when John F. Kennedy ran for president in 1960. Despite the fact that they were Democrats, they didn't want to vote for Kennedy because he was Catholic.

Growing up, George did not leave Ricefield: "I never went anyplace until I went into the army reserve. I led a pretty sheltered life, and we still live a sheltered life in Ricefield." The first Black person George saw was at the bus depot in Ricefield when he was quite young. He remembered asking his grandma what kind of person that was but does not remember her answer. Other than that brief introduction, George's first personal relationship with people of color was in the army. George asserted that he never had stereotypes about people of different ethnic or cultural groups. George considers all of his friends who are from different ethnic groups "respected and intelligent individuals."

When George attended elementary and high school, grades one through twelve were in the same building. He admitted that he does not remember much about elementary school but recalled that one of the most exciting events of his elementary school days was his first male teacher, in fifth grade. A high school experience he vividly remembered was when a teacher told him he shouldn't take algebra because he didn't think George was smart enough. "So," recalled George, "I didn't take algebra. And today, I really like math and use it a lot in my work. I hated English and the English teacher was probably the best teacher I had. I really didn't do anything in high school."

George remembered studying about Native Americans and Blacks in history books when the class studied state history and the Civil War. He further explained, "We did not talk about our own culture in school. We were all just Americans."

George was not in band because his family could not afford an instrument. He did participate in baseball and track for a while but admitted that he was a smoker and maintained that at the time "that was more important than sports." Moreover, George justified his decision not to participate in sports because the other "class of kids" was whom he would be competing against in sports, so he did not have a chance of playing.

George was seventeen when he graduated from Ricefield High School in 1960. There were fifty-one in his graduating class. Although his grandparents gave him everything he needed and were great and loving people, they did not encourage him in school: "I wanted to go to college, but there was no push. All I heard was, 'We can't afford to send you to college,' so it was an easy out. Besides, none of my close friends went to college." George explained that it is different with his children. He and his wife have made college an expectation for them, not a choice. "They wanted to go to college when they got out of high school. And two out of three have graduated from college."

After graduating, George immediately moved to Hartland to find a job. Because he was seventeen, the only job he could get was as an errand boy at a hospital supply company. George recalled, "Even in those days it was tough going to the big city to get a job." When he was eighteen, he was promoted to shipping clerk. During that same year, his grandfather had a heart attack, so he moved back to Ricefield and cut meat for a local grocer. Within a year, George moved back to Hartland and was employed in a variety of jobs. Eventually he landed a white-collar job for a hardware chain in Hartland and worked his way up to become the manager of store development. In 1964, George married a high-school friend who worked for a telephone company in Hartland. They had three children and made their home in the suburbs.

In 1976, despite being offered a promotion from his employer, George bought a hardware store in Ricefield and moved his family back to their hometown. There were two reasons for their decision. First, they wanted to raise their kids in a small town. Second, they wanted to escape the suburb in which they lived. George recounted how their suburban area changed: "Our neighborhood started out fantastic. Most of our neighbors were educated people, a pharmacist, and a couple of doctors. We just got along very, very well. But then the city started building low-income housing and with that, *they* came in the neighborhood. People who had different values than we did. They didn't have jobs and their kids ran wild."

Despite some hard times, they have never been sorry about their decision to move back home. Many main street businesses in Ricefield closed in the 1980s because of the poor farm economy and outmigration of the rural community. In 1985, George sold the hardware store and went into the insurance business. Today, George owns a successful insurance investment company that is based in Ricefield.

George clearly indicated that his education in Ricefield did not prepare him for employment. He stated, "No. High school? In Ricefield? NO. I'm sorry it didn't. And it wasn't all the school's fault. It was my attitude, too. Nope. It never prepared me for anything that I can remember, and I'm not saying that to be negative. I'm being honest with you." He went on and explained, "There was nobody there to help you. My grandparents didn't have any education. They worked hard all their life. That's what I was supposed to do. And I guess that the teachers or the school or whoever just felt that that's what George is going to do, just have a job. And that was it, and that's sad." Regardless of his perceived lack of preparation, George believes that he is "one of the most successful of all my classmates, and why? I don't know. I guess I was motivated." Aside from his success, George maintained that he lacks self-esteem "all the time" and still regrets not going to college.

George believes that schools today should have higher expectations because more is demanded of students after they graduate. He also thinks that values such as honesty and responsibility should be taught in school.

On the topic of diversity, George concluded that he was and his children are naïve: "I was very naïve and my children are, but the world is a lot tougher out there today and being naïve today is a real problem. We took our kids to Hartland when they were in high school and they saw other nationalities, the other people, but they never had any real exposure or personal relationships with them." Currently, two of George's children live and work in the suburbs of Hartland, and he worries about their safety: "In my life, if I've learned one lesson, it's that you can't trust most people anymore. And it doesn't make any difference if they are Black, White, or Red." He believes that rural schools should teach survival skills to their students. In other words, "Teach them some common sense to be careful and aware of what's out there."

In his business, George does extensive traveling. He feels sorry for the people in Hartland who have not ventured too far from home. He believes that "they do not know what is going on out there. I'm just glad that I had the opportunity to do that. I think I have the best of all worlds. I can travel the world and see what's going on and then come back to my little shelter."

Ryan

Ryan, George's older son, is thirty-one years old. He was born in Hartland and lived in its suburbs until his family moved to Ricefield when he was seven. Ryan is the oldest of three children and the only one to move back to Ricefield after college. His brother and sister work and live in suburbs of Hartland.

Ryan's mother was born and raised on a farm in Western County. After high school graduation, she attended a technical college thirty-five miles from Ricefield and received an associate arts degree. She worked for a communications company and lived in Hartland from 1963 until 1976 and, after returning to Riceland, helped George run the hardware store until they sold it. Currently, she is employed as a receptionist at the local newspaper.

Ryan and his brother played baseball or football with the kids in a three-block radius of their house. Although the town is only a mile and a half from one end to the other, most of the time they stayed in the neighborhood. Ryan recalled that he would occasionally go out to the country to spend the weekend with a friend and then his friend would come and stay in town with him a few weeks later. He also spent time at his grandma and grandpa's farm.

All of Ryan's classmates were European American. Religion was the extent of diversity in his class. He recalled that besides Lutherans and Catholics, they had two classmates who were Jehovah's Witnesses. The students in his class were curious about why these two students did not say the Pledge of Allegiance, stand for the school song, or celebrate holidays and birthdays, but this issue was never addressed in their classes.

Throughout his elementary and high school years, Ryan had a variety of jobs. He worked in the hardware store for his dad and picked rock and hauled and stacked hay bales for area farmers. From 1985 to 1992, he was employed at the local golf course, where he did ground maintenance and, when he was old enough, was a bartender. Later, he became the assistant superintendent of the golf course. This job helped him pay for college.

Ryan played basketball and football and wrestled in elementary and junior high and was on the cross-country and golf teams in high school. He enjoyed playing golf but joined the cross-country team mainly because his friends were on the team. Ryan believes that people learn discipline by participating in sports. In addition, he thinks that when students are involved in sports, it motivates them to care about their grades. He stated that students in sports "wanted to make sure they were eligible for sports, so they would work in school. Sports also curtails smoking and drinking."

Ryan described himself as "vertically challenged" (as an adult, he is five feet seven inches tall), and in high school he was the target for "a couple of guys who liked to prove they were big boys by picking on the little guy." To compensate for his size, Ryan said he "tried and was successful at being the class clown."

The first time Ryan encountered a Black person was in elementary school. One of the teachers had grandsons who were from Africa. Ryan explained,

> I don't remember what exact country it was, but her daughter married a man over there, and he was a government official. They would come to Ricefield in the summer, and you would just treat them like your friends. We would invite them to go swimming or play football. I mean we didn't leave them out because they had a different skin color. But you always hear stereotypes, and they are always in the back of your mind. I mean there is always a grain there, but it doesn't come out.

Ryan's family went to Hartland a couple of times a year to visit relatives. He pointed out that his cousin's friends, who had never been outside the metropolitan area, had more stereotypes about rural areas than he had about the metropolitan area. For example, they did not believe that Ricefield had cable television, current movies in the local theater, or popular songs on the radio. Ryan laughed as he recalled some of the fabricated "stories" he told about living in the boondocks that his city acquaintances actually believed.

Ryan pointed out that he had the opportunity in college to interact with students from diverse ethnic and cultural groups as well as to learn about stereotypes in his classes. Due to the values instilled in him by his parents, in church, and in school, Ryan concluded, "Just because a person's skin is a certain color does not necessarily mean they will act in a certain way. Everyone is a human being and, basically, you have to treat them with respect."

Ryan's favorite subject was history. When he was in sixth grade, his teacher, Mrs. Matterson, who began her career in a one-room school in Western County, integrated local history into her social studies curriculum. Ryan vividly remembers one experience in her class:

> In sixth grade, I remember we got to take a trip around Lake Andrew. We got to learn about the little towns that were along the lake, all the elevator sites. The shipping traffic was actually on this lake at one time. Right where my cabin is located, a half a mile away, there was a town called Madata. The town was along the river. It was right on top of the hill and overlooked my grandma and grandpa's farm, where my mother grew up. That's neat that a half-mile away from where my mother grew up, years before she was even around, there was a town there. One of the older ladies in the community came along on the trip and told us about where the railroad tracks used to run around the hillside on the east side of Lake Andrew. I look at our lake now and it's eight to ten feet deep and years ago, it was a main shipping lane and

there were grain elevators all the way along. I think those experiences were an integral part in getting me interested in history.

Ryan recounted that they presented a play in the same class about an 1800 train that is in a museum in Drewy. His class went to Drewy and presented the play at the museum right in front of the train.

On the other hand, art and music were Ryan's least favorite subjects. As Ryan adeptly illustrated, "I am artistically challenged! I think both my mom and Mr. Goldson thanked me for quitting trumpet. I could tell I was not going to become the next Doc Severinson."

Going from sixth grade to seventh grade was a big event in the lives of Ryan and his classmates. They moved from the elementary school on one side of town to the high school across town. The images that Ryan as a sixth-grader had concerning high school were "the little kids getting beat on, smoking in the bathrooms." Regardless of the "horror stories," Ryan found the transition to high school easy.

In high school, one of Ryan's favorite classes was biology, because the teacher used a variety of instructional methods. Ryan described him as a teacher who had a "sense of humor, I mean the class was interesting, it wasn't always straight lecture. We might go out to the wildlife area to look for different types of thistle, or dissect starfish or frogs."

Another class Ryan deemed "real life" was accounting. Rather than assigning problems from the textbook, the teacher gave each student a packet, and they had to run their own business. Ryan said, "I remember running a motorcycle shop and that gave accounting some meaning."

Ryan recalled "covering slavery in history courses. We watched old Walter Cronkite *You Were There* movies about how slaves escaped. Then we talked about how those people felt and what type of life they lived." He does not remember talking about any of the current issues of discrimination in high school. Ryan's major cultural event was a trip to Germany with his German class when he was a junior. The teacher arranged the trip and was their guide and chaperone. There were thirty students on the trip, and nine were from Ricefield.

Ryan graduated from Ricefield High School in 1986 in a class of fifty. He attended a university forty-five miles from Ricefield and graduated with a business degree in 1991. After graduation, Ryan moved to Melford, worked in retail for three years, and then moved to another city to work in insurance investment sales. In 1997, he returned to Ricefield and went to work in his father's insurance investment company. Ryan asserted that he "always intended to come back to Ricefield to work with my dad." Ryan is single and enjoys living in Ricefield. His favorite pastime is golf.

Ryan believes that he received a good basic education in Riceland. He advocated that "learning should be more fun, a field trip or actual application. There was monotony from too much straight lecture."

To help students understand diversity, Ryan suggested that we should get students "out from the shadow of the water tower a little bit." Students who grow up in a small town "have got to be aware of other cultures because every town is becoming a little bit more diverse. Even Ricefield has a growing population of Native Americans and Hispanics. That's something I've become more aware of in my line of work. I've worked with people of different ethnic backgrounds and religious backgrounds, and whatever their ethnic background is, I don't care. Their religious values or thought process might be different than mine, but I'm going to work with them."

Ryan believes that by growing up in a rural community and having a class enrollment of 50 rather than 500, you have the opportunity to build many close friendships. Ryan knows that moving back to Ricefield was the right decision for him. He is happy to be back working in his hometown.

Growing Up in a Rural Culture: Benefits, Barriers, and Changes

Growing up in a small community with a distinctive rural culture resulted in benefits and barriers for the participants. This section analyzes three categories of experience resulting from rural culture that emerged from the interviews: social life, diversity, and education. Changes—such as the declining rural economy, advancing technology, and increasingly diverse population—that occurred over the span of two generations are also addressed.

Rural Culture

Although there were individual and cross-generation differences in their lives and school experiences, the four participants expressed many similar beliefs and values. A culture, as defined by researchers (e.g., Ayalon, 1995; Nieto, 1996), includes people who have "a common history, geographic location, language, social class and/or religion" (Nieto, 1996, p. 138). In Chapter 1, Gloria Boutte used the anthropological concept of "fictive kinship" to describe the "kinshiplike connections between and among persons in a society who are not related by blood or marriage, but who have maintained essential reciprocal social, political, or economic relationships." Similarly, Coleman (1987) identified a community where "extended network[s] of kinship, friendship, and work relations pervade . . . a functional community" (p. 182).

Using these criteria, it can be said that Elizabeth, Allison, George, and Ryan grew up in a community with a distinctive culture, a rural culture. Their ancestors were immigrants who lived, worked, and raised their families in Western County for three generations or more. Although Elizabeth was the only participant who grew up on a farm, the livelihood of all the participants' families, the community, and the school depended on successful farmers. In addition, all the participants identified and were familiar with farm life because their relatives, past and present, were farmers. Ryan, for example, illustrated how important his rural roots were when he described how excited he was at discovering that an old town had overlooked his grandpa and grandma's farm, where his mom grew up. He felt a connection to his past generations. They lived and worked in a farming community with a rural culture.

The idea of family and community networks was further delineated by Coleman (1987), who used the term *intergenerational closure* (p. 186) to describe the consistent values and beliefs of an area's residents. Many of the experiences the participants shared illustrate that intergenerational closure and fictive kinship are alive and well in Ricefield. For example, Ryan expressed Coleman's (1987) idea of intergenerational closure when he said, "In a small town, you couldn't get by with anything because it would eventually get back to your parents." Indeed, a distinctive rural culture (e.g., Ayalon, 1995; Oliver & Howley, 1992; Sohn, 1994) in which residents are influenced by their social interactions, economy, religion, and education, and the changes that occur in cultures over time is evident in Ricefield.

Social Life.   One benefit of rural life Elizabeth talked about was the small network of friends and relatives with whom her family socialized. This intimate social group accepted her and gave a strong support system. In her young life, Elizabeth was exposed to very few people who had different values, religious beliefs, or socioeconomic status. Elizabeth did not have the opportunity to spend much time with her classmates who lived in town. She went to school on the bus, and when school was out, she went home on the bus. Elizabeth believed that she was never teased or discriminated against by her classmates because she did not spend much time with them. She reasoned that her children's lives were more complex than hers because they were exposed to a wider diversity of values, beliefs, and people. In addition to a broader view of the world, Allison had more opportunities to become involved with extracurricular activities and to interact with her peers. Elizabeth believed that this led to more discrimination among students in the school.

One example Elizabeth and Allison pointed out was women's sports. In the 1950s, females were minimally involved sports. By the 1980s, sports had grown in participation and popularity for young women. Women athletes were in vogue, and the schools, parents, and communities had a new focus. Although Elizabeth, like her daughter, did not enjoy or excel in sports, Elizabeth did not feel like a "nerd," whereas Allison vividly described being an outcast because she did not fit in with the popular sports crowd.

Another example of the change in social interactions with peers was illustrated when Ryan stated that he was teased about being short, or, in his words, "vertically challenged." Whereas George did not mention that being short was a source of discrimination in school, Ryan did. Ryan did not, however, perceive the teasing to be malicious. He said that after he stood up to the older students who gave him a bad time, they became his "buddies."

Although there are counterexamples, the opportunity to develop close friendships was mentioned by all the participants as a benefit of growing up in a small, rural community. They attributed long-lasting friendships to spending their entire school career with the same classmates. This idea is further clarified by DeYoung and Lawrence (1995), who state, "Ties to community, place, and family are often strong in rural communities, and it is in the local schoolhouse where many of these attachments are formed and solidified" (p. 108). Friendships were solidified even more because many of the participants' friends' parents socialized or went to the same church. The social interactions between the families of their classmates outside of school deepened the connection between friends. The network of family and friends was evident when George came back to Ricefield to open a hardware store. There was a common history between the people in town and George. Older residents knew his grandparents and had seen him grow up; others went to school and church with him. Therefore, they trusted him and became loyal customers in his store. In a like manner, Ryan felt welcome in Ricefield when he returned to work with his father. He believed that renewed and continued friendships are easily ignited when people have a common history.

Although Allison did not view herself as popular, she had a circle of close friends in high school and she chose her postsecondary institution because her friends were going there. Thinking ahead to her daughter's future, Allison wants her to attend a small school so she can build close relationships and have the opportunity to be involved in extracurricular activities.

While the rural culture certainly created benefits and barriers for the participants, its influence did not wholly determine who they are as individuals (Nieto, 1996, p. 41). Genetics, family relationships, individual personalities and emotional differences must be considered when analyzing the participants' social interactions. George, Elizabeth, and Allison talked about a lack of self-confidence and self-esteem, whereas Ryan did not acknowledge any problems with his self-concept. George, on the other hand, was more of a risk-taker than Ryan, Elizabeth, and Allison. He moved farther away from home at the age of seventeen, joined the army reserve, and had a successful career before he came home to start a new business. Ryan and Allison did not stray very far from home, and Allison had, and still has, no desire to go beyond her rural area except to vacation. Yet, Elizabeth regrets that she never left Ricefield and wonders what her life would have been like if she had taken some risks.

Diversity.   Although there has been a slight increase in different religions and family structures (e.g., Jehovah's Witnesses, single parents), the opportunity for the residents of Western County to interact personally with people of diverse ethnic groups has not increased dramatically over the past fifty

years. New technologies and improved transportation has provided opportunities for its residents to increase their knowledge of and interaction with
diverse populations, but the fact remains that Western County is still geographically isolated.

Throughout their childhoods, the participants rarely left Ricefield. One
would think that because there were better highways in the 1980s than in
the 1950s and because many families had more than one car in the 1980s
travel would be common. This, however, was not true. Travel outside of
Ricefield was minimal for all four participants until they graduated from
high school. Currently, George travels nationally and internationally for
work and pleasure and Ryan has just begun to travel with his father. Elizabeth's and Allison's travel outside their immediate area remains infrequent.

While growing up in Ricefield, George and Elizabeth's travel outside of
Ricefield was minimal, and there were very few people of color living in
Ricefield. Consequently, George and Elizabeth did not interact with people
from diverse cultures or ethnic groups until after high school. The most diversity they experienced was the religious debate between Lutherans and
Catholics. During Allison's and Ryan's school careers, diversity consisted of
one student who was Black and students of the Jehovah's Witnesses faith.
Although they both met people of color in college, accepting and understanding people with diverse cultures and ethnic groups remain illusive.
Close interactions and/or friendships with people of different ethnic groups
are not a reality for the participants.

Despite having an Indian Reservation only thirty miles away, none of
the participants had any direct interaction with the Native American population in school or in the community. In fact, any mention of Native Americans was absent from their interviews until they were specifically asked.
Elizabeth mentioned that she currently has to interact with Native Americans
in both her jobs, and George talked about a man who is Native American who
had lived in a foster home in Ricefield. At the time, George did not consider
him different because he was "just like the rest of us." Elizabeth and Ryan
did not have any recollection of any Native Americans in school or the community while they were attending Ricefield schools. Ryan and Allison, however, did recall studying about Native Americans in elementary school, but
not necessarily the tribe that was just down the road from Ricefield.

Children, like the participants of this study, who grow up in functional
communities with intergenerational closure and no ethnic and minimal cultural diversity may be sheltered to the extent that they are not prepared to
participate in the larger society. Without a variety of experiences with other
cultural and ethnic groups, many individuals who grow up in a rural culture are "less tolerant toward civil liberties, sexual nonconformity, religious
and political nonconformity, support of minority office-seekers, and racial
and ethnic groups than urban dwellers" (Ayalon, 1995, p. 3). Furthermore,
Ayalon (1995) argued that, "The isolation of rural schools, as well as their

resistance to outside influences, tends to limit students' opportunities to be prepared for the workplace and to become participating citizens in a democratic society. Without knowledge of and sensitivity to people from such cultures, workers may find that their racial prejudices and stereotyping are aggravated and the effectiveness of their efforts decreased" (p. 4).

Although Elizabeth appears to be sensitive to people's feelings and is aware of diversity issues, she admitted that she does not feel comfortable with the diverse populations she encounters at work. She is glad that she does not have to interact at a deeper level with them because she does not have knowledge of their culture. Allison explained that, in her present job, she interacts with clients from different countries and she learns about their country and culture through sessions at work. Although Allison stated that her company values diversity and that some of its clients may be from different countries, most of her colleagues at work are from the surrounding midwestern rural areas. It is interesting to note that despite her employer's claim to value diversity, it has not hired any migrant workers who have made Melford their home. George and Ryan have minimal interaction with people of color in their business.

According to Allport's (1979) "principle of last effort," stereotypes and the categories humans construct will be maintained unless information is presented that contradicts stereotypes. Throughout the participants' school experiences, they did not have a curriculum that included multicultural education and they have had, and still have, minimal interaction with people of color. Although all the participants expressed that they are not prejudiced, there are many indications that they are at Helms's (1992) contact stage of racial identity (see Table 7.1). A rural community with minimal diversity does not provide its residents the opportunity to "walk the walk." Ayalon (1995) advocated that rural schools have the responsibility to implement multicultural education approaches to help eradicate stereotypes.

Education.   Elizabeth, Allison, and Ryan believed that they received an adequate education for their time and place. Elizabeth said she had a "barebone" education. She learned to read, write, and do math, but regrets not learning more about diversity. Allison wanted to study a foreign language, but one was not offered when she was in high school. Ryan had no complaints about his education. In contrast, George does not believe that he received a good education. He blames himself for not trying, school personnel for not having high expectations for students of lower socioeconomic status, and his grandparents for not encouraging him. The participants indicated that they had some effective teachers and some ineffective teachers.

The participants' memories of their school experiences parallel those of a study completed by Herzog and Pittman (1995). The benefits of rural schools were tied to the idea of a small school where everyone knew everyone else in their class by name and the teachers knew them and their fam-

TABLE 7.1   *White Racial Identity Development Model*

Contact Stage
- Own racial group membership insignificant
- Unaware of privileges of being White

Disintegration Stage
- Recognizes the effect of racism
- Experiences discomfort
- Responses: (1) denial and/or (2) feelings of guilt and desire to act

Reintegration State
- Accepts racism but places blame and burden of change on people of color
- Relieves guilt and responsibility to work for social change

Pseudo-Independent State
- "Blame the victim" lessons
- Desire to unlearn one's own racism and begin creating positive definition of Whiteness
- Takes action: (1) develops friendships with people with similar beliefs; (2) develops relationships with people of color

Immersion/Emersion
- Intensifies efforts to create positive self-definition of Whiteness
- Seeks White role models
- Guilt and shame lessens and are replaced with pride and excitement

Autonomy Stage
- New definition of Whiteness internalized
- Expands focus to other "isms" (forms of discrimination)

Source: Black and White racial identity: Theory, research, and practice, J. E. Helms. Copyright © 1992 by Greenwood Press. Reproduced with permission of Greenwood Publishing Group Inc., Westport, CT.

ilies. There was a sense of family and community by which people cared about each other and there was a tie between the school and the community. People felt comfortable and somewhat protected.

On the other hand, like the participants in this study, Herzog and Pittman's (1995) participants also had criticisms of their rural education. One student in their study felt the same way George did (thirty years earlier) about being from a poor family. The student commented, "It was hard to get into college-prep classes if you were poor, because there was only one counselor, and she figured if you were poor, you were automatically a loser" (p. 118). Others believed that their school's SAT scores were not as high as schools in the metropolitan areas because they did not have the opportunity to take higher math and science courses. Despite the adversities in their lives, many individuals from rural schools, like George, end up leading very successful, productive lives. They overcame the adversities they encountered. Like the two people in Chapter 8, these individuals are called "resilient." Research on resiliency (e.g., Brooks, 1994; Garmezy, 1985; Rutter, 1987; Werner, 1993) found that personality factors, characteristics of the family, bonding with a caregiver, and their social environment play a role in helping children to be resilient. In addition, communities in which neighbors and community and religious leaders are supportive were found to produce children who are more resilient (Weinreb, 1997). Small, rural "functional communities" (Coleman, 1987) have many of the characteristics that help people become resilient.

It is interesting to consider that many of the students in Herzog and Pittman's (1995) study, like the participants in this study, chose to return to their hometown or a rural community to live, work, and raise a family: "They are saying that there is true value in relationships, that community is an anchor, that peace and safety lie within their rural communities. They are also telling us that their schools had good qualities but could have been better" (p. 118).

Recommendations for Change.   Based on their experiences and beliefs, Elizabeth, Allison, George, and Ryan made some recommendations that they believed would help improve the quality of education in rural schools. The recommendations were in response to their own perceived readiness for postsecondary education and/or employment.

All four stated that the curriculum should include the study of different cultural and ethnic groups. Whereas they studied the history of ethnic groups when they were in school, the participants concurred that the curriculum should be augmented with discussions and activities concerning current problems of people of color and diversity in their own rural area.

George, Elizabeth, and Allison contended that values and ethics should be part of the curriculum. Allison believes that employers are looking for people with a strong work ethic. She does not see values stressed enough in schools. The faculty, administration, and staff should model and promote values and ethics, and they should permeate the school's ethos. Elizabeth promoted the idea of teaching values by involving parents in their children's education.

The participants advocated for their own personal issues. Teachers should make learning "more fun," and it should relate to more real life situations, Ryan declared. George advocated teachers having higher expectations for all students, not just the students who might go on to college. In addition, he believed that full-time counselors are a necessity and that skills should be taught so young people from rural areas can survive in the big city. Allison pointed out that foreign languages should be offered and that there should be programs for gifted and talented students. Elizabeth suggested that the arts and sciences should be as much—or more of—a priority as sports. Elizabeth and Allison mentioned that the community and parents should be more involved in their children's education.

Change

Change is inevitable, and Erickson (1990) reminded us that cultures, too, are fluid, not static. They evolve "as people respond to new conditions and influences" (Ramsey, 1998, p. 59). Elizabeth was correct when she said her children grew up in a more complex and diverse world. The world had changed and so, too, had the culture of Ricefield. The changes that occurred in Ricefield between the 1950s and the 1990s makes it one of the "functional rural communities that is an endangered species" (Miller, 1993, p. 92). There were numerous reasons for these changes: the declining rural economy during the 1980s, advancing technology, and increasing diversity, among others.

First, the poor rural economy in the 1980s resulted in family farms going out of business, small town stores closing, and talented youth leaving their hometowns. The participants in this study were personally affected by the poor economy. During the 1980s, Allison's father closed his men's clothing store and George sold his hardware store. Currently, although both men maintain offices in Ricefield, their jobs take them outside the region. Other rural residents commute long distances to jobs in larger towns. Another kind of exodus occurred when the stores that supply the town with necessities closed and residents were forced to travel outside their community to shop. When people go outside the community for employment and services, "the community loosens the bonds that traditionally tie people together" (Miller, 1993, p. 90).

Despite the decline in the rural economy in the 1980s, there was a difference in how the generations felt about their socioeconomic status. Elizabeth said that as a child she didn't feel poor because everyone in her world had about the same things and lived the same way. It wasn't until her country school consolidated and she went to school in town that she realized she did not have as much as other children. George, on the other hand, perceived himself as poor. He talked about classmates who had all the material advantages as well as status in the community and school. George did not participate in sports because he did not believe he had a chance against the wealthy sports "stars" and future college students. Elizabeth and George believed they could not go to college because they did not have the financial resources. Elizabeth never considered it an option, and George's grandparents told him that they could not afford it.

Allison and Ryan did not believe that they were poor. Allison recalled being told many times when she asked for things that they couldn't afford it, but still considered her family middle class. Ryan felt more fortunate than most of his classmates because he had what he needed or wanted. They were never told that they could not go to college because they did not have the money. Their parents expected their children to go to some type of post-secondary institution. Payne (1998) reminded us that poverty is relative: "If everyone around you has similar circumstances, the notion of poverty and wealth is vague. Poverty or wealth only exists in relationship to known quantities or expectations" (p. 10).

A second change was the advent of information technology such as television and computers. Although Elizabeth and George grew up without television and computers, Elizabeth viewed the absence of television as positive. She said that without television, she did not know she was poor because she did not worry about what she had or did not have. A generation later, Allison and Ryan were aware of what was happening in the state, nation, and world because they had access to televisions and they had the advantage of being a part of the new computer age. Modern technologies eliminated some of the geographic isolation barriers that occurred for Elizabeth and George.

Miller (1993) pointed out that in the past, communication in rural areas was inward, but with new technologies, the focus has become outward. Rural parents can no longer insulate their children from diverse values and beliefs presented to them on television and, more recently, on their computers. Rural communities are "straddling two worlds" (p. 92). Whether one perceives technology as progress or intrusion, it has changed rural culture in many ways.

Technology has also changed the family farm. Garkovich, Beokemeier, and Foote (1995) reminded us that "new technologies, new and more complicated machines, chemicals, hybrid seeds, bioengineered seeds, and super-productive livestock are the defining characteristics of today's farms" (p. 15). Consequently, farmers have to have more education to understand the new technologies. New technologies equal more efficient, larger farms and fewer farmers. Larger corporate farms are producing more, in less time, and in a world market. Many times the headquarters of corporate farms are in urban areas, not in rural communities. These factors resulted in a decline in agricultural jobs in rural areas. To ease the economic strain, small communities hired economic developers to find industries such as food processing and manufacturing plants to move to the area. Many of the jobs in these industries are labor intensive, unskilled, and low paying. Often, new immigrants move to the rural areas to seek employment in these industries (Dinsmore & Hess, 1999; Morton, 1997).

In Ricefield, however, the industries that moved into town provided jobs for local people who lost their businesses or farms or for young people who wanted to stay in their hometown and work rather than move to a larger city. The increase in new ethnic groups remained minimal, but there was a change in the family structure. High divorce rates brought many single mothers back to Ricefield. They wanted a safe rural community and the support of their parents to help raise their children. Welfare families also moved to rural communities, like Ricefield, in search of affordable housing and established jobs.

Although Ricefield's population remains primarily White, the changes that have occurred in technology, economy, and demographics have moved them farther away from a functional community with intergenerational closure. What implications do these changes have for rural education?

Implications and Recommendations for Educators

What kind of education is appropriate for children in rural communities whose populations remain basically European American? If rural America is seen as "old-fashioned" and "underdeveloped," does it follow that appropriate educational outcomes for rural students include becoming sophisticated and more civilized? Are their needs the same as children in urban communities or other ethnically homogeneous communities (e.g., Native American, Mexican American) who also live in low socioeconomic status, high unemployment rate, geographically isolated areas? What do leading rural educational researchers, practitioners, and rural residents recommend for effective curriculum and instruction for rural students?

One of the premises of rural education is that it should prepare students "to *escape* their local community in order to pursue 'careers' wherever they may exist" (DeYoung & Lawrence, 1995, p. 107). Rural young people become "exports" of rural communities. Educators at all levels of schooling promote the idea that rural life is not as fulfilling as metropolitan life. Stereotypes of rural people perpetuate this image. DeYoung and Lawrence (1995) referred to the Hollywood film *Hoosiers* to illustrate the point that rural young people are educated to believe that in order to have successful careers, they must leave their rural area.

The most prevalent dilemma for young people who graduate from rural schools is choosing between ties to their close-knit community, family, close relationships, and place and the seduction of the big city, employment, and economic gain. Donaldson (1986) investigated the quandary young people in rural communities face. He identified three patterns of development in young adults living in a rural community: *traditional, modern-achieving,* and *questioning.* The young people he identified as traditional had limited experiences outside their town and planned to stay there. The modern-achieving youth perceived their rural community as restricting and wanted to leave town for financial gain. The questioning group had more experiences outside the community than the other two groups and valued the intergenerational support and benefits gained by living in a rural community. The questioners left their rural area for education and/or employment, experienced life in a metropolitan area, and then chose to return to live and work near family and friends. By experiencing both worlds, the questioners understood the advantages and disadvantages of both and attempted to integrate the two worlds.

Of all the participants in this study, George would be considered a questioning individual. He left Ricefield to find employment and financial gain, but rather than rejecting rural life, he returned to his hometown to raise his family in a small, supportive community with similar values and beliefs. He is an entrepreneur who believes he has achieved "the best of both worlds." He does not accept an unchanging community; he wants to see progress in Ricefield.

Like George, Allison and Ryan left Ricefield after high school. Rather than seek employment in a metropolitan area, however, they attended small higher education institutions within forty-five miles of Ricefield. After graduation, they sought employment in Melford, only ninety miles from home. Allison and Ryan stated that they planned to return to a rural community, and they did. After marriage, Allison returned to a rural area twenty-three miles from Melford because she and her husband wanted to raise their family in a small, close-knit community that has values similar to the ones she grew up with. Ryan, somewhat a questioner, always planned to return to Ricefield to join his father's business. He does not yet have a family, but he believes there is an advantage to living in a small, rural community where people get upset if you do not wave to them as you pass them on the roadway. His statement that students in Ricefield should "get out from underneath the water tower for a while" illustrates that he is on his way to becoming a questioner like his father. Due to the fact that Elizabeth never had the opportunity to experience life outside her rural community, I would categorize her as traditional. Elizabeth's life focuses on her friends, relatives, volunteer work for church functions, a Homemakers Club, and two part-time jobs.

Miller (1993) used Donaldson's framework to suggest "that the best chance for the survival of small, rural communities lies in a greater percentage of rural youth shifting into the *questioning* group. This would require a changing focus for rural schools and the assumption of greater responsibility in community affairs" (p. 93). Using Miller's (1993) and Donaldson's (1986) ideas as a springboard, I propose that a rural multicultural educational model is an appropriate choice for rural schools in primarily homogeneously white communities such as Ricefield.

At first glance, multicultural education in rural schools in sparsely populated, homogeneous European American communities seem an oxymoron. The goals for multicultural education, however, parallel many of the goals rural educational researchers advocate. First, a multicultural education (Sleeter & Grant, 1988) is an appropriate rural school model because students in rural communities and schools experience issues and concerns similar to those of other nonmainstreamed populations. These problems include inappropriate curriculum, inequality in school funding, high unemployment, low socioeconomic status, low self-esteem, geographic and social isolation, and a distinct culture (Ayalon 1995; Bell & Sigsworth, 1987; Herzog & Pittman, 1995; Oliver & Howley, 1992; Sohn, 1994; Spears, Oliver, & Maes, 1990).

Second, classroom experiences in any ethnically homogeneous school and community, whether it is European American, African American, Mexican American, Native American, or Asian American, have to compensate for the geographical and social isolation of the community's children. Ramsey (1987), when recounting her own European American educational experience, contended that her attendance at "good" public schools left her with stereotypes, with a narrowness of perspective, and unprepared for living in the "real world": "Rather than expanding my knowledge beyond my immediate experience, my school experiences had instead reinforced a narrow and Anglo-American perspective" (p. ix). Educational programs that exclude inclusiveness in their curriculum leave dominant-culture children ill-equipped to live effectively with diversity (Jones & Derman-Sparks, 1992). Jones and Derman-Sparks (1992) concluded, "We live in a diverse society in a multicultural world; not to understand and value diversity is to short change oneself and others" (p. 12).

Finally, education that is multicultural is more than a curriculum, it is a philosophy that permeates "the school climate, physical environment, curriculum, and relationships among teachers, students, and community" (Nieto, 1996, p. 313). It is effective pedagogy for all students.

However, the idea that rural education should be identical to urban multicultural education "imposes inappropriate urban models on rural institutions and denies or ignores responsibility for the health and welfare of rural residents" (Haas, 1992, p. 9). Optimally, multicultural education is a philosophy that has multiple perspectives for implementation in diverse settings. What would multicultural education look like in a rural school setting?

Rural Education That Is Multicultural

Three components are imperative in a multicultural rural educational model if its graduates are to become questioning, critical, empowered citizens of the United States no matter where they choose to live as adults. The first component is curriculum and instruction that is contextualized and based on critical pedagogy. The second component is teachers who understand the needs of rural communities and are grounded in the theories and practices of contextualized and critical pedagogical teaching and learning. Finally, the community and school must break down the walls that separate them. They must work together and become committed to an optimal education for their students.

Curriculum and Instruction

Rural education that is multicultural must have curriculum content that is relevant to and begins with the community. But, it cannot stop there. Whatever the topic, it must venture beyond the limited experiences of the students in the community. It is imperative that they have the opportunity to look at content from a variety of perspectives.

Contextualized.   Curriculum and instruction for rural school students must be contextualized. It should reflect the integrity of the relationships to the natural and human environments that constitute local cultures, economy, and meanings. By making the curriculum relevant to the lives of its students, the school is validating the community and saying, "This is a good place to live." Bell and Sigsworth (1987) recounted the importance of using the community in rural curriculum and instruction:

> The purpose of basing the curriculum substantially in the things and the people pupils are familiar with is not to persuade them to remain when their schooling is over, within their community of origin, any more than it is to persuade them that the good life will be found elsewhere. It . . . should . . . enable them to recognize that they have a choice, and thereby, to make an "informed" decision about whether to stay or to go. What it should provide them with is an understanding of the nature of community, an understanding which they can put to use wherever they choose to spend the rest of their lives. (p. 268)

One way to include the community in schools is to use the local place as a focus of study. Whether the community has dairy farms, cattle ranches, or grain farms, students can learn that "a careful study of one's own habitat reveals truths about the entire planet" (Haas & Nachtigal, 1998, p. 2). Students from kindergarten to twelfth grade can also study local places of business—such as seed stores, implement dealers, grain elevators, highway departments, and government offices—to see firsthand how local farms and businesses rely on one another. Other main street businesses—such as newspaper offices, grocery stores, or banks—may also become part of their curriculum. In turn, the people in the community become resources for the schools. By seeing and talking firsthand with the people who are stewards of the community, the students will be actively engaged in meaningful, authentic learning and gain an appreciation of their place. In turn, the community will increase its awareness of its young people (Howley & Eckman, 1997). Sometimes the most effective learning experiences we can provide our children are right in our backyard!

A Comprehensive School Reform Demonstration Program that began in rural America and incorporates these relationships among teachers, learners, the curriculum, and community is Foxfire. This approach to the curriculum has its roots in John Dewey's child-centered, experience-based theory of teaching and learning. Foxfire includes "a truckload of practical wisdom about how to make classrooms work well; a philosophy about learning and about the intrinsic relationship between schools, communities, and individuals; faith in the teaching profession and what it can accomplish; and a stubborn willingness to take risks, to look continually for more meaningful learning opportunities, and to trust in students' natural abilities" (Howley & Eckman, 1997, p. 50). Foxfire is only one example of programs that make connections between schools and their environment.

Critical Pedagogy. A problem that may occur in a completely contextualized curriculum is that its focus may be too inward. In other words, it may give students only one perspective of the world. Many times, it is the omissions in content that lead to prejudice, stereotypes, and misinformation. Pearse (1989) suggested, "It is the lack of positive images, the lack of discussion, and the lack of multiethnic perspectives, which need to be redressed" (p. 273). To counteract this potential problem, the curriculum must include a critical perspective so that students learn that there are multiple views on topics. For example, discussions with farmers about the pros and cons of using chemicals, international trade, and hybrid seeds include many ethical and environmental issues to debate. Attendance at public meetings can help students hear multiple sides of an issue; they may articulate options and learn mediation and group-process skills (Haas & Nachtigal, 1998).

Paulo Freire (1970) called this type of education education for liberation. A liberated education includes critical pedagogy that looks beyond one's own perspective. Critical pedagogy includes curriculum content that promotes numerous readings including different perspectives on a topic and instruction in which students are expected to ask questions, take risks, and take actions rather than passively accept what the teacher or the readings state. If your rural community is near an Indian Reservation, that tribe should be part of your school's curriculum. Students should visit each other's schools, read literature with different perspectives, and discuss uncomfortable issues. Nieto (1996) said, "Critical pedagogy is also an exploder of myths. It helps to expose and demystify as well as demythologize some of the truths that we take for granted and to analyze them critically and carefully" (p. 318). Gay (1995) suggested that critical pedagogy and multicultural education are "mirror images." In short, critical pedagogy is an approach that "acknowledges rather than suppresses cultural and linguistic diversity" (Nieto, 1996, p. 317).

Critical pedagogy can be used at all levels of education. Louise Derman-Sparks and the Anti-Bias Curriculum Task Force (1989) demonstrated how very young children are able to participate in discussions about diversity issues. An appropriate strategy to use with all age levels is literature. Very young children can read two or three versions of a book written by different authors and illustrated by different artists and compare them. The story of the three little pigs from the perspective of the wolf or fairy tales told by different cultures are appropriate activities to use with many age levels. Older students should read literature written by people of different ethnic groups and cultures. For example, after a visit to an Indian Reservation, students should read books authored by Native Americans on their view of Thanksgiving or the westward movement to help students understand a different perspective on issues. In colleges, liberal arts courses and teacher education programs must use critical pedagogy in their curriculum and instruction for preservice and inservice teachers. For it is only when teachers use critical pedagogy in their own lives that they can help their students view issues from multiple perspectives.

In summary, rural education should include contextualized curriculum and instruction that begins with the students' own experiences and perspectives. The next step is to make sure the curriculum includes "multiple and contradictory perspectives to understand reality more fully" (Nieto, 1996, p. 317). It is critical pedagogy that moves students beyond the boundaries of their limited world and prepares them to succeed wherever they choose to live.

Teachers

Classroom teachers implement curriculum and instruction. For rural schools to deliver an education to their students that is contextualized and includes critical pedagogy, the teachers have to be educated in the theories behind the approaches and learn how to take them from theory into classroom practice. Second, the teachers must take courses in rural sociology and rural school teaching, complete field placements in rural settings, and understand how to teach multiage levels (Miller, 1988).

One of the problems in rural schools is the ethnicity and culture of its teachers and future teachers. A study completed by the American Association of Colleges for Teacher Education from 1987 to 1994 found "seventy-six percent of the students were female, 91 percent were White, and nearly half spoke no language other than English. But even more to the point, more than 75 percent of them attended college within 100 miles of their hometowns and said they wanted to return to their suburban or rural small towns to teach" (Johnston, 1996, p. 26). Although, "home grown teachers help preserve local values and lifestyles . . . they worry that a teaching force made up largely of people who don't venture out of their home states—for training or jobs—has led to parochialism in K–12 education. . . . These teachers may lack the broad perspectives they need to serve a student population that becomes more diverse by the year" (Johnston, 1996, p. 25). "Many of the teachers in rural schools have only lived in rural White areas and have had little contact with or understanding of urban ways of living and the culture of people of color" (Ayalon, 1995, p. 4). These facts also relate to communities that have minimal ethnic and cultural diversity.

Although many teacher education institutions now include some multicultural education component in their programs, there are numerous problems. First, not all state legislation ensures that multicultural experiences occur. Second, the preparation in multicultural education varies in extent and quality (Dinsmore & Hess, 1999). And third, teachers in all-White or rural districts still do not believe they need to include multiculturalism or critical pedagogy in their curriculum. In a study that included all fifty states, Mitchell (1985) found that personnel from rural, all-White districts did not believe multicultural education programs were necessary for their schools. Marxen and Rudney (1999) found similar results in their study of first- and second-year teachers. They interviewed their teacher education graduates, who had completed field experiences in diverse settings as part of their multicultural component and were now teaching in rural communities. The teachers who were teaching in a rural setting with little or no diversity did not view multicultural education as a curricular priority. Pearse (1989) also found "an absence of personal motivation and sense of urgency" as the reason teachers did not teach with a multicultural perspective. Whether teaching in an all-White European American school or one with increasing diversity, teachers need multicultural education in their teacher education program.

The second component needed for teachers teaching in rural schools is an understanding of and experiences in rural cultures. A rural education component in teacher education programs is rare. "A survey of teacher preparation programs in twenty-seven rural states suggested that only ten percent of the 208 public and private institutions responding offered a preservice program to prepare rural teachers" (Jones, in DeYoung, 1991, p. 426). Rural schools, whether they are culturally or ethnically diverse or not, need teachers whose preservice education has prepared them to understand rural culture in addition to critical pedagogy.

The geographic isolation of many rural communities makes delivery of professional development to their teachers more difficult. Rural teachers have fewer opportunities to attend classes, conferences, and workshops then their colleagues in suburban and urban settings. Even in states where there are regional educational cooperatives, many teachers have to travel long distances to attend professional development activities. Furthermore, in larger districts, reading, mathematics, and science specialists provide professional development and mentoring for their teachers on new curricula and instructional strategies. In rural schools, teachers who are interested in subject area or new instructional strategy "volunteer" to help other teachers on their own time without pay. Or the task might be given to an already overworked principal/curriculum coordinator/community education director.

In summary, teacher education programs and professional development for rural teachers should include the theory and practice of contextualized curriculum and instruction and critical pedagogy, closely supervised experiences in diverse (rural, urban, and suburban) settings, courses in rural sociology, and education in multiage classrooms. In the process, teachers must come to realize that the curriculum begins with culture and to recognize that all learners interact with culture and construct knowledge based on their cultural experiences, biases, needs, and desires. In rural schools, learning situations or curriculum must begin with the students' rural culture in meaningful ways and then go further to look at issues with multiple perspectives. Teachers must not use their own "culture as a yardstick for other people's behaviors" (Fuller, 1994, p. 275).

Committed Communities

In a small rural town, the school and community are an intricate part of one another. Miller (1993) noted that besides providing the community's children with an education, the schools serve as a gathering place for social activities such as sports and plays. Economically, the local school system is one of the largest employers in a small community, and the school's budget is affected by local economic conditions (Howley & Eckman, 1997; Miller, 1993). Another point to consider is that small towns pay more for the education of their children but do not get as much return on their investment because the best and brightest leave their rural communities, never to return. In order to survive, schools and communities must collaborate on services from "general education to lifelong learning, from daycare programs to meals for the elderly, and from vocational training to small business development" (Miller, 1993, p. 97).

Miller (1993) described three categories in which schools and communities can collaborate both to improve the students' education and to meet the needs of the community: school-based economic development programs, school as a community center, and the school's curriculum focus on the community.

In school-based economic development programs, students complete a needs assessment of the community, propose a plan to the school and community, and set up and operate the business. Sher (1977) was one of the first people to advocate that rural schools serve as a center for economic development. Rural Entrepreneurship through Action Learning (REAL) was the organization that emerged from his idea. Examples of successful entrepreneurial collaborative school and community programs in the Midwest include managing a grocery store, a lumber yard, and an ice cream shop. On the West Coast, students gather information on water quality and fish life. Haas and Nachtigal (1998, p. 16) advocated that "rural schools should teach how to create jobs, not just how to get jobs working for someone else. Entrepreneurship education is vital to the survival of rural communities and can be offered as a community service to all citizens."

A second collaborative venture is using the school as a community center. Adult and lifelong education, delivering meals to the elderly and shut-ins, before- and after-school child care, and providing transportation for the elderly and handicapped are examples of how schools can reach out to their community and provide some much-needed services.

Miller's third category is using the community in the school's curriculum. As mentioned above, when curriculum is contextualized, it relates directly to the students' lives and is much more meaningful. The results are better education for rural students. Students learn to apply the basics and that their actions can make a difference. These three approaches can build a network between the school and the community and in the process make students aware of the "value of place, quality of environment, one's history as a member of a community, and, perhaps most importantly, a sense of belonging and affiliation among caring friends, neighbors, and relatives. It may be that this psychological sense of community provides the foundation upon which successful community development efforts are built; not the other way around" (Miller, 1993, p. 100).

Summary

When I think of a small, rural town, I think of people living in harmony with nature and other humans. People who care about each other and the land that they inhabit. Humans and nature not only in their town, but also across the nation and our planet, for we are intricately linked. Rural schools must strive to become better at educating their best and brightest to return to their hometowns to become the questioners and entrepreneurs. Rural schools must educate individuals who understand how the issues and concerns of the global world affect all of us. Rural schools must educate students to look at issues from multiple perspectives. I want my great-grandchildren to know what it is like to grow up in a small, rural town where, as an anonymous person wrote,

- You don't use your turn signal because everyone knows where you are going.
- Third Street is on the edge of town.
- The biggest business in town sells farm machinery.
- You can't walk for exercise, because every car that passes you offers you a ride.
- The pickups on mainstreet outnumber the cars three to one.
- You drive into the ditch five miles out of town and word gets back to town before you do.

And best of all

- Someone asks how you feel, and then really listens to what you say.

Editor's Commentary

As I began reading Carol's chapter, the first thing that came to my "unconscious" mind was "wholesome." Carol's lifestyle in rural, White America evoked images from Little House on the Prairie *and other images that I had digested during my childhood. I allowed my mind to reflect on other contexts that are no less "wholesome," even though they are different from the typical images that we see. Immediately, I thought of Vivian's hometown and childhood, complete with a wealth of home and community support and love. Then, in turn, I thought about aspects of all of the other chapters in this book. I revised my connotation of "wholesome" and made it broader. I concluded that in order to appreciate a diversity of lifestyles, concerted efforts must continuously be made to delete old mindsets. I am able to appreciate each context presented in this book in its own right and beauty.*

In each chapter, individuals have faced a variety of challenges. Although this chapter is set in the Midwest, where stereotypes about "perfect" lives abound, the people in this chapter faced their own unique set of challenges. For example, Carol's and Elizabeth's lives changed dramatically when they had to leave their one-room schoolhouse to go to a larger school. Major changes in schooling (such as consolidation or integration) are often done for efficiency while little serious thought is given to children's emotional and social well-being. Although Carol and Elizabeth made the necessary adaptations and seemingly turned out okay, they (as well as the other children) may have benefited from a chance to have a more gradual transition to the new setting.

This chapter stresses the importance of education that is multicultural for Whites. Many people erroneously believe that multicultural education is only for children of color (Boutte, 1999). However, as Carol notes in this chapter, nothing could be further from the truth. In fact, predominantly White settings may benefit from multicultural education more than will children enrolled in diverse schools who have opportunities to interact cross-racially with other students and, consequently, to question commonly held stereotypes and misconceptions about other ethnic groups. Also, going to school in a racially homogeneous setting increases the likelihood of developing ethnocentric beliefs because the familiar may be unquestioningly viewed as the norm.

People of color do not have a monopoly on addressing injustices. As Carol aptly noted, fighting all forms of discrimination is a challenge for all humans—not just for people of color. I hold a high degree of respect for Whites who have historically fought against racism in this country. They have fought for the rights of Native Americans, African Americans, Asian Americans, and Latino Americans. But, most important, they have fought for the rights of humanity. Whites who have had the courage to fight against racism have done so even though faced with tremendous sacrifices and public ridicule. They have resisted privileges for themselves in order to extend civil rights to all.

I think of the Whites who fought against slavery and who helped Blacks escape via the underground railroad. In contemporary times, White teachers such as like Vivian Paley, who addressed issues of race, class, and gender in her preschool and kindergarten classrooms, have gained my admiration. I also admire teachers such as the one featured in the classic video, The Eye of the Storm, *who lived in a predominantly white town in Iowa and was so incensed by the assassination of Dr. Martin Luther King, Jr., that she taught her White elementary school students what discrimination feels like. She staged a demonstration in her own classroom using the color of the children's eyes (blue or brown) as a basis for doling out or denying privileges. (The video is available from the Center for Humanities, Communications Park, Box 1000, Mt. Kisco, NY 10549, or the nearest public library).*

I also think of friends of mine such as Susan (one of this book's authors) and Sheryl and Jane (also an author of one of the chapters) and Susi and Louise. I think of the many Whites whose faces I don't know, but who have actively fought against discrimination and oppression. I think of White writers such as Peter McLaren, Jonathan Kozol, Herbert Kohl, William Ayers, Peggy McIntosh, Gary Howard, Christine Sleeter—and the list goes on and on, including critical theorists too numerous to mention. And now, I will also think of Carol, the author of this chapter, whose commitment to diversity is obvious. As noted by Freire (1970), fighting against oppression (an inherent act of violence) is an act of love. I am encouraged by this thought.

Within-race discrimination on the basis of geographic location, religion, or class is obvious in this chapter. Elizabeth pointed out that religious diversity was the only type that she experienced, "basically Catholics against Protestants." I'm struck by the word against. While Elizabeth's comment reflects the mood of the time and her experiences, it is also a powerful commentary on how we tend to view differences in adversarial and dichotomous terms. Given this stance, it is understandable why some students in my diversity classes resist and exclaim, "None of this (referring to a course on diversity) will make a difference. It's human nature. If people aren't divided by race, they'll be divided by class, gender, sexual preference, or some other issue." But as Freire (1970) and Ghandi (as cited in Fischer, 1962) note, when we give up on fighting for the human right of all individuals to be treated humanely, we also give up on humanity.

In this chapter, Allison laments that traditional holidays cannot be celebrated in schools today. (This is a common misconception, but elaboration of this point is beyond the scope of this commentary. The reader may refer to Derman-Sparks and the Anti-Bias Curriculum Task Force (1989) or Boutte (1999) for a more complete discussion about celebrating holidays in school.) But I questioned, for whom are the holidays a tradition? Using traditional in this context implies that Christian and/or White holidays are the norm (which makes everything else abnormal). Among the approximately 240 nations in the world, the United States is among the few dedicated to the ideal that various cultures can and should live together on an equal basis in the same society (the vast majority of free nations are built for and by specific ethnic groups—e.g., Japan, Bosnia, Rwanda) (Haberman, 1996). Given the tremendous amount of diversity in cultural backgrounds in this country, the traditions of citizens vary widely.

Examining what it feels like to be excluded, Allison eloquently explains how not being part of the "in crowd" undermines one's confidence. As we saw in Chapter 3, on African American males, being smart took on a negative connotation for Allison, who was labeled a "nerd." Her memories of school are overshadowed by unpleasant memories of being excluded. While some think that educators should focus only on academics, nothing could be further from the truth because academics and social welfare are interrelated. For shy children such as Allison, teachers should be particularly alert to their exclusion and try to help them find their niches.

Allison prefers to live in a small town. Many Americans tend not to venture far from their hometowns. The ethnocentric foci of schools and communities may influence this tendency. Most Americans do poorly on world geography in comparison to other countries. School curricula in the United States typically focus on the history and geography of their respective states, and to a lesser degree, on U.S. history and geography.

In my classes for potential or practicing teachers, I ask them to label the names of states in the United States on a blank map without referencing a completed map. Most do poorly—to their own dismay. Then I give them a completed map and ask them to color their maps using any color scheme they wish. Many choose the following scheme: places I've been, places I don't want to go, and places I'd like to go. Overwhelmingly I've found that most of the students have gone only to one or two neighboring states (some to none other than their own). One of the most alarming discoveries for me was that most students consistently (over the years) and strongly expressed that they had NO DESIRE to venture to more than three fourths of the United States—not to mention other countries. Most troubling was the fact that many of the students in my course are currently teaching or will be teaching in the near future. While I recognize my bias that the world should be seen, I question whether messages children get from their teachers limit their perspectives about unfamiliar people—and places! When the students in my class and I reflect on what it means that three fourths of this country and most of the world are unappealing to them, many attribute it to poor coverage of geography in school—particularly world geography. I should admit that geography is also one of my weakest subjects. I am impressed by people from other countries who know not only world geography, but U.S. geography as well. I am told by many of them that U.S. news (on television and in the newspaper) focuses primarily on the United States (versus world events). In most other countries, international news plays a central role, whereas, in the United States, world news is often limited to the last five minutes of the news broadcast. What does all of this mean when we think about appreciating diversity?

I think it means that unfamiliar people become "those people" and unfamiliar places become "over there somewhere." John Steinbeck's (1939/1992) The Grapes of Wrath *captures the essence of this phenomenon. In this novel, thousands of desperate, "decent" families who were run off their land in Oklahoma during the Great Depression traveled westward to California in hope of a better life. They were labeled "dumb Okies" by Californians and Arizonans even though all of them are White and poor. In one part of the story, a deputy sheriff describes the "Okies":*

> *"Sure, they talk the same language, but they ain't the same. Look how they live. Think any of us folks'd live like that? Hell no!" (p. 303)*

Failing to see humanity as one, and to see the beauty of our differences, allows people to effortlessly pit one group against the other (the "divide and conquer" mentality mentioned in the previous chapter). The words of the deputy sheriff in the Grapes of Wrath *illuminate this point:*

> *"Got to keep 'em in line or Christ only knows what they'll do! Why, Jesus, they're as dangerous as niggers in the South! If they ever get together there ain't nothin' that'll stop 'em." (p. 304)*

The sheriff buffers his hatred with religious references. In this chapter, George's pastor warns him that it is okay to date Catholic girls as long as he never gets serious with them. And although George speaks respectfully of people who are culturally and ethnically different than he, traces of the pastor's indoctrination can be detected when he moved because "THEY (people from low socioeconomic statuses with different values) were moving in." The deputy sheriff and George's pastor are right about one thing: if different groups ever get together, oppressive power structures can be overthrown. Hence, a built-in, self-sustaining device of oppression is to keep groups divided (Freire, 1970; Martinez, 1997).

Although the United States professes a growing commitment to cultural egalitarianism, we consistently oversimplify and misunderstand rural culture (Kirkendall, 1995). My students from the southeast often complain that they are labeled by northerners as dumb because of their southern accents. As the opening scenario in this chapter demonstrates, stereotypes about rural America abound. When I was a child in my small, rural town, our yearning to be perceived as urbane meant being called "country" was the ultimate insult. We'd admonish, "You so country!" or "Girl, he looked country!" Kirkendall (1995), in a commentary in Newsweek, contemplates America's feelings about rural life:

> America is ambivalent when it comes to claiming its rural heritage. We may fantasize about Thomas Jefferson's agrarian vision, but there is no mistaking that ours is an increasingly urban culture. Despite their disdain for farm life—with its manure-caked boots, long hours and inherent financial difficulties—urbanites rush to imitate a sanitized version of this lifestyle. And the individuals who sell this rendition understand that the customer wants to experience hillbillyness without the embarrassment of being mistaken for one. Through it all, we Ozarkians remind ourselves how fortunate we are to live in a region admired for its blue springs, rolling hills, and geological wonders. In spite of the stereotypes, most of us are not uneducated. Nor are we stupid. We are not white supremacists and we rarely marry our cousins. Our reasons for living in the hills are as complex and diverse as our population. We have a unique sense of community, strong family ties, a beautiful environment, and a quiet place for retirement. (p. 22)

Kirkendall (1995) echoes Carol's closing points that public schools in rural areas can and do prepare students to be contributors to this society and to the world. She notes that rural school systems produce successful farmers, doctors, business professionals, educators, and others. "Country folk" appreciate country music, but also like jazz, blues, classical, rock and roll, and a large variety of music. The resounding conclusion is that, in a diverse society, we must allow people to live and let live. People have the right to choose how to live, but they do not have the right to impose their choices on others.

While students in my classes are offended by the derogatory comments made about southerners, they seldom reflect on similar comments made about northerners by southerners. I remind students that they should be intolerant of racial or other epithets because their own cultural group could easily be inserted. Education that is multicultural allows students to view alternative possibilities and make choices appropriate for themselves. In the final analysis, lifestyles that are "acceptable" can range from urban, to suburban, to "out in the boondocks."

Reflective Activity ———————————————————————

At the beginning of my commentary, I noted that "wholesome" came to mind when I first read Carol's story. Write down five images or words that come to mind when you hear *rural*. Analyze these in terms of negative or positive stereotypes. How do they interfere with your understanding of the diversity that exists among rural Americans?

Resources ———————————————————————

Periodicals

Journal of Research in Rural Education
Journal of Rural Studies
The Rural Educator
Foxfire Journal for Teachers
Rural Conditions and Trends

Books

Berry, W. (1996). *The unsettling of America: Culture and agriculture* (3rd ed.). San Francisco: Sierra Club Books.
Davidson, O. G. (1996). *Broken heartland: The rise of America's rural ghetto.* Iowa City: University of Iowa Press.
Gruchow, P. (1995). *Grass roots: The universe of home.* Minneapolis: Milkweed Editions.
Haas, T., & Nachtigal, P. (1998). *Place value: An educators guide to good literature on rural lifeways, environments, and purposes of education.* Charleston, WV: Clearinghouse on Rural Education and Small Schools.
Howley, C. B., & Eckman, J. M. (1997). *Sustainable small schools: A handbook for rural communities.* Charleston, WV: ERIC Clearinghouse on Rural Education and Small Schools.
Orr, D. W. (1994). *Earth in mind: On education, environment and the human prospect.* Washington, DC: Island Press.
Peshkin, A. (1978). *Growing up American: Schooling and the survival of community.* Chicago: University of Chicago Press.
Stull, D., Broadway, M. J., & Griffith, D. (Eds.). (1995). *Any way you cut it: Meat processing and small town America (rural America).* Lawrence: University Press of Kansas.
Theobald, P. (1997). *Teaching the commons: Place, pride and the renewal of community.* Boulder, CO: Westview.
Wigginton, E. (1985). *Sometimes a shining moment: The foxfire experience (Twenty years teaching in a high school classroom).* Garden City, NY: Anchor Books.

Articles

Chu, N. L. (1993). A review of children's literature about farming and rural life. *Rural Educator, 15,* 11–15.

Internet Resources

The National Rural Education Association: http://www.ColoState.EDU/Orgs/NREA.
Organizations Concerned About Rural Education (OCRE): http://www.ruralschools.org.

ERIC Clearinghouse on Rural Education and Small Schools: http://www.ael.org/eric/.
Pulling Together: R&D Resources for Rural Schools: http://org/eric/pulling/.
Especially for Rural/Small School Superintendents: http://www.aasa.org/frontburner/rural/
    rural.htm.
Center for the Study of Small Rural Schools: http://tel.occe.uoknor.edu/cssrs.html.

Rural Literature

Young Children (Ages Three through Eight)

Anderson, J. (1997). *The American family farm.* New York: Harcourt Brace Jovanovich.
Andrews, J. (1990). *The auction.* New York: Macmillan.
Arnosky, Jim. (1996). *Nearer nature.* New York: Lothrop, Lee & Shepard.
Garkovich, L., Bokemeier, J. L., & Foote, B. (1995). *Harvest of hope: Family farming/farming
    families.* Lexington, Kentucky: University Press of Kentucky.
Gibbons, G. (1990). *Farming.* New York: Holiday House.
Hamilton, V. (1992). *Drylongso.* New York: Henry Holt.
Kalman, B. D. (1997). *Hooray for dairy farming.* New York: Crabtree.
Logsdon, G. (1995). *The contrary farmer.* New York: Chelsea Green.
McGugan, J. (1994). *Josepha: A prairie boy's story.* San Francisco: Chronicle.
MacLachlan, P. (1994). *All the places to love.* New York: Harper Collins.
McPhail, David. (1992). *Farm boy's year.* New York: Macmillan.
Mills, P. (1993). *Until the cows come home.* New York: North-South.
Mitchell, B. (1993). *Down buttermilk land.* New York: Lothrop, Lee & Shepard.
Morris, L. L. (1991). *Morning milking.* Saxonville, MA: Picture Book Studios.
Peterson, C. (1996). *Harvest year.* Honesdale, PA: Boyds Mills.
Pringle, L. P., & Garrison, B. (1998). *One room school.* Honesdale, PA: Boyds Mills.
Siebert, D. (1989). *Heartland.* New York: Thomas Y. Crowell.
Turner, A. (1993). *Apple valley year.* New York: Macmillan.
Weidt, M., Sorenson, H. (1995). *Daddy played music for the cows.* New York: Lothrop, Lee &
    Shepard.
Williams, S. A. (1992). *Working cotton.* New York: Harcourt Brace Jovanovich.

Children and Adolescents (Ages Nine through Sixteen)

Bauer, J. (1992). *Squashed.* New York: Delacorte.
Bial, R. (1999). *One-room school.* New York: Houghton Mifflin.
Bridgers, S. E. (1979). *All together now.* New York: Knopf.
Brooks, M. (1992). *Two moons in August.* Boston: Little Brown.
Carter, A. R. (1989). *Up country.* New York: Scholastic.
Cooney, C. (1991). *The party's over.* New York: Scholastic.
Fox, P. (1986). *The moonlight man.* New York: Bradbury.
Garden, N. (1986). *Peace O river.* New York: Farrar, Strauss, Giroux.
Green, B. (1991). *The drowning of Stephan Jones.* New York: Bantam.
Grove, V. (1993). *Rimwalkers.* New York: G. P. Putnam's Sons.
Hall, L. (1986). *The solitary.* New York: Scribner.
Hall, L. (1990). *Halsey's pride.* New York: Scribner.
Howard, E. (1993). *The tower room.* New York: Atheneum.
Joosee, B. M. (1989). *Pieces of the picture.* New York: Lippincott.
Kalman, B. D. (1994). *A one-room school (historic communities).* New York: Crabtree.
Kerr, M. E. (1985). *I stay near you.* New York: Harper and Row.
Kerr, M. E. (1993). *Longer.* New York: Harper Collins.
Lowry, L. (1977). *A summer to die.* New York: Bantam.
Paterson, K. (1977). *Bridge to Terabithia.* New York: Crowell.
Paulson, G. (1991). *The monument.* New York: Delacorte.

Peck, R. N. (1978). *Soup & me*. New York: Knopf.
Plummer, L. (1991). *My name is Sus5an Smith. The 5 is silent*. New York: Delacorte.
Qualey, M. (1993). *Revolutions of the heart*. Boston: Houghton Mifflin.
Rylant, C. (1992). *Missing May*. New York: Orchard.
Scopperton, S. (1978). *Happy endings are all alike*. New York: Harper & Row.
Taylor, M. (1976). *Roll of thunder, hear my cry*. New York: Dial.
Voight, C. (1982). *Dicey's song*. New York: Atheneum.

References

Allport, G. W. (1979). *The nature of prejudice*. Reading, MA: Addison-Wesley.

Ayalon, A. (1995). Does multicultural education belong in rural white America? *Rural Educator 16*(3), 1–6.

Bell, A., & Sigsworth, A. (1987). Education and community development: What can the school do? In A. Bell & A. Sigsworth, *The small rural primary school* (pp. 250–277). Bristol, PA: Falmer.

Boutte, G. (1999). *Multicultural education: Raising consciousness*. Atlanta: Wadsworth.

Brooks, R. B. (1994). Children at risk: Fostering resilience and hope. *American Journal of Orthopsychiatry 64*(40), 545–553.

Coleman, J. S. (1987). The relations between school and social structure. In M. Hallinan (Ed.), *The social organization of schools: New conceptualizations of the learning process* (pp. 177–204). New York: Plenum.

Derman-Sparks, L., & the Anti-Bias Curriculum Task Force. (1989). *Anti-bias curriculum: Tools for empowering young children*. Washington, DC: National Association for the Education of Young Children.

DeYoung, A. J. (Ed.). (1991). *Rural education: Issues and practice*. New York: Garland.

DeYoung, A. J., & Lawrence, B. K. (1995). On Hoosiers, Yankees, and mountaineers. *Phi Delta Kappan, 77*(2), 104–112.

Dinsmore, J. A., & Hess, R. S. (1999). Preparing teachers for diversity in rural America. *Rural Educator, 20*(3), 19–24.

Donaldson, G. A. (1986). Do you need to leave home to grow up? The rural adolescent's dilemma. *Research in Rural Education, 3*(3), 121–125.

Effland, A. B. W., & Butler, M. A. (1997). Fewer immigrants settle in nonmetro areas and most fare less well than metro immigrants. *Rural Conditions and Trends, 8*(2), 60–65.

Erickson, F. (1990). Culture, politics and educational practice. *Educational Foundations, 4*(2), 21–45.

Fischer, L. (1962). *The essential Ghandi: An anthology of his writings on his life, work and ideas*. New York: Vantage.

Flora, C. B., & Christenson, J. A. (Eds.). (1991). *Rural policies for the 1990s*. Boulder, CO: Westview.

Freire, P. (1970). *Pedagogy of the oppressed*. New York: Continuum.

Fuller, M. L. (1994). The monocultural graduate in the multicultural environment: A challenge for teacher educators. *Journal of Teacher Education, 45*(4), 269–277.

Garkovich, L., Beokemeier, J. L., & Foote, B. (1995). *Harvest of hope: Family farming/farming families*. Lexington, Kentucky: University Press of Kentucky.

Garmezy, N. (1985). Stress resistant children: The search for protective factors. In F. E. Stevenson (Ed.), *Recent research in developmental psychopathology* (pp. 213–33). New York: Elsevier.

Gay, G. (1995). Mirror images on common issues: Parallels between multicultural education and critical pedagogy. In C. E. Sleeter & P. L. McLaren (Eds.), *Multicultural Education, Critical Pedagogy, and the Politics of Difference* (pp. 155–159). Albany: State University of New York Press.

Haas, T. (1991). Why reform doesn't apply. In Alan DeYoung (Ed.), *Rural education: Issues and practice* (pp. 413–446). New York: Garland.

Haas, T. (1992). Leaving home: Circumstances afflicting rural America during the last decade and their impact on public education. *Peabody Journal of Education, 67*(4), 7–28.

Haas, T., & Nachtigal, P. (1998). *Place value.* Charleston, WV: ERIC Clearinghouse on Rural Education and Small Schools.

Haberman, M. J. (1996). In L. Kaplan & R. A. Edelfelt (Eds.), *Teachers for the new millennium: Aligning teacher development, national goals, and high standards for all students* (pp. 110–131). Thousand Oaks, CA: Corwin.

Helms, J. E. (1992). *Black and White racial identity: Theory, research, and practice.* Westport, CT: Greenwood Press.

Herzog, M. J. R., & Pittman, R. B. (1995). Home, family and community: Ingredients in the rural education equation. *Phi Delta Kappan, 77*(2), 113–118.

Howley, C. B., & Eckman, J. M. (1997). *Sustainable small schools: A handbook for rural communities.* Charleston, WV: ERIC Clearinghouse on Rural Education and Small Schools.

Huang, G. G. (1999, January). Socio-demographic changes: Promises and problems for rural education. *Clearinghouse on Rural Education and Small Schools* (ERIC Digest: EDO-RC-98-7).

Johnston, R. C. (1996, September 18). There's no place like home. *Education Week,* pp. 25–29.

Jones, E., & Derman-Sparks, L. (1992, January). Meeting the challenge of diversity. *Young Children,* pp. 12–18.

Kirkendall, R. T. (1995, November 27). Who's a hillbilly? *Newsweek,* p. 22.

Martinez, E. (1997). Unite and overcome! *Teaching Tolerance, 6* (1), 11–15.

Marxen, C. E., & Rudney, G. L. (1999). An urban field experience for rural preservice teachers: "I'm not afraid—should I be?" *Teacher Education Quarterly, 26*(1), 61–73.

Miller, B. A. (1988). *Teacher preparation for rural schools.* Portland, OR: Northwest Educational Laboratory.

Miller, B. A. (1993). Rural distress and survival: The school and the importance of "community." *Journal of Research in Rural Education, 9*(2), 84–103.

Mitchell, B. (1985). Multicultural education: A viable component of American education? *Educational Research Quarterly, 9,* 7–11.

Morton, C. (1997). The understanding of local context in teacher education. *Rural Educator, 19*(1), 1–6.

Nieto, S. (1996). *Affirming diversity.* New York: Longman.

Oliver, J. P., & Howley, C. (1992, August). Charting new maps: Multicultural education in rural schools. *ERIC Clearinghouse on Rural Education and Small Schools,* Document No. ED 348 196.

Payne, R. K. (1998). *A framework for understanding poverty.* Baytown, TX: RFT.

Pearse, S. (1989). Addressing race and gender in rural primary schools using two case studies. *Gender and Education, 1*(3), 273–287.

Phelps, M. S., & Prock, G. A. (1991). Equality of educational opportunity in rural America. In Alan DeYoung (Ed.), *Rural education: Issues and practice* (pp. 269–312). New York: Garland.

Ramsey, P. (1987). *Teaching and learning in a diverse world: Multicultural education for young children.* New York: Teachers College.

Ramsey, P. (1998). *Teaching and learning in a diverse world: Multicultural education for young children* (2nd ed.). New York: Teachers College.

Rutter, M. (1987). Psychosocial resilience and protective mechanisms. *American Journal of Orthopsychiatry, 57,* 316–331.

Sher, J. (1977). School-based community development corporations: A new strategy for education and development in rural America. In J. Sher (Ed.), *Education in rural America* (pp. 291–305). Boulder, CO: Westview.

Sleeter, C., & Grant, C. (1988). *Making choices for multicultural education: Five approaches to race, class, and gender.* Columbus, OH: Merrill.

Sohn, K. K. (1994). Rural Whites: A part of multiculturalism? *ERIC Clearinghouse on Rural Education and Small Schools,* Document No. ED 384 064.

Spears, J. D., Oliver, J. P., & Maes, S. C. (1990, July). *Accommodating change and diversity: Multicultual practices in rural schools.* Manhattan, KS: The Rural Clearinghouse for Lifelong Education and Development. (ED 326 262).

Steinbeck, J. (1939/1992). *The grapes of wrath.* New York: Penguin.

Weinreb, L. L. (1997). Be a resiliency mentor: You may be a lifesaver for a high risk child. *Young Children, 54*(2), 14–19.

Weisman, J. (1990, October 10). Rural America is quietly "hurting," educators warn. *Education Week,* pp. 10.

Werner, E. E. (1993). Risk, resilience, and recovery: Perspectives from the Kauai longitudinal study. *Development and Psychopathology 9*(4), 503–515.

Hidden Lives

Examining the Lives of Resilient European American Children

Susan G. Hendley

Editor's Overview

In this chapter, we travel through the author's hidden life in an upper-middle-income family. On the surface, everything looks fine. She lives in a "nice" house in a "nice" neighborhood. Her mother stays at home, her father is a pharmacist, and they even employ a maid. Beneath the surface, however, there is much pain that interferes with Susan's success in school. She wants someone to notice, but no one does. At home, the family "walks on eggshells" if Dad is around. He abuses pharmaceutical drugs, has extramarital affairs and a separate life outside their family, is verbally abusive to his wife, and ignores and rejects his two daughters. His tyrannical behavior shadows everything for Susan, but after her parents finally divorce and Susan and her mother move to another state, Susan emerges triumphant and whole after much reflection and makes peace with the situation.

We also meet Tom, who comes from an upper-lower-income family and also lives in terror—primarily of his mother. Although Susan is unable to feel safe at home or at school, Tom satisfies his need for safety at school—away from his mother. His school life is mediocre until he meets a teacher who "intoxicated" him with his words. Later in Tom's life, he engages in self-destructive behaviors such as excessive drinking. He finally recovers and is a professor today.

Susan's Story

It's hard to figure out where to start, so I'll start at the beginning. My first memories of formal schooling are of me not being able to separate from my mother in the first grade. After driving me to school, she would have to leave me screaming in the principal's office because, according to my mother, I had to go to school. Apparently, I got the nickname Wiggle-Worm because I tried to get away from the principal so I could go home with my mother. Luckily, the principal, Mr. Collier, was a loving man, so he patiently tried to calm me down so I could compose myself and go to class. I eventually made it to class without running out the door, but I only stayed there because I had to stay there, and much of the time I was there only physically. My mind was far away and definitely not on school. It seemed to twirl around. I was totally unfocused, wanting to be home because I was afraid and fraught with anxiety.

Today, I guess that feeling or experience would be called free-floating anxiety. At times, I even felt displaced for a minute or two, which caused me to panic and feel removed from reality. Whatever it was, it was terrible. Sometimes before leaving for school, I would throw up, and my stomach bothered me while I was at school. I had lots of stomachaches.

However, there were also times at school when things went well. The good times were usually associated with unacademic things like drawing or coloring and smelling the purple mimeographed ditto sheets or the scent of a fresh new book. I also enjoyed reading some of the time, but mostly I longed for the days of kindergarten (the previous year). While in kindergarten, I could get lost in a fantasy world of make-believe (in the dramatic play area) or spend time at my second-favorite place—which was the woodworking area or corner. We had an actual workbench equipped with a vice, hammer, nails, and wood. I also liked the big concrete tunnels on the kindergarten playground. The best part of kindergarten was my teacher. She was wonderful! I remember going back to see her when I was older and her telling me she'd never forget the pictures I used to draw. She said I always drew pictures of women with big bosoms. She was a warm and nurturing woman who appreciated the value of play. I loved dressing up in pretty costumes and playing with my friends. Besides my hair falling in the toilet and getting peed on by my distant cousin, Bradley Finkle, kindergarten was by far my favorite year of school. I could get lost and forget. Although I loved school during my kindergarten year because it was an escape from home, I also loved being with my mom, and she was home. The only problem was that my father was sometimes there too in the mornings.

My father wasn't home very often, but when he was there, it was tense and unhappy. My mother always had a very disgusted or disappointed look on her face when she was around my father. Whenever my father wasn't around, there were smiles and laughter and, best of all, we spent a lot of time at my maternal grandparents' house. They lived on the other side of town. I loved being able to spend the night there on the weekends because my first cousin, Mary, lived with them and we were best friends. We slept upstairs and it was quiet and calm. When I woke up the next morning, it was always peaceful. I could at least use my grandparents' home as a temporary place to escape. It seemed far away from my home. I loved seeing my grandparents get along with one another. It was obvious they were in love. They enjoyed life to the fullest, and my grandmother always had a big, beautiful, smile on her face. She radiated joy when she interacted with people. They both enjoyed socializing, too, so they had parties and family gatherings at their house.

At my house, there was unhappiness and yelling by my father—a lot late at night—because he kept very strange hours and wasn't home much during the time we were awake. He also left fairly early in the morning. My father was a miserable person who was given the gift of physical attractiveness. He was consumed with himself and trying to impress others (outside the family) at the risk of whatever it took.

I lived at 4318 St. Regis Lane, a middle-class subdivision full of families with lots of children. Our neighborhood had a large Catholic population and was located very close to one of the parochial schools. There were also several Jewish families (including us) in our neighborhood. My days usually consisted of playing with my neighborhood friends outside or playing at each other's houses. We played school a lot, hopscotch, jump rope, rode bikes, and we played at a local farm often. All we'd have to do is cross the fence at the end of our street and we could explore the farm all day if we wanted to. It was a child's dream to be free to wander safely and discover the wonders of the outdoors. There were creeks with running water that bubbled and interesting plants like milkweeds. Sometimes we'd see horses and there was always evidence of cows because cow pies were all over the place. This was the place we could play all year long. When it snowed, we would go sledding because there were great hills to slide down.

My mother and my friends' mothers did not work as I was growing up. They didn't all stay at home all day either, though. My mom had a maid who came every day so she had the freedom to do as she pleased—to be with her friends, to go out to lunch, shop, or chauffeur us around. My mother was usually at home when I returned from school. I went to the same elementary school through grade six. The school was brand new the year I started. When I adjusted to school as best as I could, I either walked to school or rode my bike. I eventually realized that I had to go to school whether I made myself sick or not.

There were two children in my family, an older sister and myself. My sister, Cathy, was the "smart one" and was artistically inclined, too.

I had three different teachers in the first grade. My mom still says to this day that I never got a good foundation in math. My first grade teacher that I remember was Mrs. Blackwell. She was really friendly and nice but she was transferred out of town early in the year. The next teacher that came got pregnant and had to leave, too. I don't really remember much about the third teacher.

The children I went to school with were from mainly middle-class homes and a few children were from low-income families. Most of the children were from my neighborhood or very close to it. Therefore, I knew many of them quite well. Some of them even went to Sunday school with me at Brith Shalom Temple.

At my elementary school, children were ability grouped only for reading. Other than that, everyone was in the same book at the same time. Feedback from teachers came in many forms. Many of my teachers used stickers that were theme related in a seasonal/holiday fashion. I loved receiving these stickers. Silver and gold foil stars were also used, as well as stamps with messages such as "Good Work," "Try Harder." Teachers used pencils that were half blue and half red to grade our papers. None of us wanted a paper returned with red marks. One of my teachers had a piece of poster board with miniature-sized books made from pieces of folded construction paper. Every time you read a book she would glue a miniature-sized book on the poster board. Little things like this were so reinforcing.

My sister taught me to read before the first grade, so I was probably in the average reading group. I don't remember my group but the "blue bird" group was the best. I read well but comprehending was a different story. I never focused on what was going on in school because most of the time I was thinking about other things or worrying. On the surface, I appeared fine. I was a very well-cared-for child. My long, curly hair was always combed and brushed and I wore pretty hair ribbons or headbands that my mother made that matched my outfits perfectly. Buying clothes was something my mom had some control over; therefore, my sister and I always looked good on the outside. If you could have sliced me open, my scars would probably have been visible because I was miserable inside and everything had to stay there hidden. My mother was a very private person. Dirty laundry was not aired and divorce was rarely heard of in "nice" Jewish families like mine. I guess we appeared fairly normal to outsiders in that my mom stayed home, we had pets, and I went to dancing school once I could separate from my mom, and we were members of the Temple. I was a Brownie and later a Girl Scout, but I didn't stick with it.

My first-grade year mainly entailed going through transitions and learning to stay at school. I eventually learned to stay all day at school until toward the end of first grade, when my mom says I decided I had gone long enough and I wasn't going any longer. However, as a child, I always sensed something terrible in the air at my home. I didn't know how to process this or had no clear idea what I was sensing, feeling, or seeing. Although my mother concealed their relationship problems, my parents did not laugh or have a sense of humor. I never saw love and affection between my parents or had the pleasure of experiencing a light, happy side at home. I think all of these factors made me cling to my mother and resist going to school. So the refusal to go to school and the struggle to separate from my mom started all over again. I did make it through first grade, and the only thing I remember hearing about was that I didn't comprehend well (I received C's in comprehension). They also thought I might have a hearing problem because when I went through the hearing screening I didn't follow directions. I was referred for further testing. It was determined that I had just not understood the directions when I was tested at school.

Writing was stressed a great deal and I liked watching the teachers draw straight lines with the chalk holder. The sound still echoes in my ears as I think about it. The teachers' writing was so perfect, too. The highlight at the end of the day was getting to wash the chalkboards and clean the erasers.

Most of my elementary school experiences are somewhat fuzzy. It seemed more of the same as the years went on. I was a well-cared-for, pretty little girl, and the teachers liked me. I basically did what I was told to do and I never wanted to do anything wrong. I guess I was somewhat fearful. I wasn't an outgoing child, and I could have been considered to be a little withdrawn from adults. Other children sometimes called me "teacher's pet," which bothered me at times, but most of the time I enjoyed the feeling that at least the teachers thought I was special in some way. I had all female teachers and liked the way they smelled.

My favorite subject was art. I was artistically inclined, too, in more of a technical way, but my sister was much more creative. She could draw free-hand, whereas I could copy anything I saw except faces or animals. I guess I loved art because I was successful at it. I remember my mother even let my sister and me take art lessons after school from an art teacher once. I thought that was exciting.

I also took Hawaiian dancing lessons from a Hawaiian woman who offered lessons after school when I was in the third grade (I think), which I really loved. She taught us about the culture and I still remember how much I hated the taste of "poi." We even got our picture in the newspaper, which resulted in my first awareness of societal ills. At that time, they put your name and address under your picture; therefore, people could look up your name and address in the phone book and call you. Unfortunately, someone who had just gotten released from a mental institution called all of the girls' homes in the picture and started talking vulgar to us once we picked up the phone. I was called early in the morning before going to school. My mom thought it was odd that a man called and asked to speak to me, so she stayed by me. He started asking me vulgar questions and I quickly told my mother and we hung up the telephone. I had never heard any of those words before. The police decided that they were going to tap our phones so they could try to locate this person. We were escorted at school going to and from the playground until this person was found. They did find him and to this day I don't know what ever happened to him. It was my first introduction to knowing there were some things to fear in society. Things like this rarely happened in our safe, little community.

While I performed okay in reading, I didn't do well in math. I remember struggling through my homework and being embarrassed about letting on in class that I didn't understand various math concepts. I wouldn't take the risk to ask questions because I was afraid I wouldn't be able to answer the teacher. I do remember thinking and knowing other kids in my class were catching on to math concepts and I wasn't. However, I'd always pass. I made average grades and thought that a C was pretty good. I hated having to go to the board to work problems—especially if we were having a math relay.

Everything we learned in school came from a textbook. I remember the teachers teaching health, but we didn't spend a lot of time on history, geography, or science. The curriculum was workbook-driven and mimeographed sheets or dittos filled up a lot of our day. We did get to do reports sometimes that were related to science. I remember most of my teachers reading aloud to us after lunch. Sometimes they would make us lay our heads down on the desk whether we were tired or not. Everyone always did the same thing, the same way, at the same time. The teachers were taught one way to teach and I guess they believed all children learned alike, so the material was taught the same way. Material was presented the same regardless of your particular learning style or level. The schedule of the day was followed closely and I don't remember many "teachable moments." I do remember that the school had at least one self-contained special class for the "retarded children," but the window on the door to that classroom was covered with paper. The regular education students rarely saw these children unless they were going to or from class. There were no special area teachers until the junior high years. We had recess, and that's where we could participate in PE types of games. I liked playing kickball and jump rope the most. I hated when it rained though, because we'd have to play games that kept us in our seats. I was bored by seat games like 7-up.

My mother went to college for a year and a half, and my father was a pharmacist. He owned a drugstore downtown until urban renewal came through the Louisville, Kentucky, downtown area and started tearing down buildings to rebuild areas. My dad then went to work for other drugstores and hospitals. He was very goal-oriented and wanted to be successful. He also had the need to feel important, and he would do things for others to look like a "big shot." He would give free samples of medicine to many people in the neighborhood, get tickets from drug representatives for his patrons, or give gifts to the people that came in to the drugstore. He strove to be the best, and, again, he wanted to be successful regardless of the costs involved. He worked seven days a week and was rarely around.

In the seventh grade, one of my closest friends, Debbie, didn't realize I had a father until she asked her mom if I had a father. My mom functioned like a single parent. She kept everything going. She made all the decisions and carried out all responsibilities by herself. My father was not involved in our daily lives. He didn't show any outward affection to my mother, my sister, or myself. I felt rejected and often wondered why he behaved in this manner. He was never at evening meals, including the weekends, and he never joined us for meals at either of my grandparents' homes unless it was a Jewish holiday. My parents never went out with each other on the weekends either. They had totally separate lives. Their relationship seemed dead. So while we had the appearance of a "normal" home, our lives were far from normal.

What I mostly remember about my father is that he was impatient and that he had a bad temper. He was self-absorbed, sarcastic, and he was a workaholic. He also seemed emotionally weak and vulnerable. He exercised a lot, to keep fit, and was always worried about having something terribly wrong with his health. One of his dreams was to go to Rio de Janeiro and the other was to get an appointment at the Mayo Clinic in Minnesota. The behaviors he exhibited were odd. He didn't want anyone interfering or talking if he was listening to the news on the radio, which was usually most of the time he was home. He was totally helpless. He wanted my mom or my sister and me to wait on him to bring him whatever he wanted or needed. He kept his white shirts folded and pressed from the cleaners, and lined up in his drawer, and if he thought someone had opened his drawers and moved them he would become irate. "Has someone been in my drawer?" he would ask. He couldn't stand the smell of onions and would not allow my mom to buy or use them. At times, he would say that he smelled onions and accuse my mother of disobeying his orders. He came from an Orthodox Jewish home and kept Kosher when growing up, but we did not keep Kosher and we belonged to a Reform Jewish congregation. However, he liked to eat bacon but would not allow my mother to buy ham because it wasn't Kosher.

My mother had to live by my father's set of rules. He took forever to get himself ready to go to work. He was extremely vain. A lot of the time, he'd take extra clothes with him and a small suitcase. It wasn't until I got older that I realized he had a hidden, separate life from us. I guess my mom thought they were clothes he planned to change into after exercising because he also went to the YMCA sometimes to exercise.

We think my dad began abusing drugs or at least began showing signs of emotional problems when my sister was around four and a half and I was a baby. When I was five or six, I remember hearing my mom trying to convince my dad to come into our bedroom and kiss us goodnight. I don't even know why he would have been home at that time, but her attempt to convince him didn't work. My sister and I remember lying in bed or being awakened and hearing my dad scream late at night. I just hated leaving my mother in the morning because I was afraid for her safety. I knew something was wrong, but I don't even think I knew how to express my feelings.

Up until my adult years, I questioned why my dad never showed any affection to me. I often wondered why he wouldn't love a cute little girl, especially since I was his child, too. I say cute because I always wondered why he rejected me emotionally since I appeared to be a lovable little girl. I couldn't understand what was wrong with me. I never asked myself what was wrong with him. It's such a personal thing. I would wonder about this so often. I would also notice other people's fathers, especially my friend Debbie's father. I longed for a father so much and relished the attention I got from my grandpa Benny (my mom's dad, who also was a pharmacist). He owned his own drugstore, which was very successful. My father resented my grandparents because my grandfather was well-to-do. My father felt like he couldn't compete financially, I guess. He was jealous of my grandparents. However, they were my salvation, and, as I said earlier, their house was my refuge.

When I think of my elementary, junior high, and high school years, I wonder how or why I managed to get that far. Things finally caught up with me around seventh grade. I probably missed more school that year than in any year. I missed around twenty or so days. I couldn't pass algebra because I had missed too many days of school. When I was there, I wasn't making passing grades. For reasons unknown to me, I had passed through elementary school as an average student, but it wasn't until my academic subjects became harder that I was discovered, I guess you'd say. In the past, I guess I got by due to focusing every so often, because I definitely wasn't concentrating on schoolwork very much. I do remember my mom having me tutored in math during the summer when I was in the fifth or sixth grade. In elementary school, I did do my homework even though math was really hard for me. In those days, parents weren't overly involved in your life like today, so they expected you to do your own homework. Parents didn't do your science projects back then. It was a different era. So, I struggled through my math homework and if I did ask my mom a question, she would try to answer me but told me to try my best. Somehow, I got by and was considered an average student.

It amazes me that not one of my teachers in elementary school had any clue that something might be going on at home that might have affected my behavior or performance in school. You would think that one teacher would wonder or catch on that something wasn't right somewhere, not because I was considered average but because of the way I began my formal school career. When I think back on it today, I guess my teachers saw my mom and me as being very fortunate. No one ever knew we were living a lie. My mom definitely looked like she came from an upper-class family. She was well dressed, most attractive, and nurturing. She was very mature and very involved in our lives. She was a Girl Scout leader for my sister's troop, an officer in the Sisterhood at the Temple, and involved at my school in things like carnivals and such. Our neat, well-dressed appearance and the fact that we didn't cause any problems in school camouflaged our home problems. In those days, if you looked the part, I guess society or teachers never thought anything could be wrong with you. It makes me cringe now, though. I suppose schools are accused of getting too involved and personal with families today, but back then, maybe they saw it as not being their business.

No one except my family knew what was going on behind the façade of our front door at 4318 Saint Regis Lane. Apparently, my sister and I were good at acting! Why did I not say anything? I'm not exactly sure. My mother never talked about it. She was not a complainer. She always kept things to herself. As a matter of fact, one of the last times I saw my mom's best friend before she died she told me she never could believe that my mom never, ever, told her what was going on in our household. She kept that part of her life hidden from her best friend, too. Her own parents didn't even know about our situation until my mom decided to leave Louisville, the only place that was home to her. She lived there her whole life except for a short time in California during my father's time in the Navy. Perhaps the social stigma of having problems in the home was too great for her to deal with or too embarrassing.

As a child, I guess I never knew I had the option to discuss anything like this. Being an educator and knowing how I have tried to get to know the children I have taught, it still amazes me that I got through elementary school without anyone knowing how I was living at home. Some children find their refuge at school because they can escape, but I wasn't one of those children. I personally think teachers perceived me as a well-cared-for child and automatically assumed all was well in my family life. After all, I had a loving mom—which, of course, she was. This may have attributed my behavior to being "spoiled."

In my seventh-grade year, I was placed in lower-level classes for math and English. I no longer was taking the math courses to prepare one for higher-level courses and I knew my English class was composed of many students who were not the type of students I was used to having in my classes. In my other courses, I was with more of my closest friends, but I still didn't excel academically. How I continued to pass, I do not know, because I did little homework if any at all after school. During junior high school (until I moved out of state), I found a way to fit in. I was popular with the girls. I stayed pretty clear of the boys because I didn't really know how to relate to them that well. In seventh grade, I appeared to be more at ease around boys, interacting with them more comfortably. However, when puberty began, I became a lot more self-conscious and awkward around boys. So, I didn't even go out with boys in high school unless I wanted to attend a certain dance or social event. Girls didn't go stag at that time either.

Since I wasn't into academics, I got very involved in social clubs. That was at least a place where I could experience success. I also started learning how to leave some of my neurotic behaviors behind and my social experiences helped to fill my world with more of a positive feeling. I was now doing more things that were fun, and I was busy and involved in a myriad of activities. Things seemed better now when I was away from home, away from the craziness. I began spending the night more with friends (especially on the weekends), so I was removed from my world at home. I also still had my grandparents' home to go to, and I still enjoyed escaping through dance.

It was about this time that my dad and mom were starting to separate and he was home even less. I remember the night before I was to take the SATs. A woman called my house and asked to talk to me and she proceeded to tell me that she was going to be with my father and I would never be welcome in their house. I have never forgotten that day and how I felt that evening when it happened. I was shocked and of course upset about this happening and wondered why a strange woman would even call my house. I didn't sleep too well, and, needless to say, I bombed the SATs. I vowed to myself that I wouldn't take them again, either. I didn't care.

Evidently, my dad had a lot of women over the years and he lived two lives. He had a small apartment he was renting. He even bought one woman a three-caret diamond ring by cashing in all of his insurance policies. I found that out at school one day. Someone had seen my father in the jewelry store.

Things continued to get worse and worse. My sister was in England for a year spending her junior year abroad, so she was far removed from the situation. My most gratifying escape from the chaos was my love of dance. If I wasn't involved in an art project, I was dancing. I never desired a quiet activity like reading because I needed to be moving—releasing energy. Through dance and listening to Chopin on the piano or my recital music, I was transported to a beautiful world. I would dance for hours and hours when most of my friends were socializing or dating on the weekend. I dreamt of one day becoming a dancer because I felt so good when I danced.

I'd get home from school and find holes in the walls or interior doors where my father had put his fist through, broken or missing furniture, including a television and chair, food on the kitchen ceiling, dented and broken handles on our pots and pans, and my favorite picture missing off the hallway wall. There were also things that were worse. My father cornered my mother in the bathroom one day and threatened her with a knife. He also threatened to hurt my mother and my grandparents. My mother would receive threatening letters and threatening calls and notes from my father. It was a nightmare.

We moved after my senior year had already started to Greenville, South Carolina. I had never moved before. We moved to Greenville because my mom wanted to move where she had relatives. She was forty-five years old, and she had never worked outside of the home. She and her best friend had a little flower business where they did everything between their two houses, but they worked it around their schedules since it was a part-time venture. We took our dog, Georgie Girl, with us, but I had to leave my two cats behind. My sister was graduating from Sophie Newcomb College that year. She had come back from Exeter, England, for her senior year. It was good for her that she was already out of the house because she escaped the worst years of living with my father. My father's behavior got worse.

We moved to a new apartment complex in Greenville. Apartment living was a new thing for us, but it was okay. My mom appeared to be doing really well. She seemed happier and still never complained. I admire her strength in being able to leave behind her support system and established roots.

I hated the first day of my senior year in Greenville. Since I started school a week or so late, it was even more awkward. It was a huge school, and I told my mom that I wasn't going back after she picked me up on that first day. Of course, I did go back, and I met a girl named Sue Marsh who lived in the same apartment complex as I did. She had just moved to Greenville and was from Bell View, Illinois. We hit it off, and we had a small group of friends we did things with. After college we remained friends, but our friendship ended several years ago after she lost her battle with cancer. It is still hard to believe that she is dead.

The most exciting thing about my move was starting over academically. I was placed in a superior English class that year and I was also in pretty good classes across the board. I didn't have to go all day because I was coming from a state that required more credit hours to graduate. I got to leave around 1:30 each day.

I'll never forget the first time I heard my English teacher, Mr. Borders, teach. I was sitting in class, and, for the first time in my life, I was able to really listen, pay attention, and focus on what the teacher was saying. It was an overwhelming experience and a wonderful feeling. I felt like the top of my head was off and everything that had previously clouded my brain and life was being lifted. I could use my brain like it was supposed to be used. There was a sense of quiet where I was free to think and process information without worrying about what was happening at home or how my mom was doing.

I began getting excited about learning. In fact, I liked learning because Mr. Borders, my "Superior English" teacher, made it exciting. He also introduced me to project work. I was able to make a Shakespearean character for one of my projects. I loved doing this project. I remember the great detail I took to make this character look authentic. I also saw myself excelling academically even though I thought I wasn't supposed to be smart. I was also drawing my cousin's lab pictures for her college biology class. Of course, art was one of my gifts and it didn't take brains to do this, I thought, but, nevertheless, I felt proud. So, I began to surprise my mom as well as myself.

I had a successful year during my senior year of high school, but I really wasn't that interested in going to college. I was going because you were expected to go, and I had no idea what colleges would accept me. I also wasn't crazy about leaving home. My sister insisted that I go to college away from home for at least a semester because she wanted me to experience some normalcy.

I received a small art scholarship from Furman University to my surprise. A local artist knew that I had won a National Scholastic Art Award for a linoleum print I had done that was sent to New York for a contest. I believe she had something to do with my being accepted. My mom didn't have a lot of money, and the fact that she never received money from my father made the situation even harder. She told me that she did have enough money for me to go for one semester, but she did not know how long the money would last. I experienced my first boyfriend (a very unhealthy relationship) the summer after I graduated high school, and all I wanted to think of was getting married until I realized how unhealthy the relationship was. The man I was in a relationship with was extremely jealous and controlling. I realized that I would not be happy with him, and I broke off the relationship.

I decided I would try the University of South Carolina (USC) in Columbia for a semester. Once I got over being homesick, which took a while, I fell in love with learning and couldn't get enough of it. I also became interested in boys, too, so everything was exciting for me. I really started enjoying myself and having fun, but school always came first. I'm sure my friends in Louisville would have never believed this major transformation I had. My sister was the academic one—not me. I was the social one. While at USC, I earned an associate's degree in child development, a bachelor's degree in interdisciplinary studies, and a master's degree in exceptional children with certification in learning disabilities. I went on to teach school for three years. I taught a self-contained class for children with severe learning disabilities and emotional or behavioral problems. I was fascinated with these children, and I was even more interested in how I could assist their families. I decided to go back to school. I got accepted to Peabody at Vanderbilt and The Florida State University.

Before going off to school, I tried to make as much money as I could. I spent the summer in Norfolk, Virginia, with one of my best friends, Linda. I had three jobs as a waitress that summer. Linda would drop me off at work in the morning and pick me up in the afternoon. I would count my tips and then I'd drive to my evening waitressing job. She wouldn't let me pay rent. I was company for her because her husband Tom was on a research ship for the summer. I spent many holidays with Linda and Tom and with my friend Melissa in Columbia. My friends were like my extended family.

I decided to go to Florida State after leaving Peabody after a day. It worked out great because Florida State started a month later and Florida State offered to give me assistance until I received my Ph.D. While at Peabody for the one day that I stayed there, I called Florida State because I still hadn't heard about my application. Dr. Rowell, Chair of the Education Department at The Florida State University, informed me that they were behind because he had just come on board. He told me that Peabody was a great school (he had received his Ph.D. from there), but he wanted me to come to Florida State. He then had Dr. Virginia Green, an early childhood professor, call me, and I was convinced I should go there. So, my mom and I packed the car and we left Nashville. Dr. Rowell helped me get a position as a Pilot Scholarship House counselor, where I lived and ate free in exchange for being in charge of twenty-one girls who were from all over

Florida who were on scholarships. It was an exciting time for me because I was thrilled to have an opportunity such as this. Before I received this offer, I was going to school, teaching with my assistantship, and working two part-time jobs. Before graduating with a degree in early childhood and a major concentration in counseling, I started seriously dating my husband, Noel. I got married before receiving my Ph.D. Nine days after I turned in all copies of my dissertation, I gave birth to my daughter, Jessica. Four years after that, I gave birth to my son, Mike, in Columbia, South Carolina.

I feel like my life's experiences have made me a more empathetic professor. The literature on resiliency research clearly points to the importance of a significant other in the child's life (Bronfenbrenner, 1981). This is referred to in the literature as a protective factor (Krovetz, 1999). Werner and Smith (1989) conducted a longitudinal study that spanned more than forty years and found that a child's favorite teacher was the most frequently encountered positive role outside of the family unit. The teacher was not only the deliverer of content skills, but also someone to confide in as well as a role model the child could personally identify with. Even though Wallerstein and Kelly (1980) advocate parents staying together for the sake of the children, I tend to disagree. I think that it is a lot healthier for all parties concerned to live in a household that is free from the undercurrents of an unhappy marriage.

Other factors also appear to contribute to the resilient child's success (Blackburn, 2000): culturally appropriate personal support, the importance of rituals, experiencing some control over an aspect of one's life, and opportunities to express one's feelings, among others. Benard (1991, 1993) found social competence and problem-solving skills to be a factor as well. Krovetz (1999) brings out the positive implications of resiliency research in his recent book, *Fostering Resiliency*. He reminds the reader that it is not uncommon for an individual to turn children's lives around. The most popular students (the winners) in high school are not necessarily the ones who will be successful later in life. Many of the students who struggled in high school become very successful in adulthood.

Even though I chose to write about my life's experiences and I do see myself as a resilient adult, I don't want to underestimate the negative effects one goes through when dealing with a most difficult childhood. Many people are responsible for my life taking a different course—my brave and courageous mother who had the willingness and determination to leave her roots and support system to move out of state so we could begin a new life; my older sister, Cathy, who insisted that I experience college, if only for one semester; my brother-in-law, Alan, who had higher expectations for me; my grandmother and grandfather, Mama Jessie and Grandpa Benny, whose house I could escape to and whose love of life, devotion for one another, and laughter showed me that life did have some happy moments; my uncle Marvin, who showed me the feeling of unconditional love and support; my girlfriend Debbie's father, Irvin Goldstein, who demonstrated what a normal father acts like; and my many friends who allowed me to relax and feel safe when I was in their homes.

Even though I charted a different path for my life before I met my husband, Noel, he has been an instrumental force in my seeing that life has opportunities for much happiness and fulfillment. If it weren't for Noel, I probably never would have had the confidence to have children. My childhood was something I didn't want to relive, and it was hard for me to see that a childhood could be good. Being a wife and a mother has been probably the most fulfilling part of my life in that it has allowed me to experience a happy home life and wonderful children. Of course we have had our ups and downs, as well as a lot of challenges, over almost twenty-one years of marriage. Some of those years were very trying. However, we are very much in love and our most important priority is our family life. Noel's wonderful sense of humor has been an asset to my life.

I shudder to think about the life I could have had and the fact that my life could have been drastically different if we had stayed in Louisville. Even though the effects of my parents' divorce was more involved because of my father's addiction, I feel very strongly about moving a child or children out of a home by getting a divorce if the situation is emotionally unhealthy or dangerous. At the same time, it's disturbing to see that intact families are no longer going to be the norm in society. Schools must continue to find ways to assist children and families so that children have the best opportunities to develop to their fullest potential.

Although my early childhood was stressful, children today experience more stress because they are so hurried (Elkind, 1981). Society is moving at a much faster pace. We seem to do everything quickly, including eating on the run. Many children have family problems to deal with as well. These difficulties can certainly affect their school performance. At the same time, teachers also need to be careful not to assume that a child's school performance will regress permanently because they are dealing with family problems. We must be aware that children, like adults, have various temperaments and constitutions and that they do not all have the same coping abilities. However, teachers need to be alert to the ways they can support children and families beyond academics.

Tom's Story

I had heard of Dr. Tom Reed in early childhood circles and had even met him once while he was working on his dissertation, but I hadn't had the opportunity to work closely with him until three years ago. Tom Reed is a University of South Carolina-Spartanburg early childhood professor. I teach at the University of South Carolina-Sumter, where we have a cooperative agreement with USC-Spartanburg to offer a four-year B.A. education program. That is how my life crossed with Tom Reed's life.

As we began to get to know one another's interests and more about each other on a personal level, I talked to him about the multicultural education project I was working on and asked if he would be interested in sharing his story for the chapter on resilient children I was writing. He kindly agreed, and I will now share his story as it was told to me on audiotapes. Even though we shared some similarities in that we are both Caucasian, close in age, and had painful childhoods, our backgrounds are different. Tom comes from an intact, "upper-lower" (Tom's words) socioeconomic status family, and his parents were both high school dropouts. Tom is from Pennsylvania. I came from an upper-middle-class family. My father went to college and graduated from pharmacy school and my mother went to college for a year. Our childhood memories evoke a painful time and neither of us ever expected to be leading successful lives with this degree of normalcy. In fact, Tom didn't expect to be alive at this age.

I will start at the point where Tom began his story. It will be told in reversed sequence because that is how he told it to me.

Somewhere between the ages of eighteen and thirty-three, Tom began to drink heavily. In his own words, he was challenging death. He drove while drinking and took many risks. He never thought he would be around to see the year 2000. He often wondered what he would be like if he were alive. He thought that he might be some kind of "worn-out-looking kind of grandpa-type of a person." The fact that he is in reasonably good health and looks as if he has lived a normal life is amazing to him.

Tom Speaks

I'm not sure why I'm still alive other than there must be some kind of use for me that I'm not totally aware of. It is 2000, and I am alive and I am contributing to society and I am on my way to doing things that are amazing to me. When I was first married, my wife asked me my five-year plan. The only thing I could think of was that I wanted to have the job I have, be married to her, and live in the house I live in. At that time, I was around twenty-seven or twenty-eight years of age. Even around twenty-eight or thirty, I didn't know how to plan for the future. I attended Alcoholics Anonymous and lived the law of the 12-step program, which taught me to live day to day, which was a very important thing.

I didn't take responsibility for the future. If I got through the day, okay, I did, and if not, shit happens. I used to live by the cliché, "eat, drink, and be merry, for tomorrow you may die." Live a good life and be happy with what you are doing is the AA focus. There are really two ways to look at this same philosophy. Now, I like to look at my days by asking myself, "Was it a good day and did I contribute to anything today?" "If it wasn't a good day, is there something that I can do to make tomorrow a better day?" That is part of the irony of this whole thing. I now feel more like I did as a kid, before I started drinking. Between the ages of eighteen and thirty-three, I seemed like a different Tom Reed. At times, when I start talking about my past I have to laugh. Everyone sees me as who I am now, not drunk as a skunk. But I remember that image well.

School was basically a fun place to be for a little while at least. We didn't have kindergarten. It wasn't something they did in my neighborhood. First and second grades were good. School was a social place for me. Academically speaking, I was horrendously average or below average, but I was doing okay until I went to third grade and met the "wicked witch of the West."

As I look back on it now, I see this woman who hated me and I hated her. I did not like what she made me do—stand what seemed like hours at the chalkboard. I am sure it was only minutes, but it seemed like hours to me. She took recess away from me because I wasn't doing well, and I am sure that I didn't do my homework either. She was mean to me, and I can't honestly say that she wasn't mean to other people. I didn't respond to her at all. It was almost like I just shut down. I promised myself that I would not let her get to me, but she did. I cried a lot. I wet my pants a lot. I was having what we would now refer to as adjustment problems in the third grade.

The school did not know what to do with me and they didn't ask me either, by the way. The decision was made to send me back to the second grade by the principal, I'm sure. The teachers and my parents had a meeting and made this decision. The walk from the principal's office back to the second grade class where I was returned to was the longest walk I've ever taken in my entire life. I experienced uncontrollable crying, shame, and confusion as to why this was happening to me, and the fact that I received no support from the teacher. I guess it was good news because they did get me back with my old second-grade teacher, who was a warm, tenderhearted woman.

I tried to please my mother. But, really, in my later elementary years is when I really began to see that my mother had some pretty uncontrollable anger and rage. So that's when school began to be a safe place to be. At least when I was at school, I didn't have to worry about her hitting me or wonder if I was going to drop something and for her to fly off the handle. I can remember being very nervous, like at suppertime. That same nervousness, instead of keeping me from getting in trouble, actually got me into trouble because I'd dump my plate or knock over my glass. It seemed like the stress that I was experiencing actually produced more and then I'd get in trouble. So, the idea of trying to be the perfect boy also started to come into play. I thought that if I didn't cause any trouble, then I was doing well. This is when I began to really force myself into that way of handling things.

My older sister was doing well in school and she was the oldest and had more privileges. My next oldest sister, Barbara, was getting in trouble left and right for things that I could never really understand. I didn't want what Barbara was getting [spankings], and I couldn't compete academically with my older sister, so it just seemed to me that the smartest thing for me to do was just to stay out of the way. In relationship to school, it worked the same way. I was never really a popular kid, nor was I a cast-off or a scapegoat or anything like that.

Our homework was ours to do, as I recall. My parents never sat down at the table with me to help me do things or to talk about things or to help me understand math problems. They would say, "Did you do your homework yet?" If I said no, then the question that followed was, "Why not?" That was their perception of their responsibility to me in regard to school. Just to see that I got the work done. So, I never really did well in school. It's kind of funny how people look at us as Ph.D.'s and think we're all smart, but actually we're probably just more resilient. We learn to take something that was a challenge to us as kids and turn it into something good as an adult. Anyway, I never really did well in school. Part of it was not having the parental support that was needed. But also I did not want to draw attention to myself. So really, I was motivated to do well enough to keep from getting into particular trouble or setting off my mother, or my father, too, sometimes.

My father, as I know now, did what he could to stay the hell out of the way, too. So it wasn't that he was so easygoing, it's just that he was miserable, too. My mother used the veil of threat—you know, "Wait till your father comes home," or, "You're gonna get it when your father comes home." So, often he ended up punishing us, but it was at my mother's insistence that he'd do something about it. It was not because it was something he decided that needed to be done, but to appease my mother. So all of us really did just enough in school to keep my parents off our backs mostly because we didn't want to get beat, paddled, grounded, or whatever it was that we got for poor grades.

On the other hand, there wasn't any support. They didn't know how to give support either. Both of my parents are high school dropouts, and they didn't know how to help us. I can remember seventh, eighth, or maybe ninth grade, I wanted to talk to my father about history, or something like that. I got kind of frustrated because he just didn't know how to help and he wanted to, but he really couldn't answer. Maybe I couldn't pose the question to his understanding, but I think it was more that he just didn't know the answer. At that point, I quit asking questions, basically because I realized that I wasn't going to get any help, and they weren't taking an interest in what we were doing anyway. Their only interest was the report card.

However, a couple of occasions in particular with my father, I did ask him for help on some things, and he did help when he was able to help. I remember an art project I did one time. It was to be a collage and he had a part-time auto welding body shop by the house and he helped me create a junk yard, and I got an A on it, but it just kind of shows you what parent involvement can help a child achieve. He didn't do all the work for me or anything like that. He just helped me understand what materials I could glue on and what would stay on this board and that sort of thing.

I decided that I really wanted to be a teacher because my seventh grade teacher intoxicated me with his words. He was talking about the Middle East and Constantinople and this is going on over here and over there and how they all merged together and the bell rings and I felt like I had just sat down. I was thinking, "Wow, that was really neat!" It really impressed me. So I hadn't decided I wanted to be a teacher until seventh or eighth grade.

In ninth grade, my history teacher was a very interesting teacher. I really enjoyed that class. I enjoyed doing well in that class. But my last year in high school or very close to it, there was a woman, I think her name was Geraldine Reid, and she started out the class by saying, "I'm Miss Reid and you spell my name "R-e-i-d" not "R-e-a-d," not "R-e-e-d." Everyone in the class was laughing. It comes to me, and I said my name is Tom Reed and you don't spell it "R-e-i-d," "R-e-a-d," etc. It cracked her up and from that moment on she understood me and it was a lot of fun being in her class.

About tenth grade, a guy named Denny, who lived very near me, started walking home with me. We lived in the same neighborhood, but he moved in the neighborhood later than me. So it took me a little while to get to know him and he was a little different than some of the other guys, too, and not some kind of a macho guy. Somehow, we started walking together and standing in front of his house talking about all kinds of stuff—the Beatles, the Pittsburgh Pirates, anything we could to stay there and chat. When we *had* to go home, we would. Neither one of us ever asked the other, "Why don't you want to go home?" Neither invited the other to their house. We would just talk right in the middle of the street.

Years later when we finally started talking about things, we realized that both of us were trying to avoid our respective houses. In a sense, we were kind of using each other to stall going home. My three sisters and I would have kids over, but we never wanted them in the house. We never had sleepovers. We were scared to death about the mood my mother might be in if anybody ever showed up.

My sisters and I had lots of ten and eleven o'clock talks in their bedroom at night. When my mother and father were gone, we would talk about all the things that were going on. We got very close in that regard. My oldest sister ended up becoming pregnant and my next youngest sister got married as soon as she possibly could and I had a lucky out—the Navy. It was a bad thing on one hand and good on the other; but I was out of my house. My youngest sister is still very hostile and very angry toward the rest of us because she really feels abandoned by us because we got the hell out of there and we didn't look back. She is now married and she has a couple kids of her own. She has a minimal relationship with me and nothing with the rest of the family.

My perception of my parents hasn't necessarily changed, but my current understanding of them has changed drastically. I can see the phases that

I went through with denial. You know, I can remember my first marriage and my wife would get so mad at me for things that I just thought were the normal things to do, like go over and help my father out on a Friday night. She'd say things like, "Come here. You know, you're married to me." I thought she was the one with the problem, not me. In retrospect, we both had a problem, but I was not willing to consider anything on my part. It was like breathing. It was just what I did and what you were supposed to do. But, anyway, I now understand why they were the way they were, who they were, and where it came from. But I didn't then, and I wasn't going to until I experienced it outside my home. I didn't start outwardly rejecting certain things my parents stood for until I was thirty-two.

I began to carve out my own path, my own way of doing things. I think that I wanted to keep peace in the family and believed that if I did something wrong, I was at fault, and it is still true today. In my family, you are either in the family or out of the family. There is really no in-between with my family. I don't have to do the stupid stuff like getting drunk every chance I got, being slack in my personal appearance, using controlled substances, and goofing off at work anymore to run the risk of being rejected. I can hide it from them rather than run the risk of being thrown out of the family like I've watched my sisters do time and time again. I would hide what I did. So being in the Navy, living out of state, away from them really gave me the freedom to go ahead and start making mistakes and I didn't have to worry about disappointing anybody.

Well, my world as I knew it was falling apart at that time. I tried counseling once, and I'd just go there and lie and then I quit going and of course my married life was crumbling apart. I got married in 1976. I didn't get a divorce until 1984. I remember I finally got tired of living the way I was living. I've had several of these moments in my life now where I've had lifelong clarity and I could see that this was not the way I wanted to live.

The lies were now catching up with me and I had to invent more lies to cover up the old ones and then forgetting what the first lie was. It got very complicated and, of course, very inconsistent. It was difficult to lie about where I was and what I was doing so often that it made my head hurt. At that time, I was losing my tolerance for alcohol, which worried me. My speech was slurring after a few cans of beer, and I thought I had some disease that alcohol activated. Little did I know that I was feeling the effects of alcoholism at the time. I also realized that I was treating my wife in the same regard as my mother, with lies, deception, not being honest with feelings, etc. At this point in my life, I figured this is just how it's going to have to be and I might as well find a way to live with it—except I couldn't.

At the beginning of my second counseling session, my therapist asked me if I thought I needed to go to AA, and I said to him, "I can stop drinking any time I want to." Which I found out every alcoholic says the same thing but he didn't push me and say, "I think you ought to seek help." But oddly enough—and again, this is one of these kind of divine interventions that people have from time to time—I got up in the morning, it was Veterans' Day I think, and I started flipping through the phone book and this was in Pittsburgh. This was in '83 and it was Saturday, and I'm dialing a number, and I didn't wake up that morning and say, "I'm going to call AA." I never planned it, and it wasn't an intention. It was an action that I really don't feel I could say I had control over. I called AA and I'm crying like mad, and I don't ever know where in the hell these tears are coming from because they came forever—I guess. These were tears I've never let out before, but anyway this woman asked me if I needed help, if I'd like for someone to come and see me now, and through all the fears and this emotional release I was having I said, "Oh no, I'm alright." Anyway I asked her when the next AA meeting would take place, and she asked where I lived, and I'm thinking it will be next month, and she said there are thirty-three meetings every day in the city of Pittsburgh. She then told me about the meeting scheduled for the next day. I went to it and I knew basically I was home.

I may not have had a physical death—whatever, I certainly had a spiritual and emotional death. It resurrected the whole thing for me. It really did. It gave me the vehicle in which to change my life, for the first time in my life I was actually around a bunch of people I could relate to and that could relate to me and people said here's what happened to me. It's the first time I started getting guidance in life. It was in 1983. I was probably thirty-three.

[As Tom reflected on racial relationships and how they influenced him, he offered the following.] It's interesting: where I lived, there weren't any Black folks anywhere. One didn't even move into the township. They were in the country and the city, but the community I lived in was just as White as it could be and I could imagine the uproar if a Black family had moved in. My parents even made me break up with this girl one time because she was Catholic. The Afro-American people lived in the city. You talk about the dominant culture or the dominant power. I was in it. I do not recall until I got much older that there was ever any talk about race relations. We didn't have to talk about it because they were there. There was really nothing to talk about.

There was a junkyard in the town called "The Jews." I grew up hearing that from everybody and I grew up thinking that was the name of the place. I didn't find out until I got older that it was called Hodges Auto Salvage. I didn't know it at the time but there were terms that were used quite freely growing up along those lines. I just thought it was like the word *red.* There's nothing wrong with the word *red*—if she looks this way, you call her red. Brazil nuts were call Jabonies, Catholics were called Mickies, and Italians were called Wops and Guinneas. I participated just as fully as anybody else did, and that might be "foolishly" now instead of fully. I did—I participated just as fully as anyone else and didn't see anything wrong with it. We finally got a "minority" in our school and he was an Indian. We called him the FBI man. Are you ready for this? He was tall. We called him the FBI man because someone decided he was a "F——g Big Indian." He didn't last long, and I never knew why he moved away, but it's no surprise any more if that's the way we treated him. Al Jordan was his name. He was a nice guy, I liked him. I didn't know what I was saying. I truly didn't know.

I had the fortunate experience of dating several Jewish women in my life, and I was scared to death my parents would find out. I did not consciously seek out cross-racially but found the difference intriguing and exciting. However, once in these relationships, I found that it did indeed place me in the "child role" by feeling that I couldn't really tell my parents what was going on in my life for fear of rejection (which was sure to happen). I carried that into my marriage as well as with finances. I didn't want to have to go through snide remarks either. Subtle comments or one made behind my back, I didn't want to put a woman through that experience. There are a couple of women that I probably could have gotten married to if I had wanted to. Particularly, there was one woman who was, I guess you might say, the more stereotypical Jewish woman, whether that's good or bad—she represented that, and I was thinking, "My God—if my parents knew who I was dating right now they'd would have snapped out. They'd wonder what happened to me." I tried to be such a good kid. Since I was raised a Presbyterian, they thought my dating a Catholic when I was 16 was a bad thing. I mean, I was going down the line of acceptability. I felt like an outsider with my parents.

I was taught by the dominant culture and I was taught not to take into consideration other peoples' thoughts or feelings. There was no need to think about anyone different than myself. We didn't have to take them into consideration, nor was it popular at the time even if somebody different was around me. We didn't have to take in other people's thoughts or beliefs. We were still working as a nation at the time [under the idea that] the melting pot [would] assimilate other people's culture into our dominant one. The rainbow theory, which I love now, didn't exist. Whites were not supposed to accept anyone else—including Jewish people. Ironically, my father was really quite skilled at welding and was asked to make a burning bush out of copper for a synagogue. But that still didn't get me any closer to understanding anything about culture. Although I was kind of fascinated by Judaism, my father did not want me to learn anything about it. His attitude was to do the job and leave. So I did.

Reflections on Tom's Story

Tom's story supports the notion that children—regardless of their negative early life experiences—can find a way to change the direction of their lives so that they can lead productive and fulfilling lives. Why and how does this happen? The issue is somewhat complex, but the majority of research studies conclude that certain factors seem to determine whether a child will be able to persevere under these circumstances. Tom grew into an individual who was much more accepting in his views about other people. Because of what he went through, he is likely a more empathetic teacher who is able to realize that people can change, grow, and develop.

After I completed my discussion with Tom, he brought up the issues of the child's lack of control under these circumstances. He questions the value of homework today because of the drastic changes that have occurred in the American family. Today's demands on the family pose many challenges to children and parents alike. Many children are being raised in families in which both parents work, and many of these children have after-school schedules that rival a busy adult's schedule. Children today may receive homework in all of their academic subjects, but because they have such a full plate of activities and commitments themselves, they are often unable to complete these assignments. Many high school students also have after-school and evening jobs that require them to work late hours.

Many children also lack the proper supervision to complete their homework assignments. Children may be the only ones home in the afternoons. Tom believes that single parents' lifestyles aren't taken into account. The dominant culture makes the rules, even if these rules don't apply to the needs of communities. Are we preparing preservice educators to work with today's families? Do teacher education programs take into account diverse populations when preparing our teachers to work with children? Are teachers equipped to work with all types of families and cultures?

Tom believes teachers need to understand their students so they will know who they are, what's important to them, and what they do in their spare time: "It's all about humanness." Both Tom and I believe that children often learn in spite of teachers. If a teacher has made the necessary connection with the student and the student really believes that the teacher believes in the student's ability to learn, students will many times surprise themselves, not to mention others. The curriculum is an important factor, but the initial atmosphere in the classroom and the comfort and trust level with the teacher are the impetus for the child's motivation to learn.

Educational Implications

Today, the buzzword we so often hear is *accountability,* and we automatically think of academic accountability. However, in looking at how universities and colleges prepare preservice educators, we cannot forget about better preparing teachers to work with the type of students who will fill their classrooms. Many teacher education programs prepare students to teach to the "ideal learner." The "ideal learner" is somewhat of a misnomer—and probably always has been. Our classrooms are filled with children who learn in a variety of ways. Children learn according to their specific styles.

More important, even if they are taught through their preferred modality, they may be dealing with family issues that cloud their capacity for learning. Just like children who come to school hungry have a hard time paying attention to learn, children who are dealing with issues that affect them emotionally or psychologically may also be unable to concentrate or focus on what their teacher is teaching them. Their minds are on what is happening at their house or to their parents or what happened the evening before or what they might find when they arrive back at home. These children may be just as bright as other students in class, but they end up underachieving academically because they cannot concentrate as well as the children who aren't experiencing problems beyond their control.

Children have different temperaments and different coping abilities, so some children may be able to persevere and focus on their learning and other children may be so distracted that they can't concentrate long enough to grasp what the teacher is saying. Many of these children probably drift in and out or tune in and out but appear to the teacher to be attending to what is being discussed. These children have learned to look as if they are paying attention, but they are really not. This may not be apparent to the teacher until test time, or maybe the teacher doesn't notice at all.

Children's affective development is equally important as their academic development. Educators receive a lot of negative press from commentators who attack education programs by accusing them of focusing only on self-esteem issues rather than on academics. This attack is rarely grounded in fact. However, these programs do focus on the whole child, and I am a firm believer that a child who is hurting on the inside does have a much harder time learning.

Schools today are much better equipped to deal with the whole child because of the multitude of services and support that can be received from the school or district level as well as from the community at large. Some districts have their own psychologists, guidance counselors, social workers, mentors, parent education programs, child study teams, and so forth. These support systems can assist the child and families who are experiencing difficulty with issues such as family addiction, abuse, and death. We must also stress the importance of teacher expectations. I recommend that, unless a child's folder is red-flagged because of an allergic reaction or illness, teachers meet their students for the first time without having read their folders. This may keep teachers from developing premature biases about the children.

The Issue of Homework

When I grew up, children were expected to sit down and do their homework on their own, but they had the time to do it. Back then, children may have had one extracurricular activity, but for the most part, they were at home in the afternoons. After they finished their homework, they were free to play outside until dinnertime. Parents or a maid were home with the children and day care was unheard of. My mother usually checked with me to see that I had completed my homework, but she was not overly involved. In today's society, after many of our children get home from daycare, their parents are busy and there is very little time to get their homework completed either before dinner or after dinner. If children aren't in day care, they are either involved in so many extracurricular activities that they don't have much time to do their homework or they are on their own without the proper supervision and help needed to do their homework. Tom and I both agree that teachers need to rethink the purpose of homework and give children only a realistic amount of meaningful homework that they are able to complete each night.

Joint Custody

Children who travel from one household to another according to a schedule may experience a lack of control over their own lives because their lives are arranged for them. There may be consistency and harmony between divorced parents, or there may be a great deal of strife, anger, or resentment between the child's parents. Children may also be experiencing the same or different emotions as their parents. Children who are used as pawns also have an undue amount of pressure put upon them. Again, with no choices, they are just expected to deal with the situation. Obviously, a child's temperament influences the way he or she is able to cope with this situation. Sensitive children often take things harder, and they may not have the coping skills needed to carry them through this difficult time. Children need help learning how to develop healthy ways of dealing with their stress.

While some research indicates that negative family interactions, drug abuse, and parental divorce may predispose a child to having future problems (Masten & Coatsworth, 1998), there is also a body of resiliency research that shows how children can persevere under difficult situations. I think that many children who do fare well by societal standards still deal with internal issues. We also need to examine the lives of children who adapt effectively in the face of adversity—children who do not get through these hard times easily but eventually learn to compensate may cover up some of the issues they deal with. Some children and adults suffer from depression after divorce. They have to learn to adapt and move forward even if this is the case.

I believe that children who adapt easier do so because of their specific temperaments. Of course, the environment plays a big part, too, but I think a child's reactions to the situation are influenced by how the child is wired.

Recommendations for Educators

1. Send out a letter at the beginning of the year asking parents to share with you during the year any life-changing events that may be affecting their child. This way, you will be more aware of what the child is experiencing and you will be able to make yourself more available to the child to help him/her through this transition.

2. Provide a mailbox in your classroom where students can leave you notes (signed or anonymous) about anything they may want to talk to you about or just let you know about.

3. Encourage your students to write in a journal about their thoughts, feelings, and ideas. They may also enjoy writing stories and writing poetry.

4. Inform parents and students alike about various support personnel in your school system who could provide assistance to the family or act as a referral system.

5. Share with your parents a list of community resources (and phone numbers) that could assist them with various services. It would be helpful to have a list of agencies that have a fee payment schedule on a sliding pay scale.

6. Provide a quiet area in the classroom where children can be by themselves to read a book or sit quietly and reflect. Make available books on a variety of issues of interest to children (e.g., books about divorce, single parenting, new baby, death). Also, have books available that are pertinent to other aspects of your students' cultures.

7. Develop a partnership with your guidance counselor, school psychologist, and social worker so you will be able to work closely throughout the school year in providing support to families.

8. Provide time to talk and listen to your students during down times such as recess, lunch, and before and after school. These are the times you can really get to know and understand your students.

9. When students are making cards or writing letters for their parents, make sure you provide several cards for students who are from blended families.

10. When discussing families and homes, make sure families are defined in many ways (e.g., one parent, grandparent, two parents, stepmother/father). A variety of descriptions for home should also be used: house, trailer, apartment, shelter, duplex, condominium, etc.

11. When parents are unable to attend school functions such as school plays, let students know they can invite another significant other, whether it be a family member, a mentor, or a special person in their life. Confer with the primary caregivers to ensure that they approve.

12. Make an informal assessment of your students to determine their emotional state.

13. Familiarize parents or guardians with community resources such as Big Brother/Big Sisters programs, mentoring programs, and services offered through the universities and colleges nearby.

14. Provide avenues for your students to express themselves through art, poetry, music, and plays. Water play is also very popular among young children.

15. Outgoing students can be very helpful in bringing out other students who are more tentative and shy when paired with them in small-group activities.

16. Make home visits to better understand your students and their families. It will provide the opportunity to talk with the parent(s) in a more relaxed setting.

17. Remember when including positive role models in your units to include people who have overcome major obstacles in their lives.

18. Hold high expectations for all of your students.

Editor's Commentary

White culture. What do we really know about it other than the generic label of Whiteness? Often, Whiteness is equated with "normal" McIntosh (1995). The two stories in this chapter zoom in on two particular dimensions of Whiteness and its complex relationship to class and gender.

Although Susan's life was "normal" for a child living with a parent who abused drugs and was verbally abusive to her mother, it did not fit the picture-book description of a little White girl living in a middle-class neighborhood. In other words, given the circumstances of Susan's home life, a child would not normally be expected to thrive. On the outside, teachers saw a well-dressed, quiet, "average" child and looked no further than that. It seems as if Susan's school never looked past the assumption that White children from homes like Susan's do well. Susan's story debunks the common stereotype that the homes of White children from two-parent, middle-income families are somehow inherently "better" than those of single-parent, low-income, and/or children of color's homes. While it is inconceivable to some teachers that a child like Susan was not thriving, children of color and children from low-income homes are quickly misdiagnosed as having problems, as we have seen in this book and as will be illustrated in subsequent chapters. So we see reluctance to label a child in one case and eagerness to do so in another.

Although Susan enjoyed aspects of White and middle-class privilege (e.g., the availability of resources in her school and being promoted each year although she was not doing well), she was not aware of them. Susan's story is an example of how a person can be privileged at the societal level, but not at the individual level (see Chapter 9 for a more thorough discussion of individual, group, and institutionalized discrimination/privilege). Yet, it is worth contemplating whether Susan's school experiences would have been different if she had been a child of color.

It is interesting that Susan's elementary school experiences are not memorable for her. In contrast to Vivian's and Curtis's stories in Chapter 2, Susan vaguely recalls details about her teachers. This could be due to Susan's emotional turmoil, but her references to the teachers she liked (her kindergarten teacher) are mundane and do not reflect the passion and respect that was evident in Vivian's and Curtis's stories. I'm not sure if this is the result of Vivian's and Curtis's enduring relationships with their teachers and close community connections or not. Likewise, Tom notes that he liked his second-grade teacher, but doesn't call her by name. He does, however, passionately remember his seventh-grade teacher, who broadened his horizons to include thinking about places such as the Middle East. He also fondly recalls one of his teachers who had a good sense of humor. These recollections convey the awesome power that teachers can have on the lives of the children they teach.

Moving to a new school changed Susan's academic trajectory. Both she and Tom were seemingly able to break the intergenerational problems that they suffered as children. Teachers played important roles in the process. We cannot speculate on the impact of White privilege, but we also cannot dismiss it.

The value given to education by Susan's and Tom's parents was displayed differently. Susan was read to and exposed to a number of extracurricular activities that are typical of middle-class homes. Although both of Tom's parents dropped out of school, their daily query about finishing homework (although this involvement was superficial in Tom's opinion) conveyed that they valued education to some degree.

While Susan's world was filled with covert messages about White privilege and their family's Jewish heritage, Tom's world was filled with overt messages regarding race and White and Christian superiority: there were taboos regarding cross-racial dating and the common and unquestioned use of racial epithets. None of the messages he received about racial cleavages are uncommon in a race-conscious society like the United States. Racism and other forms of discrimination effortlessly and endemically invade the consciousness of young children. As Tom expressed, he didn't even reflect on what he was saying. In light of the fact that children commonly pick up negative cross-racial messages, the importance of active, anti-bias approaches are evident (Boutte, LaPoint, & Davis, 1993). In sum, as Carol noted in the previous chapter, multiculturalism is needed for White children. Not only would multicultural teachers actively fight against all types of oppression and teach students to do so, but also they would seek to meet the needs of all children—even ones from homes that are stereotypically normal.

Reflective Activity

Make a list of five children's books that you were read as a child (at home or at school). How many of these primarily reflect aspects of White culture? Of the ones that reflect white culture, what messages were being conveyed about Whiteness as a model for normalcy?

Resources

Books for Children

The Cat Who Drank Too Much, by LeClaire Bissell & Richard Watherwax
Dinosaurs Divorce: A Guide for Changing Families, by Laurene & Marc Brown
The Gifted Kids Survival Guide: For Ages Ten and Under, by Judy Galbraith

The House That Crack Built, by Clark Taylor
I Can Talk About What Hurts, by Janet Sinberg & Dennis Daley
I Like Me, by Nancy Carlson
I Wish Daddy Didn't Drink So Much, by Judith Vigna
If I Ran the Family, by Lee and Sue Kaiser Johnson
It's My Body, by Lory Freeman
Just about Perfect, by Kate Green
Liking Myself, by Pat Palmer
Louanne Pig in the Perfect Family, by Nancy Carlson
Love You Forever, by Robert Munsch
The Mouse, The Monster and Me: Assertiveness for Young People, by Pat Palmer
My Body Is My House, by Jeanne Engelmann
My Dad Loves Me—My Dad Has a Disease, by Claudia Black
No More Secrets for Me, by Oralee Wachter
Nobody's Perfect, Not Even My Mother, by Norma Simon
Perfect Percy, by Bonnie Pryor
Quick as a Cricket, by Audrey Wood
The Runaway Bunny, by Margaret Wise Brown
The Secret Everyone Knows, by Cathleen Brooks
Something Is Wrong at My House, by Diane Davis
A Story about Feelings Coloring Book, by the Johnson Institute

Books for Teens

AIDS: What Teens Need to Know, by Barbara Christie-Dever
Breaking Away: Saying Goodbye to Alcohol/Drugs, by Jean Sassatelli
Can I Handle Alcohol/Drugs?: A Self-Assessment Guide for Youth, by David Zarek and James Sipe
Feed Your Head: Some Excellent Stuff on Being Yourself, by Earl Hipp
Fighting Invisible Tigers: A Stress Management for Teens, by Earl Hipp
How to Stay Clean and Sober, by Martin Fleming
In Love and In Danger: A Teen's Guide to Breaking Free of Abusive Relationships, by Barrie Levy
Making the Most of Today: Daily Readings for Young People on Self-Awareness, Creativity, and Self-Esteem, by Pamela Espeland and Rosemary Wallner
Perfectionism: What's Bad about Being Too Good?, by Miriam Adderholdt-Elliot
The Power to Prevent Suicide: A Guide for Teens Helping Teens, by Richard E. Nelson & Judith C. Galas
Walk Tall: Affirmations for People of Color, by Carleen Brice
What Teens Need to Succeed: Proven, Practical Ways to Shape Your Own Future, by Peter L. Benson, Judy Galbraith, Pamela Espeland, and Gail Galbraith
When a Friend Dies: A Book for Teens about Grieving and Healing, by Marilyn E. Gootman (Editor)
When Living Hurts, by Sol Gordon, Ph. D.
When Nothing Matters Anymore, by Bev Cobain

Resources for Teachers

The Crisis Manual for Early Childhood Teachers: How to Handle the Really Difficult Problems, by Karen Miller, Redleaf Press/ISBN 0-934111-140. Gryphon House, Inc., PO Box 2207, Beltsville, MD 20704-0207.
Practical Solutions to Practically Every Problem: The Early Childhood Teachers Manual, by Steffen Saifer, Redleaf Press/ISBN 0-9341440-61-8. Gryphon House, Inc., PO Box 2207, Beltsville, MD 20704-0207.

Books Available from Fernside

Fernside, 2303 Indian Mound Avenue, Cincinnati, Ohio 45212. Voicemail: 513-841-1012. Fax: 513-841-1546. E-mail: Fernside@fuse.net.

Fernside: Helping Children and Families Cope with Death: A description of our services (flyer)

How Can I Help a Grieving Child? (flyer)

How Can A Teacher Help A Grieving Child? (flyer)

Inside Fernside Newsletter (bi-monthly)

A Book For You, From Kids Like You (A workbook for grieving children with drawings and quotes from Fernside Kids; good for ages five through twelve)

Dealing with Death and Grief at School (A handbook for teachers and school staff covering how to explain a death, answer and questions, assist individual grieving students, a grieving class, a crisis plan, and list of resources. Developed jointly with Children's Hospital School Intervention Team)

Fernside Idea Book (A guidebook for group facilitators. Includes peer support grief group activities, descriptions of different age groupings, Rachael's World and Self-Discovery articles, and lists of books. Developed after eight years' experience with input from volunteers.)

Inside Fernside Collection (temporarily out of print). (A collection of forty-two articles dealing with grief issues that have appeared in the newsletter. Articles written in response to issues raised in children's sharing circles in Fernside. Illustrations by Fernside kids.)

Other Resources

Help for Children from Infancy to Adulthood, by Miriam J. Williams-Wilson, RN.

The Help for Children Newsletter, Edited by Miriam J. Williams-Wilson, RN.

Stress Stoppers for Children and Adolescents, by Miriam J. Williams-Wilson, RN.

Stress Stoppers Flashcards, by Miriam J. Williams-Wilson, RN. (These cards are designed to help correct distorted thinking patterns in children before they become a habit.)

The Bullying Prevention Handbook: A Guide for Principals, Teachers and Counselors, by Dr John L. Hoover and Dr. Ronell Oliver.

Project Resilience and Youth Communications: The Struggle to be Strong and The Leaders Guide to the Struggle to be Strong, Free Spirit, in press, by S. J. Wolin, W. Muller, F. Taylor, and S. Wolin.

Three Spiritual Perspectives on Resilience: Buddhism, Christianity, and Judaism in Family Therapy and Spiritually, edited by F. Walsh, Guilford Books, in press.

Wolin, S., & Wolin, S. J. (1995). Morality in COAS: Revisiting the syndrome of over responsibility. (Ed.), In S. Abbott, *Children of Alcoholics, Selected Reading.* Rockville, MD: NACOA.

Wolin, S. J., & Wolin, S. (1993) *The resilient self: How survivors of troubled families rise above adversity.* NY, NY: Villard Books.

Resilient Kids: James' Story, Attainment Co., (Video)

The Heart Knows Something Different, edited by Al Desetta.

Hotline for Families of Children with Mental Health Needs: The National Mental Services Knowledge Exchange Network: Tel.: 1-800-789-2647.

American Academy of Child and Adolescent Psychiatry, 3615 Wisconsin Avenue Northwest, Washington, DC 20016; Tel.: 202-966-7300.

"Facts for Families of Children and Teens" are short yet thorough descriptions of over sixty-five emotional/psychiatric problems that can be encountered during childhood or adolescence. These entries can be attained in languages other than English, e.g., Spanish, French, or German.

Polese, C. (1994). Resilient readers: Children's literature in the lives of abuse survivors. *School Library Journal, 40* (3), 156.

References

Benard, B. (1993). Fostering resiliency in kids. *Educational Leadership, 51* (3), 44–48

Benard, B. (1991). *Fostering resiliency in kids: Protective factors in the family, school, and community.* Portland, OR: Western Center for Drug-Free Schools and Communities.

Blackburn, C. A. (March, 2000). The Consultative Group on Early Childhood Care & Development. [on-line]. Available: http//www.ecdgroup.com/en/claudia.

Boutte, G. S., LaPoint, S., & Davis, B. D.(1993). Racial issues in the classroom: Real or imagined? *Young Children, 49*(1), 19–23.

Bronfenbrenner, U. (1981). Children and families. *Society, 18* (2), 38–41.

Elkind, D. (1981). *The hurried child.* Reading, MA: Addison-Wesley.

Krovetz, M. L. (1999). *Fostering resiliency: Expecting all students to use their minds and hearts well.* Thousand Oaks, California: Corwin Press.

Masten, A. S. & Coatsworth, J. D. (1998). The development of confidence in favorable and unfavorable environments: Lessons from research on successful children. *American Psychology, 53,* 205–220.

McIntosh, P. (1995). White privilege and male privilege: A personal account of coming to see correspondence through work in women's studies. In P. H. Collins & M. L. Anderson (Eds.), *Race, class, and gender: An anthology* (pp. 70–81). Belmont, CA: Wadsworth.

Wallerstein, J. S., & Kelly, J. B. (1980). *Surviving the breakup: How children and parents cope with divorce.* New York: Basic Books.

Werner, E., & Smith, R. (1989). *Vulnerable but invincible: A longitudinal study of resilient children and youth.* New York: Adams, Bannister & Cox.

9

Narratives from a Rural, Southern, White Woman

The Education and Work Ethic of a Member of the Class of 1931

Jane J. White and Julian L. Mims III

Editor's Overview _____

This historic chapter provides a rare glimpse into southern, rural, White, female culture during the early to mid-1900s. This chapter makes within-race variations in White Culture apparent. The authors capture the nuances and meanings of school for a woman (who is the mother of one of the authors) by sharing excerpts of conversations between the woman, Mattie Pearl, and her contemporaries. The storyline is engaging, and there is much to learn as we closely examine what the school experiences meant to Mattie Pearl and her schoolmates.

Authors' Stories

Jane J. White

Although I was born in Georgia, my parents moved north when I was three. I grew up in Ann Arbor, Michigan, and was a product of good, solid, midwestern public schools both as a child in Ann Arbor and as a college student at the University of Wisconsin. I taught sixth grade in Madison, Wisconsin, put my husband through law school, had my first child and went back for my first master's (in education) at the University of Wisconsin. I have since lived in Philadelphia, Pennsylvania, Maryland, and the Carolinas, following my husband as he moved during his practice as an environmental attorney. I have now worked in education for more than thirty-five years, first as a classroom teacher, then as a student teacher supervisor at Temple University and the University of Pennsylvania, and then as a social studies education professor and ethnographic researcher at the University of Maryland Baltimore County and the University of South Carolina.

My most significant and powerful educational experiences occurred when I was a doctoral student at the University of Pennsylvania in Philadelphia. I became bored with education courses and went sideways by taking the doctoral level coursework and comprehensive examination for cultural anthropology. I took courses on Native Americans, peasants, nomads, and African kingdoms! I was finally learning in-depth, compelling ways of making meaning about diverse groups of people across time and space. I found the concept of culture to be the single most compelling and useful idea I have ever acquired—the concept of culture as first explained in Edward Hall's *The Silent Language* (1959), in which people acquire taken-for-granted behaviors and values about what types of social relationships to establish with different types of people, how to use space (how close one should stand to another person), how to use time, what work is, what play is, how a male acts, how a female acts, how and when to use language, what is valuable in education, and so forth within the boundaries of the group into which they are being socialized. Working with Shirley Brice Heath, author of *Ways with Words* (1983), I studied how teachers and students construct knowledge about culturally different people. I had opportunities to examine how schools as a cultural institution reward and reinforce specific mainstream behaviors and values while negatively labeling and rejecting socially and culturally different students.

Yet for all my work to develop relevant and meaningful curriculum and instruction with students and teachers in inner-city, suburban, and rural schools in Philadelphia, Baltimore, Washington, D.C., Maryland, and Virginia, I was never interested in investigating my own cultural heritage. While I was growing up in Michigan (and to this day), I aggressively challenged anyone who mocked my mother's distinctive southern accent or teased about her "unusual" name, Mattie Pearl. However, I blithely assumed that my values and experiences had emerged from and were not that different from hers.

That changed while I was at the University of Maryland Baltimore County. I became frustrated as I worked with a colleague from geography to develop a middle-school curriculum unit based on how the nature of work and the work ethic changed in the United States as our country changed from a rural agrarian country into an urbanized and industrial and then a service economy. We wanted to use stories to illustrate our theme. But we

were disgusted to realize that biographies and the writings of White males—
Benjamin Franklin, Abraham Lincoln, Andrew Carnegie, and Henry Ford—
were held up as the exemplars of the American work ethic.

How had we gone astray? Surely they were not the only ones who had
worked hard and made a difference in our country's economy and history.
Other than the inclusion of European immigrants at the turn of the nineteenth century—for example, Andrew Carnegie, who worked hard, saved
his pennies, and experienced incredible social mobility—mainstream historical and geographical research had not integrated the accounts of African
Americans, Native Americans, Latino Americans, Asian Americans, and
women workers that had emerged from the texts of Black, ethnic studies,
and feminist scholarship. There were not any standard references, easily
consultable by busy school teachers, that told the story of the beliefs about
work that diverse men and women held as they worked on farms, as artisans, building railroads, in factories and then bureaucracies, service industries, and international corporations. Although the most recent set of
textbooks now abound with insets, photographs, and sometimes brief excerpts from primary sources written by a variety of people, the history and
realities of groups who have held viewpoints that differ from and may be in
opposition to mainstream history are still not sought out and studied.

Now curious about my own heritage as a worker and a woman, I began
to press my southern mother, born in 1913, for accounts of what it was like
growing up in a farming community in the South. I decided to transform
this interest into serious scholarship when I heard that my parents planned
to attend a reunion of my mother's class of 1931 of the Georgia Industrial
College.

After spending a year (1987–88) as a scholar-in-residence in the linguistics department of Georgetown University and studying with Dr. Debo-
rah Tannen, I had learned the power of stories as narrative and oral history.
Volunteering to drive my parents from Michigan to Georgia and back, I au-
diotaped more than twenty hours of reminiscences in the car on the trip to
and from Georgia. I taped and transcribed stories told on the front porches
and in the front parlors of aunts and uncles as they reminisced about their
childhood days. I collected narratives shared by the extended family that
had gathered for the wedding and reception of a cousin; I went for drives
with relatives to visit the family graveyard and to see the house where they
had all grown up. I was allowed to tape all the conversations my parents had
in a twenty-four-hour visit with their friend of sixty years, Bob Foster, who
had attended Emory Medical School with my father. And finally, I took pictures and collected all the talk that went on at my parents' table at the Georgia Industrial College reunion.

As an anthropologist, I knew that my parents were going through a rite
of passage in which they were remembering important people and reliving
key events in their lives as a prelude to saying good-bye to it all. As Neville

(1984) argued, these rites of cultural intensification are gatherings in which "cultural forms and meanings that are at other times carried in the heads of the culture bearers . . . take on social shape" (p. 161). These encapsulated bits of cultural meaning, unspoken but not forgotten, are "at every opportunity brought out and spoken with intensity and enjoyment" (p. 161). As a daughter, I welcomed learning more about what my parents' lives were like. I gained entry to this world as a child of Mattie Pearl, but as an outsider, I provided a new and interested audience for tales of what mattered to them.

As a linguist, I know that talk is much more than talk. As Labov (1972) argued in his classic article "The transformation of experience in narrative syntax," narratives do more than recapitulate past experiences. They also have a point to make, a *raison d'être* for being told, and in this case, it was particularly important that they be instructive for a family member from a younger generation. These remembrances both encode specific experiences and go beyond them. The purpose of this chapter is to analyze what was significant about the education, work, and work beliefs of a southern, White, rural woman in the class of 1931. From the particulars of her story, I hope that some of the fiercely held beliefs and practices of a community of rural, poor, southern, white women have been illuminated.

Julian L. Mims III

I was born in Augusta, Georgia, and am from a family that has lived in up-country South Carolina for over two centuries. I was educated in the public schools locally, with special interests in music and history. My college education was primarily through schools in the Palmetto State: I earned an A.B. degree with a major in history and political science and a minor in education and psychology from a small college in South Carolina and a master's degree in U.S. history from the University of South Carolina. While in college, I took education courses to become certified, had the eye-opening experience of student teaching in a rural high school, and, while completing my master's degree, taught history at a junior high school in Columbia, South Carolina.

Research for a master's thesis brought me to the South Carolina Department of Archives and History, which led to a job there. I became certified as an archivist, held national office in a professional association, published many articles and two books, and fully developed a specialty in local government records management and archival administration. This expanded to consulting throughout the southeastern United State and then to a position with the New York State Department of Education, State Archives and Records Administration.

When I returned from New York to South Carolina, I became a full-time teacher of U.S. history and Western civilization at a high school near my hometown of Edgefield, South Carolina.

During my decades of work as a certified archivist, I encountered in the records of both New York and South Carolina some of the most interesting and historic primary sources in all of America. These documents included journals for two of the most important British colonies in terms of Indian trade as well as full transcripts of slave trials, previously unresearched and soon to draw national attention as *créme de la créme* archival sources for African American history. In all these documentary discoveries, my thought was, "I can't wait to bring these resources to my students!" My archival journey led to a new dimension of classroom teaching, for the use of primary sources has become a highly developed facet of my methodology and a compelling means of engaging students. An archival career has helped me to bring history to the students in a tangible way that they can see and experience, for the copy of each carefully chosen original historical document gives them a "piece of history."

Such resources captivate students when they are imaginatively and creatively used by the teacher. The opportunity to write about resources for the study of rural, southern, white women is very interesting to me. I see the value of this effort as a teacher (whose instruction is driven by primary sources), as an archivist (whose experience with records meshes fully with social studies methodology), and as an historian (whose research interest has been rural southern U.S. history at the turn of the twentieth century).

I am a teacher. So is my wife. So was my mother. Seventeen other members of my extended family are teachers. The dimension of teaching that I bring to a family effort is a full awareness and use of resources—to add depth, meaning, variety, and glitter to instruction. The students love history that is "for real." Resources bring a beam of light to the classroom.

The Work Ethic: Acceptance of Hard Physical Labor and Pride in Competence

Mattie Pearl Weaver was born in 1913, the fourth of six children: William Session, Otis Paton, Joe Thomas, Mattie Pearl, Ada Margaret, and Luther Franklin. The Weavers lived on a hundred-acre red dirt and clay farm near the Towlaiga River in Georgia. The nearest town, Jackson, Georgia, was five miles away, an hour trip made only once a month to buy shoes, school supplies, or presents for the holidays.

The Weavers raised cotton, wheat, corn, and pimiento peppers and produced poultry and dairy products. There was always an abundance of food, but very little cash money. What little was available came into the household when the bales of cotton were sold or the milk check came. Mattie Pearl's father died when she was six, and the oldest boy, Session, at age thirteen assumed many of the responsibilities of man of the house.

All members of the Weaver family, even the smallest child, participated and shared in the work. The daily chores of the older boys, Session, Otis, and Joe, included milking the cows, separating the milk, and putting the milk into cans for collection. They fed the horses, mules, and pigs. In the spring and summer, the older boys used the mule to plow the fields, plant seeds, and reap the harvest. In the winter, they mended the machinery, repaired the fences and chopped wood.

In the fall, the younger children, Mattie Pearl, Ada, and Luther, helped pick cotton or stack wheat after they came home from school. Mattie Pearl cooked while Ada watched Luther. Their mother, Mattie, ran the chicken yard, supervised the milking of thirty cows, and helped in the fields. The three youngest children also shelled corn for the chickens, bottle fed the calves, and gathered eggs from the hen nests.

On the weekend, the girls churned the butter, swept the yard, and white-washed the hearth with white clay and water. School clothes were washed, starched, and ironed.

During my mother's childhood in the 1920s, homes in the country did not have electricity or running water. Mattie Pearl, Ada, and Luther were responsible for bringing water from the well and filling the stove bin and fireplace with wood before sunset. Cleaning the chimneys of the kerosene lamp was another task that fell to the girls. Later, when President Roosevelt created the Rural Electrification Administration in 1935, a federal loan program that eventually resulted in the electrification of 98 percent of America's farms, he became a hero to rural families.

In 1988, I drove my parents from Michigan to Georgia so that Mattie could attend the reunion of her college class of 1931 at the Georgia Industrial College. Along the way, we stopped to visit with their lifelong friends, Bob and Jane Foster. Prompted in part by the interest of an ignorant city girl (this researcher), Mattie Pearl and Bob began to reminisce and tease, displaying their intimate knowledge of the nature of farm work, in this case, milking a cow:

Bob Foster: Speaking of milking a cow, have YOU (speaking to me) milked a cow?

Jane White (author):   Nooooooo . . .

Mattie: Oh, heavens yes!

Bob Foster: When you milked a cow—well, what you do is you take your milk pail and you put about a fourth full fresh water in it. And you go toddle in there to the barn.

Mattie: Yeah.

Bob Foster: You bring the calf. You put the cow in the stall and put some feed in there and bring the calf in. And you let the calf have one quart. He can suck on one tit and one tit only. You let the calf get through he's fed. You run the calf out and wash the tit.

Mattie: And it's slick as . . . (starts laughing)

Bob Foster: A ha ha, slick as Christmas.

Mattie: That tit that he sucked is a slick as I don't know what!

Bob Foster: so then you take that water you've got and you swoosh it up under there.
Laughter.
And you try to get it relatively clean. It's somewhat less than pasteurization.
Laughter.
And you sit down on some little one-legged or two-legged or three-legged type stool. I had a two-legged stool. And you've done away with your water, and the well is a half mile away. And the cow stall is not exactly clean and neither is the cow.

Mattie: Yeah, and she's got something dried on her tail.

Bob Foster: Yeah.
Laughter.
And you got it slapping in your face. And you want to use two hands but the only way you can use two hands is to put the bucket down.

Mattie: Yup and then the cow will kick it over.

Bob Foster: And about that time flies get on the cow and she raises her hind foot up and she sets it right down

Mattie: in the bucket.
Laughter.
Oh, I've done that!

Bob Foster: And the cow manure goes everywhere.
Laughter.
There's an old southern expression that I just dearly love. It says, "Something in the milk ain't cream."
Shouts of laughter.

Mattie: And you're debating with yourself. Well it's all going to strain out. Do I dump it or

Bob Foster: Or go back to the well and start over?

Mattie: Well who's going to know?

Bob Foster: Well, it's fortunate that cow manure's not poisonous.

Description of the Era

In the rural south in the 1920s and 1930s, hard manual labor was necessary for the survival of the rural family unit. It was seen as natural that work was dirty, sweaty, and tiring, but people who grew up on farms took pride in their competence. Country folk were united by their knowledge of how to do farm chores. There was satisfaction and solidarity in the knowledge that day after day they could get up at 5:30 in the morning and put in a good day's work, in contrast to town folk, who were seen as stuck up, flighty, and soft.

Among rural families, there was a strong belief in the ability to "get ahead" through education. It is therefore not surprising that Mattie Pearl earned all A's during her last few years in the consolidated county school, which included first through tenth grade. Because of her industry and scholarship, my mother was awarded the Towlaiga Women's Club Scholarship for the Deserving Poor. Each year, this award of fifty dollars was given to the child of a "widow woman" whom the club members felt had worked hard and done well in school. Winning this award meant that Mattie Pearl could attend the Georgia Industrial College (GIC) for her senior year of high school as well as for the first two years of junior college.[1] The fifty-dollar scholarship allowed my mother to buy shoes, used books, and used skirts for the uniform. (Her mother made the middy blouses.) Mattie Pearl worked each summer at the college to earn forty-eight dollars to pay for the sixteen-dollar tuition for each of the three quarters of study.

In addition to the tuition payments, everyone in this school for 350 students worked in exchange for their room and board. There was no hired help at the college except for Minnie, a woman whose daily job was to make enough biscuits and cornbread for all three meals. All the food was grown and prepared on the college campus. The women rotated jobs each week of the month. For one week they cooked, a task they disliked because they had to get up at 4:00 in the morning. For the three other weeks, they waited tables, washed dishes, and cleaned the dormitory. The men specialized in one particular job on the farm. They grew and harvested crops, raised chickens and livestock, and prepared milk products in the dairy.

Rural men and women at that time established their identity through the work that they did. Interestingly, at the Georgia Industrial College Reunion, people were identified more than fifty years later in terms of the job they had held at school. One man was nicknamed "Chicken" because his job had been raising chickens at GIC. This man was also remembered for and teased about an incident,which took place at a recruiting picnic, in which his work was less than stellar.

---

[1]The Georgia Industrial College at Barnesville existed from 1929 to 1933. GIC was the reorganization of an Agricultural and Mechanical (A&M) School founded in 1908 with 200 students. There were five A&M's in the state of Georgia under the supervision of the Board of Regents of the University of Georgia. Their purpose was to provide training for young people that went beyond the schooling given in the one-room school houses that dotted the rural countryside. A&M's at Statesboro and Americus went on to become junior colleges and, later, four-year colleges.

Mattie: Now the only one I haven't been able to place. Somebody tended the chickens. And took care of all the chickens that were brought into the kitchen. Killed the chickens. I thought it was Weeny. Weeny?

Pug: What name?

Mattie: That's W-E-E-N-Y.

Pug: That's Steve Weeny.

Mattie: What was that?

Pug: Steve Weeny. Arthur Steve Weeny.

Mattie: Yeah, that's it!

Pug: There he is standing right over yonder!
    Pause.
    We called him Chicken. Chicken Steven.
    Laughter.
    Pointing
    Over there with the checkered coat on.

Mattie: Let me ask Matilde. She'll know.

Mattie: Cause one time Whoever it was.

Pug: Cause he can tell you.

Mattie: Cause we were supposed to go with Mr. White on a recruiting lunch recruiting for the college. Take a picnic lunch. Matilde and I fried chicken for two or three hours. And we got to the picnic. And YOU COULD NOT CHEW IT. IT WAS THE TOUGHEST THING YOU HAVE EVER SEEN!
    Laughter.
    And when we got back we found out that he had killed a hen.

Pug: Yeah.

Mattie: Instead of a fryer.
    Laughter.

Another man, T. J. Harper, was given a toy dairy farm to symbolize the work he had done there. Pug, who cleaned the boy's dormitory, laughed with my mother about how wet it was on Saturdays when students who did not go home for the weekend washed their clothes and sheets in the lavatory and hung them up to dry.

Mattie Pearl studied English, history, math, and domestic arts, which included cooking and sewing. One of the requirements for graduation was that the women had to be able to make their own graduation dress. The men took the same academic courses but instead of domestic arts had classes in agriculture and mechanics. At the GIC reunion, Mattie Pearl and her friends still remembered the professors, the textbooks, and the anxiety associated with wanting to do well on the final exam:

Mattie: Do you recall how they did the final exam in cooking?

Nita: Oh I recall.

Mattie: Do you remember that old Blue, Harrie and Lacey cookbook?

Nita: Yeah. Somebody stole mine. Or I loaned it to somebody.

Mattie: You did? I got rid of mine not too long ago I should have saved it. It had gotten so old. And I had lost a lot of pages.

Nita: Uh huh.

Mattie: In the final exam. The day before you took the final exam she er . . . oh Dykes, Dykes Nellie Dykes was the teacher's name.

Nita: That's it.

Mattie: Everybody would go up and wherever the book opened That's what you had to cook!

Nita: Mmmm . . .

Mattie: And OHHH. I remember SO WELL what I had to cook.

Nita: What'd you cook?

Mattie: Lemon pie and I haven't liked it since.

Jane: I knew you didn't like lemon pie. And now I know why. Why? Because it just scared you so much?

Mattie: Lemon pie is one of the hardest things in the world to make!

Forget chitchat about the weather. Women greeted each other with talk and memories of food. Women and indeed whole dynasties of women were associated with specific dishes. As we entered the GIC reunion and headed for the table loaded with food, my mother's first instruction to me was, "Find out where the Ridgeway girls' cake is. Their mother always made good pound cake." (And yes, Matilde Ridgeway did bring a pound cake with chocolate frosting.) As the women circled the pot luck buffet, there were cries of welcome and intense commentary on the offerings. Aunt Nita's burnt sugar caramel cake was one of the more resplendent entries and I was immediately ordered to take a picture of it by my mother. As Nita was repeatedly asked for the recipe, she modestly responded that "Its not hard to make," as she reeled off the ingredients: three cups of sugar, a stick of butter, White Karo syrup . . . Finding out that Hazel Ridgeway had brought peach cobbler launched an animated discussion of the merits of peach versus blackberry versus apple cobbler. My mother had her reputation as a visitor from far away to uphold, so she had packed the ingredients and fixed a "northern" dish the night before at Aunt Ada's. All the women tasted her cold pasta salad and exclaimed over it but some of the men were not convinced that pasta should be served cold. There was some giggling at whoever had brought "store bought" potato salad, and even worse, fried chicken from Kentucky Fried Chicken. However, the women charitably concluded that these were probably offerings from widowers whose wives had died who still wanted to contribute something to the reunion.

Women Who Were Hard Working and Smart Were Admired

Rather surprising for my generation, who thought woman's liberation did not begin until the 1970s, the American dream was held for women as well as for men in this poor, white, rural community. From the starkest poverty, women who worked hard and who were smart at school could "make something of themselves." Not surprisingly, however, their rise was accomplished within the traditional occupations available to women.

My mother had first decided to try to attend the Georgia Industrial College when another girl in the Towlaiga community, Hazel Ridgeway, who was two years older than she, had been admitted. While she was at GIC, Mattie Pearl roomed with her best friend, Matilde Ridgeway, who was Hazel's sister. Mattie Pearl, Hazel, and Matilde were remembered and respected for more than fifty years because they were smart:

Raymond Holmes (Pug):   Mattie Pearl, I am just so glad to see you.

Mattie: You tell my daughter what you used to tell me about how you used to sit between Matilde and me.

Pug: Really?
Laughter
I told them I used to try to get as close as I could to Mattie Pearl and Matilde Ridgeway. Course they came from over here, Towlaiga. Because they always were so smart in school that I hoped a little of it might rub off on me!
Laughter

. . .

Mattie: When we graduated from college in 1933. . . .

Pug: Which one of you was valedictorian or whatever it was we had? It was either you or Matilde.

Mattie: Well, Matilde was the valedictorian for the senior year.

Pug: Yeah.

Mattie: And I was salutatorian.

Pug: See I told you.

Mattie: But when we graduated from junior college we were given awards.

Pug: Yeah, right.

Mattie: And I got the medal for having the highest grade point average ever in the history of the junior college.

Pug: I don't know I must have gotten one for the lowest.
Laughter

Mattie Pearl Weaver finished the last two years of college at Mercer University in Macon, Georgia. She was able to do this because a former English teacher who lived in Macon invited Mattie to do domestic work in her home in exchange for room and board. She also worked in the local post office, and her brother Joe, who had joined the Civilian Conservation Corps, sent her (what was then seen as) the huge sum of five dollars per month from his fifty-dollar paycheck.

Mattie Pearl matriculated planning to become an agricultural extension agent, a prestigious position in the community and one that "paid well for a woman." However, although Mattie Pearl loved cooking, she could not stand all the sewing that was necessary to do well in this major. My mother switched into primary education and became a kindergarten teacher, eventually working at the University of Georgia Laboratory School so she could continue on and obtain her master's degree (an outstanding feat for a poor, White, rural woman during the Depression!).

The first question people asked when they had not seen each other since graduating from GIC was, "Well, how did you turn out? What work did you do in your life?" Both men and women claimed identity and prestige from the work they had done. Without overt questioning, I learned that the GIC alumni I met had been a Marine, an insurance agent, a farmer, a teacher, and a hospital administrator. These men and women were proud of how long they had worked, often thirty or forty years. And when they talked about when and why they had retired, the underlying presumption was that they would still be working if ill heath, good retirement benefits, and so on had not intervened.

Only after they had defined themselves by their occupation did the GIC alumni talk turn to bragging about their children. Again, their success was defined in terms of what type of work their children were doing. The women in particular also continued to define themselves by the work that they were still doing for others: cooking and cleaning for a niece who had just had her first baby, making quilts for their grandchildren, canning and sharing food they had grown in their garden, and doing volunteer work at the hospital.

Appreciation of Community Support

Rather than rugged individualism, making something of yourself was also seen as being dependent on the local community. These traditions were maintained today: The main order of business at the reunion was the announcement that forty-five alumni had contributed $914 for the scholarship fund. The scholarship recipients from last year and this year were introduced as "deserving young people" who had been valedictorians and "won about every award there is to win." They each made short speeches: "Thank all of you for choosing me in this way and helping me in my college career." The chair concluded the ceremony:

> *Hazel:* And we're glad to help the young people with their education. Because we appreciate the ones who helped us when we were way back yonder struggling to get an education.

Many narratives were about mentors along the way who recognized that their students were "deserving" and whose generosity at critical times in their students' lives made it possible for the students to achieve. Recognition and appreciation of those who had helped the students when they most needed it was highly valued.

Almost every story about a person was prefaced with a discussion of the reality of their economic situation. Poverty was not held against a person. Rather, rising from poverty by being frugal and hard working was seen as character building. The underlying maxim was that people, not things, mattered as you worked to make something of yourself.

Another woman discussed with admiration was Meta Jordan:

> *Mattie Pearl:* And Meta and I taught together at a primary school. She taught third grade. And can't you just see Meta's eyes when she said something a little naughty.
>
> *Bob Foster:* But not very naughty. Just a little naughty.
>
> *Mattie:* Meta was a girl from south Georgia like me.
>
> *Bob Foster:* Another story about Meta this one I think you've heard about Meta and the money she borrowed from the Lanes to go to school.
>
> *Mattie:* Yeah and there was something about her husband Henry wondering if he should return some money.
>
> *Bob Foster:* Yeah, Mills Lane who was the founder of the Citizen's National Bank which was a big bank in the Southeast. Old man Lane and his wife gave scholarships to deserving needy children.

And Meta was the child of an itinerant Methodist preacher from Lucia, Georgia, which is practically nowhere.

Mattie: Now I know Henry's dad was a preacher. Was Meta's too?

Bob Foster: Meta was the daughter of a Methodist preacher. And she didn't have money to go to school. And she heard about the Mills Lane scholarships which were given on an individual basis. It wasn't a structured thing. A school didn't have anything to do with it. Just go to see the lady.

Well the Lanes loaned Meta the money to go to GIC at Statesboro and to go to college. So Meta started teaching and immediately started paying back this probably very nominal loan. And paid it back in full. Not only that, on Mother's Day

Mattie: She always sent a. . . .

Bob Foster: Each year she always sent a cake to Mrs. Lane.

Jane: Oh, that is wonderful!

Bob Foster: This went on for many, many years. Well, Meta gets the cancer and gets in the hospital and it happens to be just before Mother's Day. So Henry wrote Mrs. Lane a note and said, "You're not going to get your Mother's Day Cake cause my wife is in the hospital and she can't cook. She's got cancer and it looks like she's going to die." So Mrs. Lane wrote back and said, "Is there anything I can do for you financially?" So Henry wrote back and said, No, the Lord had been good to him and he was able to take care of everything. Next thing in the return mail he gets a check for $1500. At that point he comes to see us, and says, "What must I do? I can't keep that check!" I said, "Dammit, you can't give it back!" I said, "Don't take that away from that old lady. Go put it in the bank." Which he did.

Mattie: Wait a minute. You said, "Don't give it back to the lady?"

Bob Foster: Yes, so he took it and put that money in his children's trust fund, an educational trust fund. Mrs. Lane told him that Meta was one of three that had ever paid her back. And only one of two that they knew where they were.

Humor, Quickness, and Resourcefulness

For the Towlaiga community, learning was not limited to just that which was formally taught within schoolroom walls. In the bigger context, perhaps one of the most successful, if unsung, teaching projects conducted in the history of the United States was the transformation of small farms harnessed to mule and people labor into the sophisticated, highly productive American farms we have today. State universities provided information about the latest scientific breakthroughs such as seeds, fertilizers, insecticides, and methods of crop rotation to all the farmers in the state, no matter how poorly educated and/or poor.

Although the local Towlaiga community listened with interest to these new ideas provided by the agricultural extension agents, there was also skepticism when the young and sometimes "town folk" ventured into their areas of established competence. The Towlaiga community turned out for these events with a slightly different purpose: first, to get a chance to socialize with their friends, and second, to keep an eye on each other's cooking:

Jane: I can't believe they'd[2] send somebody out to teach YOU about canning!

Mattie: Yeah. And sometimes weren't they supposed to teach sewing too?

Ada: Um hum.

Mattie: So one time they'd go would be—

Ada: sewing. And maybe the next time canning. And maybe the next time OH SHOOT! They'd demonstrate in front of the club. They'd do rolls—cloverleaf rolls.

Mattie: Yeah.

Ada: And everybody could make rolls! But you had to sit through it.

Jane: But why did anybody come if they already knew how?

Ada: Oh no, Jane, We were so glad to get a bath and get out of the house it didn't matter.

Mattie: *Laughing.* It was a social thing! We didn't really care what the woman said. We weren't going to do it anyway.

Ada: Yeah. We weren't going to follow it.

Mattie: "SHOOT!" they'd say. I'm not going to can my blackberries like that. But it was a social thing. Where everybody in the area came. And you went there. And you saw the people in the community. And you had REFRESHMENTS!

Mattie: And it was always . . . They'd start thinking months in advance. When, and two women would do it together. And they would get together and decide.

Ada: Yup.

Mattie: And then there was always a lot of comment on Miss So-and-so and Mrs. So-and-so. "OOOOoohh, they sure did serve something nice!"

[2]The University of Georgia Agricultural Extension sent out agents to teach about the latest scientific developments in canning, cooking, and farming.

Ada: Well Momma and Mrs. Singley were together. And they didn't have any fresh celery so they tied some celery seed in a little bag and cooked that in with the potatoes for the potato salad.

Mattie: *Laughing.*

Ada: And that was new. Everybody raved about the potato salad. And it wasn't a thing but a substitute! I'll never forget that. And every once in a while I'll think now that's what I want to do and give it a different flavor.

Mattie: And that was the program, the home demonstration. And then there would be contests . . . And after the contest there'd be the refreshments. Everybody always went because of the refreshments. Sometimes the refreshments . . . Mrs. Effridge always served homemade angel food cake.

Ada: Yeah.

Mattie: Because she had an egg farm and she had so many cracked eggs.

Ada: That she could make an angel food cake.

Mattie: And that was a big social thing. They'd hold it the last Friday of the month. I know what I started to tell you. I know what I started to forget. Remember that woman's name, Rosa Hultson.

Ada: Yeah.

Mattie: And she and Aunt Pearl were supposed to bring the refreshments. And they were going to make this . . . I can, I can hear my mother talking about this until this day. . . . Ada, they made this special devil's food cake, And when they started to take it out on the table,

Ada: It fell down.

Mattie: It fell all apart into a million pieces. It fell all apart. Well, it was too late for them to do something different.

Jane: Oh.

Mattie: So she and Aunt Pearl—This woman which I thought was *so clever.* She said, "Pearl, we are going to take this to the club. And we're giving it a new name." And they brought it. They made all these different servings out of all these different little pieces. And didn't they put some whipped cream on the top of it. And they named it some esoteric "Black Bottom Upside-Down Tart." And all these women were saying, 'Where did you get the recipe?' And my mother knew all along. That it was a plain ol devil's food cake THAT FAILED.

All laughing.

Mattie: Right? But this woman was so clever. She had them all thinking it was something she learned out of the *Atlanta Constitution*. And she'd had it in Atlanta one time when she was visiting there. And she had named it the "Black Bottom Upside-Down Tart." And isn't that something!

Jane: That's wonderful!

Mattie: Otherwise everybody'd be saying, "Oh my goodness. I'm so sorry your cake failed." And my momma thought she was really smart. And she'd say, "That woman, she can think up more things!"

Differences: Then and Now

Rural southern women did not go to college to get a man. They went to college to better themselves. Recognized and supported by their community, Mattie Pearl, Matilde, Hazel, Meta, and Jane Foster were women who perceived themselves as competent and serious, hard workers. They knew they could do whatever it took to get an education: manual labor and domestic work were not seen as demeaning. These women knew that they were smart and intelligent. These women in the 1930s courageously set high expectations and persevered for years to reach their educational and occupational goals.

Today, young women at college seem more focused on male/female relationships than on their personal strengths as determined, hard-working scholars. In a study at a central midwestern university, Holland and Eisenhart (1988) found that college women often do not take themselves seriously. Holland and Eisenhart found that young women genuinely perceive their abilities as secondary to those of men. Although they began classes with high aspirations, those who selected majors in math or science, where classes were dominated by men, did not allow themselves to do well.

When I reviewed the entire set of the Georgia visit narratives, I was surprised by the lack of discussion and stories about men. Men were not the featured topic of conversation as Mattie Pearl, her sisters, and her friends reminisced about their lives. When I asked about this apparent lack in their conversation, especially about how and where they met the men that they were to marry, Mattie Pearl and the others dismissed my concerns by explaining that while they were getting their education, "If a man happened along, fine. If not, they were already supporting themselves." Their common sense attitude seemed to be that, "Like children, men were a lot of work because they need a lot of taking care of." The women agreed that it was smarter to get your education, get a well-paying job, and then think about getting married and having children. All of them followed this path, with Mattie Pearl and my other informants marrying late after they had completed their own graduate or professional degrees. All of these women then worked to support their husbands in graduate or medical school.

The women did not see themselves as being economically or emotionally dependent on a man. Women did not take on their husband's identity. For example, Hazel Ridgeway was talked about, deferred to, and seen as a role model because she was one of the first local girls from Towlaiga to go to GIC. Currently the president of the GIC Alumni Association, Hazel was known for being "organized" and for being a great quilt maker. Only later did I learn that Hazel had married late to a man who had been imprisoned for murdering his first wife. He was later set free when another person confessed. The community's interpretation was that Hazel was (1) "caring" for having written to this man in prison and (2) "not dumb" for marrying a man who had money from the state (for false imprisonment). Widows whose lives were without men were not excluded from the life of the community. In fact, some widows were perceived as having an easier life because they did not have to fuss with a cantankerous old man.

In contrast to today's focus on a woman's ability to attract a man, these women's lives seemed to be built around female–female bonding and community. They based their possibilities on what they saw other women of their class and station accomplishing, such as Hazel Ridgeway winning a scholarship to a junior college. They supported each other by sharing their knowledge and experiences about how to get ahead and by rooming together. They held and reinforced common values: rather than physical attractiveness or material goods, what was admired was the energy they brought to their work and their studies, their resourcefulness, their ability to be sweet and caring but also tough, in touch with the sometimes harsh realities of life. These rural, White, women did not seem to have a sense of isolation or intense anxiety about such current issues such as time management or personal fulfillment. Rather, there was a sense of solidarity and competence bounded by humor and playfulness even as they worked at manual, physically demanding, often dreary, never-finished tasks.

These rural, White, southern young women of the 1930s did not perceive themselves to be oppressed by men, as later generations of feminists would claim. At that time and place, women saw their alternatives as more restricted than men but different. In addition to higher education, men had other routes out: for instance, the CCC, the army, or forestry. But men were also more trapped. For example, when the Weaver children's father died, Session was expected to and did become a farmer to support his mother and younger siblings.

As both men and women struggled against the reality of poverty and a national economic system that offered few opportunities to anyone, it seems as if they embodied the Puritan work ethic: a case of classic capitalism. These men and women believed that if they worked hard, persevered over time, did not indulge in conspicuous consumption, and gave back to the community, they would be worthy of achieving their educational and occupational goals. They believed that hard work builds character and that America is a country of self-made women and men. Their belief in the American dream was unquestioned: that "from the humblest beginnings" a person with "merit and industry can rise to the top" (Rodgers, 1978, p. 12).

Today, we are no longer a nation of small farmers and artisans, and both the nature of work and our beliefs about it have changed. Even though many of us still believe in and practice hard work and persistence, as members of the vast working or middle class, we did not come from humble beginnings. We, too, believe that higher education is (almost automatically) required for obtaining a job and maintaining our status. Today, we are much more sophisticated (e.g., we have traveled to many places, have been exposed to different images of people on television) and knowledgeable as contrasted with the provincialism of the women and men coming out of the rural South in the 1930s. Our lives are not burdened with the relentless demands of hard manual labor, which should never be romanticized. We have many more options and opportunities for education and careers, but our quest does not seem as urgent. Rather, as we work for salaries and are one among many in huge bureaucracies and international corporations, our task has been to find personal satisfaction in our work, and for some, to make a difference.

Educational Implications

As one of the main societal institutions of enculturation, schools will continue their primary function (albeit covert in nature) of transmitting and rewarding mainstream behaviors and values. However, this does not mean that schools have to do so through the denial, punishment, and oppression of students who enter with differing ethnicities or alternative cultures. Indeed, as "minorities" become the majority in the United States, it behooves the "establishment" to open its doors to and embrace peoples of all walks of life. It is essential that schools as institutions become truly multicultural—giving equal access to all to participate in the dominant culture of the school and workplace while teaching everyone how to learn more about the practices and beliefs of their own culture(s) as well as of the cultures of people different from themselves.

Educators, who unfortunately are becoming less diverse, are teaching an increasingly diverse population of students. Teachers first need to teach their students how to gather data about, give voice to, and reflect on their own stories as an important aspect of their identity formation. All of the students in the class need to attend to the stories of others so as to begin to understand the true diversity of participants in their society. As Boutte cites Ayers in Chapter 1: ". . . learning personal stories of individuals fights against the reduction of human beings to one-dimensional beings. As soon as one moves beyond superficial interactions and learns a little about another person's life, the stereotypes disappear. . . . We quickly learn that the range of normality is vast rather than narrow."

Learning from others about the perspectives that guide their actions and render the world meaningful for them is powerful. Students are engaged by the emotions and reactions to events inherent in the narratives. Students may be surprised as they first encounter definitions and values different from theirs about how, for example, the family is defined and treated or what types of work or learning are seen as most important. Students do not have to agree with or even like values and practices that they learn about in other cultures. However, it is important that they learn enough to find a people believable. Teachers need to structure the sharing of voices and study of others so that the students try to understand people on their own terms rather than summarily judge anything different as inferior or inadequate (White, 1988).

But teachers must help their students go beyond attending to different voices to answer the fundamental question, "So what?" Why should we study about rural, southern women living in the first half of the twentieth century? What possible relevance could it have to us today? After helping students acquire an insider's view of a culture, it is vital that students move to an outsider's perspective and place their culture and the cultures of others within the larger context of time and space.

Students learn best about what they do and what they don't do within their culture by being able to compare it to others. For example, I can see the drawing of cultural boundaries as I was gently teased about my inability as a northern city girl to milk a cow or know how to select a chicken that will be tender. By understanding better the circumstances of my mother's culture, I begin to understand that events that I would have seen as embarrassing—for example, being labeled as poor (even if it was a scholarship for the "deserving poor")—were seen as matter of factly as the reality that one was working within. I learned more about the importance of maintaining a community that first helped you and that you then participated in to help others. As a city girl who values "book learning," it was important for me to see that this particular community did not necessarily value the new information—for example, about how to cook and can—brought by the agricultural agents. Rather, this knowledge was summarily dismissed as trivial and probably not useful, although it was politely received, so that the participants could enjoy the social aspects of the meeting and maintain their traditions of competitive cooking in their evaluation of the refreshments brought. Naively, assuming that feminism had started in my generation, I was surprised to learn how self-sufficient these women were, secure in their ability to work hard, not dependent on men for their identity nor subservient to them in scholarship.

The hardest task for busy teachers will be engaging in sufficient reflection and research to be able to ask the big, important questions (that have no one right answer) so as to involve students in analysis and interpretation. As knowledge of various cultures emerges within their classrooms, teachers will constantly be studying so that they can pose questions about the significance of different cultures at different times and places. For example, in the following section, Mims asks, "Who was the southern, rural woman at the turn of the twentieth century? Why is so little known about her? Was she a 'home-concealed' woman or deliverer of the New South?" Imagine the excitement of having an entire class of students all researching primary sources to find documents to support one interpretation or the other. Finally, ethnic studies are not just for people of color but are important and significant for everyone.

Rural, Southern, White Women, 1900–1950: "Home-Concealed Woman" or Deliverer of the New South?

Who was she? Who was the rural, southern, White woman during the first half of the twentieth century? In Georgia around 1901, Magnolia Wynn LeGuin quickly bore five children and rarely left her farm home. In her own words, she was a "home-concealed woman" (LeGuin, 1991). Historically, rural, southern, White women have not been in the limelight, unlike the generous attention accorded White males. Women usually were not wealthy and often they were limited in education, opportunity, and social interaction. However, many historians agree that the southern agrarian economy could never have survived without the work of women (Sharpless, 1993). The topic of rural, southern, White women has recently gained more attention and is more focused than ever before. Contemporary historians are "painting a picture of the South that would have been unrecognizable two generations ago" (Boles, 1992, p. 1).

The South may be the most distinct section of the United States. Yet, this does not mean oneness. After all, the South includes the Mississippi Delta, Appalachia, Tidewater Virginia, and west Texas. Because of the differences in these regions, it would be a mistake to stereotype southerners. So is it also with rural, southern, White woman. As this researcher found, she may be the wife of a Georgia senator; a camp croft, a South Carolina squatter; a newly wed, despondent at the prospect of a bleak existence for life; an organizer of statewide home demonstration programs; or one who writes to escape the isolation and despondency of farm life. The dissimilarities among the lives of rural, southern, White women are dramatic. Many southern women were "seen but not heard"; however, Ella May Wiggins was so proactive that she gave her life in a 1928 Gastonia, North Carolina, textile strike (Peters, n.d.). Movie star Ava Gardner and coal miner's daughter Loretta Lynn are both rural, southern, white women; yet, they are distinctly different. Also, rural (for at least part of their lives), southern women were the mothers of presidents Theodore Roosevelt, Woodrow Wilson, Andrew Johnson, Jimmy Carter, William Clinton, and George Bush (father and son).

Two surveys conducted in Texas in the 1920s found that half to two thirds of the White women worked in the fields. The double burden of field work and house work was a fact of life. By 1925, almost 60 percent of all southern farmers, Black and White, lived on someone else's land. From the outset, the southern agrarian economy could never have survived without the work of women. What role did the South accord its women? The South's treatment of women is ironic. Patriarchy was symptomatic of the southern states, yet the South enhanced women's status by founding the first American women's club and college and passing the first married women's property legislation (Wolfe, 1996).

Although there is diversity among White, southern, rural women's roles, oral historians believe that there are also distinctive experiences of rural life: self-sufficiency, persistence through hard times, neighborhood mutual aid, and relative equality of rural folk (Walker, 2000). Poor southern women showed their defiance merely by surviving; striving, not accomplishment, often became their legacy. Ensuring the continuation of their families became no small victory (Sharpless, 1993).

In 1891, as the South looked to the beginning of the twentieth century, Mrs. W. H. Felton of Georgia attended a farmer's meeting to appeal for support toward founding a normal and industrial school for girls at Milledgeville. At the meeting, she was approached by a young woman who tearfully exclaimed, "God bless you for your sympathy. I crave learning as I never craved food, and I've been hungry many a time. I can do nothing to earn a nickel but plow, hoe, and pick cotton in the hot sun." Mrs. Felton later wrote, "My heart aches for the poor white girls in Georgia, they are nearly friendless in a cold hard world" (Felton, 1891).

Our taken-for-granted views of what life was like then may cause us to miss the mark. Women's histories and primary sources can help educators boost their understanding and instruction by putting themselves and their students in the place of others. Rural, southern, White women during the first half of the twentieth century perceived life very differently from the way we do. As a way of seeing the world through the eyes of others, few sources are equal to letters, journals, and other personal papers.

Resources enable us to make sense of the world of rural, southern, White women. Opportunities to see their experience have never been greater. If we want to understand them we take their culture seriously by studying it, employing the best truth-seeking methodology and the most revealing source material. Such material will enable us to grasp the woman's point of view, her relation to life, and her vision of her world. Resources can be a beacon that enables culture-bound twenty-first centurians to enter the first half of the 1900s. These records enable us to understand better the dramatic changes that began to occur in the twentieth century. The arrival of rural free mail delivery and the coming of the telephone, for example, were fundamental changes in the lives of southern women (Scott, 1997).

Several of the limitations of using primary sources to study rural, southern, White women's history should be noted. Principally, available materials come only from the minority who had some education (Scott, 1997). Additionally, few women left the diaries and letters that would allow historians to reconstruct their daily lives. Further, many diaries that were written have not been saved (Riney-Kehrberg, 1993). Immediately upon initiating research into the subject of rural, southern, White women, one is struck by the fact that most of the surviving sources, as well as the research and writing, relate to the colonial, antebellum or Civil War periods—as opposed to 1900 to 1950, the period that this chapter covers. Much has been said about the plantation owner, the slave, the Civil War woman, and the females of the cities. However, the twentieth-century, rural, southern, White woman is neglected in documentation and study. This chapter celebrates these women and gives voice to a group that was blatantly omitted from U.S. history.

Recalling her childhood on a farm in Depression-era, East Tennessee, Wilma Williamson exclaimed, "My grandmother could use everything about a hog except his squeal" (Walker, 2000, p. 1). Inquirers into sources on rural, southern, White women may feel that they are required to have the same earnestness—to get all you can from that which is available—for in many cases the records were not created in the first place, have not survived, or are not easily accessed. Educators interested in this topic should be encouraged, nonetheless, for there are more research materials, more easily obtained, than ever before. Further, the impact of online sources is dramatically changing educators' use of these materials.

Editor's Commentary

A common refrain heard from White students is, "I don't have a culture," or, "I'm just American." There is little or no acknowledgment of the rich legacy and cultural history that they have. They seldom realize that once upon a time, their European ancestors had distinct cultures. Nor do they see how residual effects of their heritage affect their current stances. Gary Howard (1999) reminds us that seeing others in cultural terms is difficult for many Whites because they do not view themselves in cultural terms. Howard (1999) asserts that there are many ways of being White. The current chapter provides readers with an opportunity to view White women from one of many cultural perspectives.

A prevailing stereotype of southern women is that of a southern belle whose intelligence is questionable at best. Because of the pervasiveness of this image in the literature and media, it is not difficult to conjure up an image of a southern, White woman consumed with drinking ice tea and walking leisurely under her parasol. This image neglects to portray the intelligence, determination, and diligence of women such as Mattie Pearl and, thus, calls our attention to how the range and complexity of White womanhood has been limited. Missing from historical works are common-place images that portray strong, self-sufficient, white, southern women such as Mattie Pearl and her friends. Their lives did not center on men or mundane issues such as what they would wear to the ball. Hill Collins (1993) rightly rejects simplis-tic, one-dimensional depictions of racial groups that fail to include analyses of the in-tersection of race, class, and gender (and in this case, geographic region). This chapter is important because it counters the numerous stereotypes that exist about southern, White women and allows their voices to be heard.

Contemporary White women's identities of who they are and what they can be are inevitably, albeit indirectly, influenced by images in the literature and other covert messages about White womanhood. Likewise, women of color are affected by images that portray White woman as sacred because the typical, unspoken corollary defines the roles of women of color (Hill Collins, 1993; Morrison, 1993): that is, if White women are sacred, women of color are not. However, when depictions of women of color and White women are shown through a full range of possible human behavior, the more balanced viewpoint comes closer to reality without glorifying either. Like Vivian's and Curtis's nostalgic accounts, the people portrayed in this chapter have many strengths that make them viable and positive role models for subgroups that have not fared well in school historically. Yet, as I read this chapter, nagging thoughts about White privilege and how this affected the outcomes of Mattie Pearl and her cohorts were difficult for me to reconcile with the emphasis on the work ethic. Absent in this chapter is any discussion about racial (or class or gender) discrimination, al-though the context is in the rural south only a few decades after slavery. What does this mean, I questioned myself? Is the subtext of this chapter "the American work ethic overcomes all barriers"? I have concluded that in Mattie Pearl's case, her willingness to work hard, community support, and high expectations by teachers and adminis-trators are all contributing factors to her success. Yet, "pulling yourself up by your bootstraps" may be easier for some than for others, depending on the structural bar-riers one is likely to face (Ogbu, 1993).

These reflections direct us back to the two complementary concepts presented in Chapter 1: the importance of seeing and not seeing race. We cannot narrowly contain "whiteness" under one label. There have always been Whites who are comforted by and absorbed in the notions and privileges of White superiority. On the other hand, there have always been Whites who fought side by side with blacks and others for abolition of slavery and civil rights for all. Both of these seemingly contrasting per-spectives are part of the complexity of whiteness (Howard, 1999). Mattie Pearl and her friends do not seem to fall in either of these extremes and probably would best be described as being somewhere in between. While seemingly they do not view the world through a single lens that is always right and always White, they seem to be un-informed (about race) and well-intentioned people who were probably not as widely exposed to other perspectives as were the rural, White participants in Chapter 7 (Howard, 1999). However, I hasten to conclude that, as with all of the stories in this book, the significance of Mattie Pearl's school experiences will mean different things for different people.

Reflective Activity _____

Talk with your grandparents (or a person of your grandparents' generation) to get some sense of what school was like for them. Compare and contrast other aspects of your life with theirs. Are there any themes that are common to both your experiences and theirs? Think of ways you can use the information gleaned from your discussion to personalize historical events for contemporary students. That is, think of events shared by your grandparents that may help contextualize history for students today (e.g., Who was president? What was a major political or social issue during your grandparents' era?).

Resources for Educators _____

Family, Friends and Contemporaries

The clearest and most interesting link is through relatives and friends. If you have such connections, you have the opportunity to interview them, read what they have written, study their records, and talk with their associates.

Librarians, Archivists, and Historians

These professionals have a uniquely valuable knowledge of sources. Seek out the persons who are most interested and knowledgeable in the area of the South to which you relate. Look for the archivists, as well as the collections, that are closest to your subject. Professors of history, women's studies, and/or southern studies are valuable resources.

Archives, Libraries, and Manuscript Depositories

For sources to be researched, they must first be preserved. Some of the leading archives in the United States are in the South. These include the Southern Historical Collection at Chapel Hill, North Carolina; the William R. Perkins Library at Duke University; the Alderman Library at the University of Virginia; the South Caroliniana Library; the Lower Mississippi Valley Collection, Louisiana State University; the Swem Library at the College of William and Mary; and Colonial Williamsburg, as well as numerous strong state historical societies and state archives (Scott, 1997).

Not only these fine archives, but also repositories everywhere are generating improved finding aids to reveal their holdings and provide more ready access. This preservation and description of research materials, together with improved accessibility, is of inestimable value to educators.

Records on Individuals

Primary sources include diaries, letters, journals, ledgers, account books, photographs, and scrapbooks. Published sources include newspaper articles, biographies, autobiographies, and obituary notices. These sources are available in a greater variety of media than ever: hard copy, microfilm, and CDs, as well as being online. The resources with which you may most strongly identify are personal data. Of primary sources, personal papers of individual women offer great appeal. Virginia Woolf once wrote that when writing a letter, one tries to reflect something of the recipient (Nicholson & Trautman, 1979). Consequently, researching letters may be regarded as second in importance only to conducting interviews for illuminating the life of a person. An expanding variety of personal papers, especially letters and diaries, shed light on the everyday exigencies of southern women. In the privacy of their diaries, for example, some women admitted to a passionate longing for knowledge: reading clubs, in one case, were described as "a peace offering to a hungry mind" (Chamberlain, n.d.). Examples of records on individuals include the following:

1. The work of a home economist of Rock Hill and Laurens County, South Carolina who was State home demonstration agent and organizer of the State Council of Farm Women (Winthrop University, Dacus Library, Archive and Special Collections Department, Rock Hill, South Carolina).
2. Nannie Stillvell Jackson Diary and Store Ledger, 1890–1908, University of Arkansas Libraries, Special Collections, Fayetteville, Arkansas.
3. There are 390 cubic feet of records in but one records series of the Women's Bureau, 1918–1956, National Archives Records Administration, Office of the National Archives, Washington, D.C.

Online Sources

A breakthrough for educators is the online availability of resources. Today, millions of documents are as accessible as the nearest "wired" computer. The advantages of this expanding source for educators are (1) a growing breadth and diversity of materials and (2) more readily available information describing these sources (the meta-data of finding aids, catalogs, indices, and related links). The payoff of online sources, succinctly stated, is indexed/screened/described sources that can be readily accessed and printed out—in your home, office, school library, or classroom. Online, powerful meta-data is a boon to women's history research. Examples include the following:

1. CIS Representing LEXIS-NEXIS in the academic and public library markets (see http://www.lexis-nexis.com/cispubs/guides/womens_studies/southern_women/swmnd4.h). Relevant subject headings, or combinations thereof, in using these indices include: farm life diaries, personal narratives, rural conditions, rural education, rural women, social life and customs, southern women's history, women in agriculture, women farmers, women teachers, women writers, and work ethic.
2. Library of Congress, or the National Archives, or the University of Virginia Library, or the South Historical Collection at Chapel Hill are new breakthroughs for educators.
3. The Ker Papers. This collection covers three generations and spotlights a family member who began a full-time career as a teacher at the age of fifty-eight and continued to teach well into her eighth decade. (Scott, Anne F. Southern Women and their Families in the 19th Century, Papers and Diaries, Series D. Holdings of the Virginia Historical Society. Part 4: District of Columbia, Florida, Georgia, Kentucky, Louisiana, Maryland, Mississippi, Missouri, and Tennessee, p. 6–7.

Added to Web May 1997. CIS Women's Studies, http://www.lexis-nexis.com/ cispubs/guides/womens_studies/southern_women/swmnd4.h. The finding aid is online, and the collection itself is available on microfilm: the Mary Susan Ker papers, 1785–1923, 25 reels, Southern Historical Collection, University of North Carolina, Chapel Hill.

Full-Text Sources

Publications are increasingly available in the full text. For example, the Women's History Review Web site provides scholarly articles retrievable in full text. Articles of interest may not only be identified, but also read in their entirety online.

Online Document Images

Increasingly, actual images of original documents are available. This enables educators and students to see the original and, if desired, to print it out—providing the information, as well as the "look," of the original document. Online documents allow educators to bring "a piece of history" into the classroom. This is a proven method of engaging students and enriching instruction.

Articles

Articles are easily accessed in published journals. Examples of journals are *The Journal of Women's History* and *Oral History Review.* Useful articles include the following:

Bialeschniki, M. D., & Walbert, K. L. (1998). You have to have some fun to go along with your work: The interplay of race, class, gender, and leisure in the industrial new south. *Journal of Leisure Research, 30*(1), 79–100.

Faragher, J. M. (1981). History from the inside out: Writing the history of women in rural America. *American Quarterly, 33,* Winter, p. 550.

Gilbert, D. (1983). Patchwork: Oral histories of grandmothers. *Southern Exposure, 11*(5), 54–59.

Hall, J. D., & Scott, A. F. (1987). Women in the south. In J. B. Boles & E. T. Nolen (Eds.) *Interpreting southern history: Historiographical essays in honor of Sanford W. Higginbotham* (pp. 454–509). Baton Rouge: Louisiana State Press.

Litoff, J. B., & Smith, D. C. (1992). Writing is fighting, too: The WWII correspondence of southern women. *Georgia Historical Quarterly, 76*(2), 436–457.

Osterud, N. G., & Jone, L. A. (1981). If I must say so myself: Oral histories of rural women. *The Oral History Review, 17*(2), 1.

Quinney, V. (1976). Textile women: Three generations in the mill. *Southern Exposure, 3*(4), 66–72.

Wheeler, W. B., & McDonald, M. J. (1986–1987). The communities of East Tennessee, 1850–1940: An interpretive overview, *East Tennessee Historical Society Publications 58–59 (1986–1987),* 3–38.

Bibliographies

Cline, Cheryl. *Women's diaries, journals and letters: An annotated bibliography.* New York: Garland Pub., 1989.

Filardo, Peter M. "Labor History Bibliography, 1998." *Labor History,* Nov. 1999 v40 i4 p483.

Goodfriend, Joyce D. *The Published Diaries and Letters of American Women: An Annotated Bibliography.* Boston: G. K. Hall, 1986.

Notable Women in American History: A Guide to Recommended Biographies and Autobiographies. Westport, Conn.: Greenwood Press, 1999.

"Southern History in Periodicals, 1996: A Selected Bibliography." *Journal of Southern History,* May 1997 v63 n2 321 (50).

"Women in the South: A Bibliography." *Southern Exposure,* 1977 4(4): 98–103.

Wardell, John. "Rural Education and Small Schools." *Rural Sociology,* Spring 1991 v56 n1 p161 (14).

Books

Allen, Ruth. *The Labor of Women in the Production of Cotton.* Austin: University of Texas Bulletin, no. 3134, September 8, 1931 (26).

Bleser, Carol, Ed., *In Joy and in Sorrow: Women, Family, and Marriage in the Victorian South.* New York: Oxford University Press, 1990.

Hall, Jacquelyn D. & Anne F. Scott, "Women in the South," in *Interpreting Southern History: Historiographical Essays in Honor of Sanford W. Higginbotham.* ed. John B. Boles and Evelyn T. Nolen. Baton Rouge: LSU Press, 1987, 478 (6).

Hagood, Margaret J. *Mothers of the South: Portraiture of the White Tenant Farm Women.* NY: Greenwood Press, 1969 (reprint of Chapel Hill: University of North Carolina Press, 1939).

Kahn, Kathy. *Hillbilly Women: Mountain Women Speak of Struggle and Joy in Southern Appalachia.* Garden City, NY: Doubleday, 1973. 230 p.

Kirby, Jack T. *Rural Worlds List: The American South, 1920–1960.* Baton Rouge: LSU Press, 1987, 390 p.

Korenman, Joan. *Internet Resources on Women: Using Electronic Media in Curriculum Transformation.*

Maman, Marie & Thelma H. Tate. *Women in Agriculture: A Guide to Research.* NY: Garland, 1996. 298 p.

Thomas, Jeannie B. *Featherless Chickens, Laughing Women, and Serious Stories.* Charlottesville: University Press of Virginia, 1997.

Collections of Primary Sources

Barthelme, Marion K., Ed. *Women in the Texas Populist Movement: Letters to the Southern Mercury.* College Station, TX: Texas A & M University Press, 1997. 248 p.

Fairbanks, Carol & Bergine Haakenson, Eds. *Writings of Farm Women, 1840–1940: An Anthology.* NY: Garland, 1990.

Rasmussen, Wayne D., Ed. *Agriculture in the US: A Documentary History,* 4 vols. NY: Random House, 1975.

Diaries

American Women's Diaries: Southern Women [microform]. New Canaan, CT: Readex Film Products, 1988. 34 microfilm reels (35mm) + guide (by Jane D. Begos, 44 p.)

Woodell, Harold, Ed. "The Shattered Dream: A Southern Bride at the Turn of the Century: The Day Book of Margaret Sloan." In Carol Bleser, series ed. *Women's Diaries and Letters of the Nineteenth Century South,* vol. 3. Columbia: USC Press, 1991.

Guides to Primary Sources

Begos, Jane D. "Southern Women's Diaries, A Guide" (44 p.). *American Women's Diaries: Southern Women* [microform]. New Canaan, CT: Readex Film Products, 1988. 34 microfilm reels (35mm) + guide.

Fischer, Gayle V. & Kathryn W Fuller. "Edited Collections of Primary Sources in U.S. Women's History: An Annotated Bibliography." *Journal of Women's History,* Winter 1995 v7 n4 206 (24).

"A Guide to Uncovering Women's History in Archival Collections." *Choice: Current Reviews for Academic Libraries,* August 15, 2000 v37 supplement 161(1).

Masstrom, Kathryn L., Ed. "Women's Voices in the Southern Oral History Program Collection." Cited in Gallagher, Connell B. "Assessing Published Collection Guides." *Oral History Review* 1993 21 (2): 81–88.

Terry, Gail S., comp. *Documenting Women's Lives: A Users' Guide to Manuscripts at the Virginia Historical Society.* Richmond: Virginia Historical Society, 1996.

Wilkins, Cary C., Ed. "Guide to the Kentucky Oral History Collection." Cited in Gallagher, Connell B. "Assessing Published Collection Guides." *Oral History Review* 1993 21 (2): 81–88.

Indexes/Abstracts

Women Studies Abstracts. Rush, NY: Rush Pub. Co., 1972–
Women's Studies Index. Boston: G. K. Hall. & Co., 1989–

Oral Histories

Jones, Lu Ann. "Mama Learned Us to Work": An Oral History of Virgie. St. John Redmond. *The Oral History Review,* Fall 1989 v17 n2 p63 (28).

Unpublished Sources

Here, the search for materials moves to a higher level of challenge (and likely, a higher return). Unpublished primary sources include letters, diaries, journals, and speeches found in archives, manuscript collections, historical societies, private collections, or family albums or scrapbooks. While the search into unpublished material can be time/money-consuming, it is important to note that such demands are not necessarily prohibitive. Universally, finding aids to document collections are improving. Many have computer indices and are online. Practically every repository of any size has some index, catalog, or other finding aid that will facilitate access.

Autobiographies

Chamberlain, Hope Summerell, "What's Done and Past," unpublished autobiography, William R. Perkins Library, Duke University.

Women of Color and Southern Women: A Bibliography of Social Science Research, 1975–1995, produced by Research Clearinghouse on Women of Color and Southern Women at the University of Memphis.

Oral History Transcripts

Jones, Lu Ann. Interviews for an Oral History of Southern Agriculture. National Museum of American History's Oral History of Southern Agriculture project. Natural Resource Section of the Division of History of Technology at the National Museum of American History, Washington, DC.

Walker, Melissa. Interviews. McClung Historical Collection, Lawson-McGhee Library, Knoxville, Tennessee.

Online Sources

Articles

Walker, M. (2000). Narrative themes in oral histories of farming folk. *Agricultural History*, 74(2), 340. http://web1.infotrac.galegroup.com/itw/i.ral+history-united+states?sw_aep= usclibs.

Bibliographies

Danborn, David B. H-SHGAPE Bibliographies: Agricultural and Rural Life during the Gilded Age and Progressive Era [online]. February, 1997. http://h-net2.msu.edu/~shagape/ bibs/rural.html.

Effland, Anne B. & Mary Gold, comps. Women in Agriculture and Rural Life: An International Bibliography [online]. February, 1997. http://www.nal.usda.gov/afsic/wia/ women.htm.

Finding Aids, Guides, and Catalogs

Duke University, Rare Book, Manuscript, and Special Collections Library, Durham, North Carolina National Agricultural Library. http://scriptorium.lib.duke.edu:8000/dynaweb/ findaids/warburt/.

Web Sites

American Women's History: A Research Guide, Digital Collections of Primary Sources: Farm Work and Life http://www.frank.mtsu.edu/~kmiddlet/history/women.wh-digcoll.htr. lArchivesUSA: http://archives.chadwyck.com.

Web Sites for Academic Libraries, Social and Behavioral Sciences: History, Geography and Area Studies: North America. http://www.lib.utsa.edu/Archives/links.htm; http://www. frank.mtsu.edu/~kmiddlet/history/women.html.

State History Collections

Florida State Archives Photographic Collection

Kentuckiana Digital Libary

Lewis Hine Photographs for TVA

Library of Virginia Digital Library program

Journals

Agricultural History: http://www.public.iastate.iastate.edu/~history-info/homepage.htm.

Rural History: http://www.public.iastate.edu/~history-info/homepage.htm.

Oral Histories

Today's Pioneer Women Oral Histories, Jane Hanneman interviewer. Center for American History, University of Texas Library, Austin.

Voices of American Homemakers Collection. National Extension Homemakers Council. Center for American History, University of Texas Library, Austin.

Research Centers

Center for Research on Women, Newcomb College, Tulane University, New Orleans, Louisiana: http://www.tulane.edu/~wclib

References

Boles, J. B. (1992). "The new southern history." *The Mississippi Quarterly, 45*(4), p. 368.

Chamberlain, H. S. (n.d.). "What's done and past." Unpublished autobiography. William R. Perkins Library. Duke University.

Felton, R. L. (1891). Letter from Bartow County, Feb. 16, 1891 in "Country Life in Georgia in the Days of My Youth," 271. Documenting the American South. Web site. University of North Carolina at Chapel Hill Libraries: http://docsouth.unc.edu/felton/felton.html

Hill Collins, P. (1993). Toward a new vision: Race, class, and gender as categories of analysis and connection. *Race, Sex, & Class, 1*(1), 25–45.

Holland, D. C., & Eisenhart, M. A. (1988). Moments of discontent: University women and the gender status quo. *Anthropology and Education Quarterly, 19*(2), 115–138.

Howard, G. (1999). *We can't teach what we don't know: White teachers, multiracial schools.* New York: Teachers College Press.

Labov, W. (1972). The transformation of experience in narrative syntax. In *Language in the Inner City.* Philadelphia: University of Pennsylvania Press.

LeCompte, M. (1978). Learning to work. *Anthropology & Education Quarterly, 9,* 22–37.

LeGuin, C. A. (1991). *A home-concealed woman: The diaries of Magnolia Wynn LeGuin, 1910–1913.* Athens: University of Georgia Press.

Morrison, T. (1992). *Playing in the dark: Whiteness and the literary imagination.* New York: Vintage.

Neville, G. W. (1984). Learning culture through ritual: The family reunion. *Anthropology & Education Quarterly, 15,* 151–166.

Nicholson, N., & Trautman, J. (Eds.). (1979). *The letters of Virginia Woolf, Vol. IV: 1929–1931.* New York: Harcourt, Brace, & Jovanovich.

Ogbu, J. U. (1993). Differences in cultural frame of reference. *International Journal of Behavioral Development; 16*(3), 483–506.

Peters, E. G. (n.d.). Southern bells: Voices of working women. A telling in three parts. DAI, 58 (98), 4046A, DA 9812108.

Riney-Kehrberg, P. (1993). Separation and sorrow: A farm woman's life, 1935–1941: Analysis of Martha Schmidt Friesen's diary. American rural and farm women in historical perspective. *Agricultural History, 67* (2), 185.

Rodgers, D. T. (1978). *The work ethic in industrial America 1850–1920.* Chicago: The University of Chicago Press.

Scott, A. F. (1997, May). Southern women and their families in the 19th century. Papers and diaries, Series D. Holdings of the Virginia Historical Society. Part 4: District of Columbia, Florida, Georgia, Kentucky, Louisiana, Maryland, Mississippi, Missouri, and Tennessee, p. 2. CIS Women's Studies. http://www.lexis-nexis.com/cispubs/guides/womens_studies/southern_women/swmnd4.h. (This collection is available on microfilm: the Mary Susan Ker papers, 1785–1923, 25 reels, Southern Historical Collection, University of North Carolina, Chapel Hill).

Sharpless, R. (1993). Southern women and the land. American rural and farm women in historical perspective. *Agricultural History Spring, 67*(2), 30.

van Gennep, A. (1908, 1960). *The rites of passage.* Translated by Monkia Visedom and Gabrielle Caffee. Chicago: University of Chicago Press.

Walker, M. (2000). *All we knew was to farm: Rural women in the upcountry, 1919–1941.* Baltimore: Johns Hopkins University Press.

White, J. J. (1988). Becoming a southern woman. In K. Bennett (Chair), *Women's realities: Voices from schools and communities.* Symposium conducted at the annual meeting of the American Anthropological Association, Phoenix, AZ.

White, J. J. (1989). Student teaching as a rite of passage. *Anthropology & Education Quarterly, 20,* 177–195.

White, J. J. (1991). War stories: Invitations to reflect on practice. In B. R. Tabachnick & K. Zeichner (Eds.) *Issues and practices in inquiry oriented teacher education* (pp. 226–252). London: Falmer.

Wolfe, M. R. (1996). Revisiting the ruins: A feminine retrospective on Dixie's past. Dialogue: Southern women in history and historiography. *Journal of Women's History, 8*(3), 175.

10

Education in the United States

Puerto Rican Perspectives

José R. Figueroa-Britapaja

Editor's Overview _____

This chapter takes us on a journey from the island of Puerto Rico to New York City and back to Puerto Rico. The author and his friend share aspects of their school experiences in New York that fell short in terms of meeting their needs as students who primarily spoke Spanish when they arrived here. In school, both were subjected to low expectations, stereotypes, and irrelevant curriculum. They were also intimidated by gang members and/or other children in the school. The connections between the school and community were basically nonexistent, and the physical environment of the school was less than adequate. Yet, returning to Puerto Rico was empowering for both of them. They were able to regain a positive sense of ethnic identity, self-respect, self-determination, and pride. The experiences in the United States and Puerto Rico made a definite impact on their lives, and both men (at the time this book was being written) were currently engaged in emancipatory teaching—the author at the university level and his friend as a public school teacher in New York.

My Personal Story:
José R. Figueroa-Britapaja

"José Ramón, ven acá," my mother called, and I knew that it was serious. Mother always called me by my first two names, but this time there was something different in her voice, and it felt uncomfortable. I walked into the house through the kitchen door and she was patiently sitting next to the window that looked out toward the tall mango trees. "Papito . . . ven acá por favor" (*Honey . . . please come over here*), she said in her soft warm voice. I closed the screen door behind me and walked toward my mother. "Papi . . . como te gustaria mudarte a los Estados Unidos?" (*Honey . . . how would you like to move to the United States?*), she asked.

I looked down toward the kitchen floor, paused a little, and slowly but surely told her that I didn't see the need to go away and leave my friends. "Que va a pasar con abuela, Mami?" (*What will happen to Grandmother, Mom?*), I asked. I told her that Puerto Rico was where I wanted to be and that I really didn't see the need to leave our home. She turned around and said, "Pero así puedes aprender Inglés" (*But this way you can learn English*). I smiled and said, "Pero ya yo sé Inglés Mami . . . quieres ver? Mira . . . (*But I already know English Mom . . . do you want to see?*). And suddenly the following sounds came out of my mouth: "Wishi, washi, wishi, washi . . . " Surely this wasn't English, but to a five-year-old native Spanish speaker, that was precisely how English sounded.

I continued with what I believed to be an eloquent demonstration of my linguistic skills, but to no avail. I soon realized that Mom was not convinced of my language prowess, so I did the next best thing I could think of, and said, "Te quiero mucho, Mami" (*I love you very much, Mom*). She smiled and hugged me tightly in her arms and whispered, "No te apures, papito . . . todo va a salir de lo mas bien" (*Don't worry, honey . . . everything will be just fine*).

Until then (1969), I had experienced the life of a monocultural society on the island of Puerto Rico. The concepts of social class, language, and skin color and the word *spic* were totally unknown to me. My father, whom many years ago had experienced this same fate, was having a sense of déjà vu. The pattern of migration that had forced his mother in the late 1920s to immigrate north to the city of New York was reemerging in his own lifetime; this time, it was affecting a second generation. As in the case of many Hispanic/Latino children, the migratory pattern began early in my life.

Our first city dwelling was a sofa bed in my aunt's living room. We shared a small two-bedroom apartment with my aunt, my uncle, and her two sons. The noise was unbearable and the pollution was awful, but it was the only place in town. Later that summer, fate took us into the Bronx, and a new awakening took place. While we were living on 166th Street, a racial feud erupted between the African American community and the New York Police Department. One very warm morning, a four-year-old African American girl who was quietly playing in the public playground with her preschool friends was harassed and physically assaulted by two White officers.

The incident prompted a new sense of reality for me. How could a police officer represent all that is feared in a child's life? At what point do citizens need to fear those who are to protect them? I wasn't sure what I was experiencing, but it definitely represented a new way of interpreting the world. Before I could say a word to my mother, a crowd of parents and neighbors were pushing and beating the two officers under my window. Suddenly, six patrol cars appeared on the scene, a fire erupted in the playground, and two gasoline canisters exploded in close proximity to the squad cars. Fireballs were flying everywhere, people were screaming, two injured bodies were lying next to my window, and all I could hear was my mother screaming angrily as she pulled me away from the window and into the bedroom. Welcome to America, José.

Once again, my parents had decided that it was time to move to another location in the city; this time, it was 1206 Powell Avenue in the Bronx. As the morning light came about my bedroom window, I was nervous thinking of how my new school would receive me, but I had no choice in the matter. The process of involuntary migration had been repeated once more in less than two months.

Children rarely have a say as to where their parents intend to live; yet they are expected to adapt to their new surroundings without a second thought. Parents rarely examine how a child processes these difficult life changes in order to regain his or her concept of self and personal identity in the face of total uncertainty. Every day, children around the world are expected to accept these social and psychological changes without any resistance. For the most part, children are voiceless in the process of immigration and migration from one country, state, or neighborhood to another.

My father knew very well that schooling in America would become an uphill battle, but he had no choice other than to drill and practice with me the basics of the English language as best he could. Before long, that awful day had arrived, and I found myself being dragged to school by my mother. I remember praying to "Papa Dios" (*Holy Father*) to release me from the nightmare, but the prayer went unanswered. The school building was just getting larger as we got closer, and the strange noises around me (students speaking English) were simply becoming unbearable.

We approached the steps of P.S. 36 (Public School 36) in the Bronx, and I found myself experiencing an anxiety attack. The palms of my hands were sweating and all I could do was clench my blue tie with my right hand as Mom helped me through the entrance. Confused and dazed at the complexity of the events, I stumbled through the halls as my mother attempted to find my room. When I finally faced the door of my assigned first-grade room, I simply lost control and instinctively locked my hands and feet onto the frame of the door.

I used my small arms and legs as best I could, for I was determined not to die on that day. "Me quiero ir pa casa, Mami. . . . No me hagas esto, por favor" (*I want to go home, Mom. . . . Don't do this to me, please don't*), I pleaded to my mother. To this day, she clearly remembers how difficult it was for her to leave me in a strange school, filled with strange people who did not speak her language, or mine. To this day, she refuses to comment on the incident, for I truly believe that it was harder for her than it was for me.

The cultural shock of this experience had a profound influence on the way I was to perceive the process of education in the United States. What does a child do in such a foreign setting? What do school officials decide when there is a lack of appropriate assessment tools and resources? Ridiculed by my peers for not speaking the English language and excluded from most of the class activities, I was immediately diagnosed as being mentally challenged. In less than a week, I was classified, through the exclusive use of teacher observations, as being a candidate for special education. I was lowered a grade level and forced to sit in a corner so as not to disturb the other children.

Can you imagine the surprise in my father's face when he received the reclassification letter? He could not understand how a child's educational and mental condition could change overnight. Ironically, his confusion was only exacerbated when he approached the school officials. When pressed for some answers, the school blatantly stipulated the following terms: (1) your child must acquire total English proficiency in less than thirty days; (2) he must be able to acculturate himself to the American school system within that time; (3) we have no resources and/or ideas on how to accomplish such a task, so it is your parental responsibility to carry out this endeavor; and, finally, (4) failure to comply with our educational recommendations will result in your child's placement in a special education setting and possibly another school.

As I reflect on this process, I begin to wonder just how many parents are left with the uncertainty of their children's educational well-being. Let's consider the context for a moment. How does a family, without resources, manage to overcome such an educational dilemma? What kind of an educational system systematically classifies students without the appropriate assessment procedures and resources? Most important, do such events still occur today in our nation's schools? Sadly, the answer to this last question continues to be a resounding yes.

To the surprise of the school officials, I was able to succeed within the so-called "normal" classroom setting. I overcame the language barrier and gradually made my way into the social context of the school. However, language is but one of the many obstacles that children face in schools. For example, how does a child protect himself/herself from bullies in a school? What can a child do when teachers dismiss the existence of discrimination and harassment practices? How would you feel if you experienced a beating every morning just before class and then after lunch by a group of kids who call you "a F——g spic?" Is it possible for a child to gain a desire to learn in a school community that is prone to harassing and taunting with such phrases as "Why don't we throw you over the fence and onto the Cross Bronx Expressway, you Puerto Rican bum!"

Slowly, a child begins to wonder what is the true purpose of schools and sometimes reaches the ill-fated conclusion that it is an instrument of torture rather than a step toward success. With time, I associated myself with a group of African American students who were being bused from other parts of the Bronx. For a brief moment, I had successfully managed to find refuge from those who harassed me and to gain access to a place of inclusive peace and safety. What had begun as a childish activity in the playground had suddenly emerged as a racial and social class division within the elementary school. To my surprise and that of my persecutors, I had been able to form a coalition of like-minded individuals who shared a common sense of oppression and discrimination.

In light of this newly found power, I was able to repel the harassing forces that existed within the student population. Ironically, my liberation was short lived, and I soon found out that some classroom teachers were simply large carbon copies of those playground bullies that I so feared.

Largely because of my shyness and my unwillingness to place myself in a compromising situation by being ridiculed and called names as a result of my limited English skills and the fact that some kids did not accept me as an equal, some teachers viewed me as being slow, dumb, unworthy of high expectations, or simply not worth the effort. Because of such beliefs, I endured being systematically placed in the slower, nonacademic groups, constantly questioned as to whether I had copied my work from someone else, and, on several occasions, being forced to relieve myself in class because I was not to be trusted alone in the halls of the school. And who can forget the day, in third grade, when I brought forth the notion that the current inhabitants of the Americas had unjustly occupied and destroyed Native communities. I was immediately ridiculed and corrected by the teacher with the following remarks: "We are all Americans, my dear. Don't you remember that these lands were fairly bought with beads and necklaces? Besides, what would the primitive Indians do with all that land anyway? They needed to share it with someone."

Nevertheless, as my mother always says, "No hay mal que dure cien años, ni cuerpo que lo recista." Roughly translated, this means that all oppressive conditions have limitations. To my benefit, there were several teachers who were very special to me and who saw the need to help me succeed. These teachers encouraged me to feel a sense of pride for my native language and my culture and to cultivate my cultural heritage as part of the educational experiences of the school. As a result of their efforts, I was appropriately assessed through the use of interviews, manipulatives, reading samples, and a variety of other instructional strategies and later placed in the gifted program. For this, I applaud their efforts, their professionalism, and especially their humanistic view of education.

Several years had gone by, and I was finally able to succeed academically and socially in school. However, my parents were concerned that I was gradually losing my native language and that a college education in the United States was a financial impossibility. Once again, I found myself migrating to another land, this time to face yet another set of challenges on the island of Puerto Rico.

For years, I had lived in the United States with a somewhat distant and naive understanding of what it meant to be a Puerto Rican. Now that we had moved back to the island of Puerto Rico, things would take on a slightly different, yet familiar, twist. One day as I walked with my mother to my new school in Puerto Rico to register for the next academic year, I heard one of my neighbors say, "Mira, ese es el Nuyorican" (*Look, that's the Nuyorican*). At first, I had no idea what she was referring to, but later I learned that people on the island referred to non-island-born Puerto Ricans in certain terms, terms that are undoubtedly discriminatory and stereotypical. For the first time in my life, I was to experience the rejection and discriminatory views of my own people—here, in my own land. How ironic: I became an outsider in my own country.

Unfortunately, in the eyes of many islanders, a Nuyorican is a kind of cultural hybrid who exists within two cultures, the American and the Puerto Rican. Many islanders cannot see the complexity of this process and as a result formulate a stereotypical image around their notion of what constitutes a Nuyorican. According to this construct, a Nuyorican is seen neither as a full "American" nor as a complete Puerto Rican. In essence, such an individual experiences the duality of two cultures and two languages and, for the most part, views both societies from a somewhat outsider's perspective. In my case, the mere fact that I had lived in the States qualified me to be classified and ostracized as one of those individuals.

In Puerto Rico, these seemingly simplistic cultural distinctions carried a strong connotation. For many community members on the island, I was a "culturally and socially detached" member of society. According to some of my fellow classmates, neighbors, and teachers, I was to fulfill the mythical and stereotypical role of the Nuyorican. To my surprise, I became the target of a discriminatory practice that perceived "cultural outsiders" as (1) people who would be unable and unwilling to speak the Spanish language; (2) people who would have a preference for the so-called American lifestyle, along with fast food and an individualistic view of life; and (3) people who would undoubtedly exhibit a dislike for the traditional love of country, culture, social structure, and overall social consciousness of the island. In fact, the main concern of many of my teachers was that I might somehow "infect" my new classmates with a variety of unwanted social behaviors and attitudes that were incompatible with those of the island culture.

To understand the distant view that many island-born Puerto Ricans have toward the United States, we need to examine briefly the events that prompted such cultural constructs to evolve on the island. After four hundred years of Spanish domination, Puerto Rico was finally granted self-autonomy by Spain in 1887. Yet, this freedom was short lived, for in 1889, under the treaty of Paris, Puerto Rico was ceded to the United States as a result of the Spanish American War.

In 1917, as the United States prepared to enter World War I, Puerto Ricans were granted U.S. citizenship, but only with certain limiting conditions. For instance, Puerto Ricans who live on the island are not allowed to vote in U.S. presidential and congressional elections. In fact, their only representation is that of a resident commissioner who is allowed to voice his/her opinion but has no right to vote in congressional matters. As a result of this political arrangement, Puerto Rico has no representation in the United States Congress. However, a Puerto Rican is able to completely exercise his/her constitutional rights to vote and have equal representation if he or she resides in the U.S. mainland—not on the island.

Ironically, this limited citizenship status does not limit the use of Puerto Ricans living on the island as a military resource. In fact, many Puerto Rican historians would argue that Puerto Ricans were conveniently granted U.S. citizenship at a time when the United States was in no condition to enter World War I. At a time when the U.S. military barely counted on the world stage—with fewer than 20,000 men and no armed divisions—a draft law, the Selective Service Act, was enacted on May 18, 1917. Immediately following the enactment of the Selective Service Act, over 20 percent of Puerto Rican males living on the island were sent into combat in the fields of Europe.

The impact of these historical and current social and political events has created a unique perception amongst the islanders as to the nature of the United States' relationship with Puerto Rico. For example, the vast majority of Puerto Ricans refuse to see themselves as Americans, and instead call themselves Puerto Ricans or Boricuas (derived from the word *Borinquén*, the Taino Indian name for the island of Puerto Rico). Puerto Ricans see this social and political relationship as a result of a military, economic, and political imposition rather than of choice. Hence, they continue to speak Spanish as the main language of commerce, education, and social interaction and elect to consciously distance themselves from anything that may be considered "American," even while living on the U.S. mainland.

The critical factor that needs to be considered here is that these historical, social, and political events have the capacity to negatively affect the educational experiences of children not only in U.S. mainland schools, but also on the island of Puerto Rico. The existence of such social and cultural misgivings concerning foreign-born Puerto Ricans (who are seen as partial Americans) plays an important role in the educational experiences and opportunities of Puerto Rican students who migrate back to the island schools.

As a result of our returned migration to the island, I was to relive some of the same frustrations that I had experienced in New York public schools. In my case, the school system in Puerto Rico became a mirror image of the

New York educational process. The lack of resources needed to deal with a child who was not fluent in the Spanish language and unable to cope immediately with the mainstream Puerto Rican community was readily apparent. As in the Bronx, the school district in Puerto Rico gave me a limited amount of time to demonstrate language and grade-level knowledge proficiency. This time, however, it was my mother who had the difficult task of helping me with the reading, writing, and speaking of the Spanish language before grade placements were done at the end of August. As expected, I started the learning process by learning the kindergarten basics and gradually moving up to my grade level. It was altogether a miracle that I was able to comply successfully with the school deadline and begin my academic year in the correct grade level. However, the stigma of being a Nuyorican was ever present for years to come.

Whenever an incident occurred amongst the student population, the administration was quick to question the nearest Nuyorican. If something was missing from a classroom or a closet, you certainly knew whom they would call. And guess who would find themselves in the office if a fight broke out? According to the school principal, "It had to be one of those aggressive U.S.-born kids with bad ("American") social habits. The lack of social respect for others is a result of those individualistic values that these kids learn in American schools." As some administrators and teachers were fast to point out, "These kids (Nuyoricans) are a bad influence on the school community and someone has to do something about it. In fact, these foreign-born kids should have stayed in the United States where they belong."

Even though there existed a number of inconveniences and prejudiced views at the school, there also existed a greater sense of self and personal connection to the community of the island. The curriculum reflected the culture of my family, the significance of my last name, my family history, the richness of my culture, my role within the broad social sphere, and my relationship to the world community. In other words, it allowed me to see myself as a contributing and valued member of society, as a descendent of a rich civilization and culture, rather than a tolerated outcast and a refugee in a foreign land.

Most important, I was able to see the world from a different perspective. For example, have you ever taken the time to think about how we tend to view the world, and through what lens? If you live in the United States, you tend to have a culture-centric view of what happens in the rest of the world. You are taught in schools that the most significant world events have occurred in the United States, that all major human achievements can be traced to the United States and that all relevant historical, political, and social movements have taken place in the United States of America. In fact, America, for the students of U.S. schools, is just the fifty states.

In Puerto Rico, the center was no longer the United States of America. History was in accordance with Latin American historians, and we concentrated on world history, rather than U.S. history. There was special emphasis on Latin American literature, arts, music, history, philosophy, and culture. The examination of Europe and the rest of the world was critical in understanding our current cultural role and significance in the world. England was not the central focus of migration to the Americas. And, of course, who can forget the new idea that the Americas are not the fifty states but two very large continents in the Western Hemisphere of the world. What a different view of the world. For the first time in a history class, I was taught that all those who live in the Western Hemisphere of the world are Americans, because these are the Americas. All of a sudden, classic literature was not relegated to English-language authors. In essence, the world was a different place to live in, and it was much broader than I had previously imagined. Unlike in U.S. schools, the world revolved not around the accomplishments of the United States, but rather those of the global community.

Suddenly, my life had changed in ways that I had not imagined. I wasn't followed in stores, nor treated differently in society for being a Puerto Rican or just having a different skin tone. In school, I was expected to achieve my potential and live up to the standards of my cultural icons. I had experienced the literature and achievements of my ethnic group, and in doing so, I was expected to attain those same ideals. The meaningful use of proper and challenging role models made a significant impact in my life. The world was a different place, and I was eager to live up to the challenge and mirror the accomplishments of those before me.

A Friend's Story

Twenty-two years ago, I walked into a small ninth-grade classroom and stumbled into a tall fellow by the name of Felipe Rangel. Aside from sharing a homeroom teacher and the fact that both our families had migrated from the states, we really didn't have much in common. Nevertheless, we developed a strong friendship, and, to this day, his family has become an extended family of my own.

One day, as we shared a cup of coffee at his kitchen table in Queens, I mentioned the purpose of this chapter, and he was eager to become a part of the project. We scheduled a time and place for a quiet conversation, and what follows is a glimpse of the triumphs and tribulations that go along with being a child in a racially, socially, and politically challenging society. The story that follows is completely told by Felipe Rangel, a teacher, parent, and role model to so many children in his public school in New York City. What you are about to read is his first-person account of his life experiences and struggles as well as his triumphs and dreams.

Felipe Rangel Pissini

It's been five years since I began working as a dual language teacher in Central Park West. Unlike the transitional bilingual programs of my former school, the dual language program encourages all students to become fluent in two languages. It allows both Spanish and English speaking students to immerse themselves in two languages and, hence, two cultures. Sadly, not all schools see the need to work towards greater cultural awareness, and this is one of the reasons why I think life is so complicated in the United States.

I was born in the Bronx and lived at 142nd Street and Willis Avenue for several years. My brothers and sister were all born in New York, with the exception of my youngest brother, who was born in Puerto Rico. We spent all of the 1960s and early 1970s attempting to cope with life in the Big Apple, until one day, my mother decided that it was time to leave the madness and return to the island of her parents. The reasons for the move were simple; the level of violence and moral decay was fast approaching a level that was hard to handle. The city was rapidly changing, not only in terms of the economic decay but also in ways that were no longer acceptable to the family. Everywhere we looked we saw social decadence and it was clear at the time that something had to be done before it was too late.

School, for example, was both an interesting, yet frightening place to be. It was a place that really did not lend itself to children and the kind of educational experiences that we have come to expect from such a powerful nation. For example, our neighborhood did not encourage us to play outside, like we would expect from those TV commercials. The reality was that we could not even dream of playing without the constant supervision of our parents. The very existence of gang activity in the community made it very difficult for any parent to feel safe and secure. Gang activity was an everyday event that represented an undoubtedly dangerous condition for children and adults alike. My childhood playground was surrounded by gangs associated with the Scorpions and the Latin Kings, and you really had to respect the consequences of confronting such people. This, along with an increasing drug culture in the area, made it very difficult to live the life of the "American" dream that is depicted on TV and the media.

Violent incidents were not foreign to the school, and this made it all too easy for violence to spread into the playground. The use of glass bottles, knives, broken glass, and even blades were at times common at the elementary school. Elementary school kids were assimilating the kinds of behaviors typically associated with gangs. Children would wear colored jackets to represent the appropriate gang colors of the neighborhood, and gang members would harass students and teachers both inside and outside of the school grounds.

On several occasions, students were dismissed from school during the noon hours simply because of the level of gang activity that was present in the region. Many of the older kids in the neighborhood would escalate their gang activities to the point of forcing the school to shut down their operations for the day. Can you imagine the kind of pressure that existed in a place like that? This was a place where young kids were able to manipulate the system simply because the school was unable or unwilling to aggressively deal with the issue of gangs. The basic premise of the school was to dismiss the students and avoid getting involved with the community. You see, the school never saw itself as an integral part of the community, so why should it get involved with the families and their struggle against such a terrorist attack?

I can remember how the school premises and the playground were constantly filled with broken glasses and bottles. Because the school was so detached from the community, people felt that it was just okay to throw bottles and physically assault the school premises. Somehow, their environment and the conditions of their lives desensitize people, and then you begin to see a negative kind of behavior taking over your neighborhood.

There was a lack of social responsibility toward the school grounds and its contents. Many of the young boys simply did not care for the school premises and would break windows and fences, destroy the doors of the school, and, if they had the opportunity to enter the school, they would steal things and break whatever they could. This place was like a war zone, it was violent, and it was a place where people simply lost all notions of what is private property and what needs to be done to take care of your local community resources.

I still carry the souvenir of the times in the form of a scar or two. I clearly remember how terrified I was to find myself bleeding on the way to the hospital simply because I wanted to play. Do you know how scary that incident was for a child whose only wish was to play with his friends, but finds a playground filled with broken glass and bottles? Listen, I never saw or heard anyone from the school attempt to clean the place up. In fact, things were simply left to be as they were and nothing else.

Like I said, life was difficult in the community and people were constantly becoming victims of violence in the area. I can remember a morning when I was watching television with my mother, when suddenly a large number of young men walked past the house throwing bricks at all the windows of the houses on both sides of the street. It was incredible to see close to 100 men on foot, throwing bricks at everything and anything that was present. Car windshields were broken, people were hurt, and a large number of homes had lost their front windows by the time the incident had concluded. Life in the city was definitely going down a spiral, yet we had to endure more of this for some time to come.

Life in the classroom was not far from that of the streets. On many occasions, I would become the victim of racial slurs as I would hear children calling, "Get out of here, you little Puerto Rican!" I was constantly persecuted by a variety of people at school who did not want me at all in their neighborhood. Some of my problems were racially based, while others were of a social and economic nature. A number of kids and even some teachers were simply not interested in seeing me in the classroom. More than once, I found myself being chased after school by a group of children who did not like the fact that I was different looking.

As a child, it is very difficult to understand why there is such a thing as harassment on the basis of being different in terms of race and/or ethnicity, yet you are forced to deal with such concepts whether you like it or not. The fact that I was harassed and at times beaten at the hands of my aggressors only made me feel insecure and unable to appreciate who I was as a person. I felt fearful that I might somehow suffer at the hands of other kids who did not appreciate who I was. Sadly, the end result of this condition was that of establishing a link with several gang members who promised protection and self-assurance.

In order to alleviate the constant harassment, I searched for help from outside sources, specifically gangs. These new friends were not a part of the school environment, but did belong to the neighborhood and hence provided a safety net. Unfortunately, this involvement only prompted a series of fights and only furthered the already unstable condition of the school.

An interesting thing about racial and social conflict is that it doesn't follow established guidelines. You see, racism, discrimination, and oppression have no defined boundaries or limitations. Racial conflicts can occur between any number of groups or individuals. All that is needed is a sense of power over another human being, and the result is basically the same: oppression and persecution of those who are perceived as being weak. In this particular community, the African American children were the majority and they therefore wielded the power. They set the rules and the manner in which others had to follow. If you questioned their power, you would receive a beating from the bigger kids.

I can clearly remember the psychological and physical abuse that some kids had to endure simply because of their skin color. The racial makeup of the school prompted an open war against the few White students that attended class. White kids were constantly experiencing the harsh reality of being a minority, and, for the most part, they could not understand why this was so. For example, "Apache," a White kid who attended school, was always considered to be an aggressive and violent child. We called him Apache because of his warrior nature. Of course, we all know that such a nickname reflects the discriminatory nature of Hollywood and its depiction of Native

Americans. Nevertheless, as children, we all bought into that ideology and the child was nicknamed in accordance to our racist views of the world.

Anyway, in the case of Apache, nonWhite students would constantly intimidate and commit acts of aggression simply because of the White color of his skin. This was pure and simple racial discrimination on the part of the students of color, who were the majorities in the school. This White child was as poor as the rest of us, was suffering from the same educational injustices, and never experienced any help from either the school or his family; yet he was seen as being different, and, for that, he had to pay the price. This was a sad lesson for me, and to this day, I can see how harmful it is to become blinded by color or race. It is very easy to discriminate and hold people in an imprisoned state of existence based on how we perceive them.

Sadly, my educational misadventures did not end with the social experiences within the community. I also endured what I currently consider to be a kind of educational mistreatment on behalf of the school officials. While attending school in the Bronx, I never experienced a formal curriculum as such. I always felt that something was lacking from school. Now that I am a teacher, I can understand what was missing from my education—a formal educational process that takes into consideration the needs and experiences of the children.

My education in New York basically consisted of endless and mindless routines that revolved around the use of worksheets. I never felt a connection to the real world. It wasn't until we moved out of the city that I was able to experience a formal and meaningful curricular approach to learning. I had to wait until the sixth grade to experience science and social studies. Can you imagine all those years without ever learning a single thing about science and social studies? In fact, social studies was only mentioned when it was time to make a picture of Lincoln or Washington and the celebration of Thanksgiving. How can you expect children under these conditions to make it in their lives? What kind of an educational process is this where students are left without the benefit of a working knowledge in the field of social studies?

Like I said, social studies was drawing and painting cardboard papers to help us understand how a given president looked. To me, this was a total waste of time. I could never see myself doing such damage in my classroom. As in the case of the social studies curriculum, science was never a part of my school experiences in the Bronx. In fact, I was first introduced to a formal science book when I began school in Puerto Rico. Now, can you tell me who is the third-world country in this case: the little island in the Caribbean or the wealthy city that neglects its children?

As a child, I did not realize that such an educational process was limiting and systematically oppressive to all students. As a teacher, I can clearly see how this process of education serves only to hinder a child's capabilities and prevent him or her from fully achieving in a competitive world. My personal experiences in school were simply preparing me to attain a minimal level of competency and not a well-rounded education. To this day, I find myself questioning the level of personal and professional consciousness of my teachers.

Even as a child, I was very aware of the difference a school is able to make in a child's life. For example, the private school children whom I knew had a very structured and demanding school curriculum while we had a loose system that encouraged mediocrity. In a very broad sense, I feel as if the public school children were being mistreated by the system. I spent countless hours drawing and telling stories; singing and working on worksheets that had no relation to what was being done throughout the day. How does this compare to someone who is presented with an academically oriented and challenging curriculum? What does this say about a child's educational opportunity? How can this represent equality in education when we know of the existence of differentiated educational practices? Does it mean that we are severely limited by where we live and how much we are able to afford?

In my view, the public school system was undoubtedly mistreating its children in the way it constructed and implemented its curricular experiences. Marginalized children, whether marginalized on the basis of race, social class, or culture, tend to be treated as second-class citizens in many of our schools. How can this occur in a country that proclaims itself a leader among all nations? I can't recall a single instance where the school was doing something to partially overcome the educational misfortune of the children. It is clear to me now that our social conditions automatically forced us to be at the mercy of a mediocre school which did not care for the welfare of its children.

I believe ghettos exist because many of its members fail to recognize the existence of an alternative life. A person who is born into such a system is not allowed to know other forms of life intimately and therefore develops a lack of hope and aspirations. There is no light at the end of the tunnel, just an endless journey. Because of a lack of awareness, people fail to realize that there may be other things in life. People need to elevate their level of consciousness to a degree that can accept change. An individual must be able to reject his/her personal state of existence in order to begin a life of self-reliance and self-dignity. The difficult part of the solution is that of showing and teaching people how to become self-sufficient and to develop a sense of dignity. For many, *dignity* is just a word without any true relevance in their lives.

However, we need to understand that our current social system has been created on purpose to promote and maintain the existence of the ghetto. It was created to maintain the existence of poor communities that only serve a self-perpetuating system. It doesn't get any better. You can see it over and over again, as ghettos around the nation continue to exist and how new ghettos are being created on a daily basis. The government invests in a variety of projects to eliminate such communities, only to create a new one down the road. I left the city nearly twenty years ago, and it still remains as bad as it ever was; nothing has changed.

Only after leaving the city did I learn what it meant to have a sense of personal dignity. As I came in contact with people who cherished their own cultural identity, I began to see what it meant to be a respected member of society. It is very easy to develop an internal sense of self-reliance and self-respect if you feel pride in who you are. These new friends were working, expressed a personal sense of stability, and they were openly proud of their community. These were the kinds of things that were missing during my formative years.

When I was a child I did not know who I was. I knew that I was Latino and I knew that I was marginalized, like many others who live in the Bronx. As time went by, I began to identify myself with my true origins, my sense of Puerto Rican affiliation. Not immediately, but this was significant during my high school years and later while attending college.

When people ask me what I am, I simply reply, "A Puerto Rican." Occasionally, someone would say, "Well, don't you feel American?" My response is, "I choose to call myself a Puerto Rican because society will never see me as anything else but a Puerto Rican. So why should I go through the trouble of calling myself anything else?"

In this country, color and/or perceived racial and ethnic background carry a lot of weight. Curiously, I have found that the white community will treat me in accordance to how they see me rather than how I choose to be seen. For that reason, it really doesn't matter what I say, but what people believe. You see, there are well-established cultural, social, and racial barriers that need to be broken in this country.

American society has a standard that needs to be upheld and at times championed by the establishment. In the United States, being an "American" is an elusive condition. If you have money and power, society immediately becomes colorblind. It's a different story for the middle-class folks, and let's not forget the poor in America. You see, race is not always a prime factor in the acceptance game, but rather the social and political platform that you are able to sustain. People in America seem to be able to win the race or ethnic battle against prejudice or at least limit its effects greatly when they have money or social mobility and power. You see, the people in power, no matter what color they are, are better suited to accept anyone whom they perceive as having an equal level of power or money. Let's put it this way, you have better chances at being tolerated if you have money than if you don't have a penny, no matter what color you are. This society is purely capitalistic and hungry for money and power.

Just because you choose to identify yourself with one group or another doesn't change the fact that you will always be seen as different. For instance, I am not White, and to say otherwise would only represent my own ignorance. It doesn't matter how I identify myself; people will treat me and classify me in accordance to their standards. So why fool myself into believing that I am just like everybody else when I can be happy with my very own ethnic identity? The key to happiness is self-awareness, self-reliance, and the development of personal dignity and pride in yourself as an individual.

As a public school teacher in the New York school system, I feel that all my students have the potential to understand, appreciate, and learn from the struggles of self-determination and self-worth. I would like my students, both Latino and non-Latino, to cherish their own identity and experience the wealth of their cultural basis. If you wish to maintain a high level of education within the public schools, we need to establish a grass-roots movement that attempts to build the self-worth and self-respect of those children. They need to see the benefit and worth of who they are, what they can accomplish, and how they can relate to and affect those around them.

Throughout the years, I have noticed that many of my classroom kids don't have the level of self-respect and self-worth needed to succeed in the world. As teachers, we need to create a powerful level of consciousness that is geared towards the goal of self-awareness, personal pride, and righteousness. The essence of an individual is directly related to his or her own culture. If you attempt to destroy an individual's culture in the name of education, you will eventually marginalize that person's self-worth and self-respect.

As teachers, we need to share our own personal cultures and views about the world and help our students to develop a strong sense of personal identity and dignity. Without such things, our children will be lost in a world that is screaming for direction and purpose.

What Can We Learn from These Life Experiences?

The purpose of these stories is not to create a generalization, but to provide a window into the lives of two individuals, whose experiences may serve to guide the future steps of educators, parents, and community members. I trust that these stories may somehow serve to initiate a dialogue of hope and to clarify some of the complex events that exist within our school communities. It is my hope that you will revisit these life stories and gain a new insight and perception as to the importance of knowing your Latino students—or any member of your community, for that matter.

My personal vision of education is based on the notion that schooling and education coexist in a framework of constant tension and resistance. A classroom experience, for example, represents not only an educational practice, but a social and cultural experiment that involves many participants. As we have seen in the stories presented, there are a number of critical life choices that may conflict with the best interest of a child's educational and life experiences.

In both cases, we see the significance of the migratory process. Almost without warning, both children are faced with the harsh realities of moving into what is perceived as a foreign land. In such instances, these lands are, for the most part, socially and culturally unprepared to deal with their needs and concerns. In the case of many Latino and Hispanic children, the process of migration and/or immigration is a violent one, to say the least. In many instances, children are either left behind with other family members in their home countries or brought under severe conditions to what is for many a frightening and alien environment.

To help us understand the significance of immigration on the educational experiences of children, we need to consider the theory of voluntary and involuntary immigration. For years, John Ogbu, an anthropologist, has argued that student achievement is affected by the way children perceive themselves within society. According to Ogbu (1993), there is a distinct difference between voluntary minorities—or immigrants—and involuntary minorities—who enter the U. S. mainstream culture against their will or as refugees. In other words, students who elect to immigrate to the United States are more likely to succeed academically than, for example, African American, Native American, Mexican American, and Puerto Rican students, all of whom share a number of historical experiences that begin with the process of forced colonization and end with the systematic implementation of oppression, discrimination, and eventual dehumanization.

By definition, Ogbu's theory provides us with a new way of analyzing our stories. If by "involuntary immigration" it is meant that a child is forced to cope with preexisting social and historical conditions, we must consider the possibility that most, if not all, children may be victims of the involuntary immigration process. For example, when a family decides to relocate or migrate from one state to another, the child is simply expected to come and to cope with the consequences of such a decision. Regardless of whether the child's family has elected to migrate or immigrate to this country, the harsh reality remains that children's needs are rarely considered in this final equation. Consequently, we may be forced to reexamine the way in which we view our communities and the way our children perceive the processes of schooling and community development.

As teachers, we must do our best to listen and pay close attention to the needs and views of our students. Often, we expect children to act and behave as adults when, in reality, they are not. They are members of a social order that at times fails to see the need to nurture and closely monitor their development. In doing so, we may have begun to jeopardize the welfare of our future generations. As we acknowledge these factors, we must be cautious not to forfeit our sense of humanity and to strive continuously to provide all children with a profound and socially conscious learning experience. I therefore urge us all to begin to reflect on our practices and to experience the wealth of knowledge that comes from helping a child to develop a sense of community and self-identity. Let us not contribute to the process of oppression by forcing our students to comply with our notion of who they are in society. Rather, let us attempt to construct new ways of learning that encourage cooperation, mutual respect, and appreciation.

The classroom setting often relies on its shared sense of beliefs and values in order to maintain its function and efficiency. However, those same beliefs may also play an important role in the exclusive repression of alternative forms of teaching and learning. Schools have a tendency to create restrictive and unwelcoming environments that are counterproductive, rather than instrumental, in the development of their children. On many occasions, we see the creation of a cultural environment that is congruent with the interests and needs of several individuals to the point where it excludes a vast majority of its population. In doing so, these individuals create an educational culture that imposes a series of negative meanings and perceptions.

Often, we are witnesses to a process of dehumanization that exists within and beyond the boundaries of our own classrooms (Freire, 1970). As educators, we too become entrenched and narrowly focused by the external influences and pressures of society, not to mention our own deeply rooted biases and personal prejudices. How many times have we, as teachers, been influenced by the negative views or ideals of another community member? When was the last time that we were personally subjected to a stereotypical notion or a racial comment? How many times have we been guilty of judging a child based on our false assumptions or biases? These are some of the fundamental understandings that warrant our immediate attention.

When I was a student in high school, a friend of mine asked me why some teachers simply failed to continue with their original ideals and had fallen into the trap of indifference and neglect. I thought about the question, and I found myself without an answer. Several years later, I had become a teacher, and when the question came up during one of my graduate classes, I found myself providing the following statement: Many teachers have become victims of a systematic culture of oppression and misinformation. That is, many, if not all, of our colleagues have been socially, politically, and culturally oppressed into thinking that they are incapable of changing their working environments or their approaches to teaching and learning. In other words, they have been acculturated, assimilated, and melted into a single frame of mind that is repressive and limiting.

By no means am I creating an excuse for teachers; however, we need to consider that teachers have themselves been a part of our educational system. In essence, we too have been socially and culturally molded to believe that children are incapable of achieving their potential. For example, let us examine some of the following ideas or assumptions that permeate our classrooms, communities, and even early childhood playgrounds:

- All Latino children are illegal aliens.
- Latino children are illiterate in the English language.
- Most Latino families are poor and live in large urban areas.
- Latino culture encourages laziness, arrogance, taking siestas, eating tacos, and a lack of appropriate work ethics.
- Latino children are genetically and/or culturally inferior and/or deprived.

These are a number of social, historical, and political assumptions and beliefs that continuously affect and alter our notion of children and others. In the case of Latino students, teachers may assume that Spanish-speaking children are culturally deficient or incapable of having a culture altogether. Many teachers immediately conclude that most Spanish-speaking children are intellectually inferior to their English-speaking counterparts because they assume that anyone incapable of acquiring a second language would be automatically categorized as being intellectually inferior. If this assumption were true, the vast majority of the U.S. population would undoubtedly have to be classified as intellectually inferior, for only a small percentage is able to speak in a language other than English. It is ironic that such a false theoretical construct continues to pervade in a nation that is essentially monolinguistic. Undoubtedly, this clearly reflects an irrational and conflicting social understanding that serves only to dehumanize others while protecting the interests of a few.

Sadly, these oppressive views are not limited to teachers, for they also become a part of the integral fiber of American society. As was experienced by both children in this chapter, the forces of oppression can also often be found in the hands of those who are oppressed. As Paulo Freire (1970) so eloquently argued, "The oppressed must not, in seeking to regain their humanity (which is a way to create it), become in turn oppressors of the oppressed, but rather restorers of the humanity of both" (p. 28). That is, oppressed individuals or communities at times become the oppressive force within the system. In the case of the Puerto Rican community on the island, the existence of internal distrust and prejudice is alive and well. Our human tendency to categorize and distinguish that which is perceived as different or unknown is sadly played out within the social constructs of our own ethnic groups. In fact, the argument can be made that no group is immune to the devastating forces of discrimination and oppression, for they know no boundaries and have no allegiance but to themselves. For this reason, we must be vigilantly aware of the fact that we may at one time or another be active reinforcers and promoters (consciously or unconsciously) of the negative and oppressive ideologies that others have set in motion.

In their quest for power and liberation, students can also become entangled in their own web of subjugation, prejudice, and oppression. Many times, the lack of guidance and proper nurturing allows for the development of subordinate groups within schools and surrounding communities that only serve to perpetuate the preexisting conditions of rejection, prejudice, hate, ignorance, and oppression. In their struggle to achieve a sense of liberation and self-identity, those who are themselves oppressed become the oppressors, and, in the process, they dehumanize those with less power (Freire, 1970). In essence, students, children, parents, teachers, and communities at large may fall prey to the overarching subtlety of power. If not cautious, we may all fail to reflect on our own dehumanization and on the consequences of our individual and collective actions, only to become what we loathe.

Our goal as educators and mentors of our students is to provide a clear relationship between the formal or social standards of our current and historical experiences and the individual life experiences of our students. Our daily struggle should be that of encouraging our students to develop the kinds of values, powers, and skills necessary for the successful debate of our social conditions. We need to guide and facilitate in our communities the kind of change that is active, cooperative, and socially responsive to the needs of all within the community (Shor, 1992). As teachers, we need to provide all members of our community with the sense of dignity and respect that allows us all to develop the skills and resources needed to change our society in a positive and proactive manner (Gintis, 1989).

What better way to allow ourselves to become active in the change process of society than to listen to our students, to our parents, and, most important, to ourselves carefully and genuinely. As teachers, we need to consider that each and every one of us has a history, a story to tell, a life to share, and a world of wisdom to explore. We must allow our own ideas to emerge and to be critically analytical of our actions and the actions of others. Our profession is not one of mere economics, but of a moral character that is formulated on the supposition that all of humanity is entitled to an educational experience that provides for a heightened state of consciousness and a true sense of self-determination. Our goal is not to continue to enforce the old myths and assumptions, but to move toward a society that is based on our free will to improve, to empower, and to evolve as a democratic and socially just community.

Teachers must come to the realization that one's power and authority is not given by virtue of one's profession, but by one's own construction of knowledge, one's personal and professional accomplishments, and the failures of one's attempts (Ashendon, Connel, Dowsett, & Kessler, 1987). We must be wary of our tendencies, our biases, and the impact that myths and assumptions have on our collective efforts. Our goal as educators is to become socially conscious participants within our communities. Our students, fellow colleagues, and parents all have stories and notions concerning what "the others" are like. It is our moral and ethical responsibility to break away from these repressive ideals and move forward into a new era of knowledge.

Editor's Commentary

> *Never in history has violence been initiated by the oppressed.*
> —Paulo Freire (1970, p. 37)

José and Felipe (both who are of Puerto Rican heritage) experienced rather hostile school settings in New York. Consequently, Felipe astutely advises educators, "The essence of an individual is directly related to his or her own culture. If you attempt to destroy an individual's culture in the name of education, you will eventually marginalize that person's self-worth and self-respect." The attempts made by school officials to destroy José's and Felipe's culture (particularly their language) were acts of violence—well intentioned, but no less harmful. As was the case when José and Felipe entered school in the late 1960s and early 1970s, educators are still not prepared to deal with students (White students included) in cultural terms (Haberman, 1996). This will be discussed in more detail in Chapter 13.

José and Felipe entered schools whose cultures were diametrically opposed to their group-oriented (versus individualistic) culture. Their language and cultural habits were viewed as deficits rather than strengths, thus elevating the school's Eurocentric cultural perspective as the only "right" way. This is culturally assaultive. But cultural relativism is widespread, as we saw when José returned to Puerto Rico. He was ridiculed for being "too American," which calls our attention to the general ethnocentric nature of humans. Most societies teach individuals to survive in their environment and to favor the familiar (culture). Yet when José returned to Puerto Rico, he was comforted by the Latino versus the English influences in the curriculum. A challenge for us as humans is the development of the ability to confirm the strengths and beauty of our own cultures as well as of those that are diametrically different.

The program that Felipe currently works in encourages students to become fluent in two languages and, hence, two cultures. In a recent e-mail to me, José reflected on bilingual education and the nature of programs that are most helpful. He noted,

> *I am not sure I would be in the right position to debate whether bilingual education has made a positive impact in schools. The range of bilingual programs is extensive, and this has created a number of concerns for those who wish to measure its effectiveness. I would rather concentrate on discussing the need to establish well-staffed ESL and bilingual programs that are seriously supported by the district rather than programs that are half conceived and ill managed by paraprofessionals. In my opinion, the major problem with educational programs lies in the manner in which they are implemented and supported. Most programs are implemented to react to an overwhelming situation. I see very*

little strategic planning on behalf of school districts. Most of their work is dedicated to managing whatever the state requirements are and to trying to survive the financial burdens of their schools. Therefore, little effort is truly made to conceptualize solid programs that are gradually implemented and monitored in schools. They simply work with what they have, when they have it.

I think that either ESL or bilingual programs can make a positive impact in the lives of students. The true issue at hand is how they are going to be operated and whether the school truly has an interest in helping all students to succeed. For example, what are administrators looking for when they hire someone to work in a diverse context? What are the professional characteristics of teachers working with diverse populations? In other words, this question can be a hot issue that I need to reexamine.

The question as to what the schools could have done to better facilitate my success needs to be related to the one on bilingual education and ESL programs. I think they are both related and need to be discussed in terms of program support and district mission. Community involvement is one particular factor that few schools manage to foster. But this is mostly due to the fact that the personnel of such programs are ill trained or lack the appropriate school district support to conduct outreach programs and integrate the natural support systems of the community into the school setting.

José noted that he had better access to bilingual materials in Puerto Rico than in New Jersey, even though they are from the same authors and publishing companies (he was a professor at a university in New Jersey when we started this book project). So it would seem that although there are promising programs for bilingual children (like the one Felipe teaches in), there is still much coherent work to be done toward learning to appreciate and utilize languages other than English in schools. As Samuel Betances, Puerto Rican educator, often emphasizes, bilingual education is simply "understandable instruction" (teaching in whatever language is necessary to help children understand and learn).

In the chapter, José's insights about alternative interpretations of the historical plight of Native Americans in this country vis-à-vis European "explorers" was met with ignorance and ethnocentrism by his teacher. Imagine what it felt like to have everything you knew disconfirmed and challenged on a daily basis. The cultural invasion noted in Chapter 6 is apparent here, although it escapes the teacher's consciousness because she clings to her indoctrination. Educators seeking to provide education that is multicultural must challenge and interrogate beliefs that have been deeply ingrained for most of their lives. This is a daunting, but inevitable, task for liberatory pedagogy.

Readers may have been taken aback by the descriptions of violence within the public schools and neighborhoods described in this chapter. But as Freire explained, the violence (even turned inward) is a response to the inhumane treatment by society (including schools). Like the two African American males in Chapter 3, José was greeted by his U.S. school with the diagnosis "mentally challenged." In Chapter 4,

Min-Woo's parents were also surprised by the school's assessment of their son. José's father recognized that this classification was incorrect and immediately protested to school officials, who were anything but accommodating. Like Min-Woo's mother, José's mother actively assumed the role of teacher to help him relearn Spanish when they returned to Puerto Rico.

The negative experiences encountered by José and his family in his New York school led him to question the true purpose of schools. Aren't schools in a democratic society supposed to be equalizers? Fair and equitable places? Hardly. As each chapter thus far has illustrated, schools vary widely in terms of what they offer to their students. Kozol's (1991) careful analysis of schools across this country revealed startling differences in the type of resources, facilities, per-pupil expenditures, curriculum, and other necessities found in schools, demonstrating that schools typically perpetuate the social class structures that exist in society. In particular, schools do little to help children from low-income and working-class backgrounds break the cycle of poverty and achieve the "American dream."

Felipe was bullied by African Americans who held the power in his school. He astutely notes that, "Racial conflicts can occur between any number of groups or individuals. All that is needed is a sense of power over another human being, and the result is basically the same: oppression and persecution of those who are perceived as being weak." Felipe's experienced three levels of discrimination: individual, group, and institutional.

On an individual level, any person can engage in discriminatory or oppressive acts. While these actions may be personally hurtful, they do not typically carry any political, economic, or social ramifications or consequences in the larger societal structure. Felipe's harassment by a single child who disliked him and called him racial epithets would be an example of individual discrimination. However, when groups that are in power (e.g., African Americans in Felipe's school, who represented the numerical majority and therefore had a degree of power) use this power to their advantage and to another person outside the group's disadvantage, the group possesses a level of power that could affect the "outsider's" well-being. Yet, in terms of structural power, the African American students had little power beyond the school and/or community in which they resided. That is, as a group, African Americans do not possess political, economic, or other forms of power in general society. Specifically, Blacks are in the minority among government officials, CEOs, and so on. Their worldview is not prominent in most schools or in the media. These power structures do not favor them. Therefore, African Americans possess little collective power on the larger societal level, which directly affects who will do well in school, who will be given preferential employment opportunities, and whose viewpoints are put forth as legitimate.

The third level of discrimination is represented by the institutionalized discrimination that Felipe encountered in the school setting. The rules for succeeding in society (schools included) are largely based on the White power structure. Hence, the curriculum and school practices favor White culture (or those who are willing to assimilate into this culture). In other words, while anyone can commit an individual act of prejudice or discrimination, these acts do not carry the power that leads to structural inequities. *This does not condone individual acts of discrimination, but we should recognize their political, economic, and social limits. On the other hand, individuals can inadvertently contribute to institutionalized discrimination without conscious intent. This is the case of the teachers whose actions advantaged White culture and disadvantaged Latino culture. This level of discrimination is the most insidious because it is not often apparent to the perpetrator but contributes to institutionalized discrimination. The challenge for educators is to recognize that even well-intentioned, nice people can and do contribute to institutionalized racism, classism, sexism, and other forms of discrimination. The good news is that contributing to structural inequities in schools and society does not have to be a foregone conclusion. Engaging in critical pedagogy is a viable alternative.*

Reflective Activity _____

Both José's and Felipe's voices were silenced by schools. Think of what it was like when you were a child and you had valid things to say and an adult (with privilege) said that you didn't know what you were talking about or told you to be quiet. How did it feel? What recourse did you have? What implications does this reflection have for teaching?

Resources _____

What follows is a collection of readings and resources that can help promote a greater sense of self-identification and awareness for Hispanic children in U.S. schools. Although the materials are specifically tailored to mirror the experiences of Hispanic communities, they are nevertheless valuable tools for cross-cultural teaching and learning activities. Such resources can be used to help non-Hispanic children understand the ideas, views, and values of the Hispanic children who live and share their communities.

In many instances, many of the following books are readily available in both English and Spanish. This dual language approach to literature provides both Spanish-speaking and non-Hispanic children opportunity to engage in the study of a foreign language. It also promotes the creation of choice in literature and the development of critical literary skills. Children learn how to examine literature in more than one language and to gain a knowledge of literary styles not available otherwise. Spanish-speaking children can benefit from reading in their own language yet also being able to contribute to the classroom discussions of the text. Finally, the use of dual-language books provides children with an additional avenue for self-expression and creativity in a second language or their native language while studying in the United States.

Hispanic Literature for Elementary Children

Preschool–Kindergarten
The Desert Is My Mother (El Desierto Es Mi Madre), by Pat Mora
Angela's Wings, by Eric Jon Nones

Grades One through Three
A Birthday Basket for Tia, by Pat Mora, illustrated by Cecily Lang
Calling the Doves (El Canto de Las Palomas), by Juan Felipe Herrera, illustrated by Elly Simmons
Carlos and the Cornfield: Carlos y la Milpa de Maiz, by Jan Romero Stevens, illustrated by Jeanne Arnold
Chato's Kitchen, by Gary Soto, illustrated by Susan Guevara
Family Pictures (Cuadros de Familia), by Carmen Lomas Garza
Fiesta, U.S.A., by George Ancona
The Gift of the Poinsettia (El Regalo de la Flor de Noche), by Pat Mora & Charles Ramirez Berg, art by Daniel Lechon
Pepita Talks Twice (Pepita Habla Dos Veces), by Ofelia Dumas Lachtman, illustrated by Alex Pardo DeLange
Prietta and the Ghost Woman (Prietta y la Llorana), by Gloria Anzaldua, illustrated by Christina Gonzalez

Grade Four through Six
Crazy Weekend, by Gary Soto
Alicia's Treasure, by Diane Gonzales Bertrand
The Pool Party, by Gary Soto, illustrated by Robert Casilla

Easy Readers—Hispanic Authors—Ages Six to Ten

Paloma and the Secret of the City of the Pyramids (Paloma y el secreto de la Ciudad de los Pirámides), by Monica Zak
Carahigo the Bandit (El Bandido Carahigo), by Fernando Almena
A Cricket from the Year 2000 (Un Grillo del Año Dos Mill y Pico), by Ramón García Dominguez
My Friend the Painter (Mi Amigo el Pintor), by Lygia Bojunga Nunes
Juan Bobo: Four Folktales from Puerto Rico, by Carmen T. Bernier-Grand, Ernesto Nieves, and Ernesto Ramos Nieves
Juan Bobo and the Pig: A Puerto Rican Folktale, by Felix Pitre, illustrated by Christy Hale
The Valley of the Colorful Bird (El Valle de la Pajara Pinta), by Dora Alonso
Vejigante Masquerader, by Lulu Delace

Easy Readers—American Authors—Ages Six to Ten

I Know a Lady: Mi Amiga, La Señora Mayor, by Charlotte Zolowtow

Fables and Old Tales

Stories by Charles Perrault (Cuentos de Perrault)
Stories by the Grimm Brothers (Cuentos de Grimm)
Fontaine's Fables (Fabulas Fontaine)
Aesop's Fables (Fabulas Esopo)
Fables are Forever (Fabulas para Siempre)
Twelve bilingual fables in English and Spanish.
Stories That Must Not Die (Historias que no Deben Morir), edited by Juan Sauuageau Mexican American and Southwest stories in both English and Spanish.

Hispanic Literature for Middle School Children

The Girls from Playa Blanca, by Ofelia Dumas Lachtman
Juanita Fights the School Board, by Gloria Velasquez

Maya's Divided World, by Gloria Velasquez
Pacific Crossing, by Gary Soto
Walking Stars, Stories of Magic and Power, by Victor Villasenor
The Secret of Two Brothers, by Irene Beltran Hernandez

Hispanic Literature for High School Children

Across the Great River, by Irene Beltran Hernandez
The House on Mango Street, by Sandra Cisneros
Macho!, by Victor Villasenor
Shifting Loyalties, by Daniel Cano

Adult Fiction—Hispanic Authors

Author: José Donoso
    The Coronation (Coronación)
Author: Montserrat Roig
    Good Times (Tiempo de Cerezas)
Author: Sandra Cisneros
    Woman Hollering
    My Wicked Wicked Ways
    Third Woman
Author: Rudolfo Anaya
    Bless Me Ultima: folk stories
    Heart of Aztlan: Chicano urban experience
    Tortuga: trilogy of mystical stories
    Albuquerque: recounts the father quest of a Hispanic boxer
    The Adventures of Juan Chicaspatas: epic poem
Author: Laura Esquivel
    Like Water for Chocolate
Author: Gabriel Garcia Marquez (Nobel Prize Winner)
    One Hundred Years of Solitude
    Chronicle of a Death Foretold
    The General in his Labyrinth
    Love in the Time of Cholera
    The Autumn of the Patriarch
    Leaf Storm
    Strange Pilgrim
Author: Sergio Troncoso
    Short Stories
    A Rock Trying to be a Stone
    The Snake
    Espiritu Santo
Author: Himilce Novas
    Mangos, Bananas & Coconuts: A Cuban Love Story
Author: Rosario Ferree
    The House on the Lagoon: Puertorican literature
Author: Arturo Carrion
    Puerto Rico: A Political and Cultural History
Author: Roberto Santiago
    Boricuas Influential in Puerto Rican Writing: An Anthology
Author: Luis Antonio
    A History of the Puertorican in the USA, Vol. I

References

Ashendon, D., Connel, B., Gary Dowsett, G., & Kessler, S. (1987). Teachers and working class schooling. In D. W. Livingstone et al. (Eds.), *Critical pedagogy and cultural power*. New York: Bergin & Garvey.

Freire, P. (1970). *Pedagogy of the oppressed*. New York: Herder and Herder.

Gintis, H. (1989). Education, personal development, and human dignity. In H. Holtz, I. Marcus, J. Dougherty, J. Michaels, & R. Peduzzi (Eds.), *Education and the American dream*. New York: Bergin and Garvey.

Haberman, M. J. (1996). In L. Kaplan & R. A. Edelfelt (Eds.), *Teachers for the new millennium: Aligning teacher development, national goals, and high standards for all students* (pp. 110–131). Thousand Oaks, CA: Corwin.

Kozol, J. (1991). *Savage inequalities*. New York: Crown.

Ogbu, John U. (1993). Differences in cultural frame of reference. *International Journal of Behavioral Development, 16*(3), 483–506.

Shor, I. (1992). *Empowering education: Critical teaching for social change*. Chicago: University of Chicago Press.

11

Finding Our Voices, Finding Ourselves

Becoming Bilingual and Bicultural

Susana M. Sotillo, Ph.D.

Author's Overview[1]

This chapter describes and explains the societal and educational experiences of three individuals from different cultural traditions and socioeconomic backgrounds who learned English as a second language and struggled with the process of accommodation to American sociocultural norms. The unifying theme in all three stories is the process of acquiring a second language and culture in an educational system that does not officially recognize the importance or value of speaking two or more languages.

I will begin with my own story as a middle-class immigrant from Lima, Peru. Next, we will hear about Monique, a nineteen-year-old undergraduate student who grew up speaking three languages. Finally, we will hear from Yolanda, a twenty-three-year-old student from the Dominican Republic who came to the United States mainland at the age of two. Both are undergraduate students at Montclair State University in New Jersey. Pseudonyms are used to protect the students' privacy.

My Educational Beliefs

Congruent with the conceptual framework of this book, I understand education as a tool for social change and a means of furthering the democratic

[1]The overview for this chapter was written by the author.

principles of social justice across national and global learning networks. Education is a compartmentalized societal process that provides opportunities for intellectual growth for all students only when it takes into consideration their own cultural and linguistic experiences as members of a multiplicity of American communities. In trying to understand our own experiences and the changing nature of American education, I will draw upon Sonia Nieto's (1992) pedagogical orientation articulated in *Affirming Diversity.* From this perspective, students are viewed as critical thinkers capable of creating change in their own lives as members of a particular community and responsible for effecting change in the broader society.

Scholars such as Cummins and Sayers (1995) have described how students whose cultural and linguistic diversity is incorporated into the school curriculum develop respect for both their own cultural identity and the identities of others and are thus capable of collaborative work in the construction of knowledge. Cummins and Sayers (1995), Nieto (1992), Peterson (1995), and other scholars committed to the process of empowerment and social justice view multicultural education as a process of comprehensive school reform and creative intervention strategies for the education of all students. It is a tool that permits educators to explore alternatives to the current educational system in place in many of the nation's public schools that, as Anyon (1997) has carefully shown, has short changed far too many of its students. As she explains in her book *Ghetto Schooling,* the economic and political devastation of cities has negatively affected inner-city schools. Many of these children spend countless hours filling out worksheets and working on repetitive tasks that have no real connection to the outside world. They are not presented with an academically oriented curriculum or challenged to think critically and engage in problem-solving activities. As a result of their repeated exposure to negative educational experiences, close to 30 percent of children in inner-city schools drop out, severely limiting their opportunities for social and economic advancement (Anyon, 1997).

My School Experience: Encountering Cultural and Linguistic Differences and Coping with Hostility

I first arrived in the United States in 1960. I was eleven years old when my father, who had been studying for a master's degree in metallurgy at Columbia University, decided it was time for us to join him. Unbeknownst to us, he had made arrangements in advance to register us in Catholic schools. There were six of us: three boys and three girls. There was a ten-year gap between my oldest sister and myself, the second oldest child. Our oldest sister was more like a substitute mother to the rest of us.

The next day following our arrival in the United States, my father brought us to school. I clearly remember my terror at finding myself in a strange land, where people spoke a language I could not understand. I was placed in a classroom where an elderly music teacher kept asking me something about a book. Since I lacked a basic knowledge of English, I could not respond to her questions. I looked around to other Spanish-speaking girls in my class, but they all ignored my requests for help. This elderly teacher proceeded to hit me over the head, uttering words I could not understand. When I returned home after this awful day, I cried and begged my father to send me back to Peru. I was terrified at the prospect of having to go back to school. My parents could not understand how I felt to be yelled at in a language you could not decipher. Every morning I had a gnawing feeling at the pit of my stomach. I was terrified at having to attend classes in a hostile and alien environment.

After three months of struggling to make sense of the sounds and rhythm of a foreign language, I managed to develop more than a survival vocabulary. I could put phrases together and eventually managed to write intelligibly. The former strange sounds finally made sense. I could talk back and did not need to rely on others for help in understanding the teacher's instructions. Six months later, I was excelling at spelling and vocabulary. I was so proud of the A's that appeared in my report card! My success in reading, speaking, and writing stood in sharp contrast to my abysmal failure in mathematics and elementary algebra. I could not figure out what was going on. I was used to the metric system, but in the States we had to learn how to use a different system of measurement. What are called functors, a special class of words whose role is largely grammatical, such as "divide *into*," "multiply *by*," three quarters *of*," "*twice as* much," added to my mental confusion. I was hopelessly behind in math, earning nothing but F's.[2] The importance of decoding the meaning of these words has been carefully documented by Orr in her 1987 study of the influence of the African American language (also known as black English vernacular) and the performance of black students in mathematics and science. Failure to understand the role of functors and the grammatical relationships entailed would prove damaging to my academic performance in science courses.

It was very painful having to experience cultural clashes. North American cultural norms indeed differed from my own. In Peru, I had been taught by nuns in a rigid private Catholic school. Morning services started at 8:00 in the chapel and were over by 8:30. We then had classes until

---

[2]The importance of decoding the meaning of these words has been carefully documented by Eleanor Orr in her 1987 study of the influence of the African-American language (also known as the Black English vernacular) and the performance of black students in mathematics and science. Failure to understand the role of functors and the grammatical relationships entailed would prove damaging to my academic performance in science courses.

noon. At noon, we would march quietly into this enormous dining room where we had to wait until Mother Superior gave her benediction before we could eat. Classes resumed after lunch and were over by 4:30. We would then form two straight rows separated by grade levels and march down to the chapel where we would say the rosary. Our school day did not end until 5:00.

The nuns were very strict when it came to our dress code. Everyone wore the same uniform. If the skirts were above the knee, the nuns would send us home and demand that we conform. Silence was the rule at all times. We were only supposed to speak in class and in the dining room. During recess, speaking was forbidden and we were required to play sports.

In New York City, we lived on the six hundred block of West End Avenue, between 90th and 91st Streets. My experience at Saint Gregory the Great, a parochial school in Manhattan, was truly liberating. Girls could wear short skirts and study side by side with boys. I had never studied with boys and found this aspect of education fascinating. My classmates could talk freely and did not have to line up in perfect rows or march down the hall. This was truly different from the kind of environment in which I had grown up. It also created problems for me. I did not know how to socialize with other boys and girls. Most of the Cuban and Puerto Rican students were not really interested in befriending me. This was a time of crisis in Cuba, and most of the Cuban students did not want to be singled out. I remember the many times I asked my Cuban classmates for help with math and music only to be ignored and pushed away. They were obviously embarrassed by my presence and lack of English skills. Fortunately, I managed to make some friends during my year-long stay in the United States. One of my best friends was an Irish American, Ann McMorrow, whose father was a trolley car conductor. The other girl was Magda Rodriguez, a Puerto Rican classmate who would often come to my house to play with me.

When my father completed his graduate studies in 1961, we all returned to Peru with him. I had been under the impression that my father wanted me to continue my studies in a bilingual school. I certainly did not want to lose my English language skills. Unfortunately, my parents decided to put me back in my old school. I was devastated at the prospect of having to go back to a caste-like atmosphere where wealthy students discriminated against those of us whose parents did not have enough resources to live in mansions. I was ashamed of my parents' modest house and old Studebaker. I dreaded going back to a rigid educational environment. As a result of my parents' decision to put me back in the same religious school, I was seriously depressed for many months and took out my frustration on them. I deliberately neglected my studies and had managed to flunk just about every other course. If it had not been for my mother's persistence, the nuns would have forced me to repeat an entire academic cycle.

My failure in math and elementary algebra in the United States had serious repercussions when I went back to Peru. The equivalent of one's freshman year in U.S. high schools was quite demanding in Peru. Most of my classmates had mastered intermediate and advanced algebra and were beginning to study precalculus and science. Since I had flunked most of my math courses, I had no choice but to attend summer school. It turned out that I would be attending summer school for the next four years. I did manage to catch up with my classmates in the humanities and social sciences. To my parents' delight, I excelled in literature, history, and philosophy. These small successes encouraged me to envision myself as a future scholar.

My father wanted his daughters to be able to earn a living. Although he was a successful college professor and dean, who eventually became the rector of the National Engineering University in Peru, his salary was not enough to cover his numerous financial obligations. My father worked seven days a week to provide the best possible life for all his children. He stressed reading and academic achievement at home and set up a competitive environment among us. My earliest recollections are sitting on my father's lap at the age of four deciphering newspaper headlines.

In spite of financial difficulties, he managed to pay for my tuition at a very prestigious secretarial school run by American nuns. This was an excellent investment in my future. It allowed me to learn skills that I would later use to finance my college education in the United States. I first worked for the Maryknoll Fathers and Brothers in Lima for about six months. In March, 1968, I was hired by IBM to work as a secretary in the engineering division. It was there that I met engineers and other high achievers who encouraged me to go on to college. I was thinking of leaving Peru because most of my classmates had gone either to Europe or to the United States to pursue higher education.

I felt terribly alone and discouraged by what I perceived as a highly patriarchal and rigid social system. Women were not allowed to live on their own, and there were few career opportunities available to them. I decided to apply to two American universities: Temple University and the University of Pennsylvania. I had chosen the Philadelphia area because my oldest sister lived in southern New Jersey, forty-five minutes from Philadelphia. I wanted to live with her while attending college.

When I received my acceptance letters from both universities, I showed them to my father and asked him to help me finance my education. I can still remember his words. Although he was very proud of my being accepted at those institutions and knew that I was capable of completing my education, he told me in very strong terms that his primary duty toward me had been fulfilled. He would only pay for the boys' university education because they were the future breadwinners. Since I was a girl, I would eventually marry and become my husband's responsibility. His responsibilities toward me ended when I graduated from high school. I knew right away that I would have to borrow the money from someone willing to help me finance my education.

My Undergraduate Education at Temple

Two wonderful individuals lent me the money to attend Temple University. One was a gifted engineer with whom I worked at IBM who had earned numerous scholarships as both an undergraduate and later as a graduate student and understood the value of a university degree. My other mentor and friend was a Maryknoll priest who took out all of his savings, $550 at that time (1968), and gave them to me unconditionally. I owe these two wonderful human beings what I am today. If it had not been for their financial support and encouragement, I would never have been able to study in the States.

I first moved in with my sister, but the commuting distance and family misunderstandings that arose proved detrimental to my well-being. Luckily, the university's foreign student advisor found a foster family with six young children to take me in. I stayed with this family for approximately two years. As a pampered middle-class teenager in Peru, I had expected my family and others to take care of me. This family demanded that I find a job and fulfill my responsibilities toward them. We had serious misunderstandings and confrontations because I had not understood the cultural norms of behavior in America. My only way of coping with a stressful situation was to run away.

This was the first of many moves as an undergraduate attending Temple University. These were exciting and challenging years. Since I had experienced considerable language loss by not attending a bilingual school, I had to relearn English. Though I tried to imitate the sounds and rhythm of English faithfully, my pronunciation never reached nativelike norms. Gradually, I was able to master the complex syntax and morphology of English. For the first two years, my grades fluctuated between Bs and Cs. I was quite good at world history, literature, and communications. My writing skills evolved gradually in freshman composition.

I could not understand why I was doing so poorly. After all, my grammar and spelling were excellent. It took me a long time to realize that the way text is organized in English is considerably different from the way text is organized in a romance language, Spanish. This process involved a different set of rhetorical rules which were grounded in cultural ways of being. I had never heard of the thesis statement, organizational rules, cohesion, coherence, or other features of discourse. (See Kaplan, 1967, for an explanation of contrastive rhetoric and teaching of composition.)

To complicate matters further, it was difficult for me to concentrate on my studies because I had to work thirty hours a week in order to pay for my meals and a room I was renting near campus. I did not enjoy having to work so many hours each semester because this prevented me from participating in many of the culturally enriching experiences a university offers. I could not attend talks by famous scholars and barely participated in ongoing student events.

I made a decision to major in communications and theater, specifically journalism, some time during the end of my sophomore year. After meeting a charming and gifted graduate student, I was married in 1971 and later gave birth to my only son, Ivo Gabriel Daniele. Though my son had been born before the end of my senior year, I managed to complete my undergraduate studies and earn an undergraduate degree in journalism.

Upon graduation, I decided to apply to graduate school. I chose urban geography because I wanted to imitate one of my favorite role models, Marilyn Silberfein, a well-respected professor of geography. I really had not given this area much thought but found the field to be quite challenging because of its emphasis on complex statistical models. After completing my master's degree, I found two part-time jobs teaching introduction to geography and urban studies at two different institutions. I had the stamina and ambition to commute back and forth between jobs, although this eventually created tensions and conflict in my family.

In the mid-1970s, it was difficult to find employment in academia. I was very lucky to find part-time employment teaching at a local community college. I supplemented my part-time salary with a full-time job as an administrative assistant at a data processing outfit. I really detested this job and wanted to go back to graduate school because I missed the intellectual challenge of being a university student. In 1978, I decided to enroll in a master's program in international relations at the University of Pennsylvania.

After I had worked for two years as a part-time instructor of journalism and geography, an opportunity opened up for an administrative position at the Community College of Philadelphia. I was hired on a temporary basis to coordinate the English-as-a-second language/bilingual program. This position eventually turned into a full-time appointment.

I learned so much while working at this two-year institution. As an administrator, I learned how to write grants, schedule courses, establish literacy programs in the Latino community, and work closely with training and service providers who worked exclusively with Southeast Asian refugees. These were challenging and exciting years during which I traveled extensively, presented many papers at various conferences, and eventually decided to enroll in a Ph.D. program in educational linguistics at the University of Pennsylvania. I was politically active in the bilingual education movement and worked closely with the Philadelphia school district. I remember the few victories and many defeats in our struggle for a viable model of bilingual education.

In retrospect, I would never have been able to pursue a doctoral degree if I had not been employed full-time at the Community College of

Philadelphia. While I gave my heart and soul to this institution and the students I served, they also reciprocated by allowing me to participate in the forgivable loan program. It took me exactly nine years to complete all the course work and dissertation requirements for my doctoral degree. I wish I had had the time to engage in long philosophical discussions about the nature of language learning while a graduate student at Penn. But I did not have that luxury. I was always running from one place to another, shuffling papers endlessly, and performing administrative tasks. This gave me very little time to engage in serious academic writing. Every semester, it seemed that as soon as I finished one grant, I had to start writing another. The days turned into months, and the months into years. It now all seems like a huge blur, but this is how I chose to spend my young adulthood. My political advocacy work and inability to say no sidetracked me from my main goal: to join the ranks of the academy.

One sunny morning, March 16, 1989, as I was enjoying my drive to work, I was involved in a head-on collision that forever changed my life. I remember looking up to some anxious police officers who were trying to restrain me. I had severely bitten my tongue and was bleeding profusely because of the impact of the collision. I ended up in the hospital in the intensive care unit for a week.

It was then as I lay in pain in my hospital bed that I began to take stock of my life. I was dissatisfied with my accomplishments. I suddenly realized that what had once been an exciting career opportunity had turned into an unbearable, dead-end job. I was constantly at odds with the administration, faculty, and students. The more I did to produce quality work and meet others' expectations, the less I accomplished. I felt constantly under siege. It was then that I made up my mind to leave and finish my dissertation. I saw this unfortunate turn of events as a second chance to fulfill a lifelong dream.

I was hired as an assistant professor of linguistics at Montclair State in the fall of 1989. For the first three years, I worked almost exclusively with ESL and Latino students and was gradually assigned to work with all types of students. The most challenging assignments involved teaching graduate courses in linguistics and second language acquisition, which is my area of expertise. In 1993, I was appointed coordinator of the ESL program and gradually began to incorporate computers in education, especially the use of e-mail in encouraging language learning partnerships.

My research interests have shifted from ESL and bilingualism to critical discourse analysis, which is a multidisciplinary approach to the study of discourse and communication in their social, political, and cultural contexts. My most recent research has focused on the linguistic aspects of political discourse in a working-class town in New Jersey. As a scholar and citizen, I am deeply committed to effecting political and social change in the community where I live. I am politically active at both the local and state level.

As I became computer literate and acquired expertise using the Internet as a tool for research, learning, and teaching, I expanded the scope of my work. In addition to teaching content matter, I also teach my students how to use the new technologies in acquiring general knowledge and learning languages. As the 1990s came to an end, I had mastered new tools for coping with the demands of a twenty-first-century education. My desire to explore the world and acquire knowledge has not diminished in the least. In spite of some serious setbacks, I remain hopeful and optimistic, and await the challenges of this new millennium.

Other Stories: Monique and Yolanda

Monique was born in Booton, New Jersey, into a multilingual immigrant family with a rich multicultural tradition. She has a younger brother. Her mother speaks Macedonian as a first language, and her father is perfectly fluent in both English and Italian. Currently, she lives with her parents in West Caldwell, an upper-middle-class suburb in Essex County, New Jersey, where the median income is $65,920 (1994 Census estimates). Monique is currently attending a large state university and majoring in linguistics.

Monique's Linguistic Resources in a Monolingual School System

I am nineteen years old and I was born in Booton in New Jersey. I lived in Parsippany for about ten years and then moved to West Caldwell and finished the fifth grade there and middle school and high school.

In Parsippany we were—I guess you could say we were middle class. We lived in an apartment. There were different races in the schools. There were Indians and not too many Blacks at the time. Now there are a lot of Blacks. The schools basically put you in special programs if you did not have English as a first language. You automatically were tested and put into a class for English and math skills.

Kindergarten was fine, and then when I moved to second grade, they tested me for English and math and said that I was very low in these skills and I couldn't be put in with the normal class. So they had taken me out and there was a special room where you would have two different teachers, a math and an English teacher. We would spend an hour to two hours doing English and math. That means I was taken away from my regular class period while doing this. They did that all the way up to fourth grade. They did that for two to three years, and I was put into the low reading group all through elementary school. I was always put into low reading and low math, always starting from the bottom because they figured that since I spoke so many languages, I was a retard.

I spoke three at the same time. I knew all of them practically the same. Of course English was the best one that I could understand—better than Italian and Macedonian. To tell you the truth, I don't know why they thought I was retarded. There were kids who were kind of slow and they needed the special attention. For me, I just spoke different languages. I didn't think that was fair. My mom, she kind of fought the school about it, but they said, "I am sorry, we have to do that." She didn't like that at all, but she couldn't really say much.

I hated it! I hated it because I felt I was stupid. They treated me like an idiot and they would say—every day they would pick me up in the middle of class and everyone would see that I was leaving. That's what I remember. They would pick me up at a certain time and all the kids knew that I had to go there. I was seven or eight years old. You want to be with your friends, and play around, and they would start mimicking me. They imitated me, like they did with the retarded kids, the real retarded kids. It puts you kind of on the outs.

We all got a chance to share our backgrounds when we were in elementary school, you know, where we came from. We did have a few Chinese, a few Indians, but primarily White students. Then gradually it became primarily Hispanic and Black. My best friend was a Chinese girl. I always got along with the different-background kids. Actually, my other best friend was Black, too. Since I was different, I always went with the different people. I always made them feel comfortable. These girls were not in special classes. The Chinese girl was in the high class, and I was in a couple of classes with the Black girl, but we had the same teacher in the third grade and in the fourth grade. We kind of stuck together all through elementary school.

Compared to European schools, the schools here teach nothing. In Europe, they are teaching you algebra in second grade. Algebra you don't really learn until nearly sixth or seventh grade, maybe even eighth grade. So we are pretty much behind, and then we wonder why the Europeans mock the Americans. We really don't have a strong education system. So I had no choice. Teaching was just normal like in any elementary school, but it could have been better.

There were these two girls who had come over to America from Macedonia, probably ages fifteen and seventeen at the time. One was one year older and the other was two years younger than me. They had no knowledge of English. They gradually started learning English rapidly and got straight A's in school. Now they speak what you would call flawless English. When you speak to them in Macedonian, they pretend as if they don't know it and that they were not born there. They don't understand you. They try to forget something that is there. I don't know why they do that. Maybe they had bad memories—a bad past that they are trying to forget now that they have a new life. One of these girls is going to be a psychiatrist. She got straight A's in school. They all progressed very well, but they always pretend that they don't know their language, and I know that they know it better than I do because they were born there, whereas I was not. They always try not to speak the language. I don't like that because you were born there and that is your language. Even if you are a citizen now, but that's still your culture. I treat my mother's and grandparents' culture respectfully. I always try to speak their language at home. But for them to pretend to forget, that is just ridiculous! I don't think that's right. That's disrespectful to your parents.

I started off with negative feelings from kindergarten through the middle of fifth grade in Parsippany. They were very discriminatory toward minorities and toward bilingual kids. So I didn't like it. I moved to West Caldwell in the middle of my fifth grade year and everything just went upscale. They put me with normal children. I started off with low math, and then I went to middle math and then to high math and gradually accumulated the high math grade and then reading because they gave me a chance. See, the others schools didn't give me that chance; they just automatically assumed that I was dumb towards English because I was bilingual.

Although I generally had negative feelings about elementary school, my favorite teacher was my second grade teacher. I was like a teacher's pet. She was like in her forties, I think. She was a little kooky. I found out after I was older because I didn't know at the time. But she was my favorite teacher. I would sit after school and mark papers with her—like correct homework. She would give me her pen. She took me to Friendly's twice, maybe three times. She loved me. I saw her maybe a couple of years ago, but she wasn't there. She retired finally. I heard she went a little crazy. She had some kind of a mental problem. But I was a teacher's pet and I'll never forget that. My mom says she once said to her, "Your daughter one day is going to be running some company. She's gonna be a big-time boss." She says she could tell the way I acted in class what was gonna happen to me. That's really positive, actually.

In the middle of fifth grade in West Caldwell, when I told them I was in these special ed classes, they thought that was hideous: "That's absurd! We are not putting you in those classes." And I ended up being in the high math, and high reading I think, all the way up until like eighth grade. They didn't believe in special education or anything like that. I mean they did have a low, middle, and high math. And what I did is I started in low math, and went to middle math, and then to high math. I gradually went up. There were certain levels, and if I did all my work and knew everything and I passed the test, they would move me up. They would move the kids up there. They don't just keep you there. So that was a very good thing about West Caldwell School. It is a middle- to upper-middle-class area. So it's a little bit different from the other school system in Parsippany.

I struggled in middle school because it was a little bit tougher. In middle school, when I started in eighth grade, I enjoyed French and math. And that's it. I really wasn't too crazy about history or science. I never really was but always liked math and different languages. I love math.

There was a reading book that we used and that had lots of plays like *Oliver Twist*. We did that in eighth grade. I loved that. We saw the movie, everything. *Les Miserables* stands out, too. We went to the play. *Oliver Twist, Les Miserables*—those were the things that stood out because we always did more for it. We did four different things. We did like a project, a research paper, picture drawing, watched the movie, went to the play, or did one of the other. That stood out a lot.

In seventh grade, while studying the Renaissance, we read about a love story between two people that happened a long time ago. It was a book and I did whole pictures on it. I got an A+ on it. I still have it. I just don't remember the title of the book: *Isolde and Tristan*? [It was] about two lovers.

Science and history were my least favorite subjects. With history, I don't know. I liked some of it—like when we talked about all the different painters and artists and stuff. But overall, it was hard enough for me to comprehend history, I don't know why. Even in college, I am taking it finally this semester, but I've tried to avoid it for a while. Because it's just hard to comprehend in the readings.

And in high school, I was basically average, you know. I was in regular math, regular English. I wasn't in honors. I could have been if I really wanted to, but I didn't because I knew it was tough. I stuck with my languages. I took five years of French, three years of Italian, and one year of Spanish just starting off.

In high school in my freshman year, we had two classes. A history and an English that was combined together. It was a program—world cultures and English. The world cultures teacher was very, very tough. I'll never forget her name. She was just very tough. She didn't care about you. She was very much into herself. She was always favoring other students, which was not fair. She was very mean, very mean. I had other mean teachers, but I liked them. Like I had one teacher in college who was so mean. Everyone was, like, always saying, "Oh we hate her, we hate her." But you know what, for you to get on her good side all you had to—I would always like— even kiss butt a little bit because she, she would always say this is wrong, this is wrong, but I would try harder and harder and I would prove her wrong. She liked me. Even to this day she asks about me. She is still tough, but a good teacher. I learned a lot from her.

I believe that everyone should be in the same class. ESL is different. If certain kids need certain attention, you really shouldn't pull them out during the school day. They should have like a tutor. Even if the school can provide a special tutor that goes to the house maybe for an hour, three times a week. For example, I tutor two hours a week—two hours, three days a week. That's it! A teacher with certification would do it on the side, but just don't take the kids out of the class. I think that just kind of discriminates. People start cliquing and the clique starts saying, "She is in retarded class. Let's not play with her." And that's not fair.

In high school, there were about 600 students. We had different ethnic groups, but there were few Blacks. We had two or three Black students. They weren't left out. The students weren't racists or anything like that. Definitely not! Schools shouldn't separate the different races or nationalities. That's wrong. Because if you are going to teach a child from when he's a child that he can't play with certain people, that's what happens when he becomes seventeen, eighteen, or nineteen and they're in gangs and they are killing, or they are in the Ku Klux Klan. That's where it all derives from. You learn everything from when you're a child.

Children pick up a lot. They know. They'll hear and then they will repeat it later. My parents always told me to play with everyone. My father almost married a Black woman—he told me that. So I would never be against anything. I had friends who were from a different race, backgrounds, and nationalities. And all my friends speak at least three different languages.

Teach children how to get along together. Teach them about the different races that we have, and how everyone should be together more, and there should be no discrimination. Make them understand that at a very early age, even kindergarten and the first grade, as soon they start school so they know from that point.

As to methods of teaching, lecturing I didn't like. If you just sit there and talk. I like discussion—lots of discussion. Maybe watching some film and then discussing about it. Maybe getting—getting into a deeper discussion. It gets you to talk and learn, and then that's when the teacher comes in. That's when you get your ideas and then write like a reflecting paper on it. How you reflect on watching this film. Group work I like also because you share the work or divide it up, and then you learn what they wrote, and they learn what you wrote. I like group work. You can't just sit there and lecture at students because it's going to drain them.

One year, I picked Macedonia and did a whole report on Macedonia because there's a big controversy, you know, between the Greeks and the Macedonians. My paper that I sent to all the colleges was about my Macedonian background and the experiences I had. So I ended up fighting with my teachers because they were saying, "No, it's Greek [giving the Greeks credit for Macedonian achievements]."

I have been to Italy thirteen times. From ages one to ten, we were there from June to September. We have a house there, down the shore. And then what we do is take the boat from Bari which is down there and go on the boat. And only my mother would drive us through Greece up to her country for two weeks. Then we would come back to Italy. We did this for ten years, and as we got older we kind of took turns. We did Macedonia one year for three weeks [and] Italy the next summer. Lately, it's been Italy a lot. I've pretty much experienced everything because I have been there. I've even been to France, Sicily, and Italy.

So everything kept getting better. My freshman year of college was a little rough because it was the first. This semester I did great, and last semester I did great. So I have been trying and everything has been just upscale—everything since I left the school system. Everyone has treated me better. And everything changed from the time I was young to now. So there are more opportunities, and groups, and places to meet with teachers and discuss certain things that you need help with.

My future plans include choices. I have a choice of either working for the United Nations or working for a company that involves traveling around the world, interpreting, and translating for companies. I would love to translate and travel. Those are my two favorite things. Actually, I would like to work for a company, for someone that would involve me in translating and making business deals in different languages for them. I've always wanted to do this since freshman year. I knew exactly what I wanted to do!

Yolanda's Story: Experiencing Discrimination in America

Yolanda is twenty-three years old and is the daughter of Dominican immigrants. Her parents speak Spanish at home and have very close connections with relatives in the Dominican Republic. The family of four (mother, father, Yolanda, and her brother) live in Paterson, New Jersey, a city of over 140,000 residents. Paterson is best described as a working-class city with a large Black and Latino population where the median income is $26,960 (1994 Census estimates). Yolanda graduated in May 1999 from Montclair State University.

Learning in Urban Public Schools

I'm twenty-three years old. I was born in Paterson, New Jersey, and moved to the Dominican Republic when I was about six months old. I lived there until I was around five years old, going on six. Then we came back to Paterson and I've lived here ever since.

I didn't like primary school at all, especially junior high. I guess I just didn't fit in with everyone else. High school was a little different. It was more of a mixed crowd, so I liked that better. That was a better experience for me. I didn't fit in. I guess the way I looked, I mean, the way I dressed. I mean, my parents never had money to send me to school wearing the latest styles or whatever. And kids really pay attention to that over here. So I really just didn't fit in. I have gone to public schools all of my life.

Teachers in primary school tended to show favoritism toward certain students. Growing up in Paterson, I mean, the population has been mostly African Americans and Latinos—like the whole time. It's not like when I was in kindergarten—it was mostly White—and then in fifth grade, it was mostly African Americans. It's just always been African American and Latinos. If anything, I'd say [there's] favoritism toward African Americans. In thinking back on it, the students were—they either hung with African Americans during the school year or mostly Latinos during the school year because people tend to clique. Cliques were usually segregated in that way.

I liked when teachers would have us write about ourselves or just write our opinions about something. I think that I always liked that. In high school, I don't know about everyone in general, but I myself just thought it was an intermediate period. I mean, you just feel that you are just forced to study certain things. Some things you liked for some reason and disliked for others. Gym I didn't like. I didn't like having to change for that. Spanish I liked because it was the easiest. I was OK at math. It wasn't like my forte or anything. Those teachers are kookies, it's all I could think of. They basically taught what they had to teach. I mean they were just going by what they had to do. They didn't stray from what they had to do in any way. It was like they had a set plan and that's what they stuck to. The only time minorities were discussed was during African American month, which is what? February? And then of course you had to write reports in all of your classes and you'd hear about people, but other than that, no one went out of their way to talk about minorities, especially about Latinos.

I don't really like to read. I think maybe in junior high I—for a while—I got into reading, like, little books. You know how they write books for the teens? I got into those. My dad didn't like those, and after a while, I just only read what I had to read. As a matter of fact, I don't think I had ever read a book by a Latino author until I came to college. In high school, you read stuff like Shakespeare. The traditional stuff didn't really include Latino or other writers.

Social studies was my least favorite subject, which was really, I mean, social studies always translated into American history basically. That was basically what social studies was. They covered slavery maybe in one of the topics of the book briefly, very briefly. And I mean, every once in a while you'd get that one teacher that was, you know, into it. Like I remember in the eighth grade, my teacher was injured so we had a permanent substitute, and she was really educated as far as African American studies went, so she would always talk to us about stuff like that and that was the most exposure any of us ever had to the subject—nothing about Latino history or culture.

In elementary school, my favorite teacher was my fourth grade teacher. I actually go back and visit her every once in a while, but it wasn't really because of her knowledge. I think it was her classroom management skills that I admired the most because she was just the kind of teacher you couldn't get over on. From the fourth grade to the eighth grade I only had that one African American teacher and that was the permanent substitute. And then from first to third grade, my, actually my kindergarten teacher or my first grade teacher, I don't remember, she was Latina. But other than that, my teachers have pretty much been White.

I went to high school in Wayne, New Jersey, but it's Wayne Technical and Vocational school now. I studied accounting. It really doesn't interest me anymore. I chose vocational school because other than that, the choices were Eastside High School. I don't know if you've ever heard of it, but it's pretty much like. . . . It's craziness. I mean, you know, pretty much like Joe Clark and that whole thing. [Readers unfamiliar with Eastside High's legacy may be interested in viewing the movie *Lean on Me*.] And that was not an option for me. And there was an arts high school, the Rosa Parks school, but I didn't get into that. You had to apply and go through this whole process. And then there was Kennedy High School. I didn't really consider that.

I never went to a vocational school thinking that that was it. To me, it was just high school. I never understood when I was in high school how people would be like, "Well, this is it for me, no more school," because that was, that was just the way I was brought up. You go to high school and then you go to college. My father, the family he grew up in, the boys had to work in the family business, but all the girls went to college. So it's like all of the women are professionals but all of the men are blue-collar workers. And my mom, she had to leave school very young—when she was very young to go work in someone's house or something. But that was just the way it was. I mean you go to high school and then you go to college. My relatives—they all live in the Dominican Republic. I have an aunt who is a gynecologist. One is a dentist. There's a set of twins. One of them does hair, the other one does nails, which is really odd. I have an aunt that's a pediatrician. I also have an aunt that's an architect.

With the field that I have chosen in particular [teaching], I feel that, really the exposure will be on me. I will be totally exposed to people that aren't of this culture. As of yet, I have no idea what to expect once I get into a classroom. But I think—it's really important for people to know that just— I mean, it is important for them to learn English because they're here, and, let's face it, they're gonna be faced with having to go places where they just won't be accepted for not being able to master the language. At the same time, it's of utmost importance for them to remember their culture. I mean being here does not mean having to adopt all of the belief systems of this country as far as I'm concerned.

Really, my biggest goal or the ultimate goal is to be able to teach outside of the United States for me. So that really I'll be teaching English as a foreign language and not as a second language. I haven't any place in particular in mind, but I just know that I don't want to stay here for the rest of my life. One of the main reasons I came to college was to be able to go study abroad sometime because, I mean, my very first year I went into my Educational Opportunity Fund (EOF) counselor's office and I was just telling her how I wanted to go abroad. But then, there was one semester when my grades went down, and it was just really hard to get it up to where I would be able to go abroad. And then finally, I was able to bring it up to a point where I would be able to go abroad.

I've chosen linguistics, but so far, in all honesty, I think the class that has interested me—that has held my interest the most has been urban anthropology. I guess, I've never really liked the country and am pretty sure that if I do stay in this country, I'll be staying in New York. I don't know, I just really love the city and everything that's in it—all the people, all the different peoples, different cultures in the city. And that class actually touched up on that. We didn't just talk about New York the whole time. My project was on different night clubs in the city, so I actually found myself going to clubs by myself and reporting on them. It wasn't that bad. I had fun. I had fun writing that paper. My teacher was a great teacher.

And I also had her for native Latin Americans. That was another class also that was pretty good—native Latin Americans—because I also got to learn about the Arawak and Tainos and I really didn't know that much about them. I mean, I knew, those were the Indians in the Dominican Republic. Oh, I got to write about Christopher Columbus, one of my favorite things, and get a grade for it. Basically, I wrote that he's glorified in a way that—that's just not right. I just know that at the end of the paper I wrote that anyone who thinks that Christopher Columbus really did all of these great things should take the data they give us every year and then go down to the library and educate themselves on him. He was just atrocious.

I don't think my culture played that much of a role in my education. A lot of times, people always thought that I was African American or that I was mixed [that I had one African American parent and then a parent that was maybe white or Latino]. African Americans and Latinos in high school pretty much kept separate unless—it's hard to explain, like let's say a Latino that spoke Black English or African American vernacular—a Latino that spoke African American vernacular could probably hang out with the clique that was African American, stuff like that.

I think that schools and teachers should try to help students come to terms with who they are. Going into a school and just learning about one particular culture, and one particular system, that's, I mean, I don't think that helps the student in any way when they are not from that culture, when that's not really their culture or their system. You get students who, after a while, they don't know what to identify with anymore. And then you get students that feel like other students should only identify with certain things. And you even see that in college. I mean I've heard of like, this organization, LASO. I knew this girl, a Latina, and she was telling me how she—there were people in that organization who looked down upon her because she was dating an African student.

All through my schooling, no one asked about my culture. I guess in this area, most of the Latinos are Puerto Rican. I mean, I have students asking me things like, "Do you speak Puerto Rican?" I go to the Dominican Republic at least every two years. No one ever asked me about my culture in high school or throughout my schooling. Only once I was asked to bring a souvenir from our culture. That's the only thing I can remember.

In Paterson in particular, or in Passaic County, education is pretty much odd. It was geared toward a student that just was not in that classroom. And I can't imagine that anybody got a lot out of any of it—K through twelve. I mean, it was just crazy. What was being taught was not something that all of us could relate to. Actually, the majority of us wouldn't be able to relate to what was being taught. When you are that young, you just figure that this is what we are supposed to be learning.

Reflecting on Our Stories

Our stories reflect commonalities in the way we were brought up. We were raised in two-parent homes where education was valued as an end in itself. Our parents were actively involved in our lives and encouraged us to pursue higher education. These are traditional middle-class and lower-middle-class values. In spite of financial obstacles, our parents clearly understood the importance of pursuing education beyond high school. All three of us have indeed internalized our parents' values and worldview.

Our educational experiences differ considerably with respect to the modes of learning and structure of our educational environments. I was educated in an all-girls school. This was a very structured, authoritarian learning environment. Following the traditional European model of education, we were expected to memorize massive amounts of information and display our knowledge by repeating as much as we could possibly recall in essay exams or oral presentations. I was never taught to think critically or to question authority.

Monique's earlier educational experiences in Parsippany negatively affected her self-esteem:

I hated it! I hated it because I felt I was stupid. They treated me like an idiot and . . . every day they would pick me up in the middle of class and everyone would see that I was leaving.

Fortunately, her parents remedied this situation by moving out of the school system that viewed cultural and linguistic differences as pathologies. When she angrily describes being treated like a "retard," Monique is displaying social prejudices she has internalized by being exposed to an insensitive educational environment where she was initially classified as learning disabled. Educational policies such as tracking and ability grouping are most commonly found in large, racially diverse, and poor communities and are based on discredited hypotheses of cultural or genetic deprivation (Persell, 1977; McDermott, 1977; Gould, 1981).

When Monique was placed in an educationally progressive, upper-middle-class environment, her outlook on life changed radically:

> I started off with low math, and then I went to middle math and then to high math and gradually accumulated the high math grade . . . because they gave me a chance. See, the other schools didn't give me that chance; they just automatically assumed that I was dumb . . . because I was bilingual.

There were more opportunities for her to engage in rewarding educational activities, such as learning foreign languages, acting in various plays, and doing creative research projects.

Yolanda, on the other hand, grew up in Paterson, New Jersey, a working-class city with a large Black and Latino population. Because her parents had limited economic resources, Yolanda often felt ostracized by her classmates:

> I didn't like primary school at all, especially junior high. . . . I didn't fit in. I guess the way I looked, I mean, the way I dressed. I mean, my parents never had money to send me to school wearing the latest styles. . . .

She also resented the fact that teachers in primary school showed favoritism toward African American students and that her own ethnic background was not acknowledged. Latino culture and Latino writers were not part of the mainstream curriculum.

When reflecting on her own educational experiences, Yolanda felt that she was "forced to study certain things." She also noticed the limited educational choices available to her and the mechanistic approach to teaching followed by most of her teachers:

> I mean they were just going by what they had to do. They didn't stray from what they had to do in any way. It was like they had a set plan and that's what they stuck to.

A similar experience is described and critically analyzed by Felipe Rangel Pissini in Chapter 10 when he compares an educational system that encouraged mediocrity among poor children in the Bronx with the highly structured and demanding educational system available to children attending private schools. Thus, for Yolanda, learning became a chore rather than a challenge. Because her parents could not afford to move away from Paterson, she remained in a school system that did not address the aspirations of many of its culturally and linguistically diverse student population. Yolanda's academic achievement was partly affected by what she perceived as discriminatory and marginalizing practices in school. This is in keeping with Ogbu's (1993) theory of the correlation between student achievement and children's self-perception within the larger society.

The quality of education in poor, urban districts has been the subject of many court battles related to New Jersey school funding. For example, there have been nine major court decisions related to school funding in New Jersey. The first one, *Robinson v. Cahill 1973*, "declared that New Jersey's system of financing public schools was unconstitutional because it violated the state constitutional mandate for a thorough and efficient education by basing school funding on local taxation" (Anyon, 1997, p. 135). In the last major court decision, *Abbott v. Burke 1997*, the Supreme Court determined that the regular funding provisions of the 1996 Comprehensive Educational Improvement and Financing Act (CEIFA) were unconstitutional as applied to the special needs (poor urban) districts. The judges ordered the legislature to assure by the start of the 1997–98 school year that per-pupil expenditures be equivalent to the average per-pupil expenditures in the wealthy suburban districts.

Jean Anyon (1997), who has written eloquently about the schooling of working-class and minority children, points out that New Jersey, along with Illinois, New York, Massachusetts, and Michigan, remains "one of the most segregated states and has had one of the most segregated school systems in the nation for more than a decade" (Anyon, 1997, p. 133). As Yolanda's experience shows, the concentration of Blacks and Hispanics in New Jersey's cities is accompanied by the concentration of children of color in the poorer urban school districts, such as Camden, Newark, and Paterson. The legislative response to the numerous court cases has resulted in the imposition of caps on local school district expenditures, and, more important, in a requirement that calls for a minimum curriculum of basic skills for all students (*Abbott v. Burke 1990;* Centolanza, 1986 as cited in Anyon, 1997, p. 136).

What this means is that minority children are subjected to a basic skills curriculum that emphasizes rote learning and skill-drill exercises. As Anyon (1997) critically observes, such a curriculum is relatively inexpensive because it utilizes workbooks and worksheets and does not require that the state invest funds in hardware and software for computers, state-of-the-art laboratory equipment, textbooks, or other expensive curriculum materials for urban schools.

In contrast, property-rich suburban schools continue to offer sophisticated and challenging curriculum and a range of enrichment courses for their students. The unequal educational experiences of Monique, who attended an upper-middle-class school district, and Yolanda, a product of a poor urban district, reflect these unjust socioeconomic disparities.

Monique and Yolanda also differ with respect to their choices of favorite and least favorite subjects in school. Yolanda states that she really did not like to read in junior high, "For a while—I got into reading, like, little books. You know how they write books for the teens? . . . and after a while, I just only read what I had to read." In contrast to this experience, Monique was exposed to Western literature and enjoyed reading *Oliver Twist* and *Les Misérables.*

Yolanda's most memorable experience of a creative teacher was when she was in eighth grade:

> My teacher was injured so we had a permanent substitute, and she was really educated as far as African American studies went . . . and that was the most exposure any of us ever had to the subject.

Both narratives seem to indicate that the schools did not capitalize on Monique's or Yolanda's cultural background and knowledge of languages. Their sharing of cultural experiences in school was limited to what Peterson (1995) has called the three F's: "facts," foods, and faces. Monique went on to learn two additional languages, French and Spanish, and became fluent in both. Yolanda concentrated in Spanish because it was offered in her school. Because of the limited curricular choices available in her district, Yolanda had no choice but to attend a vocational school where she studied accounting. She had wanted to attend the Rosa Parks School of Art but was not able to gain admission.

Monique's least favorite subjects were history and science because these required the tedious task of memorizing facts and formulas. Her preferred style of learning includes team work or collaborative learning, group discussions, and writing reflection papers. She strongly dislikes the teacher-fronted approach because "You can't just sit there and lecture at students because it's going to drain them." Her favorite teacher was a second grade teacher who showed interest in her. This teacher encouraged her to develop self-confidence and assigned meaningful tasks, such as inviting her to grade papers with her. She also encouraged her creativity and active participation in class:

> She says she could tell the way I acted in class what was gonna happen to me. That's really positive, actually.

The need for emotional support from parents, community members, and educators is crucial to children from bicultural or multicultural backgrounds in making the transition from their home traditions and culture to the mainstream culture. As Lee (in Chapter 4) points out, children can build a strong psychological foundation for high self-esteem and a strong sense of identity "by adopting a bicultural approach in which children add new values while keeping their original culture." However, the original immigrant culture undergoes changes as a result of prolonged cultural and linguistic contact (Edwards, 1994).

Yolanda's educational experiences in elementary and secondary school were quite different. She felt left out, confined to a basic curriculum that limited her creativity and discouraged critical thinking and self-reflection. Her least favorite subject was social studies because it always translated into European American values and history and ignored other cultures and races. In high school, Yolanda read Shakespeare and other Western writers but was never exposed to non-Western or Latino authors:

> No one ever asked me about my culture in high school or throughout my schooling.

In analyzing her own schooling, Yolanda concludes that many of her fellow students never got much out of the education available to them:

> And I can't imagine that anybody got a lot out of any of it—K through twelve. . . . What was being taught was not something that all of us could relate to.

This is a powerful statement that confirms what many scholars and writers have been saying about the schooling of minority students in urban districts. As Anyon (1997) states, "although nationally we spend a great deal of money on urban education, we are still failing to educate inner city youngsters. We spend far less on city schools than we do on suburban schools— and given the relatively large percentages of city school budgets that are removed from the regular education program for special needs purposes, the disparity is even greater" (p. 148).

One of Yolanda's favorite teachers was her fourth grade teacher. She still visits her every now and then. What is revealing about her story is that she liked this teacher,

> [not] because of her knowledge. . . . I think it was her classroom management skills that I admired most because she was just the kind of teacher you couldn't get over on.

This statement appears to indicate that Yolanda admired a teacher who could control her class and provide some structure for learning, which is precisely what children from poor urban schools say is lacking in their classrooms (Fullan, 1993). In the urban schools she attended, Yolanda had limited exposure to collaborative learning activities or to academic tasks that included a research skills component. Her primary motivation for going on to college came from her own family. In her father's family, the boys had to work in the family business, but all the girls were encouraged to go to college. As she states,

> It's like all the women are professional but all of the men are blue-collar workers.

Yolanda's relatives include successful professional women: a gynecologist, a dentist, a pediatrician, and an architect. Their accomplishments inspired Yolanda to move beyond the limitations imposed by a mediocre school system.

Although a linguistics major with a concentration in English as a Second Language, her most rewarding learning experience was studying urban anthropology and Latin American history. Her instructor was a gifted lecturer who assigned creative projects that taught students how to engage in ethnographic observations, gather, and analyze data. She has also been exposed to the value of using primary sources in researching the role of Christopher Columbus in the discovery of the Americas. This enabled her to separate fact from fiction by interpreting data and analyzing historical sources.

Our perspectives on culture and multiculturalism are very similar. I came back to the U.S. mainland as a young adult after having been raised in a Latin American environment. Yolanda and Monique were born in the United States. Although both have traveled extensively and lived in their parents' countries of origin, their cultural experiences and educational training differ from mine considerably. It took me a long time to acquire communicative competence in American culture. This was not a matter of learning grammatical English or imitating near-nativelike American English speech, but being able to decipher the appropriate rules of behavior that accompanied specific speech acts.

Unlike Monique and Yolanda, I had a very difficult time relying on my own judgment for making decisions or selecting options. I relied on authority figures and was unable to understand what was expected of me during my first two years in college. For example, my foster family wanted me to find a job and become self-sufficient, but I was afraid of leaving the security of their home.

Yolanda and Monique encountered different types of cultural dissonance in American schools. Monique is very proud of her heritage and of the fact that she speaks five languages fluently. Although she was initially unwisely placed in classes for the learning disabled for speaking Macedonian and Italian as first languages, once her learning environment changed,

Monique made remarkable progress in all subject areas. She focused primarily on languages and math.

Monique strongly believes in preserving her parents' language and culture and sharply criticizes immigrants who choose to forget their language and culture. She criticized two young immigrants who pretended not to understand her when addressed in Macedonian:

> I don't like that because you were born there and that is your language. Even if you are a citizen now, but that's still your culture.

She views language learning, cultural diversity, and living abroad as valuable learning experiences that have helped expand her worldview. Monique's learning experiences exemplify the positive and enriching aspects of multilingualism.

With respect to multicultural education and race relations, Monique understands that parents are responsible for inculcating tolerance of and respect for other cultures in their children. She reflects on her own upbringing and parents' attitudes:

> Children pick up a lot. They know. They'll hear and then they will repeat it later. My parents always told me to play with everyone. . . .
> I had friends who were from a different race, backgrounds, and nationalities.

She believes that schools ought to bring together the different ethnic groups and nationalities, thus eliminating the discriminatory educational practices that she endured as a young child.

Although Yolanda recognizes how important mastering English is for immigrants in order to avoid stigmatizing forms of speech and modes of behavior, she is aware of the importance of retaining one's language and culture:

> I mean being here does not mean having to adopt all of the belief systems of this country as far as I'm concerned.

Like Monique, Yolanda understands that all students need to be exposed to the history and culture of each major geopolitical group in the United States: European Americans, African Americans, Latino Americans, Asian Americans, and Native Americans. But her own schooling did not provide this exposure to her:

> I think that schools and teachers should try to help students come to terms with who they are. Going into a school and just learning about one particular culture, and one particular system . . . I don't think that

helps the student in any way. . . . You get students who, after a while, they don't know what to identify with anymore.

Yolanda often felt alienated from the majority culture because she experienced cultural imperialism and discrimination. People often assumed that she was either African American or that one of her parents was white or Latino. In both high school and college, she did not feel comfortable in cliques that formed around racial groups to the exclusion of others.

As in Yolanda's case, I have also experienced discrimination in the classroom as an undergraduate student. Back in the early 1970s, graduate teaching assistants would come into the classroom and ask the instructor for permission to count "minorities." Although I had a foreign-student visa, my instructors insisted on having me stand up to be counted as a "minority." I protested in one of my journalism classes when I was asked to stand up by the instructor by reminding him that I was a foreign student, to which he replied, "It does not matter. You are Hispanic." This was painfully humiliating.

Another incident involved insulting and racist remarks by fellow classmates. In one of my favorite courses, Political Existentialism, the instructor read from one of my papers and acknowledged the quality of my work. I felt very proud and happy to have my work publicly recognized. Two of my classmates remained after class and told me that the instructor had shown favoritism toward me because "it was fashionable to give A's and B's to minorities." Like Wenju in Chapter 5, I felt deeply offended by their insulting remarks and condescending attitude.

Monique and Yolanda differ in the way they envision their futures. Monique knows exactly what she wants to do upon graduating from college:

> Actually, I would like to work for a company, for someone that would involve me in translating and making business deals in different languages. . . . I've always wanted to do this since freshman year. I knew exactly what I wanted to do!

This self-assurance, enthusiasm, and ability to pursue her goals are partly the result of the educational choices available to her in a suburban school environment. She had a wide range of educational choices in school and was able to thrive in a nurturing environment. Her parents were able to afford private tutors and brought her up in three different cultural environments: the United States, Italy, and Macedonia. Monique is outgoing, optimistic, and emotionally independent.

Yolanda has often expressed interest in teaching English as a second language but seems uncertain as to what she wants to do after graduation:

> As of yet, I have no idea what to expect once I get into a classroom.

She does not sound as optimistic or self-assured as Monique. Her educational experiences were very different from those of mine or Monique's. Limited choices in school and lack of encouragement from teachers and administrators prevented her from experiencing different ways of learning. One could say that she was shortchanged by New Jersey's unequal educational policies and the political exploitation of poor urban school districts. Her curriculum did not include the sophisticated math and science programs, foreign languages, and arts and music courses offered by property-rich suburban school districts. Lack of exposure to a variety of ways of learning has affected her performance in college.

She also expresses a certain degree of alienation from American culture:

> [M]y biggest goal or the ultimate goal is to be able to teach outside of the United States for me. So that really I'll be teaching English as a foreign language and not as a second language. I haven't any place in particular in mind, but I just know that I don't want to stay here for the rest of my life.

Although hard working and friendly, Yolanda is shy and dislikes speaking out in class or leading group discussions. Like Monique, Yolanda is eager to become self-sufficient and emotionally independent. She welcomes the challenge of teaching abroad and has already demonstrated that she can handle uncertainty and cultural differences by participating in the college's study-abroad program for one semester.

The three of us have had different educational experiences in the United States. All of us experienced cultural clashes and different forms of discrimination. In Yolanda's case, discriminatory behavior in schools was compounded by socioeconomic differences. Monique's setbacks were temporary, but she eventually succeeded in articulating her needs and aspirations. She found her voice by transferring to a progressive learning environment in an upper-middle-class neighborhood. Finding our voices and articulating our goals took longer for both Yolanda and me. As a young adult past the sensitive period for language learning, I had to struggle with the process of relearning a second language. Our stories describe how each of us has managed to achieve many of our personal goals by taking chances, making choices, and persevering in the face of obstacles.

In my own case, I have accomplished many of my long-range objectives, but learning remains an ongoing process. Both Yolanda and Monique graduated from college in 1999 and have accomplished a major goal in their lives. What they will be able to do after graduation will depend on their own efforts, the work environment and choices available to them, and their ability to plan and forge ahead in spite of temporary setbacks. All of us were raised in two-parent families that provided the love, support, and encouragement crucial for coping with daily challenges of a hostile school environment. This is not the case with many students attending urban schools in America, where the percentage of families headed by single parents is rapidly increasing. Often, the primary caretaker holds two jobs and has to work long hours. This leaves little time for family quality time. Socioeconomic obstacles interfere with the learning process. When this happens, children do not get the loving attention and support they need from parents, teachers, and administrators to develop their full potential.

By learning to negotiate the gradual process of accommodation to U.S. cultural norms, we have managed to integrate our individual cultural experiences and perspectives into the overarching and complex U.S. cultural framework. However, this process of accommodation, which involves re-thinking and modifying some of our own cultural values and working toward common societal goals, was at times seriously strained. Individuals need access to the power structures of society in order to become agents of change. This can only happen in a participatory type of democracy (Chomsky, 1997). Teachers and administrators need to incorporate students' cultural and linguistic resources into the formal curriculum and envision the school as an integral part of the community.

Educational Implications

Our stories describe our school experiences and the obstacles encountered during the process of accommodation to the cultural and linguistic values of the dominant society. We consider ourselves successful in so far as having accomplished important goals we set for ourselves. Graduating from college and finding challenging jobs are important measures of success for both Monique and Yolanda. The interpretation and analysis of our diverse educational experiences should prove valuable to teachers and administrators who have the obligation to meet the needs of an increasing number of bilingual and multilingual children.

Three major themes have emerged from an analysis of our individual stories that seem to account for our academic success and ability to accomplish personal goals:

1. The importance of family, role models, and school in providing nurturing environments that are conducive to success.
2. The crucial role of language and culture in sustaining our sense of self-worth and optimism, which facilitated our successful accommodation to the culture of the classroom and permitted us to stay in school.
3. Our differential exposure to a variety of ways of learning and the availability (or lack) of a wide range of courses and academic enrichment programs which affected our subsequent academic performance.

In the past, success in U.S. schools implied "Anglicization" of immigrant children. It usually meant not only learning English but also forgetting our parents' native language and culture. That was my experience the first time I arrived in the United States in the early 1960s. José in Chapter 10 had the same experience. Yolanda and Monique can self-identify without having to exclude their cultural heritages. The choices today need not be clear-cut and rigid, but involve making an accommodation between cultural and linguistic, social, and national identification. These choices are now possible because the demographic makeup of the United States is rapidly changing. America has become a multicultural society where individuals enjoy a broader view of the world and move freely in a variety of different settings.

In order to overcome some of the problems we encountered, such as the lack of educational choices experienced by children attending poor urban school districts, we need to develop an inclusive model of multicultural education. As defined by Nieto (1992), "multicultural education is concerned with equity and social justice for all people, and because basic values of different groups are often diametrically opposed, conflict is inevitable. Passively accepting the status quo of any culture is inconsistent with [the goals] of multicultural education (p. 277)." This type of education accepts the culture and language of students and their families. It also recognizes the difficulties inherent in negotiating common assumptions and expectations and the means to accomplishing mutual goals. Multicultural education also involves developing tools for dealing with conflict and divergent agendas.

But this model cannot be implemented as long as poor families and families of color are isolated. As Anyon (1997) points out, in New Jersey, as in other states, significant economic and educational decisions are made by legislators who seem to feel that wealthy suburbanites have no responsibility for the education of urban Black and Latino students because these are "other people's children" (1997, p. 134).

Structural change in urban school districts can only come about by the concerted efforts of grass-roots groups, enlightened educators, and compassionate and committed individuals in policy-making positions. But change is possible, as Peterson (1995) explains in his account of "La Escuela Fratney" in Milwaukee, Wisconsin. Six major factors accounted for the transformation of the Fratney school: (1) grass-roots movements; (2) multiracial unity in which all groups are represented and work together; (3) finding time for educators and parents to reflect, learn, and negotiate curricular changes; (4) empowering parents to become involved in their children's education; (5) institutionalizing structures that foster change in the public schools and in the teaching profession; and (6) ensuring that school reform takes place within the context of broader social changes.

It is the last factor that is crucial for successful school reform and the implementation of multicultural education. Progressive pedagogical approaches, curricular innovations, and new learning methods will not change poor urban schools unless the broader problems of poverty, chronic unemployment, inequality, and violence are addressed by society at large. As Peterson (1995) states, "the improvement of our schools generally must be linked to changes in society" (1995, p. 81).

Families that value education and encourage and support their children play an important role in their academic development. But our own stories also clearly show that academic success and the ability to find employment for self-growth and advancement are inextricably linked to socioeconomic factors. Children whose parents can afford to live in property-rich school districts will succeed and thrive regardless of cultural or linguistic differences. They will be better prepared to overcome temporary setbacks or major obstacles than those who are shortchanged by the lack of educational choices and opportunities to excel.

Editor's Commentary

All three stories in this chapter highlight the need for culturally relevant pedagogy. Like Felipe in the previous chapter, Yolanda lamented the mindless instruction used by teachers who never strayed from the predigested lesson plans. Diversity was covered pseudomulticulturally (Boutte & McCormick, 1992)—the only mention of people of color was during Black History Month. There was a sense of total invisibility in regard to Latino influences in the curriculum (Martinez, 1997).

Adding to the assault of being invisibilized in the curriculum, the women in this chapter did not have the advantage of having a teacher who shared her ethnic heritage (Yolanda did have one Latina American teacher). This scenario is inconceivable to most Whites because approximately 88 percent of the teaching profession is White. As I have pointed out in previous chapters, sharing the students' ethnicity is not sufficient for effective teaching; however, many parents of White children would likely object if all of their children's teachers throughout their thirteen years of schooling were people of color. Likewise, they would resent the invisibility of Whites in the curriculum.

Freire's conception of cultural invasion and manipulation, introduced in Chapter 6, is apparent in this chapter. In Monique's and Yolanda's schools, myths that glorified Whiteness were the norm (e.g., presenting Christopher Columbus as a hero). However, later, in a college course, Native Latin Americans, Yolanda was able to expose some of the common myths that she learned in elementary, middle, and high school. After carefully researching Christopher Columbus, she exclaimed, "He was just atrocious."

As noted by Susana, school becomes a hostile place when one has to fight for the right to be who one is. Monique observed that some girls from Macedonia assumed raceless personae in order to avoid exclusion at school (see Chapter 4 for a fuller discussion of this concept). As Toni Morrison, Nobel Prize novelist, warned, losing one's language means losing one's culture (and culture anchors, sustains, and strengthens us). It frightens me to know that one of the young women who assumed a raceless persona planned to become a psychiatrist. Will she view cultural behaviors as pathological? Will she recommend total assimilation as the way to psychological health for her clients?

As we have seen in previous stories in this book (e.g., Chapter 4, Chapter 10), cultural behaviors are too often mistaken for academic problems (Boutte & DeFlorimonte, 1998). Too often, children of color are erroneously placed in special education courses or low-ability groups, as we have seen in other chapters in this book. Monique seemingly internalized the negative label associated with her special education placement. The sense of disempowerment and embarrassment is evident in her description of school experiences. Contrastingly, when she went to a new school that held high expectations for all children, she excelled. She recalled, "They gave me a chance." What a profound statement, because a chance is all that many students need and deserve.

What does it mean to have to psychologically divorce oneself from one's culture, language, family members, and ancestors? This is essentially what the three women in this chapter were urged to do. Telling a child not to speak her native language implies that there is something negative about one's history, family, and, by extension, oneself. Although schools tend to view having a first language other than English as a deficit, the ability to speak more than one language is a strength. The more languages one understands, the more possibilities of humanity one can imagine.

I was appalled by the insensitivity and ethnocentrism of Susana's university when university personnel routinely interrupted classes to count the "minorities." Using their token approach, the university's personnel made no distinction between international students and students of color born in the United States. The university was concerned about how they looked statistically on paper, but not about substantive issues of inequities and respect. Susana's story, like Wenju's in Chapter 5, also reminds us to be cognizant that international students may have the extra demand of working and going to school.

Both Monique's and Yolanda's comments conveyed that it felt good to be on the receiving end of favoritism by a teacher. However, both resented observing other students as the teachers' favorites. The challenge for educators is to make each child feel special. In order to do this, educators will have to be aware of their biases and preferences. For example, when I taught, I realized that I gave special preferences to females—particularly those who were assertive. Therefore, quiet males got the least amount of attention from me until I recognized my biases. With concerted and continuous efforts, I was able to teach in a more equitable manner.

As Susana points out in her analyses, each of the women came from homes that viewed them as capable (although Susana's father did not pay for college for his female children). Discovering the nature of families' and communities' impressions of their children is an important part of teaching.

Both Monique and Yolanda respected their "strict" and "mean" teachers, confirming Delpit's (1995) assertion that students who do not come from the "culture of power" appreciate explicit communication regarding the rules for that culture. Messages that are put forth in an indirect manner often miss their mark and leave students uncertain of what the rules are, thus setting them up for failure. When the rules are clear rather than disguised, students who are not intimate with the culture of power are not confused, misled, and excluded. Instead, they are empowered to soar and find and use their multicultural voices!

Reflective Activity

Turn your television to a channel that is in Spanish only (if you do not speak Spanish). Alternatively, you may rent a movie in a language other than the one you speak (e.g., Chinese, French) or get a book that has been translated into a language other than English. Spend at east an hour listening to the television or movie or "reading" the book. How does it feel not to be able to comprehend the language? If you went to a place where you were suddenly immersed in another language, what are some of the frustrations you would have? What strategies could others use that might be helpful? What implications does this have for teaching children whose first language is something other than English?

Resources

The following is a list of books and articles that will be useful to administrators and teachers who need to understand the cultural values and linguistic resources of immigrant children learning English as a second language in North American schools. Online resources and Web sites focusing on Macedonia, Peru, and the Dominican Republic are also included as tools for cross-cultural teaching and learning activities. This list also includes up-to-date textbooks and Web sites that will be useful in teacher training workshops and courses.

Bilingual Education and Multilingual Resources

Baker, C. (1996). *Foundations of bilingual education and bilingualism* (2nd ed.). Clevedon, UK: Multilingual Matters.

Castellanos, D. (1983). *The best of two worlds: Bilingual-bicultural education in the U.S.* Trenton, NJ: New Jersey Department of Education.

Edwards, J. (1994). *Multilingualism*. New York: Routledge.

Freeman, R. D. (1999). *Bilingual education and social change*. Clevedon, UK: Multilingual Matters.

Carrasquillo, A., & Rodriguez, V. (1995). *Language minority students in the mainstream classroom*. Clevedon, UK: Multilingual Matters.

Franklin, E. (Ed.). (1999). *Reading and writing in more than one language*. Alexandria, MD: TESOL Publications.

Roca, A., & Jensen, J. B. (Eds.). (1996). *Spanish in contact*. Somerville, MA: Cascadilla Press.

Rosenthal, J. W.(1995). *Teaching science to language minority students*. Clevedon, UK: Multilingual Matters.

Taylor, C. (1992). *Multiculturalism and "the politics of recognition."* Princeton, NJ: Princeton University Press.

Teaching English as a Second Language Methodology

Long, M. H., & Richards, J. C. (Eds.). (1987). *Methodology in TESOL*. New York: Newbury House.

Williams, J. D. (1998). *Preparing to teach writing* (2nd ed.). Hillsdale, NJ: Lawrence Erlbaum Associates.

Teacher Training

Brown, H. D. (1994). *Principles of language learning and teaching* (3rd ed.). Englewood Cliffs, NJ: Prentice Hall Regents.

Goodlad, J. I. (1994). *Educational renewal.* San Francisco: Jossey-Bass.

Culture and Language

Dominican Resources

Fernández, Jorge Max. (1980). *Sistema educativo Dominicano: Diagnóstico y perspectivas.* Santo Domingo, RD: Instituto Tecnológico de Santo Domingo.

Malagón, Jacqueline. (1994). *Palabras en acción: Una visión de la educación Dominicana.* Santo Domingo, RD: Editora Corripio.

Veloz Maggiolo, Marcio. (1980). *Sobre cultural y política cultural en la República Dominicana.* Santo Domingo, RD: Editora Alfa y Omega.

Dominican Republic 1996: Results from the demographic and health survey. *Studies in Family Planning, 29*(4) (December, 1998), 423–427.

Macedonian Resources

Stolz, B. (1991). *Studies in Macedonian language, literature and culture: Proceedings of the first annual North American-Macedonia conference on Macedonian studies.* Ann Arbor, MI: Michigan Slavic Publications.

Peru Resources

Delgado Tresierra, W. (1977). *Peru Eterno* (Volumes I and II). Barcelona, Spain: Ediciones Americanas, Escudo de Oro, S. A.

D'Ornellas, M., Florez, R., Gonzalez, M., Barrionuevo, A., Carreño, P., & Vite, O. (1997–1998). *Literatura Peruana.* Lima, Peru: Expreso Fasciculo Coleccionable.

Internet Resources

Dominican Republic

Culture and Geographic sites: http://www.Caribbeansupersite.com/domrep/culture.htm.

History and Politics: http://Pegasus.cc.ucf.edu/~jtorres/domrep/domrep.html.

Páginas Dominicanas: http://www.asd.k12.ak.us./HomePages/Mpolanco/dem-rep.html.

Ethnic Studies: A Dominican Place in the Sun; Research Institute: http://www.elibrary.com.

Macedonian Culture and Language

http://www.unet.com/mk/mian/eco.htm.

http://www.erc.msstate.edu/~vkire/faq/politics/president.html.

Contemporary Macedonian Culture: http://www.unet.com.mk/mian/macult.htm.

Peruvian Culture and Society

http://ekeko.rcp.net.pe/CARETAS/

British Council—Education in Peru: http://www.britcoun.org/.

Universities and Colleges in Peru: http://www.freecoolcash.com.

Civic Organizations and Education Programs: http://civnet.org/orgprog/.

References

Anyon, J. (1997). *Ghetto schooling.* New York: Teachers College, Columbia University.

Boutte, G. S., & DeFlorimonte, D. (1998). The complexities of valuing cultural differences without overemphasizing them: Taking it to the next level. *Equity and Excellence in Education, 31*(3), 54–62.

Boutte, G. S., & McCormick, C. B.(1992). Avoiding pseudomulticulturalism: Authentic multicultural activities. *Childhood Education, 68*(3), 140–144.

Chomsky, N. (1997). *Media control.* New York: Seven Stories Press.

Cummins, J., & Sayers, D. (1995). *Brave new schools.* New York: St. Martin's.

Delpit, L. (1995). *Other people's children: Cultural conflict in the classroom.* New York: New Press.

Edwards, J. (1994). *Multilingualism.* London: Routledge.

Freire, P. (1970/1999). *Pedagogy of the oppressed.* New York: Continuum.

Fullan, M. (1993). *Change forces.* London: The Falmer Press.

Gould, S. J. (1981). *The mismeasure of man.* New York: Norton.

Kaplan, R. B. (1967). "Contrastive rhetoric and the teaching of composition." *TESOL Quarterly 1*(3): 10–16.

Martinez, E. (1997). Unite and overcome! *Teaching Tolerance, 6*(1), 11–15.

McDermott, R. P. (1977). Social relations as context for learning in school. *Harvard Educational Review, 47*(2): 198–213.

Merriam, S. B. (1988). *Case study research in education: A qualitative approach.* San Francisco: Jossey-Bass.

Nieto, S. (1992). *Affirming diversity.* New York: Longman.

Ogbu, J. U. (1993). Differences in Cultural Frame of Reference. *International Journal of Behavioral Development, 16*(3), 483–506.

Orr, E. W. (1987). *Twice as less.* New York: W. W. Norton & Company.

Persell, C. H. (1977). *Education and inequality: The roots and results of stratification in America's schools.* New York: Free Press.

Peterson, R. (1995). La Escuela Fratney: A journey toward democracy. In M. W. Apple and J. A. Beane (Eds.), *Democratic schools* (pp. 58–82). Alexandria, VA: Association for Supervision and Curriculum Development (ASCD).

12

I Can *Feel Your Pain*

Multicultural Mentoring in Academe

Rhonda Jeffries and Carson Singer

Editor's Overview _____

This chapter is written by two authors, an African American and a Crow Indian. They share the narratives of American Indian high school students who participated in a research study with them. This chapter is unique because of the African American author's contribution, which will be explained in the chapter. To locate authors for this book, the initial authors who convened at the ACEI conference used a "snowball" approach and invited people in academia we knew who had done work in the area of diversity. We had extreme difficulty locating American Indian authors. The American Indian woman who was part of the initial conception was unable to write her proposed chapter on Iroquois Indians for a number of reasons—one being she was enrolled in a doctoral program. Another writer who originally identified himself as American Indian revealed, after seeing that we had a chapter on biracial Americans, that he was biracial and would rather write for that group (although he was unable to complete his chapter).

While I realize that there are American Indian authors and do not want to contribute to the rhetoric about not being able to find one, Table 12.1 illustrates that Native Americans make up less than 1 percent of the population of faculties at universities in the United States. As this chapter will address, many of these faculty members are overburdened with professional and community demands and responsibilities. We feel somewhat comforted by the fact that the American Indian writer of this chapter emphatically expressed that he did not feel silenced or misrepresented by co-authoring this chapter.

TABLE 12.1   *Full-Time Faculty and Administrators in Colleges and Universities, by Ethnic Groups (1991–1992)*

	Total	Native American	Asian	African American	Latino/a	White
Faculty	520,551	1,655	26,545	24,611	11,424	456,316
Executive, Administrative, Managerial	136,908	503	2,163	11,886	3,453	118,903

Source: U.S. Equal Employment Opportunity Commission (cited in *Chronicle of Higher Education Almanac,* September 1, 1995, p. 22). Copyright © 1995, *The Chronicle of Higher Education.* Reprinted with permission.

Multicultural Mentoring (Rhonda)

Multicultural mentoring relationships improve the personal and professional lives of the individuals involved in the relationship as well as the organizations in which the individuals contribute. Mentoring across culture unites diverse people through developmental experiences that encourage *new lines of questioning* and *unique methods of problem solving* (Crosby, 1999; Thomas & Ely, 1996).

New Lines of Questioning: Can Outsiders Be Used Effectively?

As a person of color who wants to see other people of color overcome the oppression that sometimes accompanies the color, I can feel Karen Swisher (1996) as she advocated for American Indians to own their knowledge. She strongly stated her position in a postcolonial framework that begs those in power to step aside and provide space for oppressed groups, in this case American Indians, to tell their own stories. She also clearly believes that American Indian scholars need to produce research rather than simply be subjects and consumers of research. Efforts of this type will more accurately portray Indian experiences that may inform classroom practice (Swisher, 1996). By publishing their knowledge, American Indian scholars and the communities with whom they conduct research can be empowered, especially through the aspect of role modeling.

Swisher (1996) strengthened her position by crediting numerous non-Indian scholars who have produced accurate, sensitive, and in some cases beautifully written pieces about the American Indian experience. Wanting in this work, in her opinion, are an articulated authority and a fundamental passion for the American Indian experience that can come only from in-digenous people.

While I reiterate my empathy for Swisher's position, I see so much difficulty in the actualization of her desires through this methodology. My own personal empowerment as an academic came from one who could have easily been seen as a White, middle-class, male oppressor. Quite the contrary, he provided guidance, support, information, opportunity, and friendship that allowed me to flourish and take ownership of my scholarly pursuits. We crossed many cultural borders to build a professional relationship that strengthened my position as a scholar of color and buttressed his credibility as a person who happens to be White, middle-class, and male and—more important—committed to the struggle of assisting people from traditionally oppressed groups. To have non-Indian scholars removed from the pursuit of empowerment because they are non-Indian weakens their struggle to overcome oppression. There are many people who are or may be willing to commit to the struggle if the opportunity presents itself.

The American Indian struggle was not a priority on my list of issues to address. However, when the opportunity presented itself, I embraced it. The American Indian struggle became my struggle entirely by default, but I easily accepted it and added this specific aspect to my goal of increasing understanding among cultural groups.

I met Carson, a Crow Indian from Montana, while I was on the faculty at the University of Wisconsin—Milwaukee. Because Carson and I were in the same field of study and are both people of color (I am African American), I was asked to mentor him as an emerging, pre-service educator. Carson was part of the Ronald E. McNair Scholars Program, which is designed to use intense support from faculty mentoring to help underrepresented "minorities" pursue graduate education and become academics. Carson had not been able to find an American Indian scholar to mentor him so I was as close as they could get. It was an opportunity to help Carson, but also to help myself. Through Carson, I would pursue new lines of questioning that were not on my agenda for many reasons. The Ronald E. McNair program provided an opportunity for me to participate in the American Indian struggle. Most apparently, these questions were missing from my agenda because there had been no obvious person to answer the questions about American Indians, and prior to knowing Carson, there had been no one who needed me to address and consider the questions for them.

Unique Methods of Problem Solving: Why Mentor Cross-Culturally?

I see a natural connection between the work of all marginalized people and as an African American female in academe, I am sometimes marginalized.

Alternatively, as an African American female academic, I have professional power that so many nonprofessional African American females do not have. Consequently, I see no barrier to the ability of Carson and myself to cross racial and gender borders and help each other as marginalized people. Furthermore, I see no barrier to using what professional power I possess as an academic to assist Carson in his quest as a new educator en route to an academic career. Contrary to more conservative theories, the most appropriate method for emerging from oppression is not always for oppressed people to help themselves in isolation. This is not to suggest that marginalized people should wait for those in power to bestow power upon them. Most marginalized groups possess nonlinear, shared power that is simply not in accordance with conservative, Western notions of power. And certainly, having more people from marginalized groups redefine power and establish new theories about power will assist in changing the status quo. In the meantime, how do marginalized people enter the academic playing field?

Like most cultural groups, academe is steeped in tradition with particular communication patterns and acquired, value-laden behaviors. Culture is not easily exchanged and is much like a security blanket for many members of any cultural group (Spradley & McCurdy, 1990). Many within this cultural group are reluctant to embrace new theoretical considerations and alter their established behavioral norms by opening the group to new and different types of members. Thus, academe has been reluctant and slow to diversify. Considering this, diversification of the academic ranks and empowerment for marginalized groups can progress through a variety of methods. A more productive form of diversifying the academic work force is through cross-cultural mentoring.

Cross-Sectioning a Cross-Cultural Relationship Through Research

Identifying Research Ideas.   The work Carson and I began together became important as I realized how little I knew about American Indian people. We decided to conduct a study of cultural contributors to high school dropout rates because dropout rates are highest among American Indian students. This is becoming increasingly difficult to document because the National Center for Education Statistics (1996) ceased reporting American Indians as an individual group after its 1996 report, which shows 1994 data. Furthermore, although these statistics have existed up until recently, the literature diminishes the impact of this phenomenon by rarely mentioning American Indians in discussions on educational disenfranchisement among people of color (Farmer & Payne, 1992) or by generalizing the American Indian cultural experience in schools to that of other marginalized groups (Woods & Clay, 1996).

Carson's concern about this lack of focus on American Indian educational issues coupled with his personal and research interests led him to volunteer in an American Indian school with a primary mission of high school completion for culturally marginalized students. The McNair program required that each scholar being mentored in the program participate in original research; therefore, Carson selected the American Indian alternative school as his research site. This school uses American Indian cultural norms and strategies as a method for reconnecting high school students who are considering leaving school or have already done so. Carson had an established research agenda when we met, and as a way of assisting his academic growth, I agreed to pursue any research study upon which he wanted to focus. Carson had established entree at this school, and his relationship with them supported and enabled our research, and we were ready to begin data collection shortly after we agreed upon the topic and field site. Carson began to review the literature on American Indian schooling and the high dropout rates among American Indian students. I began to develop an interview protocol that we could use for qualitative interviewing, and I also began a crash course with Carson on taking field notes and conducting participant and nonparticipant observations and collecting effective interviews. He was overwhelmed, and I was challenged. I took my charge from the McNair scholars program sincerely and was determined to assist and guide Carson toward pursuing his career as an academic or in whatever other direction he was motivated.

Collecting and Analyzing Data.   We chose to conduct a qualitative study of Spotted Eagle High School in Milwaukee, Wisconsin, an alternative partnership high school that has become a haven for many American Indian students who have given up on "traditional" schools. Spotted Eagle was established based on a philosophy of values that promote a sense of community, self-esteem, ethnic identity and pride, and an appreciation of all cultures and their relevance in today's society. Spotted Eagle uses a culturally integrated curriculum and coordinated community services to meet the needs of the students and their families—two aspects the school believes are the cornerstones of an alternative high school format. Students attending Spotted Eagle are in grades nine through twelve and are from age fourteen to eighteen.

After observations and discussions between Carson and myself, we focused the study on the life-history narratives of three students and the professional-history narrative of the principal. Carson's extensive history with the school provided perceptions upon which I could balance my interpretations, and my research background on marginalized people became a backdrop for Carson's observations. Simultaneously, we were learning and sharpening our qualitative data gathering techniques and strengthening our data collection by trying to achieve such measures as "balance, fairness, completeness and sensitivity" (Wolcott, 1990, p. 133).

Carson and I conducted the interviews together so that he could learn techniques that enhance the interview process. Lots of head nodding and lack of overt facial expressions are essential to capturing narratives that are true to the narrator's experience and not simply what the interviewer wants to hear. The students were initially reticent to speak, and, at times, I am certain Carson was unsure of my ability to get them to reveal painful or controversial information to me. Carson was having difficulty believing that I could successfully interview the students because they did not know me, and I was untrusting of my success at having given Carson adequate instruction to successfully interview as well.

Carson seemed surprised in one interview with an American Indian female when she appeared as comfortable with me as a woman as she did with him as an American Indian. During our interview event, Carson entered the dialogue to ask her whether she was not revealing information because she was uncomfortable with me as an African American person.

Student: When I started here, I had like really good grades. I was averaging about 3.0. Things were pretty good. But then after that, it started going down, down, until I just quit school. I used to do really good in school.

Rhonda: It sounds like you have a really stable experience. You went to one elementary school, one middle school, one high school, and then something just went wrong. Was it one big thing or a lot of little things?

Student: A lot more of the little things, like the fighting . . .

Rhonda: Did you have any direct contact? Were you involved in any fighting?

Student: (long pause)

Carson: Is there any reason that you might possibly have, yet are not comfortable to share, because I might be a male, and she might be African American?

Student: No.

The student denied that race or gender was an issue for her in the interview process. She may have paused because she did not want to answer the question truthfully and admit to fighting; neither did she want to overtly misinterpret her experience. Whatever the case may be, she also denied race and gender as issues that affected her educational experience. When I asked her whether she would have done better in traditional high schools if there had been an American Indian counselor or American Indian teachers on the staff and faculty, she replied,

There wasn't anything wrong with the counselors who were there. It's just that at that time in my life, I was really depressed for a long time. I really kept to myself. I really don't think it would have mattered if it were an American Indian person or not. I still would have kept to myself and wouldn't have felt comfortable talking to anyone about what was going on in my life.

For this student, the personal issues to which she alluded were too overwhelming for her to discuss with anyone, including Carson and myself, and she doubted anyone's ability to understand or assist her with these problems. However, she readily cited organizational problems such as the size of the school and the lack of closeness which is a byproduct of a large high school as factors that contributed to her leaving traditional school:

It's just like you are a number. It's not like they really know you personally or anything. To them you are just a student and nothing more. They are here to teach; they are getting paid; and that's it. It's not like they take time out personally to sit beside you. They don't really talk to you about it. It's like they talk to everybody at once and that's it. It's like a whole group thing.

The schools' inability to acknowledge who she and others were as American Indian people as cited as reasons why students from this study decided to leave traditional school. Other students' narratives revealed similar themes about feeling disconnected and being part of a group that ignored their needs or being part of a subculture that is never mentioned in the curriculum. A male student expressed feelings of alienation:

. . . Egypt and Africa . . . that's all you really learn about in public school. We never did do the United States. I was wondering when that would come in. The first two chapters are usually in Egypt and Africa and the United States is usually toward the back. And, there is never anything about Native Americans in those books.

The female student conveyed similar thoughts in her narrative about the curriculum:

I didn't like the fact that they'd teach you history from a book and not from their own experiences. So it's like they are just . . . how can I say this? They give you a book and say read this. And this is what's supposed to have happened. It's not like that. There are a lot of things in textbooks that they don't focus on or talk about very much. I mean how is a chapter about Native Americans supposed to cover all the years of what happened?

The female participant, along with the male students, easily cited school-based issues such as culturally inappropriate curriculum as barriers, but they were less likely to discuss personal issues that were situated with themselves and their families as barriers to their academic achievement. Earlier in her narrative, our female participant denied race and the lack of American Indian personnel in public schools as factors that contributed to her educational failure. However, toward the end of her interview, she revealed the contradictory nature of her experience and admitted that race and other cultural subtleties do matter:

> Being Native American, I think that more people like myself need to get educated because there are not many Native American doctors. You don't see many Native American lawyers and other things of that sort. So, [getting an education is] like being able to do something with my life that younger Native American people can look and say, "She can do it. So can I." It's kind of like being a positive role model to the people that are Native American. It's like helping to contribute to the community.

As Carson and I unpacked the complicated experiences of the participants, three compelling issues were revealed. The data in its entirety show that the format and size of traditional schools and the racial composition of a school's professional personnel create significant barriers for American Indian students. Moreover, the education of the participants' families and the economic position of the student created more barriers to success than the racial categorization of being American Indian. Our student participants alluded to these factors, but they were much more hesitant to elaborate on perceived personal barriers than on perceived organizational barriers. Finally, identifying any of these factors as barriers in the participants' narratives does not remove the impact of existing in any organization as a person of American Indian heritage. We are still struggling to understand the full impact of the intricacies of being people of marginalized status in these cases are affected by the multiple marginalization of race, class, and gender. Optimally, these discussions help us expand our conceptualizations of best educational practices for people of color and specifically for American Indians.

Managing Marginality: An American Indian Confessional

During the time that Carson and I worked together, it was unclear how our relationship would evolve. We met often in my office on campus and discussed our personal experiences with racism in our personal and professional lives. We discussed my ignorance about American Indian people and the limited amount of knowledge I possessed considering I had grown up in a state with a significant concentration of American Indian people. Carson's understanding of my ignorance made it easier for me to learn, and our relationship evolved into a reciprocal exchange of professional and personal knowledge. During our time together, and more important, after I left Milwaukee, Carson and I relied mainly on electronic mail to develop our professional and personal discussions. The data shared in this section is from electronic mail dialogue between Carson and myself.

Issues similar to those identified by the high school participants in our study were apparent in Carson's educational experience. He talked to me initially about how difficult merging himself into the culture of "elementary school teacher" had been and often exhibited anger about the lack of knowledge his fellow students and professors possessed about race, class, and gender:

> Yes, too many times throughout my "education" in the teacher education program I was the only male person of color. To top it off, what little they knew of my culture was very inaccurate and stereotypical! Though I challenged many White, male professors and White female classmates on what they characterized as "White versus them" issues, I floundered in their eyes.

Many times, the mentoring aspect of our relationship took precedence over the research project. It was clear to me that Carson had the ability to persevere, but he began to overtly speak about leaving the program. He often questioned his ability to finish despite his resolve to do work in which he deeply believed:

> Having seen and experienced cultural, social, economic, and academic failure as a child and a young adult, I promised myself NEVER to give up in attaining a college education. This is a field that would allow me to assist and guide those who were and are in situations similar to what I have [experienced] and am experiencing.

Still, he expressed dismay at what appeared to be the university's apathy concerning hiring American Indians—even if for no other purpose than to exhibit a physical role model:

> During my first year in this teacher education program, I thought it strange that it did not have one American Indian professor! Sure, the university had its usual, stereotypical history and sociology American Indian professors. Yet, according to local, state, and national statistics, American Indian children in kindergarten through grade twelve are failing academically at an alarming rate. So, why do they not have an American Indian education professor? This was in the mid 1990s and today, in the year 2000, the teacher education program still does not have one!

The university was aware of this shortcoming and the McNair Scholars Program is an attempt to address that phenomenon. Unfortunately, the program was not enough, and near the end of my first summer with Carson, he dropped out of the program. I lost all contact with him. I was unable to connect with him via e-mail, and he was not returning any of my calls. When the McNair Program could not reach him, they turned to me for help. I was unable to do any more than explain the pressure Carson was under from existing in an academic program that simply did not acknowledge who he was and what he planned to contribute to the profession. As for our students in the research study, the system was not prepared to work with Carson and his support systems were not properly in place. In terms of his support system, I was failing, as well. As he struggled with family issues and financial stability, the added stress of this teacher education program was the final blow. I was disappointed in myself and worried about him for the remainder of the summer. I was responsible for repairing the cultural breach in his educational experience and now, he was gone.

Fortunately, Carson returned to the university in the fall semester, and we continued to meet sporadically. I recommitted myself to working with him, and we decided we would work on the research project as time allowed during the fall and spring semesters. With my encouragement and the program's support, Carson reentered the McNair Program the following summer, and we decided to try it again. When I accepted a position at another university, 1,000 miles away, I was concerned that Carson would lose his momentum and perhaps leave the program again. Nevertheless, I packed my bags and assured him we would survive the distance and get the work done.

Technology unquestionably enabled and enhanced the mentoring experience. Carson and I e-mailed, faxed, and phoned each other during our second summer together, and we were professionally closer than we had been when we were within ten miles of each other. We were highly productive, and Carson presented our work, "Cultural Discontinuity and High School Dropout Rates among Urban American Indians," at the McNair Summer Research Symposium. He was nervous about presenting his first research project and disappointed that I was not physically there for moral support. But he succeeded. When I read his report in the symposium proceedings, I realized that it was among the best—and that is my professional, not personal, opinion. I may be a little biased, but since his impressive presentation, we have collectively presented our research numerous times at national refereed conferences. Because of his success, I confirmed that cross-cultural mentoring works. Cross-cultural mentoring *has to* succeed—because at this juncture, this method may likely be the most effective alternative for assisting marginalized students, increasing the number of American Indian academics, and diversifying academe.

Cross-cultural mentoring works: Carson not only finished the McNair Program, but also graduated from the university's teacher education program and recently began his teaching career as an elementary educator in a predominantly American Indian school. He speaks on his teaching experiences:

> The past three weeks have been bloody chaotic. Thus far, my first year teaching has been great. Yet, often times I feel like I don't know what I'm doing and am cheating my students out of an education! Believe me, I would not want to be anywhere else due to the fact that I see and feel the severe need for committed American Indian males in ensuring our children reach some semblance of socioeconomic success. I have a meeting before the kids come in and lessons to prepare—you know the routine, ha!

As Carson rushed from the e-mail to keep pace and reach for success, he appears to be experiencing what any new, first-year teacher would feel. However, he expenses the added concern of mentoring his students and providing more than a basic academic experience for them. Carson is flourishing as a first-year teacher, and I like thinking that our mentoring relationship has played a part in that success. We still talk regularly and continue to work on academic projects. In our correspondence, he confirms my belief that this cross-cultural mentoring effectively addresses the struggles and assists the progress of oppressed people.

> I thank the Good Lord for your patience, understanding, and mentorship with me! I definitely see the past couple of months/year as being quite hectic yet overall moving in a positive direction personally and professionally. Of course, you've been a factor in where I'm going and want to go personally/professionally. I do wish I had more time to explain this but my kids are coming in and they need my attention! This is the last week of extended day activities for two weeks, which will give me more time to focus on our presentation and for applying to graduate school (I'm leaning towards exceptional education or curriculum and instruction). I'll write soon, Carson . . .

It has been my quest to assist Carson in the creation of options for his professional future. Encouraging him to apply to graduate school, successfully proposing and presenting research jointly for professional conferences at the national level, and writing and publishing our research have been some of the more overt things that I have been able to do with Carson. A less obvious thing that has been significant for Carson is my understanding of his complicated life. In these times, we all live complicated lives, but life is sometimes played in high volume for people of color. I understand that all too well. I have benefited in many ways from the mentoring relationship. Continuing to encourage him after he has made it clear to me that he is overwhelmed is an artful performance that I enjoy giving. Our last electronic correspondence conveyed Carson's apologies for not completing work on a project that we had been adjusting for several months. He begged for my forgiveness and hoped his negligence had not broken the friendship. My response was,

> don't even consider that i am mad at you. i will continue to help you create options for your professional future. i don't want to create extra burdens for you, just trying to help. that's what a mentor does ;-) take care and keep in touch, r

Final Questions

This chapter has explored how marginalized individuals can realize greater gains through educational reforms more importantly, the chapter alludes to ways in which people from various cultural groups can combine our efforts and build bridges from within that might span into mainstream America. According to Swerdlik and Bardon (1988):

> Mentoring exists when professional persons act as resources, sponsors, and transitional figures for another person entering the professional world. Mentors provide less experienced persons (mentees) with knowledge, advice, challenge, and support in their pursuit of becoming full members of a particular segment of life. . . . Mentors welcome less experienced persons into the professional world and represent skill, knowledge, and success that the new professionals hope someday to acquire. . . . " (as cited in Crosby, 1999, p. 12)

Perhaps I have not been all of these things to Carson. I have, however, introduced many of these opportunities to his professional experience. Additionally, we have been able to become what many forced mentoring partnerships cannot—a productive professional relationship, as well as, a friendship. While I am not American Indian, this "limitation" has not precluded me from possessing a genuine interest in and passion about Carson and American Indian issues. In spite of Swisher's (1996) admonition for American Indians to publish more research themselves about their own people, the chapters of this book demonstrate the need for more collaborative work among people from diverse cultural backgrounds to address issues of oppression. Many of the issues negatively affecting American Indian students affect most students of color, as well as White students who are poor, gay or lesbian, or marginalized for reasons I do not yet comprehend. The ultimate goal within the philosophical tenets of this chapter is that marginalized people must be acknowledged, served, validated, and prepared to live productive lives. It is everyone's responsibility to reach out and embrace this task. Ultimately, if more people from inside various cultural groups do not embrace the "stranger" (Shabatay, 1991), we will make little progress in changing the face of education and society. Not only must we embrace the stranger, we must also continue to work toward creating spaces for the stranger to thrive, rather than simply exist.

Editor's Commentary

My first interaction with Carson was via e-mail. I had mailed all of the authors a summary of feedback from the reviewers. One reviewer suggested that we get a Navajo writer since they were one of the largest groups. Carson's e-mailed response to me was astute and passionate:

> *Hi, Gloria. The request for the "typical" Indian did and does not surprise me in the least bit. I think first of all you need to realize that just because an individual (Indian person) is from a larger, more numerous group (Navajo, or as they call themselves, "Dine"), does not necessitate that their experiences with the non-Indian world/culture is representative of all Indian people and nations.*
>
> *There are well over 500 different and unique "American Indian" domestic nations in America. Yes, we all share similarities, i.e., unfair relationships/dealings with the U.S., yet each of these relationships differs vastly from one nation/tribe to the other. Moreover, the differing relationships have resulted in some nations/tribes experiencing greater socioeconomic challenges than others. A prime example is with the federally approved, legalized gambling venture. Few tribes in America have been successful with their casino halls; contrary to the popular belief that "all" Indians benefit from this "unfair" venture! That is total B.S.! My tribe, the Crow, has a casino; however, neither I nor the vast majority of Crow Indians (and Indians in the U.S. in general) have ever benefited from the supposed millions of $$.*
>
> *Free education? I'm up to my full-blooded neck in debt in student loans. Ironically, many non-Indian students conveniently decide to claim "Indian ancestry" by enrolling in a particular tribe to take advantage of certain tribes who offer full financial help for enrolled tribal members who claim at least one-quarter blood of "Indian-ness." Funny though, many of these "Indians" who were active in the Indian community during their "higher-ed" days, are no longer to be found working or living in or near Indian communities. Free health care? Never had it during my twelve years of living off the rez (reservation). Contrary to common belief, statistics show that the majority of Indians live in urban areas. I thank the Good Lord immensely for my health, since Montana is practically across the nation and it is much too expensive to travel home often for this much needed service many Indian people need. Yes, there are "Indian" services in urban areas, yet for a fee.*

Racism? Encountered and endured it strongly not only from white peo-
ple, but also from blacks, hispanics, etc. . . .

You know, I could go on and on with the problems I have faced and am
facing as a Native person, yet I feel this is not the time or place. In my experi-
ences and in my educated and noneducated opinion, there are far more Indians
(non-Navajo specifically) in the U.S. like me who have had similar experiences
in the academic and nonacademic environments that differ from those who
come from a "larger group"! Of course, as the tentative titles roughly say,
"Silent Voices," I'm convinced that this perpetuation of leaving "others" out of
the story will continue until the "right" person comes along. . . .   Carson

I appreciated receiving Carson's candid e-mail, which reiterated how many
groups have been silenced. When I received Rhonda and Carson's chapter, I worried
that his voice may have been silenced in the coauthoring process. He responded by
e-mail:

To whom it may concern: I in NO WAY am silenced nor FEEL silenced
by Rhonda Jeffries writing said chapter by herself. I do, however, regret not
being able to directly contribute to the actual writing due to a new teaching as-
signment and attending to my new family.

I attended two American Indian reservation elementary schools and one
elementary school located off the reservation in a white community. In the off-
reservation elementary school I attended, they (white teachers) put me back a
grade and in all special education classes. Placing Indian children in special ed-
ucation classes was the norm in this school. I corroborated this practice years
later upon speaking to fellow educationally successful Indians! Many of them
had endured the same treatment. Interestingly, the same overt racism I endured
in this supposed respected, white community still survives strongly today. Un-
fortunately, I attended and endured junior high and 30 days of high school in
this same community before dropping out, disgusted with "white history and
culture," or commonly known as a "good ol' American education," ha! I even-
tually attended adult high school (GED '83) in a larger city where ethnic di-
versity was just a notch up from where I attained my "formal education."
Additionally, I attended a technical school in this larger city and graduated
from their accounting/bookkeeping program. I began my undergraduate edu-
cation in the state of Wisconsin and received my degree from the university of
Wisconsin—Milwaukee. I majored in "white history & culture" (commonly
known as elementary education—if you think about it, isn't that what we teach
children throughout america—white, euro-american subjects through white,
euro-american eyes?). Not surprisingly, I also encountered prejudice, narrow-
mindedness, and ignorance toward nonwhite peoples not only from future
teachers, but professors as well! As far as the three students interviewed, I have
not seen nor heard about their educational successes or failures. Forgive my dis-
organized composing, but in a few minutes I have a health lesson to teach and

am not sure when I'll be able to sit down and thoroughly answer your questions. Hope all is well.   Carson . . . .

P.S. Write back for further info . . . .

P.P.S. My son Noah is a few days from being 4 months. He's quite the blessing!!

Because I am well aware that the voices of people of color are frequently silenced or misrepresented—especially when the power differential does not favor the person of color (Delpit, 1995; Hill Collins, 1993), I still worried about contributing to the problem of further silencing Native peoples. While I believe that it is possible for a person outside a culture to obtain an emic view of the culture, I e-mailed Carson once again and asked whether I could share his e-mail (the first one presented here) in the book in an effort to ensure that he concurred with Rhonda's perspective. His response convinced me that he did not feel pressured and that it is unlikely that he would allow me (or anyone) to silence him. I also realized that he and Rhonda had worked together for years and had developed a level of trust and understanding that he felt comfortable with. He wrote,

> *Hi Gloria, yes you may use my e-mails. However, in my old e-mail I said (or meant to say), "non-Indian" writers typically write about the larger Indian nations such as the Navajo (Dine), Sioux (Lakota, Nakota, or Dakota), Cherokee, etc. You need to be aware there are hundreds of other nations, each with their unique relationship with the federal government. This continual focus on a few larger nations unfortunately perpetuates stereotypes that are deeply ingrained in the collective american psych! I could go on about the inaccurate information and/or stereotypes that are still being taught in K–12 and higher ed., but I'm sure you're aware (possibly guilty also?) of how non-Indian people view us. Take care and will talk to you later, Carson . . . .*

As Carson's e-mails suggest, the voices of many Indian people go unheard. Academic research on the status and needs of American Indian families continues to lag far behind research on other families of color (Mindel, Habernstein, & Wright, 1998). Additionally, research often does not have a long-term commitment to the community and has tended to buttress the assimilatory model by locating deficiencies in Indian students and families (Deyhle & Swisher, 1997). As Deyhle and Swisher note, most studies on children have focused on negative outcomes, such as drug addiction, alcoholism, and suicide, while few have addressed positive and competent Indian adolescents, who represent the majority of Indian youth.

A thorough review of research found that although the body of research on this topic is substantial, very few studies asked Indian students, "Why did you leave school?" (Deyhle & Swisher, 1997). Rhonda's and Carson's ethnographic inquiry talked and listened to American Indian youth rather than sent them questionnaires to complete. Most studies place the blame on deficits of the students and their families rather than on the deficiencies and characteristics of schools producing dropouts. Many Indian youth, like Carson and the female interviewee in this story, feel "pushed out" of school (Deyhle & Swisher, 1997). Indian students report mistreatment by teachers and administrators and they also label the schools' academic offerings as dull and unconnected to their lives. Based on an ethnographic study of Navajo and Ute students, Deyhle (as cited in Deyhle & Swisher, 1997) concluded that

> *Mistrust of teachers was often justified. A past superintendent explained the "cultural problem" to me, "Some of our older teachers hold traditional views of Indians," and "wiping the slate clean" of these teachers would help the Indian students. . . . Our Indian students learn which teachers don't like them and avoid them.*
>
> *Indian students didn't trust their teachers, even good teachers who cared deeply about their students. The teacher represented a member of the outside Anglo community, a community that has actively controlled the economic, religious, and political lives of the Navajo community. Tensions in the larger community were often mirrored inside the classrooms. . . . The only path to "success" for Indians was to become "non-Indian." It was a path many Indian youth rejected. (p. 131)*

Directly related to the high "pushout" rate of Indian high school students is their disproportionately low enrollment in colleges and universities (see Tables 12.2 and 12.3). We should be mindful that estimates show that fewer than one-half percent of all students enrolled in college are Indian. These estimates may be inflated by individuals claiming Indian ancestry for financial purposes only (as noted by Carson). Hence, the situation may be even more dire than it already looks. It is unfortunate that our current educational system continues to disinvite Indian youth. Indian students actively or passively resist the Eurocentric instruction and content that public

TABLE 12.2   *Student Enrollment at Institutions of Higher Education, by Ethnicity and Gender*

Ethnicity	Enrollment
African American	1,410,300
Native American	121,681
Asian American	724,124
European American	10,603,746
Latino/a American	988,960
International Students	456,847
Total	14,305,658

Source: U.S. Equal Employment Opportunity Commission (cited in *Chronicle of Higher Education Almanac,* September 1, 1995, p. 5). Copyright © 1995 *The Chronicle of Higher Education.* Reprinted with permission.

TABLE 12.3   *Student Enrollment of Women, Minorities and International Students*

Social Group	Percent of Students Enrolled
Women	55.1%
Minorities	23.4%
International Students	3.2%

Source: U.S. Equal Employment Opportunity Commission (cited in *Chronicle of Higher Education Almanac,* September 1, 1995, p. 5). Copyright © 1995 *The Chronicle of Higher Education.* Reprinted with permission.

schools offer. Given the history of cultural invasion and genocide of Indians by Europeans, resistance among indigenous people is justified.

American Indian nations flourished long before the invasion of the Americas by European immigrants (DeGenova, 1997). "The complex civilizations of the indigenous peoples featured advanced architecture, sophisticated agrarian systems, and effective herbal medicinal cures. Each American Indian tribe had a distinctive language, spiritual belief system, and history, which were transmitted from generation to generation in oral or sometimes written form" (DeGenova, 1997, p. 15). Upon contact with the Europeans, conquest, manipulation, and cultural invasion ran rampant. The Europeans' complete disregard for the complex civilizations already existing in the Americas was disrespectful and dehumanizing. Cultural cohesion was subverted when the U.S. government refused to recognize some tribes as distinct, autonomous, self-governing entities, forcing them to adapt to the political, legal, and religious systems of the European immigrants (DeGenova, 1997). "One of the most effective strategies of this forced change was the system of boarding schools set up by a combination of government and religious institutions, which separated generations of children from their families" (DeGenova, 1997, p. 23). This effect is still felt, because those who went to boarding school often knew little of traditional customs, thus causing generational disconnections.

Currently, almost one half (48.6 percent) of all Native Americans reside in nonmetropolitan areas (U.S. Department of Commerce as cited in Mindel et al., 1998). Another 23 percent live in central cities, and the remaining 28 percent live in metropolitan areas outside central cities. Seventy-five percent of all Native Americans live west of the Mississippi River. Four states—Oklahoma, California, Arizona, and New Mexico—have over 100,000 each, together accounting for 43 percent of the total Indian population (Mindel et al., 1998). A closer look at these demographics reveal that

- *approximately 22 percent live on American Indian reservations*
- *10 percent live in tribal areas of Oklahoma*
- *3 percent live in areas (not in Oklahoma) that are inhabited by a federally or state-recognized tribe that does not have a land base*
- *2 percent live in an Alaska Native Village Statistical Area (Mindel et al., 1998).*

Difficulties in the census enumeration procedures make it difficult to get an adequate count because self-identification as Indian has only been allowed since 1990. Accuracy of the census data continues to be debated, but definitive growth has been noted in the Indian population.

The government and society have the power to dehumanize a race or to declare it nonexistent. One method of dehumanization that has been particularly effective is the dissemination of negative stereotypes regarding Indians. The following excerpts from widely circulated books used during most of the 20th century in schools illuminate this point (as cited in Barron, 1980).

Denigration of Indian Spiritual Belief/Elevation of Christianity
The missionaries are doing a good job in changing this. But a good many of the Indians still have their old beliefs.
    Smiley, V. K. (1958). *Swirling sands.* New York: Dodd, Mead, p. 136.

They went toward their cottage, glad of the way things were moving. It gave them great courage to try for still greater things in the days ahead, in spite of the many old ideas that were still holding the boys and girls back from living free and happy lives. Would Denny choose to be a Christian? Would Lester give up being a Medicine Man?
    McGavran, G. W. (1952). *Yakima Boy.* New York: Dodd, Mead, p. 102

But we've got to choose between the wise ways and the foolish ways. And we can't be real for sure Christians and believe all the things our ancestors did who'd never even heard of Jesus.
    McGavran, G. W. (1952). *Yakima Boy.* New York: Dodd, Mead, p. 102

Assaults on Indians' Sense of Industriousness
Get an Injun a job, build him a house, treat him as White as you can, and he'll throw the whole thing out the window the first day the weather's right for fishing.
    Butler, B. (1976). *A girl called Wendy.* New York: Dodd, Mead, p. 52

Myths about Indian Appearances and Character Traits
Do you mean to say you gave those filthy Indians my father's homestead?
    Wilson, H. (1972). *Snowbound in Hidden Valley.* New York: Harcourt, p. 21

I've read that Indians are great at stealing horses.
    Erickson, P. (1959). *Wildwing.* New York: Harper & Row, p. 52

You can't trust an Indian. They'll steal your eyeteeth if you give them half a chance.
    Craig, J. (1972). *No word for goodbye.* New York: Coward, McCann & Geoghegan, p. 75

Belittling Comments about Indian Names and Dress/Glorification of Anglo Names and Dress

I cannot write that your name is Little No Feather. What will the principal say? No, I will call you Johnny. That is a real American name. You want to be a real American don't you?

> Steiner, S. (1961). *The last horse.* New York: Macmillan, p. 1

Nanabah suddenly felt uncomfortable with her long braid and Indian clothes. She wished it were fall when she, too, would go to school and dress like an American.

> Thomas, E. W. (1959). *Torch bearer.* New York: Franklin, p. 4

Imposition of Europeanized Descriptions of Beauty

Rachinda knew that her eyes were softer in tone with more goldish flecks than the black eyes of most of her people. She knew too, that her hair and complexion were a shade lighter than the usual type of Indian.

> Carroll, V. (1966). *White cap for Rachinda.* New York: Washburn, p. 33

Her face was too skinny and her teeth stuck out. She wished her eyes were blue and her skin pink and gold like the girls in the books. She was ugly and clumsy.

> Embry, M. (1971). *Shadi.* New York: Holiday House, p. 26

. . . seated beside him was the most beautiful lady Rose had ever seen. She had dimples, a dazzling smile, and her head was covered with golden curls. . . .

> Lampman, E. S. (1956). *Navaho Sister.* New York: Doubleday, p. 114

Miss Hansen had eyes like bluebells and hair like goldenrod thought Alice, deciding to make up a new poem about her teacher. She thought Miss Hansen was the most beautiful person she had ever seen and that she would study twice as hard as ever and never do anything wrong.

> Carlson, N. S. (1960). *The Tomahawk family.* New York: Harper & Row, p. 46

Never had Nanabah seen anyone so beautiful. Her hair was as golden as the autumn leaves.

> Thomas, E. W. (1959). *Torch bearer.* New York: Franklin, Watts, p. 4

This teacher had hair the yellow of the sky when the sun was setting.

> Means, F. C. (1969). *Our cup is broken.* (Boston: Houghton-Mifflin, p. 96

Disparaging Commentaries about Indian Languages vis-á-vis English

"School man speaks with much swiftness," Deer Woman said as Mr. Slagle drove away.

> Forsee, A. (1955). *Whirly bird.* Philadelphia: J. B. Lippincott, p. 16

"Many good luckies," Deer Woman called as the wagon rolled off with a lurch and a heave.

> Forsee, A. (1955). *Whirly bird*. Philadelphia: J. B. Lippincott, p. 16

"Me got full oatmeal box before," complained Grandma. "That bad stealer stoled most my five centses."

> Carlson, N. S. (1960). *The Tomahawk family*. New York: Harper & Row, p. 46

One Navajo boy when asked where he came from replied: "Much away from this place."

> Erno, R. B. (1969). *Billy Lightfoot*. New York: Crown, p. 29

Expressions of Thankfulness for Better (European) Way of Life

I very glad I never more have to cook in yard over cook fire with smoke making plenty tears for my eyes.

> Ball, Z. (1967). *Sky diver*. New York: Holiday House, p. 26

Criticism of Indian's Adaptation to Inadequate Lifestyles Created by Europeans

Poverty brought him the pain of an empty stomach, the nipping coldness that lingered like an invisible blanket to the Indian's badly constructed homes.

> Rhodes, J. (1972). *The way of Charles speaks soft*. New York: Criterion, p. 26

As these excerpts indicate, cultural invasion of Indian cultures has been widespread, blatant, and deliberate. These attacks on all aspects of Indian cultures served to promote White superiority. Published books filled with culturally invasive perceptions and images gave the myths and misconceptions a sense of legitimacy and officiality. Rampant myths and misconceptions appeared in literature throughout most of the second half of the twentieth century and continues today, albeit under more sophisticated disguises. Evidence of this can be seen in the widely read book The Indian in the Cupboard, *which is required in many schools even though it is filled with stereotypes about Indian savagery and inaccurate information about various Indian nations. While all books have value and it is not possible to remove all inflammatory books from classrooms (nor is this a goal), educators must be cognizant that they must actively mediate the racist messages in books. Otherwise, educators may unconsciously contribute to racism. Students also need to be encouraged to critically evaluate the books they read in terms of their stereotypes. Additionally, book collections in classrooms should be balanced to reflect contemporary images of Native Americans (as opposed to historical books/folktales only) as well as books written by American Indians (Boutte, 1999).*

In addition to negative depictions in the literature, parenting types of American Indian parents have also come under attack. Viewed through the lens of the Eurocentric research on parenting types mentioned in Chapter 4, American Indian parents have often been labeled "permissive" or "apathetic" (Deyhle & Swisher, 1997; Mindel et al., 1998). An alternative, emic perspective of this parenting type indicates that many American Indians value the inviolability of the individual, which dictates light discipline, ridicule, or shaming in opposition to corporal punishment or coercion. At the very center of this parenting style is a respect for the child's relationship to the family. Adults respect children enough to allow them to work things out in their own manner (Mindel et al., 1998). Problematizing the European cultural value of interference, a Northern Alaska Inupiat researcher provided a native's perspective on the differences in child-rearing practices: "Our perspective is that Western child-rearing practices are overly directive and controlling, essentially interfering and intruding in the development of the child. The development of individuality is constrained and childhood is prolonged in Western society" (as cited in Deyhle & Swisher, 1997, p. 142).

Understanding Indian perspectives has tremendous implications for disciplining Native American children in school settings. Little Soldier (1992) cautions educators about singling out Indian children for disciplinary actions. The value of interdependence versus individualism makes singling out one child (to praise or ridicule in public) culturally assaultive.

In sum, I agree with Rhonda that people of color are all brothers and sisters and should and can work collaboratively (Freire, 1970/1999; Martinez, 1997). This theme has been echoed in several chapters in this book. And as the stories in this book come to an end, we should heed Freire's and Martinez's words to "Unite and Overcome" the existing oppressive power structure!

Reflective Activity

What are some of your stereotypes of Indian people and where did they come from? Locate current books about Native Americans and examine them for negative stereotypes. What did you learn from school about American Indians? Compare it to the ideas from this chapter.

Resources

Billman, J. (1992). The Native American curriculum: Attempting alternatives to teepees and headbands. *Young Children, 47*(6), 22–25.

Foerster, L. M., & Little Soldier, D. (1981). Applying anthropology to educational problems. *Journal of American Indian Education, 20*(3), 1–6.

Greenberg, P. (1992). Teaching about Native Americans? or Teaching about people, including Native Americans? Ideas that work with young children. *Young Children, 47*(6), 27–38, 79–81.

Haukoos, G., & Beauvais, A. (1996/1997). Creating positive cultural images: Thoughts for teaching about American Indians. *Childhood Education, 73*(2), 77–81.

Kasten, W. C. (1992). Bridging the horizon: American Indian beliefs and whole language learning. *Anthropology and Education Quarterly, 23*(2), 108–119.

Katz, J. B. (1996). *Messengers of the wind: Native American women tell their life stories.* New York: Ballantine.

Little Soldier, L. (1992). Building optimum learning environments for Navajo students. *Childhood Education, 68*(3), 145–148.

Little Soldier, L. (1997). Is there an 'Indian' in your classroom? Working successfully with urban Native American students. *Phi Delta Kappan, 78*(8), 650–653.

Little Soldier, L. (1989). Sociocultural context and language learning of Native American pupils. *Journal of Rural and Small Schools, 3*(2), 2–6.

Locust, C. (1988). Wounding the spirit: Discrimination and traditional American Indian belief systems. *Harvard Educational Review, 58*(3), 315–330.

Medicine, B. (1982). Native American (Indian) women: A call for research. *Anthropology & Education Quarterly, 19*(2), 86–92.

Ramsey, P. (1979). Beyond 'ten little Indians' and turkeys. *Young Children, 34*(6), 28–32, 49–52

References

Barron, P. (1980). *Characterization of Native Americans in children's literature.* Unpublished doctoral dissertation, Florida State University, Tallahassee.

Boutte, G. (1999). *Multicultural education: Raising consciousness.* Atlanta: Wadsworth.

Crosby, F. (1999). The developing literature on developmental relationships. In A. Murrell, F. Crosby, & R. Ely (Eds.), *Mentoring dilemmas* (pp. 3–20). Mahwah, NJ: Erlbaum.

DeGenova, M. K. (1997). *Families in cultural context: Strengths and challenges in diversity.* Mountain View, CA: Mayfield.

Delpit, L. (1995). *Other people's children: Cultural conflict in the classroom.* New York: New Press.

Deyhle, D., & Swisher, K. (1997). Research in American Indian and Alaska Native education. From assimilation to self-determination. In M. W. Apple (Ed.), *Review of research in education* (pp. 113–194). Washington, DC: American Educational Research Association.

Farmer, J., & Payne, Y. (1992). *Dropping out: Issues and answers.* Springfield, IL: Thomas.

Freire, P. (1970/1999). *Pedagogy of the oppressed.* New York: Continuum.

Hill Collins, P. (1993). Toward a new vision: Race, class, and gender as categories of analysis and connection. *Race, Sex, & Class, 1*(1), 25–45.

Little Soldier, L. (1992). Working with Native American children. *Young Children, 47*(6), 39–42.

Martinez, E. (1997). Unite and overcome! *Teaching Tolerance, 6*(1), 11–15.

Mindel, C. H., Habernstein, R. W., & Wright, R. (1998). *Ethnic families in America: Patterns and variations.* Upper Saddle River, NJ: Prentice Hall.

National Center for Education Statistics. (1996). *Dropout rates in the United States, 1996.* Washington, DC: U.S. Government Printing Office.

Shabatay, V. (1991). The stranger's story: Who calls and who answers? In C. Witherell & N. Noddings (Eds.), *Stories lives tell: Narrative in dialogue and education* (pp. 136–152). New York: Teachers College Press.

Spradley, J., & McCurdy, D. (1990) Culture and the contemporary world. In J. Spradley & D. McCurdy (Eds.), *Conformity and conflict* (7th ed.) (pp. 2–13). New York: HarperCollins.

Swerdlik, M., & Bardon, J. (1988). A survey of mentoring experiences in school psychology. *Journal of Social Behavior and Personality, 10,* 265–272.

Swisher, K. (1996). Why Indian people should be the ones to write about Indian education. *The American Indian Quarterly, 20*(1), 83–90.

Thomas, D., & Ely, R. (1996, Sept.-Oct.). Making differences matter: A new paradigm for managing diversity. *Harvard Business Review,* pp. 79–90.

Wolcott, H. (1990). On seeking and rejecting validity in qualitative research. In E. Eisner & A. Peshkin (Eds.), *Qualitative inquiry in education* (pp. 121–152). New York: Teachers College Press.

Woods, P., & Clay, W. (1996). Perceived structural barriers and academic performance among American Indian high school students. *Youth & Society, 28*(1), 40–61.

13

Conclusion

Voices of Humanity

Gloria Swindler Boutte

In the preface, I mentioned that one member of the ACEI committee that conceived this book said that in order to effect education, you have to touch the hearts of people. We hope that the stories in this book achieved this goal. Having the pleasure of experiencing each chapter as I edited, I feel enriched. Mikhail Bakhtin, the Russian theorist, wrote about the plurality of experiences and how every dialogue with others (including books that we read, music we listen to, and so on) influences our own ideas in some way.

Indeed, the stories in this book have added new dimensions to my repertoire of knowledge concerning different ethnic groups. Whenever I think or talk about any ethnicity, my thoughts will include experiences discussed in the stories in this book. For example, I will remember what life was like for African Americans in the rural South or Black males in urban cities. But I will also recall the trials, tribulations, and joys that accompany immigrating to a new land and trying to adapt. My memories now also include the challenges of trying to merge two different cultural orientations—both of which are a part of oneself. I will incorporate different dimensions of what it means to be White in rural America or middle-class and privileged on the surface and suffering underneath. And I cannot forget what it is like to feel demeaned because my way of speaking is different from the mainstream's. And finally, how can I forget the historical and contemporary pain and suffering (as well as the triumphs) of Native peoples. And so, when I'm talking to my students about diversity, I have to capture all of these dimensions and more.

The stories in this book were like a breath of fresh air for me. The voices were not the typical, aloof, objective (the "I have no biases" approach) approach that is still too common in education. Although each story was unique and passionate, we also sought to ensure that the stories had fidelity. Fidelity describes what the story means to the person telling it (Blumenfeld-Jone, 1995). Fidelity is distinguished from "the truth" or "what happen in a situation" (p. 26). Blumenfeld-Jones (1995) notes that when the tale-teller entrusts his or her story to a receiver, the worth and dignity of the teller is expected to be preserved. Maintaining fidelity is a moral obligation to the people who willingly shared their stories with us. We sought to honor the stories by being as honest as possible and trying to capture the essence of what the stories meant to the tellers of the tales. We hope we succeeded in this task by not imposing our interpretations on the interviewees' actual stories. And yet, in our own analyses of the stories, we remained faithful to our own perspectives.

We hope that the narratives presented in this book transform not only the lives of its readers, but also of those who come in contact with these readers. Emihovich (1995) advises that "the key for transformation through narratives lies in collaboration; of constantly testing our meaning against that of others, . . . and ensuring that as many voices as possible are included. . . . Becoming comfortable with narrative accounts means accepting the idea that the world has no fixed rules for assigning meaning to behavior" (p. 45). Personal narratives defy positivistic notions about grouping everyone into universal categories or finding consensus. They can be, metaphorically, tools used in the struggle against marginalization. As Audre Lorde (1984/1998) eloquently noted, the "master's" tools will not dismantle the master's house. That is, the gross misconceptions and myths concerning marginalized people cannot be dismantled using the academy's own tools—traditional modes of research inquiry or pedagogy. As social scientists and educators, we are reminded that we cannot—like "hard" scientists—be discovers of *true* knowledge. Emihovich called for more "passionate criticisms" . . . which privilege more writers on the margins to use emotion in the service of rational action—to share our insights, where knowledge and art and caring are intertwined" (p. 45). We need not discard our own knowledge to hear the stories in this book; but we need to be open to local knowledge, narratives, and "truths" of children and families (Hartman, 1992). We need to be careful about privileging our "professional" knowledge to the point that we cannot hear information from worldviews that challenge our perspectives. Quoting Poet Imamuu Amiri Baraka, Hartman (1992) emphasizes, "I can't say who I am unless you agree I'm real." Some will doubt the realness of the stories in this book and, hence, silence the tellers' heartfelt experiences.

What is refreshing about this book is that the stories highlight many individuals who are not typically slated to succeed in school or society (or whose eventual positions are expected to fall within certain perimeters). These individuals demonstrate that they refused to be defined by educational literature or societal expectations that expect their failure.

Every ethnic group in this book cited problems with schools. Although no institution is without flaws, at some point we have to question just *whom* schools are for. It seems as if they are prepared and operate for some hypothetical person who doesn't exist. Schools barge forward with business as usual because reconsidering systemic change would devastate the status quo—even though the status quo is inadequate (Nieto, 1996). However, there are schools that have taken the system head on with promising results (Eakin, 1992). Asa Hilliard's (1991) research examined effective schools throughout the nation in a variety of rural, urban, central city, and suburban settings. While there is no single recipe for success, several components were apparent in all the schools examined by Hilliard and Barbara Sizemore (as cited in Eakin, 1992): ongoing staff development, strong instructional leaders, high expectations, parent involvement (often this increased as schools improved), productive climate and culture, monitoring of student progress, effective instructional strategies, and students' learning essential skills. So schools do have the potential to meet the needs of all children.

When discussing diversity and equity issues, White students frequently proclaim, "But I didn't look like Sally, Dick, and Jane" (in primers used in primary grades during my schooling). Their comments deny the reality of institutional discrimination, implicating individual differences instead. As noted in several chapters, books for school curricula are still predominantly Eurocentric (Boutte, 1999).

Comparing oppressions (e.g., arguing over which ethnicity, class, or gender is more oppressed) is fruitless because we can all claim oppression if we look long and hard enough and none of us chose our race, class, or gender when we were born (Hill Collins, 1993). We are all caught in an oppressive system that pits classes, races, genders, and other groupings against one another. However, institutionalized discrimination privileges Whites as a group and disadvantages people of color. For those of us who were raised on the perceived periphery of the elusive mainstream society, our trials and tribulations may seem greater than those of others. The closer one is to the imaginary norm (White mainstream), the better one is likely to fare. When distinctions are made between individual and institutional discrimination, it becomes apparent that an individual can be disadvantaged as member of a group, but privileged on an individual level, or vice versa. In other words, Whites can face discrimination and people of color can be privileged, but the levels of discrimination and privilege on an institutional basis differ and cannot be ignored.

What conclusions can we draw from the stories about schools and the role that educators play in the lives of the students they teach? For some children, schools are safe havens from the terrors at home, as in Tom's case in Chapter 8. For others, schools are hostile environments, as they were for Harold and Ray in Chapter 3, José and Felipe in Chapter 10, Susana, Monique, and Yolanda in Chapter 11, and Carson in Chapter 12. Some children feel unsafe at home and school (for example, Susan in Chapter 8). For still others, like the Chinese family in Chapter 5 or the rural, White children in Chapter 7, schools may not overtly help or hurt the students. Or schools may have no idea what to do differently for children like Min-Woo in

Chapter 4 or Janet, Ruth, and Terry in Chapter 6. Yet, schools have the potential to educate all students in an equitable manner and to impact their lives positively and open up new possibilities to them. To do so requires that schools stop engaging in benignly culturally assaultive practices. As Felipe in Chapter 9 warns, if schools continue to destroy students' cultures in the name of education, they will continue to marginalize students and damage their self-worth and their self-respect. Elevating Eurocentric lifestyles and accomplishments to pivotal places in the curriculum while omitting substantive and important contributions of people of color is harmful to White children and children of color.

Educators must learn to be careful observers and listeners and to go beyond the conventional "wisdom" gained in teacher preparation programs, according to a Black teacher cited in Delpit (1995): "There's got to be a dialogue. My instructors [in a historically black college] knew what you knew because they talked to you. They *knew* their students. That's really the only way to teach. . . . Teaching is all about telling a story. You have to get to know kids so you'll know how to tell the story, you can't tell it just one way" (p. 120).

Schools are not neutral or apolitical places. They put forth agendas that go unnoticed by unobservant educators (who inadvertently contribute to the demise of too many students). Believing that schools are apolitical contributes to oppression. Continuous reflection on one's pedagogical strategies is required. Educators will have to look beneath the surface to determine whether they are really doing what they intend to do—give all children a chance to succeed. I'm convinced that if educators carefully examined classrooms and schools, in many cases it would be obvious that the process of education has gone awry.

In each story in this book, there were teachers who were glimmers of hope. These teachers positively impacted the lives of their students and resulted in the authors' and participants' success. If these efforts can become collective versus isolated instances, education can really be the equalizing institution that it purports to be in our democracy. Otherwise, we will continue to "educate" a few students who come from homes and communities where they would succeed regardless of the input from schools.

Many of the authors in this book were successful *despite* school officials' efforts to thwart their success—not *because* of their efforts. Some people in this book were able to turn their lives around because of the influence of a single educator or of a person in their homes or communities. Yet, as Freire (1970/1999) notes, collective efforts are more powerful, deliberate, and sustaining. Hence, systemic changes are needed. We recognize that schools are microcosms of society and do not operate in isolation. However, this book is centered on what schools *can* do.

It is important that educators—who are often silenced themselves—also learn to collectively advocate for themselves and actively engage in changing the system rather than allow the system to impose rules on them. Simply put, educators must become more outwardly political rather than passive. Emancipatory and liberatory education, by its very nature, extends beyond the walls of schools. When it does, the voices of educators will be heard and systemic changes can be made.

But the absolute necessity to be more responsive to the needs of children does not fall only on educators in public schools. Teacher education programs in colleges and universities must also meet the challenge. Like schools, teacher education programs reflect society (Haberman, 1996). Haberman outlines five obstacles that tend to prevent university-based teacher education programs from becoming multicultural:

1. Future teachers are not just ill prepared to deal with diverse populations; they are ill prepared to deal with any population of children and youth in cultural terms.
2. People do not choose to be teachers because they want to deal with children and youth in cultural terms. This problem is an important precondition for the first one.
3. The knowledge base in teacher education uses personality constructs, not cultural constructs, to explain human behavior.
4. Teacher educators who guide practice (student teaching, field work, etc.) rely on explanations other than cultural ones to understand and predict children's behavior.
5. The approach in traditional preparation programs is to educate the neophyte that *normal behavior* and *normal development* in children and youth are synonymous with "healthy and desirable behavior and development." (p. 112)

Teacher education programs that use lecture as the primary method to prepare teachers fall short of the goals of praxis (the integration of theory and practice with ongoing reflections and thoughtful actions in real settings). As noted by Freire (1970/1999), this antidialogical approach (lecture) encourages replication of the existing hierarchies. Students in teacher education programs need to understand that the range of normality is wide and that they therefore need reflective experiences with many different populations and settings. Teacher education programs must also immerse students in communities like the ones they will work in so they can gain a better appreciation and deeper understanding of various groups.

Trying to decide what to take from the stories in this book may be a challenge for some readers. In terms of educational implications, there are no equations or simple solutions. Teaching is as complex as the lives presented in this book. Even when the stories appeared simple on the surface, we discovered that they were not. There are no simple explanations for why people succeed or make the choices they do. There is no one correct way to grow up. As the stories in this book have shown, people in the same family can take decidedly different trajectories. The solution lies in figuring out how to offer liberatory pedagogy that empowers all children. As educators at all levels, we need to carefully examine what we do in our classrooms—who we silence, overlook, or glorify.

A common complaint of students in my classes who read the work of critical theorists such as Lisa Delpit is that they sound "angry." Undoubtedly, some readers may have had the same sentiments about authors in this book. It is important to clarify that critical theory addresses difficult and political issues directly. People uncomfortable with this approach can easily mistake intensity for anger. But what is heard in critical theory is more accurately described as active confrontation of moral inequities. Addressing issues of oppression is a way to fight for humanity; it is an act of love—not anger (Freire, 1970/1999). The attacks are not personal—they address institutional issues of oppression. Many educators and potential educators believe that as nice people, they will not contribute to oppression. But being nice is insufficient to the task, because nice people can benignly contribute to oppression. We hope that the stories in this book touched your heart enough that you will take action and fight on behalf of the humanity of us all. Let the voices resound for as long as they may.

> I've come to the frightening conclusion that I am the decisive element in the classroom. It's my personal approach that creates the climate. It's my daily mood that makes the weather. As a teacher, I possess a tremendous power to make a child's life miserable or joyous. I can be a tool of torture or an instrument of inspiration. I can humiliate or humor, hurt or heal. In all situations, it is my response that decides whether a crisis will be escalated or deescalated and a child humanized or dehumanized.
>
> Haim Ginott

References

Blumenfeld-Jones, D. (1995). Fidelity as a criterion for practicing and evaluating narrative inquiry. In J. A. Hatch & R. Wisniewski (Eds.), *Life history and narrative* (pp. 26–35). New York: Falmer Press.

Delpit, L. (1995). *Other people's children: Cultural conflict in the classroom.* New York: New Press.

Eakin, S. (1992). *Every child can succeed: An action guide.* Bloomington, IN: Agency for Instructional Technology.

Emihovich, C. (1995). Distancing passion: Narratives in social science. In J. A. Hatch & R. Wisniewski (Eds.), *Life history and narrative* (pp. 37–48). New York: Falmer Press.

Freire, P. (1970/1999). *Pedagogy of the oppressed.* New York: Continuum.

Haberman, M. J. (1996). In L. Kaplan & R. A. Edelfelt, (Eds.), *Teachers for the new millennium: Aligning teacher development, national goals, and high standards for all students* (pp. 110–131). Thousand Oaks, CA: Corwin

Hartman, A. (1992). In search of subjugated knowledge. *Social Work, 37*(6), 483–484.

Hill Collins, P. (1993). Toward a new vision: Race, class, and gender as categories of analysis and connection. *Race, Sex, & Class, 1*(1), 25–45.

Hilliard, A., III. (1991). Do we have the *will* to educate all children? *Educational Leadership, 49 (1),* 31–36.

Lorde, A. (1984/1998). *Sister outsider. Essays and speeches by Audre Lorde.* Freedom, CA: The Crossing Press.

Nieto, S. (1996). *Affirming diversity: The sociopolitical context of multicultural education* (2nd ed.). London: Longman.

Appendix

A Legacy Defied

Growing Up Black in the Rural South during the Civil Rights Era (Gloria Boutte's Story)

In my early youth a great bitterness entered my life and kindled a great ambition.

—W. E. B. Du Bois (as cited in Copage, 1995, no pagination)

As I have pointed out elsewhere (Boutte, 1992), it is extremely difficult to write about one's personal experiences. On the surface, it may seem as if all one has to do is recall events and write them down. However, writing about my school experiences, determining the most salient events, and making sense out of them proved to be a difficult task. Sharing my experiences is an emancipatory exercise for me, as the reader will soon detect. It represents my political resistance to and defiance against the systemic, endemic discrimination that I and many others experienced in school. Telling my story allows me to contribute in a small way to the dismantling of racism and classism. Like Freire (1994), my rebellion against every kind of discrimination—from the most explicit to the most covert and hypocritical, which is no less offensive and immoral—has been with me from my childhood. Freire emphasized, "I have reacted almost instinctively against any word, deed, or sign of racial discrimination, or for that matter, discrimination against the poor, which quite a bit later, I came to define as class discrimination" (1994, p. 144). My sentiments echo Freire's, as will become apparent in my story.

My story seeks to reveal and expose structural inequities in schools. Mahatma Gandhi regarded secrecy as the enemy of freedom (Fischer, 1962). For this reason, he believed in revealing himself—including those innermost personal thoughts that individuals usually regard as private. While I am in no way equating my life with Gandhi's, I do believe that issues of discrimination in schools should be personified and should not be glossed over.

As I provide glimpses into my life, I offer the following comments and explanations to support the validity of my recollections:

1. Traumatic and exceptional events are usually more memorable than typical ones. I remembered some events because, as an impressionable child, they caused me to be embarrassed about some aspect of my life. I also consulted old report cards, certificates, and school albums and had discussions with family members to help me recall and/or verify events.

2. Examples are presented through the lens of a child. Hence, my perceptions of events are as real to me as the actual event. Only the individual who experienced an event can truly understand the significance of that experience. As noted by Gandhi (as cited in Fischer, 1962), no one can describe oneself with fidelity, but one can reveal oneself. My biases, preferences, and worldview are revealed in my story.

3. Numerous African Americans and individuals from low-income backgrounds have had similar experiences, according to their accounts and interpretations. Over the years, my memories have been unexpectedly triggered by examples in the educational literature recounting similar experiences among low-income and African American children.

Segregation

On a day that was neither too hot nor too cold, I was making mud pies in our detached garage beside our white, two-story home. I was playing with my older sister, Linda, and a friend, "Tump," when we were called into the house and told that our daddy had been killed. At that moment of my three-year-old life, my future took on a whole new direction. As a "Negro," being raised in a rural town in the South in 1961 was a challenge in itself. Coupled with being raised by a single parent (a Black female at that!), I'm sure that my future seemed gloomy at best to most educators. But as a child, I had no awareness that an ill twist of fate would affect my educational experiences.

As in many small towns and urban areas alike, railroad tracks symbolically separated "Black" and "White" neighborhoods in my town. We lived in a Black section of town—"across the tracks." Four railroad tracks ran in front of our house. However, the negative connotation of "across the tracks" was not apparent to me as a child—it was simply my HOME, "the temple of my familiar." There were three children in my family at the time. My mother later remarried and had another child.

The primary industry in my small, southern town was cotton mills. Before integration, social roles were clearly set. Jobs in the mills were primarily for Whites, except for janitors who cleaned the toilets or lifted heavy bales of cotton. Even Whites who worked in the cotton mills hired Black women to clean their homes and cook and paid them two dollars per day. There were also a number of lumberyards, and men cut trees down from nearby wooded areas and processed the wood. This was the primary occupation of Black men. Before his death, my father had been a driver and owner of one of the lumber trucks ("pulp wood trucks"). Due to the outdoor nature of the work, inclement weather prohibited men from working at unpredictable intervals. In the 1950s, there were few jobs for Black women except working as domestics in the homes of Whites or as custodians in the hospital. Many Black women worked as caregivers for White children. My grandmother ironed clothes (at our home) for a White woman, and we joyfully got their hand-me-downs when the White children outgrew them. There were no industrial jobs, so the only alternative was to "go up north," which many Blacks did.

Segregation was so deeply entrenched in my hometown that it was seldom questioned. Blacks stood outside (whether it was hot or cold) a small, unpainted shack/store/restaurant to order hot, juicy hamburgers with chilli from the White owner while Whites sat comfortably inside on smooth, vinyl-covered kitchen chairs with chrome legs.

I attended segregated schools until 1969, when I was in sixth grade— which was apparently the earliest my hometown felt it could respond to *Brown vs. the Board of Education*'s 1954 mandate to integrate the schools *with all deliberate speed.* There was only one Black elementary school in town (named after the street it was located on) and, except for two or three Black children who later went to "the White school," all of the Black children attended the same school. Going to school before first grade was not even a consideration for most of the Black children because kindergartens were privately owned and required payment. The elementary school comprised several older, but nicely maintained, red brick buildings.

Since my older brother and sister were already in school, I was eager to attend school. Each day when they came home, I would ask questions about school and enthusiastically listen to their stories. Finally, the day came for me to receive my vaccination for school. The immunization that was given before entering school left an ugly sore on the upper part of the arm. Although I still have a scar from the shot, I was very proud of my big, scabby sore because to me it meant that I was going to school! I could not wait to learn to read and write.

My classroom was located in a large, old building with shiny hardwood floors. The school smelled sterile, like the green disinfectant (which looked like eraser shavings) that was used when sweeping the floor. My first-grade classroom seemed huge, with high ceilings, large windows, and endless hardwoods. Contrary to today's classrooms' bright ambiance, the classroom seemed cold, being absent of plants, paintings, fluorescent lighting, and so on. A long, narrow, dark coatroom was in the front of the classroom. I don't remember whether coats were ever stored there, but corporal punishment was administered there. Being a child who was afraid of "whippings," I did everything in my power to avoid any punishment and, indeed, do not remember being paddled until fifth grade, when I was hit in the palm of my hands in front of the entire class.

There was only one first-grade class, so Tim, my neighbor, and I were in the same classroom. Both of Tim's parents were teachers, and, as I will point out later, he received preferential treatment. Mrs. Schumpert, my first-grade teacher, was, through my first-grade eyes, a wonderful and beautiful teacher. She had light brown skin, a long ponytail, and a brilliant smile. I do not remember her ever speaking a harsh word to us. Mrs. Schumpert's presence added to my joy at attending school, and, coupled with a cozy home life, my educational foundation was solid.

After my father died, we lived with my grandmother and grandfather in a two-bedroom, wood home. Doing well in school was stressed in our home. We had to do our homework and share it with Mama Nell, our grandmother. Other household routines included eating breakfast and dinner together (lunch, too, if school was out) and going to church *every* Sunday for what seemed like the entire day.

One of my earliest inklings that money was an issue for our family was when I brought Carolyn, a friend of mine, home with me after school one day. Neither of us had consulted our parents. We enjoyed each other's company so much that we decided that we wanted to play together longer. So Carolyn rode the bus home with me. When we got home, Mama Nell (my grandmother) pulled me aside and scolded me for bringing Carolyn home and fussed about having to feed us both. As we ate peanut butter sandwiches for our after-school snack, I recall thinking that my grandmother had never complained about food before. The message that stayed with me was that I should never bring anyone home with me again because we could not feed him or her. The only link I had between my friends at school and at home was my next-door neighbor, Tim.

School plays were an important part of elementary school. In our first-grade play, Tim was chosen to play the main character, Jack Frost. Tim and I loved each other dearly and played together at home every day, so I naturally wanted to play the lead female. However, Regina, another teacher's daughter, was chosen instead. *I* got to be a daisy. Tim proudly sang, "I am Jack Frost. You know. You know. I laugh ha ha! I laugh ho ho!" Although I remember Tim's song, I cannot remember the brief, insignificant lines that the rest of the daises and I sang. An accumulation of experiences like this one contributed to my current role as an advocate for children from low-income homes. The teachers were simply following the "social order" and probably gave little thought to the roles that the children played or to my feelings of disappointment.

I am amazed and pleased that these experiences have remained with me after all these years and after I have achieved some level of "success." The poignancy of my memories corroborates my beliefs that teachers are extremely powerful individuals. The unfortunate part is that many do not realize the power that they hold and exert. Nor do they seem to be aware of the possible long-term effect that they have on the lives of vulnerable children. In my case, the bitterness of my experiences kindled my ambition. More times than not, however, children of color from low-income homes do not defy the negative legacies that are bequeathed to them.

Teachers often give preferential treatment to children from middle-income homes and disregard children from low-income homes. As a first-grader, I had no understanding of the social dynamics that come into play in classrooms. However, each year they became clearer to me. I never got to speak or sing solo in the school plays. In a democracy, all children should be given opportunities to participate and *lead.* Each child has a gift to offer, and educators can never predict which children will be successful in life. Even in a school with all African American teachers and students, racism and classism can thrive.

Teachers' children, children with lighter skin, and children from middle-income homes were held in high esteem in a number of other ways as well during my elementary years. For example, Tim, Regina, James, and other teachers' children always received lavish praise for their work. In first grade, our assignment was to write one entire page of three straight letters, *I, T,* and *L.* Mrs. Schumpert held up Tim's work for all to see. I became embarrassed about my work and took Tim's work home (instead of my own) to show my grandmother. Of course, I was punished when my grandmother discovered that I had *stolen* Tim's work. Mrs. Schumpert (albeit a nice, well-intentioned woman) was probably a victim of classist beliefs. She had not given me or my other classmates any positive feedback about our hard work. I felt ashamed of my efforts even though I initially felt proud of my letters.

Although I was a good student, I was always on the periphery. I don't remember much (if any) positive feedback from Mrs. Schumpert even though I adored her. Overall, I believe that I was successful *despite* school—not because of it. My keen desire to learn and my family's emphasis on learning probably contributed to my motivation to do well.

I now recognize the residual effects of being raised in the midst of the "melting pot" era, during which White, middle-class standards were held up as the norm. Racism and classism are so insidious in their nature that they creep into one's mind and existence without one's conscious awareness. On the surface level, my negative school experiences may seem innocuous. However, beneath the surface, the damage can fester unless it is addressed or counterbalanced. As early as first grade, I had internalized the message that some people are *better* than others. In a society where such messages abound, no one wants to be on the bottom. Therefore, even the "lowliest" person must find someone to pick on to ensure his or her "superiority." It is both amazing and regrettable how a classist and racist system (school and society) transforms innocent children into malicious, competitive individuals. In my first-grade class, Melvin was usually the recipient of all the jokes.

Melvin was bigger than the rest of us because he had been retained. Everybody knew that he was poor because of his tattered clothes and the skimpy lunches that he brought to school (usually fried egg sandwiches). He often had thick mucus around and inside his nostrils, so the kids called him "Snot." Melvin was from a large family who lived in what we called "the country," outside the "city" (ha!) limits. All of the children brought their own lunches to school, but we could buy milk from school (for two or three cents, I think!). The students always laughed at Melvin's lunches and inability to buy milk. One day, someone offered Melvin a carton of milk. Melvin was eager to get the milk because he never got to drink milk at school (and milk was a status symbol). However, before the little boy gave the milk to Melvin, he spit in it. Everybody knew this except Melvin. I remember being horrified but did not dare speak up. Kids in the class would also shoot spitballs at Melvin and taunt him in other ways. I felt sorry for Melvin.

Other poor kids were subjected to the same treatment. Apparently, I was perceived as being okay economically, probably because my clothes were in good condition and I was quiet. At any rate, I was never picked on. It could have been that although I was "low" according to the societal pecking order, other children with less status assumed the brunt of the ostracism.

Poor kids are still chastised in our society, and I believe that the invisibility of diverse lifestyles in schools and society contributes to this problem. My lifestyle certainly did not resemble that of Mom, Dad, Dick, Jane, Sally, Spot, and Puff in my primers! The images presented in basals also sent strong, but subtle, messages about my physical appearance. However, the negative messages about Black skin, hair, lips, and eyes were tempered later thanks to the Black Power movement, Black history lessons and films in school, and novels by African American writers later in high school (particularly, *The Autobiography of Malcom X*). *Malcom X* had a powerful effect on me because it was the first book that I had read that explicitly deconstructed the pervasive Eurocentric messages.

Clinton was another classmate who was treated badly and called "dumb" because he had been retained. He was larger than the rest of us. His skin color was what the Black community commonly referred to as "jet black" (the color of dark chocolate). Children called him "Smut" (referring to the black soot from burning coal in the commonly used stoves). Ostracizing dark-skinned children was not uncommon due to the notions of White superiority that surrounded our daily lives. Clinton also smelled bad, and his family was poor. His hair was "nappy," thick, and matted.

Surely Mrs. Schumpert had some idea that children in her classroom were being picked on, but I do not recall a single incident in which she addressed the issue. Yet she had the power to diffuse the negative behavior and attitudes. There is no room in school for condonation of discrimination.

Some children do not really have a fair chance to succeed in school. Numerous odds imposed by society are against them. By the time Clinton got to fifth grade after being retained several times, he probably hated school and had turned into a bully. He was significantly bigger than the other boys, so it was easy for him to bully them. Eventually, Clinton dropped out of school (around fifth grade). I am convinced that he really wanted to learn when he initially entered first grade; however, circumstances prevented him from doing so. Educators often send strong messages to children that they do not belong in school—especially Black males (Kunjufu, 1985–1995). As a result, they turn to negative behavior such as stealing, doing drugs, and the like. I am sure that in first grade, Clinton had no conception that there was an unwritten message that poor children would have a harder time in society and school.

My trajectory was different from Clinton's in several ways. First, I was never retained and was generally thought of as smart. While there are certainly times when children should be retained, there is enough literature that graphically illustrates the general ineffectiveness of retention (Shepard & Smith, 1990). Teachers routinely retain children without thinking of the long-term effects or of how another year of the same type of instruction will be effective when the first year was not (Shepard & Smith, 1989, 1990). Many teachers think that the children need "more time to develop" but fail to examine alternative instructional strategies (Walsh, 1991).

Second, my school experiences as a female raised in the 1960s were different from those of males. As a quiet female who tended to be compliant, I fit in better at school than boys who often had to fight to defend their egos.

Third, many of my family members frequently complimented me about being smart (which indicated that they expected this from me). Also, I often saw my mother and older siblings reading. Based on what I know about Clinton's family from my experiences with them over the years (they later ended up living downstairs from us in low-income apartments), his mother spent most of her time ensuring that the children were physically safe, clothed, and well fed. For a single parent raising six children, this alone is an awesome task. To Clinton's teachers, it may have appeared that his mother did not care. On the contrary, I believe that she cared about her children very much and did as much as humanly possible to ensure their welfare.

Fourth, in some instances, teachers' expectations of children can be influenced by the teacher's perception of the children's physical attractiveness (Brophy & Good, 1970). In the era we were raised in, Clinton was defined by society as an unattractive child because he was the polar opposite of Eurocentric notions of beauty. Implicitly, his color, hair, socioeconomic status, and family composition were diametrically opposed to those of Dick, the main character and prototype presented in our primers (Morrison, 1993). By today's standards, he would be considered "fine." Clinton rarely smiled, if ever. It is a sad commentary on society, but my "long hair" and quick smile made me more appealing according to these prescribed standards. Later, when Clinton started to rebel against school and society, he was viewed as a troublemaker. By then, Clinton apparently realized that school was not a positive place for him and that it would be simpler to seek satisfaction outside the school. (See Richard Majors and Janet Billson's (1993), Janice Hale-Benson's (1986), and John Ogbu's (1990) discussion of this phenomenon.)

Fifth, I received good grades and liked school. Many teachers prefer to work with children who seem eager to learn versus those who do not. However, children like Clinton need educators the most. We must learn how to reach these children. Not only will the children benefit, but society as well.

African American children from working-class homes like mine may succeed in school despite numerous odds when they have "buffers" such as the ones that I have outlined. Despite my slight advantage over children like Clinton, I doubt Mrs. Schumpert ever expected me to become a college professor! It is ironic to think that if she were still alive, I could be *her* professor! The satisfaction of my own accomplishments is shadowed by my awareness that many other potential professors, doctors, electricians, and the like did not reach their fullest potential.

In many ways, Clinton's and my stories are familiar to many children of color and poor kids. Recently, one of my students, who is a teacher married to a dentist, relayed an experience that her husband had had. A patient who had been one of his teachers expressed surprise that he had "made something of himself." In school, because he was poor, she had treated him with disdain even though education professes to be the equalizing force in society. Although he had defied the teacher's low expectations and succeeded, each time the dentist saw his teacher-turned-patient the pain of her low expectations reignited.

Children do not select the families that they are born into. If a person happens to be born into an economically viable family, then he or she should be thankful—because it was certainly through no effort of his or her own. If children chose their socioeconomic status, race, or gender, many would probably choose the one that is preferred in their sociocultural context. As educators, we should be humble about our social standings and work toward helping all children have a true opportunity to succeed in this DEMOCRACY. Educators do not have to come from the same ethnic or socioeconomic backgrounds as their children to be able to appreciate them as humans having great potential (Ladson-Billings, 1994).

My recollections coupled with teachers' comments on my report cards indicate that I was generally viewed as smart by my teachers and classmates. I loved attending school and had perfect attendance several years. I usually won the spelling bees or came in second or third. I was also good in math, was an avid reader, and often went to the public library (alone) to check out books to read. Recalling my weekly walks to the library evokes memories of my detour to the dime store on Main Street using my weekly allowance to buy hot popcorn, two chocolate pecan turtles, or chocolate-covered peanuts and a drink. Anticipating reading the books, I walked home with my book bag filled with the two- or three-book limit and munched on popcorn and candy.

The exposure to literature and field trips broadened my horizons and revealed many possibilities. My favorite books were from a series about people who lived in far-away places such as Egypt and India. I read these books and dreamt of living lavishly like the characters in the books. Although I was influenced by the stories I read and yearned for a lifestyle that was dramatically different from my own, I had no plans for getting there. Neither did my family, whose goal (consistent with the times and our socioeconomic status) was for me to finish high school and get a job. This was not because my family did not want anything more for me or did not believe that I could achieve it, but because they were also limited by their own circumstances. The goal of completing high school seemed satisfactory—better than the norm, in fact. Since children's outlook for the future seldom includes realistic goals beyond their own worlds, it is crucial for guidance counselors and other school officials to steer capable students into the courses that prepare them for college. Teens from low socioeconomic backgrounds may not know what their options are until it is too late, and then they will not have the necessary preparation.

The frequent exposure to African American heroes and heroines during my elementary schooling had a significant impact on my life and views. We frequently watched films about famous African Americans. I unconsciously internalized the idea that Blacks could achieve despite many obstacles. This strong background in the history of people of the African diaspora who live in America empowered me and buffered me from racism that I would face later in an integrated school. Because of the Eurocentric nature of school curriculums, White students have the privilege of constant exposure to the heritage and accomplishments of people from the European diaspora. All children's heritages should be included in the classroom (Boutte & McCormick, 1992).

One of my most salient fourth-grade memories was of my friend, Regina, who was my teacher's daughter. We played together in school and enjoyed each other's company. One day, she invited me to her house to play with her (I am sure that this took much convincing, but she was the baby of the family and could be quite persistent). When I went to her extremely large house (in comparison to our four-room house), I was impressed. We played Monopoly and had snacks (I don't remember what they were, but I do recall loving them). Regina's lifestyle seemed closer to the families in the books that we read than to my own. After that visit, I was never invited to her house again, and Regina and I eventually stopped talking in class. In class, her mom showed a definite preference for the more financially advantaged and/or light-skinned children, although she tolerated me because of my intellect.

I suspect that Regina's mother went to great lengths to keep us apart because she did not want her daughter to associate with a person whose mother was a "blue-collar" worker. Her mother, like others, was confined by societal expectations and practices. Throughout high school, Regina and I continued to like each other and speak casually, but we both realized at that point that our friendship was futile.

My elementary school would be considered substandard by today's standards, although we did not view it that way. Despite attending a school where the facilities were undoubtedly inferior to the White schools and the books were probably substandard as well, I exited elementary school at the end of fifth grade with my soul, intellect, and self-esteem intact. Although most children come to school with a natural interest in learning, many African American and poor children lose their motivation to learn by the time they are in fourth or fifth grade (Hale-Benson, 1986; Kunjufu, 1985–1995, Vol. II).

Segregated schools and Black teachers will not necessarily reverse the "fourth grade syndrome." Because of systemic racism and classism that are deeply embedded in our social mores, "educated" African American teachers (or "miseducated," as Dr. Carter G. Woodson [1933/1990] would say) or teachers who come from poor backgrounds conveniently forget their backgrounds when they regard poor and Black students with disdain. Many African Americans have learned to identify with the dominant European (mainstream) culture and to view aspects of African American culture negatively (Fordham, 1996). Therefore, Black teachers are not necessarily better teachers of Black children on the basis of color alone. Teachers who are culturally aware and care for all children regardless of their ethnic or socioeconomic backgrounds can positively affect the lives of the children they teach (Ladson-Billings, 1994). This does not imply that Black children do not need Black teachers as role models, for they are in dire need of them; but it does imply that all children need teachers who hold high expectations for them. The within-race classism that I confronted during my elementary years at segregated schools was intensified by racism during my middle and high school years at integrated schools.

Integration

Still I Rise
You may write me down in history
With your bitter, twisted lies,
You may trod me in the very dirt
But still, like dust, I'll rise

—Maya Angelou

If someone asked me what integration felt like, I'd say it felt pretty much like segregation in my small town. But in some ways, integration gave Blacks in my town a voice in places where I had not witnessed this before.

One day, my mother and I were shopping for luggage in a smaller, local version of Kmart. Mama found a piece of luggage that she liked and asked the White store clerk to open it so she could examine it more closely. The man adamantly refused and told my mother to buy the luggage if she wanted it. This incensed my mother, and she replied that she would not buy "pork inside the pig." Finally, the man relented and opened the luggage. We didn't buy the luggage, and I learned a valuable lesson. At first, though, I was embarrassed about the scene but felt a sense of pride when my mother insisted that the man open the suitcase. Such assaults on our dignity were common—in school also. However, we *were* now permitted to go inside the hamburger joint and enter the front of the bus station! Integration had come to Smalltown, U.S.A.!

By the time school was integrated during my sixth year in school, Tim and Regina (teachers' children) had attended the White school for two to three years. I am not sure how they were able to attend the White school, but I suspect that their parents legal knowledge of the *Brown vs. The Board of Education's* ruling coupled with their middle-class status enabled them to enroll. Tim and Regina had seemingly assumed what Fordham (1988, 1996) refers to as a "raceless" persona and sought to assimilate and disassociated themselves from many aspects of Black culture (see Chapter 1 for a fuller discussion of fictive kinship). At the time, I regarded them with envy because they were always in the limelight. Now, I worry about how the process of assimilation affected their psyches. I wonder how denouncing an important and immutable part of their being (their racial identities) affected them in the long run—and their children. Emotional well-being is equally important as performing well in school and later careers. Today, as an educator, I'm amazed that any of us exited such a racially charged situation with any degree of sanity.

A graduate student (a White, male principal) in my diversity course concluded that integration is theoretically a good concept. However, having had the experience of being one of a few Whites in a predominantly Black high school setting, he had been picked on endlessly. His analysis of the situation is that children—whichever children were the numerical minority—were thrown into the lion's den, so to speak, with little support from adults. The adults did not know what to do because they were also dealing with the ugliness of racism. Black and White children were ordered to attend school together and presumably to ignore the fact that we could not even eat in the same restaurants outside the classroom. We were supposed to become "color-blind" (Schofield, 1997) amid the bomb threats intended to prevent full integration of schools. Perhaps there was no way to ease the process. Even today, when teachers teach children who are culturally different from themselves without adequate preparation, we are setting both teachers and children up for failure, frustration, and anger.

Knowledge about oneself and one's culture can be a powerful emancipator. In high school, *The Autobiography of Malcolm X* somehow ended up in my hands. Perhaps I chose it because I had read the book *Roots,* by Malcolm's coauthor, Alex Haley, The book had a significant influence on me, although I didn't realize at the time. To this day, I don't know where I got the book. I still have my original copy, though. I'm sure I didn't get it from school, and I don't remember buying it. I can't imagine my school requiring or even having a copy because the racist, tyrannical principal would never have tolerated such a "radical" work. It's amazing that the book was even allowed to remain in my hometown! No kidding. *The Autobiography of Malcolm X* taught me to love Blackness and to defy negative messages.

On a positive note, there were several teachers, White and Black, who helped students reach their fullest potentials. Miss Way, my sixth-grade teacher, was an older, White, petite woman with short, gray hair and a stern look. She did not smile much, but she was a good teacher. Most of the children thought that she was mean; however, I always felt that she liked me. We learned a lot in her classroom, and she was a demanding teacher. As far as I could tell, she expected all of the children—Black and White—to perform well. We spent a lot of time diagramming sentences and learning grammar. All of the students were called to the board to diagram sentences or perform other grammatical exercises, and Miss Way did not show favoritism. Because I excelled in English, I think that I may have been one of Miss Way's favorite students. She often allowed me to wipe and clean the chalkboard, a privilege.

One spring day in Miss Way's classroom, I was stung by a yellow jacket. The bee landed on my thigh near my knee. As a reflex, I quickly brought my knees together, and the yellow jacket was smashed. Miss Way sent me to the school nurse. Afterward, she continued to show concern about the bee sting, which made it feel a lot better. In fact, she even joked about it being the bee's last sting. It was uncharacteristic for Miss Way to joke, so everybody in the class was thankful that I had gotten stung.

Miss Way accepted the responsibility to teach all children—not just a select few. She focused on all children and held high expectations for all and *demanded* that we did our best. With this task in mind, she refused to blame the children for their shortcomings. She seemingly did not regard ethnicity and low socioeconomic status as excuses. Many teachers want to teach only children who come to school most prepared and who do not offer many challenges. That is, many children from mainstream homes will perform well regardless of what the teacher does in the classroom, but the teacher readily accepts the glory by making comments such as, "*I* taught him." In contrast, saying, "*She* can't learn," shifts the blame to the child. The role that teachers are supposed to play in this process is forgotten by these teachers. They give up on children, lamenting, "These children can't learn." Teachers like Miss Way believe that each one of their students will learn! They welcome such challenges and view them as part of teaching.

Another implication of Miss Way's teaching is that all children must exit school with a sufficient proficiency in reading, writing, mathematics, social studies, and science. As Delpit (1988; 1995b) assertively and convincingly argues, this is particularly true for mastery of standard English. Many teachers, in their attempt to show an appreciation for children's natural vernacular, often neglect to ensure that children are proficient in standard English—especially African American children. Delpit notes that such negligence relegates these children to lower socioeconomic statuses later in life because they do not have mastery of the language used by mainstream society. Unintentionally, then, teachers perpetuate vicious cycles of racism and classism. However, I hasten to add that Delpit makes an argument for teaching standard English within a relevant context rather than taking a skills-only approach.

A final point that I would like to make regarding Miss Way is that she modeled acceptance of all of the students. Teachers set the tone for race- and class-based acceptance or intolerance in their classrooms. Educators must consciously reflect on the messages that they are sending when they call on White and/or middle-class children more frequently, give them more positive feedback, allow more time for them to respond, or send positive nonverbal feedback to them. Children are very adept at figuring out whom teachers regard in high esteem and whom they do not.

Not surprisingly, the curriculum that I encountered in school was primarily Eurocentric. For example, we took a field trip to Fort Sumter, where the first shot of the Civil War was fired. Everything that we learned about the Civil War was from a Eurocentric perspective, primarily the White South's view. We learned about Civil War heroes from the South, but the perspectives of slaves were not shared. The implicit message was that the Civil War resulted in the fall of the South's wonderful way of life. The perspective that African Americans were elated about the war because it meant to end slavery was not mentioned.

In music, we learned lots of songs about our state, South Carolina, and the nation. Given my current knowledge of diversity, I retrospectively know that all of the songs catered to a Eurocentric taste in music. One song about American inventors focused only on White inventors. It was not until I was in college that I realized that there are and have been numerous African American inventors as well. This type of glaring omission in the curriculum (intentional or not) sends subtle, negative messages about one's ethnicity. As students, we were being taught that White men were the only people who made important contributions to this country's development. I am not sure whether we internalized this message right away, but after years of repetition, we learned it. Unlike in the Black elementary school, we did not learn about heroes of color. Such omissions hurt not only children of color but White children as well because it gives White children a false sense of superiority (Howard, 1993) and children of color a sense of invisibility and insignificance (Spencer & Markstrom-Adams, 1990).

Being raised in the midst of the Civil Rights Movement and sit-ins helped me to understand the injustices that we faced. Before the movement began, many Blacks were angry about the blatant racism in school but had little power to address it in a significant way. Occasionally, we did not attend school on Black holidays, but I do not remember resisting oppression otherwise. The movement taught me that we had a voice and could actively fight oppression. I've been doing it ever since.

Some teachers found their own ways to fight racism. Miss Golden, a petite, soft-spoken, White teacher, uniformly demonstrated that she cared for all children. Ironically, a young, White, student teacher was placed with Miss Golden but seemed terrified and had no idea of how to teach Black children. The student teacher remained remote for the entire season.

On Halloween, Miss Golden invited *all* of her students to come by her house for treats. She lived right in the middle of the downtown area in a huge, two-story, white house. To say that the house impressed me would be an understatement. Although my initial childhood home had been as large as Miss Golden's house, those memories had faded years ago. Miss Golden's home mirrored my images of lavish homes in novels that I read or in movies that I had seen. I was not unhappy with my own home; however, I was intrigued by the possibility of living in a similar home in the future.

While Miss Golden fought racism with kindness, Mrs. Nobles apparently detested integration and believed that Blacks were inferior to Whites, often referring to us using pejorative terms such as "you people." She was a tall, energetic teacher who wore glasses. She taught science in an exciting way, but it was clear that she spent more time with the White students and held higher expectations for them. Whenever the Black students asked questions, she seemed impatient and rude.

One of the few C's that I had received up to this point was given to me by Mrs. Nobles. Although I worked hard on my leaf and insect projects (and learned a lot from both of them), she gave them low grades. Teachers like Mrs. Nobles do a disservice both to themselves and to their students—especially if a student is already academically marginal and ambivalent about school. With a teacher like Mrs. Nobles, many students would simply confirm her negative expectations and give up. Due to family support, strong willpower, and positive experiences with other teachers, I did not.

Recess in middle school was segregated for the most part, although there were times when we interacted with each other. (For a more thorough discussion of this subject, read Beverly Tatum's (1997) *Why Are All the Black Students Sitting Together in the Cafeteria?*) Classes were tracked by race. The home economics class, taught by an African American female, was filled with Black girls. Black females needed to know how to cook, sew, and iron. This was our formal indoctrination to our legacies. Black boys were herded into shop classes.

In eighth grade, I noticed that some of my White classmates took algebra while we took regular math classes. I assumed that they were simply smarter than the other kids. Now, I realize that this may or may not have been the case. Their parents were probably more aware of the preparation that they needed to prepare for high school and college. At any rate, many of the African American children who were not included in advanced classes were probably equally qualified. Tracking is often unfair and ineffective (Oakes & Lipton, 1990). Moreover, school officials find it difficult to change a practice that is so deeply entrenched in the system. When we expose some children to advanced classes and others to remedial classes, the gap between the two groups becomes cumulatively larger. By middle school, the gap has often become so large that it is almost too late to combine students in heterogeneous groups.

At the end of eighth grade, the guidance counselor, Mrs. Floyd, who was Black, helped me with my high school schedule. She suggested that I enroll in the vocational track. Although I was an A and B student (report cards verify this), she saw only a child from a working-class family who would not attend college. When I later became a professor at a historically Black university in the same state, some of my colleagues who were alumni of the same institution spoke highly of my middle school guidance counselor and were proud that she was making a difference for Black children in schools in my small town. From my standpoint and experience, the guidance counselor could have been White for all practical purposes. She apparently saw little promise in Black children from low-income homes, the vast majority of Black students in my rural hometown.

Schools and teachers teach much more than academics. They also teach what society thinks of you and what "your place" should be. I learned that my family and community were not favored. For a long time, I carried around a deep sense of shame about something that I had no control over—my home setting and family status. Ironically, I learned to assume the common classist posture of "being better than someone else," and for a while felt that my home setting was better than others "below" me (those who had less economically). Indeed, as this example illustrates, the ability to replicate itself effortlessly is the true power of the virus called oppression. The glorification of European values (e.g., the dominance of information regarding European and European American accomplishments, literature, music, and so on) sends the message of White superiority loud and clear, although it is never stated outright that people of color are inferior. Hence, people like my guidance counselor sought to identify more with White culture in an unconscious effort to avoid feeling at the "bottom of the barrel."

When I entered high school, several classes sounded interesting to me (e.g., journalism, algebra, French, and English composition), even though I had been placed in a vocational track. Therefore, I went to talk to the high school guidance counselor about taking the courses and was able to switch to the college preparatory track. If I had remained in the vocational track, it is likely that I would not have been ready for college. My mother was not aware of the different career tracks. She knew that I was a good student, and, given the dynamics of our town, she probably had no idea that I might go to college and one day teach at a university. Although my mother is a very bright and extremely literate woman, like many working-class parents, she was not savvy when it came to school politics. Additionally, she was inundated by the job constraints and economic realities of being a single, Black mother in a small town. She believed that by going to integrated schools, our education would be better than her generation's. I am still not sure what was gained and lost in the process of desegregation. None of this should have mattered: schools should be fair places that parents can trust to prepare all children for life in a democratic society.

As adults, my brother, cousin, and I retrospectively lament that our school experiences did not include making us aware of opportunities to go to college. We knew about the local college and technical schools. We knew little about others inside and outside South Carolina. Our parents could not give us this information. They had finished high school, which was unusual in the rural South of their day, when Blacks still worked unusually hard and long hours and had few professional opportunities. They actually walked three miles to school and back and had to work in the fields daily after school. My mother recalls walking to school and have White children on buses passing them and throwing things and yelling racial epithets and obscenities at them. Most of her cohorts did not finish high school due to such dire circumstances. My mother married immediately after high school and my uncles (her three brothers) fled to the military—one of the few opportunities available to Black men at the time. College was therefore not even a consideration for them or for us.

I think that I was expected to get a "good job" at a textiles plant or in another industry or get married. My first cousin, whose father had traveled more and became an insurance representative, expected him to go to college. In fact, his sister was already attending a small, historically Black university in North Carolina that I would also later attend. Without my uncle's help in completing financial aid forms, it is doubtful that I would have been able to attend college. Had I accepted my destined place in life, I would not have left our small town or experienced my current level of success. Life is full of ironies, and teachers would be wise to remember that they cannot determine a child's future based on his or her socioeconomic status.

I wouldn't be surprised to learn that the principal of my high school, was a card-carrying member of the Ku Klux Klan. He was a blatant racist who never attempted to hide his beliefs. He said the word *nigger* with such ease that it must have been the first word that he uttered. I heard him refer to Black students as niggers frequently and was deeply angered by it. Given that racism was transmitted from the top down in this school, it is not surprising that there were frequent fights between Blacks and Whites. During one fight between a Black girl and a White girl, the principal walked up and immediately interceded by grabbing the Black girl and yelling, "Nigger, leave this White girl alone!" The Black girl was suspended from school and the

White girl was not. The principal had not seen the fight start and simply assumed that the Black student had started it. Such inequitable disciplinary practices were commonplace. We sought an education in the midst of hatred, prejudice, and low expectations. There were only one or two Black teachers and a Black assistant principal, who seemingly had little power. The overriding message was very clear: White students are superior and "niggers" had better stay in their place. Still, despite frequent negative experiences, I remained optimistic about my future. Hale-Benson (1986) points out that many African American students form their impressions of themselves based on experiences within the Black community rather than internalize often negative messages from Whites.

Not surprisingly, most Blacks and Whites remained socially segregated at school. However, the Black and White athletes socialized with each other. Stories abounded of White cheerleaders being intimate with Black athletes. These rumors tingled with excitement about the societal taboo of interracial dating. To the best of my knowledge though the White females (cheerleaders) were not stigmatized and the Black athletes boasted their "conquests." Except for athletes, most of the "popular" students were White. Whites held most of the student government offices and other popular roles (e.g., homecoming queen and cheerleader). There were no active efforts to seek representations of diverse racial and socioeconomic populations in school events. Instead, Regina, Tim, and one or two other students were often used as token representatives of the school's black population for various roles or events. When one race is glorified, as Whites were in my high school, subtle messages about definitions of beauty, intelligence, athletic prowess, and the like are conveyed.

Because of my enhanced sensitivity to racial inequities in school programming, I am particularly alerted to these issues when I visit schools today. Amazingly, even today in integrated schools, most of the speaking roles often go to Whites and/or children from middle-income families. It is not unusual for Black and poor children to be placed in the back row during programs. Unless schools consciously seek to provide equity in all endeavors, it is likely that they will convey unintentional, but powerful, messages about who is valued and who is not. Such messages may affect the future performance and attitudes of Whites and children of color. Although some educators do not consider these issues to be substantive and underestimate their effects, racism, classism, and other types of discrimination should never be taken lightly (Boutte, LaPoint, & Davis, 1993). Interestingly, many critics undermine and label multicultural efforts as attempts to make children of color "feel good." These opponents conveniently forget that public schools have been glorifying and elevating Whiteness since their inception. Moreover, these critics of multiculturalism also often disregard substantive issues such as educational equity and cultural relevance.

Schools are not the only institutions that perpetuate racist and classist attitudes: these attitudes are pervasive in our society. Television shows about African Americans that were popular during the 1970s, when I was in high school, were of *The Jeffersons, Good Times,* and *Sanford and Son* genre, and presented stereotypical images of Blacks. Although we watched and enjoyed these shows, only recently have I realized the imbalanced images of Blacks that they presented. Even in the new millennium, the images of people of color are still limited in the media.

Throughout high school, I earned mostly A's and B's and was named to *Who's Who among American High School Students* during my senior year. I also graduated with honors with little effort or realization of the long-term implications. My thoughts about future endeavors vacillated between joining the Air Force and attending college. My primary goal was to escape my small, oppressive town. My senior book notations indicated that I planned to major in either education, French, or sociology if I attended college. My visions of success included living in an apartment (as opposed to owning a house). My entries in my senior book detailed that I also wanted to get married and have three daughters. I envisioned a small home to accompany this dream.

Most of my closest friends had no intentions of going to college. They planned to either get married or go to work. Many of my friends did well in school and had potential to do well in college. Yet, only one of my closest friends attended college, and she did not finish her degree program.

Because my hometown was basically an industrial textile town, I enrolled in a "textiles" course in eleventh grade. You had to be sixteen to enroll because, as part of the course, students were employed at one of the three cotton mills in town for sixteen hours a week (four hours a day, Monday through Thursday). The pay was four dollars an hour and I was excited about the possibility of earning such good money.

I worked in the weaving room of a mill and worked from 4:00 to 8:00 P.M. four days during the week, after school. My job was to keep several rows of weaving looms running. The noise of the machines was deafening, even with the mandated earplugs. The machines broke down often and I was supposed to keep them threaded. Eager to do well on this "good job," I put forth my best effort. The first day, I was assigned only a few machines and did fairly well, although I was extremely fatigued at the end of the day. By the second week, my supervisor notified me that I was terminated because I couldn't keep up. I was embarrassed and disappointed in myself. I cried about losing my first job. Now, I realize that the supervisor did *me* a favor. It would have been easy to stay on a job that paid "well" instead of going to college (typically, the mill hired the students who did well). I couldn't realize as a teenager what a dead end this job would have been for me and how little my pay would have increased over the coming years. Now I laugh about my termination, although I shudder to think of how many of my classmates did well at the mill and could not envision anything better. To date though, I have never been terminated from another job! Perhaps my eighth-grade home economics teacher's comment about marrying a rich man indicated that she recognized that I was not cut out to do manual labor!

However, I wonder what she thought my future *would* be; obviously, given the circumstances, my marrying a rich man was a long shot.

After my short stint in textiles, I focused on more academic subjects. French was one of my favorites. During twelfth grade, the French Club visited a French restaurant in Columbia, the capital of South Carolina, about forty-five minutes away. We ordered our meal in French. Because we did not have any upscale restaurants in my hometown and most people dined at home anyway, this was my first time eating in an elegant restaurant. Even when my family went to Columbia to go shopping, we ate at the dime store or grabbed a hamburger from a fast-food restaurant. The experience of eating at a formal restaurant, though intimidating, broadened my horizons.

Opportunities to participate in activities that will expand cultural experiences and outlooks are critical for students who come from nonmainstream backgrounds. Because I was an avid reader, I was familiar (theoretically) with the script for dining at an elegant restaurant. Also, at home, we sat at the table and ate together every day and my mother would serve special meals such as roast duck or leg of lamb occasionally. Yet, my classmates who ate at such upscale restaurants regularly had an advantage over me, and the experience, while exciting, was tense for me as well. I tried to enjoy the unfamiliar foods even though they were not pleasing to my ethnocentric palate. "Soul food" with a southern slant was more to my liking. "La Petite Château" served steak (*le bifteck*) broiled rather than deep fried.

Another senior year experience that was pivotal was a field trip to the university that I eventually attended. The university was a historically Black university in North Carolina. The first thing that caught my attention was the fact that Blacks were in charge of everything! All of the tour guides were Black, as were the speakers, band members, and cheerleaders! After surviving life at my oppressive high school, I felt liberated!

There were 178 graduates in my high school class. Both the salutatorian and valedictorian were White. It is surprising to see how many of the White student "stars" have fared over the years. Most are living lifestyles that fall short of my expectations and those of their teachers, I'm sure. It is one of life's ironies that I felt like a celebrity at my fifteen-year high school reunion because everyone was so impressed by my accomplishments.

How did my African American elementary school classmates fare? Tim, my neighbor during first grade, played football and was involved in many other school activities. He was also named "Mr. Senior." He lived in California as a medical researcher and an artist (on the side) for a while and now teaches at a historically Black university. Since Tim came from a home where both of his parents were teachers and he was usually shown favoritism throughout school, it is no surprise that he is doing well. Additionally, his parents knew enough about the school system to ensure that he was successful. They were also both college educated and were cognizant of the trajectory to success (as typically defined by society). In my senior memory book, Tim wrote, "To Gloria, My childhood sweetheart and one of my closest friends. May you always have mucho happiness and success in the future! Yours, Truck" (his high school nickname). The income differences between our families undoubtedly interfered with our friendship. Yet, as adults, none of this is significant.

Regina, my elementary school friend, was very popular throughout high school. She was one of the only Black cheerleaders for a while and was named "Miss Senior." In an effort by the school to appear fair and to appease Black students, both she and Tim were frequently selected as representatives because they came from the "right" type of families. None of the other class "kings" or "queens" were Black. I question whether their selection was based on actual votes by the student body. Call me a cynic, okay? Regina is now an attorney in North Carolina. Again, it is not surprising that she fared well given that her mother was a teacher and guided her education. Class differences interfered with our friendship, also. In my senior book, she wrote: "Gloria, This year it seems that you have changed a lot, but I always knew you were a beautiful person. I wish you all the success in the world. And I will *never* forget you. Love, Regina." It is shameful that both Tim and Regina had to assume raceless personae in order to be successful in school. It is also unfortunate that social class divided us in a democratic society.

Melvin, the first grader who brought egg sandwiches to school, played football in high school. I don't think that he excelled academically, but he is now gainfully employed in New York (not in a professional position). I wonder whether Melvin's career choice was affected by his school experiences. He came from a very large family who lived in a small, unpainted wood home in the "country" area of the community. Both of his parents were present in the home, but neither was formally educated. They would probably have been classified as a low- or working-income family. His mother stressed Christianity and allowed Bible study to be held at her home. Unlike Regina's and Tim's parents, Melvin's parents were not involved with school and did not know how to negotiate the system for his benefit.

Clinton, who was later labeled a special education student, dropped out of school before middle school; he was about seventeen at the time. Special education students were stigmatized during this era. As an adult, Clinton has been unemployed most of his adult life. I ponder whether he ever had a chance to succeed in school.

Educators' influence and impact extend far beyond the walls of the school. When we fail to give our best to help children succeed in school, we inadvertently contribute to the demise of society. Students, like Clinton, who cannot find their niche or any hope in school may resort to socially unacceptable ways of seeking satisfaction. In fact, many students like Clinton turn to drugs and crime (Majors & Billson, 1993). As humans, our lives are inextricably interrelated. Therefore, students who exit school unprepared affect the quality of life for all of us.

After graduation, I attended Johnson C. Smith University in North Carolina and majored in early childhood education. Later, I went to Iowa State and earned a master's degree in child development and attended the University of South Carolina for my Ph.D. degree in educational research. I taught in a lab school at Iowa State, worked in a clinical setting in Oklahoma, and returned to South Carolina to teach young children. I have held professorships at four universities and am currently at professor a the University of North Carolina—Greensboro. I have authored several articles, and this is my second book. Ironically, I ended up teaching at a major university that would not admit Blacks in the 1960s.

There is no way that I could have predicted what I would be doing today. It was totally beyond my realm of imagination and reality. I doubt that any of my teachers, friends, or family members would have predicted this career for me. I am certain that I have as much intelligence as Tim and Regina; however, I did not have the same resources and could not benefit from numerous educational opportunities, even though I attended a public school in a democratic society. Additionally, Tim's and Regina's early exposure to an integrated setting may have given them an edge in terms of knowing how to negotiate the system.

I am happy in my chosen profession, a very important outcome. However, at the same time that I emphasize that I am happy with my career choice, I also emphasize that many possibilities were not offered to me. Had I had the exposure that Tim and Regina had, it is likely that I would have attended an Ivy League or other top-ranked school. Also, if I had known about other career possibilities, it is likely that I would have become a pediatrician. We did not have any pediatricians in my hometown, so this possibility was nowhere in my repertoire! I would love to hear Tim's and Regina's stories because I cannot imagine that it was as easy for them as I thought it was. Disassociating themselves from others who looked like them and faced similar obstacles could not have been easy.

Most teachers probably believe that there is no way that a student like me would be overlooked today. I disagree. I witness it all too often. I read about it constantly (Singham, 1998; Steele, 1992). Unless teachers consciously work to avoid and reverse these trends, it is too easy for them to get pulled into an inherently inequitable system.

Why did I defy the legacy that was intended for me? My level of success can be attributed to a combination of factors, including my family, a few outstanding teachers, and intrinsic motivation. Good teachers can help students develop the intrinsic motivation and determination that they need to succeed in life (Delpit, 1995a; Ladson-Billings, 1994).

Teachers have the awesome task of reaching students from all walks of life. Most teachers enter the education profession because they want to teach all children. However, if teachers carefully examine their practices and observe which students are succeeding in their classrooms, they may realize that students who need the least amount of help are the only ones who excel. Continuous reflection on teaching practices is an ethical obligation.

When I first started teaching, I held deeply ingrained biases against males. They were the ones least affirmed in my classroom. I had to make a conscious effort to overcome my biases and resulting discriminatory acts, for example, being less tolerant of boys' misbehaviors, giving them less response time and fewer positive comments, and interacting with them less. Subconsciously, my biases toward females (probably a result of being raised in a family of three girls and only one boy) influenced my instruction and interactions with the children. It is ironic (or perhaps a result of my teacher preparation) that I easily forgot the awesome power of teachers.

Concluding Comments

Incident

Once riding in old Baltimore,
Heart-filled, head-filled with glee,
I saw a Baltimorean
Keep looking straight at me.

Now I was eight and very small,
And he was no whit bigger,
And so I smiled, but he poked out
His tongue, and called me, "Nigger."

I saw the whole of Baltimore
From May until December;
Of all the things that happened there
That's all that I remember.

——*Countee Cullen (1925)*

Many of my racially related school experiences are as poignant as the one conveyed by Cullen's poem. I suspect that this is so for many other people as well because racism can be devastating for individuals of all races. Both the perpetrator and the victim are often harmed. I wonder how the Baltimorean child in the poem felt when the Black child smiled at him. Did it touch his life or change it in any way? Was his response automatic or learned? Did his brief encounter with the Black child cause him to reflect later on his views? On the other hand, did the experience cause the Black child to become bitter? Did it prompt the Black child to dislike nonBlacks? Did it dampen his spirit?

Many renowned African American and European American authors lament that Black and poor children's educational trajectories are filled with obstacles (Hale-Benson, 1986; Hilliard, 1991; Irvine; 1990, and Kozol, 1991, among others). I was one of those Black children from a working-class family. Instead of adopting the negative legacy of nonsuccess, I adopted a self-disconfirming prophecy. That is, I was determined to show that "they" were wrong and that I could achieve much more than they predicted. I am thankful that I did not internalize the negative messages and develop a distaste for school, as too many African American children do by third or fourth grade (Hale-Benson, 1986; Kunjufu, 1985–1995, Vols. I–III; Morgan, 1980).

On February 17, 1995, edition of *The Oprah Winfrey Show,* Oprah discussed how racism causes people to behave in a way that is unnatural to the spirit of who they are. She powerfully described the damaging and cumulative effects of racism: "If every day of your life you walk down the street and you are suspect and people treat you differently, that, whether you realize it or not, has an impact on the way you live and move through the world. And that's what racism is. It's not just the Ku Klux Klan burning down your house—it's the day-to-day wearing down of the spirit." Institutionalized racism and classism are so insidious that they effortlessly invade the consciousness and actions and operate on automatic pilot in schools.

Although I achieved a level of success in my school experiences despite many odds, old mindsets die hard. A few years ago, I visited my old high school and ran into the assistant principal, who is also African American. He was excited that I was teaching at a university. He proudly introduced me to several teachers and administrators. However, I distinctly remember the pain I felt when he introduced me to a young, White, female teacher by saying, "She was one of the kids from over there in the projects." Underneath his words was the strong insinuation that it was incredible that I had done something positive with my life. Why had it mattered where I was from? What about my good grades? Didn't that matter? It seemed to me that the sum total of my worth was that I was a kid from a low-income housing project who had—surprisingly—made it. In case the reader has conjured up a large, high-rise building, the housing projects he referred to were only two stories high and there were just four apartments in each of the fourteen buildings. These apartments were supposed to provide "nice" homes for low-income families. Because my father died when I was three and my mother reared four children alone, my family was "economically challenged," despite her working full time and receiving Social Security benefits because of my father's death.

As a child, I was not aware that I was considered "this poor little child from the projects." I was content with my family and community. I think this is what people mean when they say, "We didn't know that we were poor." Children tend to see the world from their community orientation, and, typically, everyone around them lives as they do. That is, young children judge their worth in comparison to others in *their* community (Hale-Benson, 1986). At home, I felt comfortable. In school, I was made to feel ashamed of my parents, home, and community by many—not overtly, but implicitly by the books I read (or didn't read), my treatment by many teachers, and verbal and nonverbal feedback from teachers, administrators, and other students.

Seldom does the system recognize that it is designed in such a way that it does not promote success for all of its citizens. This lack of recognition of the problem is the most insidious type of racism, classism, or other forms of discrimination. Before one can dismantle discrimination, one must be able to recognize it.

Even today, because of my personal experiences, I am still greatly perturbed when teachers talk about "poor project kids" without realizing that they are talking about me. Ironically, many of these teachers have come from similar backgrounds but have forgotten their struggles. At the very least, many teachers currently have or have had family members who were not privileged enough to be born into a middle- or upper-class family. Educators must realize that children do not have the luxury of choosing the families into which they are born; therefore, each child's home environment should be appreciated. Teachers should also seek to expand children's horizons so that eventually they will become proficient in the "mainstream" culture as well as in their own.

I hope that my story has touched the hearts of educators and prompted them to reflect on their teaching practices and possible contributions to negative outcomes for students. Many simply fail to examine the political nature of teaching. In the long run, I hope that the experiences that I share will make a difference in the lives of poor and African American children. I hope this book serves to inspire wonderful teachers who encourage and believe in students no matter where they are from or how much money their families earn.

Like many teachers, I pursued teaching because I wanted to be a positive influence in the lives of children—regardless of their ethnicity or socioeconomic status. The "good" teachers that I encountered were instrumental in my educational success and later decision to become a teacher.

Negative portrayals or omissions of poor children and people of color contribute to the failure of many students to reach their fullest potential. The power of continuous negative imagery on children should not be underestimated (Spencer & Markstrom-Adams, 1990).

Teachers should seek to leave a positive, indelible impression on children's desire to learn. The fact that I cannot remember some of my teachers is a powerful statement regarding their influence on my learning and development. Yet, other teachers (both positive and negative ones) are permanently imprinted in my mind. The positive ones undoubtedly contributed to my later success. Perhaps positive teachers cancel out the influence of the negative ones. Nevertheless, one negative teacher at an impressionable and pivotal time in a child's life can sway the child away from school and future success.

For every child like me from a working-class home who survives and excels later in life, there are probably 1,000 more who do not (Wilcox,

1982). Kozol (1991) poignantly pointed out the "savage inequalities" in schools across the nation. To address inequities, many communities are establishing educational advocates who serve as ombudspersons for low-income and working-class parents. These advocates apprise parents of the opportunities and rights that their children have and help parents negotiate equitable academic placements and disciplinary actions for their children. All educators, in fact, should be ombudspersons for all children and defy any negative legacies that we encounter.

I have come to the conclusion that racism and oppression in my small, rural hometown were so endemic and insidious that both the Black and White children[1] basically had only two options: to defy them or succumb to them. There was little middle ground. Most of my Black classmates succumbed to it. I did not live "down" to teachers' and society's expectations that I would become pregnant, incarcerated, or the like. Retrospectively, I realize that, in the larger scheme of things, the White students that we held in high esteem are labeled by the general society as "hicks" or "rednecks." They suffer the effects not only of their own racism but also of regionalism and other oppressing prejudices in the larger society. An oppressive culture has some oppressive effect on each of its members.

The importance of literature in nurturing dreams of freedom and liberation cannot be overemphasized. Books can be vehicles for releasing hopeful imaginings (Greene, 1995; Kohl, 1995). Teachers should make available stories that encourage young people to fundamentally question the world as it is and dream it as it might be otherwise. That's what books did for me—open up a world of possibilities. It was not until I read *The Autobiography of Malcolm X* that I looked at the issues beyond personal liberation. A commitment to larger issues of discrimination provided the moral impetus that motivated the struggle to eliminate victimization during the Civil Rights era. Living through this era taught me that reality was not fixed and that justice and fairness could be achieved.

I still feel pain and anger every time I visit my hometown. Although my children can now play there, I cannot ride past Mollohon Park without remembering that it was once for Whites only. The neighborhood where my mother now resides was for Whites only when I was a child. The lessons that I learned there will likely stay with me forever. It is my hope that my lessons will help others learn.

> *If you know from whence you come, there is no limit to where you can go.*
> —*James Baldwin*

---

[1]It was not until 1972 that Vietnamese students, refugees from the Vietnamese War, were enrolled in my high school, extending the racial categories beyond Black and White.

References

Boutte, G. S.(1992). Frustrations of an African-American parent—A personal and professional account. *Phi Delta Kappan, 73*(10), 786–788.

Boutte, G. S., LaPoint, S., & Davis, B. (1993). Racial issues in education: Real or imagined? *Young Children, 49*(1), 19–23.

Boutte, G. S., & McCormick, C. B. (1992). Authentic multicultural activities: Avoiding pseudo-multiculturalism. *Childhood Education, 68*(3), 140–144.

Brophy, J., & Good, T. (1970). *Teacher-student relationships: Causes and consequences.* New York: Holt, Rinehart, and Winston.

Copage, E. V. (1995). *Black pearls for parents: Meditations, affirmations, and inspirations for African-American parents.* New York: Quill.

Delpit, L. D. (1988). The silenced dialogue: Power and pedagogy in educating other people's children. *Harvard Education Review, 58*(3), 280–298.

Delpit, L. D. (1995a). I just want to be myself: Discovering what students bring to school in their blood. In W. Ayers (Ed.), *To become a teacher* (pp. 34–48). New York: Teachers College Press.

Delpit, L. D. (1995b). *Other people's children: Cultural conflicts in the classroom.* New York: The New Press.

Fischer, L. (1962). *The essential Gandhi: An anthology of his writings on his life, work and ideas.* New York: Vantage.

Fordham, S. (1988). Raceless as a factor in black student's school success: Pragmatic strategy or Pyrrhic victory? *Harvard Educational Review, 58*(1), 54–84.

Fordham, S. (1996). *Blacked out: Dilemmas of race, identity, and success at Capital High.* Chicago: University of Chicago Press.

Freire, P. (1994). *Pedagogy of hope: Reliving pedagogy of the oppressed.* New York: Continuum.

Greene, M. (1995). *Releasing the imagination.* San Francisco: Jossey-Bass.

Hale-Benson, J. (1986). *Black children: Their roots, culture, and learning* (rev. ed.). Baltimore: John Hopkins University Press.

Hilliard, A. G. (1991). *Testing African American students.* Morristown, NJ: Aaron Press.

Howard, G. R. (1993). Whites in multicultural education: Rethinking our role. *Phi Delta Kappan, 75*(1), 36–41.

Irvine, J. J. (1990). *Black students and school failure: Policies, practices and prescriptions.* New York: Greenwood Press.

Kohl, H. (1995). *Should we burn Babar? Essays on children's literature and the power of stories.* New York: The New Press.

Kozol, M. (1991). *Savage inequalities.* New York: Crown.

Kunjufu, J. (1985–1995). *Countering the conspiracy to destroy Black boys* (Vols. I–IV). Chicago: African American Images.

Ladson-Billings, G. (1994). *Dreamkeepers: Successful teachers of African American students.* San Francisco: Jossey-Bass.

Majors, R., & Billson, J. M. (1993). *Cool pose: The dilemmas of Black manhood in America.* New York: Touchstone.

Morgan, H. (1980). How schools fail Black children. *Social Policy, 10*(4) (January–February), 49–53.

Morrison, T. (1993). *The bluest eye.* New York: Knopf.

Oakes, J., & Lipton, M. (1990). Tracking and ability grouping: A structural barrier to access and achievement. In J. I. Goodlad & P. Keating (Eds.), *Access to knowledge: An agenda for our nation's schools* (pp. 187–203). New York: College Entrance Examination Board.

Ogbu, J. U. (1990). Overcoming racial barriers to equal access. In J. I. Goodlad & P. Keating (Eds.), *Access to knowledge: An agenda for our nation's schools* (pp. 59–89). New York: College Entrance Examination Board.

Schofield, J. W. (1997). Causes and consequences of the colorblind perspective. In J. A. Banks & C. A. M. Banks (Eds.), *Multicultural education: Issues and perspectives* (pp. 251–271). Boston: Allyn and Bacon.

Shepard, L. A., & Smith, M. L. (1989). *Flunking grades: Research and policies on retention.* London: The Falmer Press.

Shepard, L. A., & Smith, M. L. (1990). Synthesis of research on grade retention. *Educational Leadership, 47,* 84–88.

Singham, M. (1998). The canary in the mine: The achievement gap between black and white students. *Phi Delta Kappan, 80*(1), 8–15.

Spencer, M. B., & Markstrom-Adams, C. (1990). Identity processes among racial and ethnic minority children in America. *Child Development, 61*(2), 290–310.

Steele, C. M. (1992). Race and schooling of Black Americans. *The Atlantic Monthly, 269*(4), 68–78.

Tatum, B. (1997). *Why are all the black kids sitting together in the cafeteria?* New York: Basic.

Walsh, D. J. (1991). Extending the discourse on developmental appropriateness: A developmental perspective. *Early Education and Development, 2*(2), 109–119.

Wilcox, K. (1982). Differential socialization in the classroom: Implications for equal opportunity. In G. Spindler (ed.), *Doing the ethnography of schooling* (pp. 268–309). Prospect Heights, IL: Waveland.

Wilson, M. N. (l986). The Black extended family: An analytical consideration. *Developmental Psychology, 22,* 246–258.

Woodson, C. G. (1933/1990). *The mis-education of the Negro.* Trenton, NJ: Africa World Press.